Six Years
of Hell

CHESTER G. HEARN

# Six Years
# of Hell

## Harpers Ferry
## During the
## Civil War

Louisiana State University Press
Baton Rouge

Designer: Melanie O'Quinn Samaha
Typeface: Trump Medieval
Typesetter: Impressions Book and Journal Services, Inc.

Library of Congress Cataloging-in-Publication Data
Hearn, Chester G.
    Six years of hell : Harpers Ferry during the Civil War / Chester
G. Hearn.
        p.    cm.
    Includes bibliographical references (p.    ) and index.
    ISBN 0-8071-2090-1 (cloth) ISBN 0-8071-2440-0 (pbk.)
    1. Harpers Ferry (W. Va.)—History.   2. West Virginia—History—
Civil War, 1861–1865.   I. Title.
F249.H2H47      1996
975.4'99—dc20                                                      96-21738
                                                                        CIP

To Ann, my wife, who endures my hours of isolation,
to Chet and Dana, and their life together,
and to the beloved memory of Wendy

# Contents

# Illustrations

John W. Geary
Nathaniel P. Banks
Dixon S. Miles

*following page 211*

John E. Wool
Lafayette McLaws
James A. Walker
Julius White
Joseph B. Kershaw
Ambrose P. Hill
Ambrose Burnside
Benjamin F. Kelley
Robert C. Schenck
George B. McClellan
Henry H. Lockwood
Albion P. Howe
Washington L. Elliott
Max Weber
Franz Sigel
Jubal A. Early
John D. Stevenson
David Hunter
Jeremiah C. Sullivan
John S. Mosby
John R. Kenly
Winfield Scott Hancock
Philip H. Sheridan

# Preface and Acknowledgments

Harpers Ferry, West Virginia, is a fascinating place to visit. It is more than a town. It is a forgotten field of many skirmishes and engagements and is central to some of the greatest battles of the Civil War. Today the town is best remembered for John Brown's raid in October, 1859. However, the horrors of war that began to infest the town in the spring of 1861—the first year of the Civil War—have largely been overlooked by historians. John Brown may have hurried the South's secession, but he did not destroy the town's industry, burn the lower town, or force a mass exodus of its citizens—but the constant passing of Union and Confederate armies through the area did.

My fascination with Harpers Ferry started forty-five years ago when I was a freshman at Allegheny College in Meadville, Pennsylvania. One of the college's history professors, "Skipper" Knight, shouldered the task of indoctrinating freshmen in dormitory behavior, and one evening he gathered our group together and talked about John Brown, who in the 1830s operated a tannery near the college. I never forgot that interesting fragment of Brown's history and carried it with me for many years.

Several years passed before I visited Harpers Ferry, and during that period I developed an interest in the Civil War. Although Professor Knight and historians employed by the National Park Service at Harpers Ferry credited Brown with hastening the Civil War, nobody could provide a clear account of what became of the town after the raid—or why. After doing some initial research, I became intrigued by the importance of the town during the war and fascinated by how often it entered into the strategies of the

Union and Confederate armies. Every battle fought in northern Virginia, Maryland, or Pennsylvania in some way involved the Ferry, and nobody suffered more than the civilians who lived there.

Many years ago I discovered the archives at Harpers Ferry. At the time they were not well organized, but today they are—with drawers filled with old maps and files laden with documents and manuscripts written during the war by the soldiers encamped there and by the townspeople living there. Bruce Noble, the park historian, along with Michael Antonioni, Nancy Hatcher, and Peggy Bethany, has been most helpful in making maps and documents available to me in the carefully guarded archive on the third floor of the John Brown Museum.

I located another enormous source of soldiers' letters, diaries, and manuscripts at the U.S. Military History Institute in Carlisle, Pennsylvania, and I owe a debt of gratitude to Dr. Richard Sommers and his staff for their kind and useful help. The institute's library in Upton Hall contains one of the finest collections of Civil War books in the country, and with the considerate help of John Slonaker I found much out-of-print primary-source material that is virtually unobtainable today.

Closer to home, Susan Brandau and Marry Harrison of the Milton Public Library and Evelyn Burns of the Brown Library in Williamsport, Pennsylvania, have provided help not only on this book but on everything I have ever written. They help reduce my travel a good deal by finding source material through their interlibrary network.

I am also indebted to James Hutson and Mary Ison at the Library of Congress, Michael Musick at the National Archives, Linda McIlveen at the Ontario Historical Society in New York, J. R. Richards at Gettysburg College, Ellen Stack at the Historical Society of Pennsylvania, and to the staff at the Corry Library in Pennsylvania—all of whom have furnished me with or guided me to documents and letters pertaining to Harpers Ferry in the Civil War. To those whose names I have forgotten or misplaced, I sincerely apologize, for without the help of all, this short history would be incomplete.

# Abbreviations Used in Notes

| | |
|---|---|
| *B&L* | Johnson, Robert U., and Clarence C. Buel, eds., *Battles and Leaders of the Civil War*. 4 vols. New York, 1887–88. |
| CHS | Chicago Historical Society, Chicago, Ill. |
| CPL | Corry Public Library, Corry, Pa. |
| HFA | Harpers Ferry National Park Archives, Harpers Ferry, W.Va. |
| *HTI* | Faust, Patricia L., ed., *Historical Times Illustrated Encyclopedia of the Civil War*. New York, 1986. |
| JCCR | Jefferson County Court Records, Charles Town, W.Va. |
| LC | Library of Congress, Washington, D.C. |
| MLGC | Musselman Library, Gettysburg College, Gettysburg, Pa. |
| *OR* | *The War of the Rebellion: A Compilation of the Records of the Union and Confederate Armies*. 70 vols. in 128 books. Washington, D.C., 1881–1901. |
| USAMHI | U.S. Army Military History Institute, Carlisle, Pa. |
| VSL | Virginia State Library Collection, Richmond, Va. |
| YUL | Yale University Library, New Haven, Conn. |

Six Years
of Hell

# Prologue

By most accounts, the Civil War began at 4:30 A.M. on the morning of April 12, 1861, in the harbor of Charleston, South Carolina. But for the townsfolk of Harpers Ferry, the fighting started on the night of October 16, 1859. The first skirmish occurred outside the enginehouse of the U.S. Armory, and the battle was won, like so many that came thereafter, by Robert E. Lee. The leader of the raid, an abolitionist named John Brown, swung on the gallows six weeks later in a town of a similar name—Charles Town, in Jefferson County, Virginia. The residents of Harpers Ferry thought Brown's execution would mark the end of their trouble, but for a nation driven by sectional differences, his death hurried the beginning of the destruction of their properties, their livelihoods, and nearly a million American lives.

What made Harpers Ferry so important was its location, its industry, and the Baltimore and Ohio Railroad. The town's name suggests a quaint, picturesque village set in a peaceful valley rimmed by sparkling rivers flowing between lush wooded mountains. This is much how Thomas Jefferson viewed the landscape when he stood on a rock overlooking the sparsely settled valley in 1780 and wrote: "It is as placid and delightful as that is wild and tremendous. . . . This scene is worth a voyage across the Atlantic."[1] Peter Stephens, however, had built a home below Jefferson's Rock and referred to his solitary settlement as "The Hole."

Among the early settlers was an architect named Robert Harper, who came to Pleasant Valley in 1747 to build a Quaker

---

1. Thomas Jefferson, *Notes on the State of Virginia* (2nd American ed.; Philadelphia, 1794), 23, 24.

meetinghouse a short distance downriver from where the Shenandoah River flows into the Potomac. Standing at the base of towering Maryland Heights, Harper could look across the river at a rocky tongue of land that rose gradually between the southern shore of the Potomac on one side and the western shore of the Shenandoah on the other. For fifty guineas he bought the rough-hewn home of Peter Stephens and 125 acres of land that comprised most of the future town. With a sturdy flatboat he went into business transporting travelers across the Potomac, and "The Hole" became Harpers Ferry.[2]

"The Hole" was certainly not a very elegant name for the picturesque settlement described by Jefferson, but in another century—about a hundred years later—thousands of soldiers would write home to loved ones that the dirty little town of Harpers Ferry was nothing but a "godforsaken, stinking hole." And to any military man with an ounce of tactical sense, a hole it was.

Directly across from Harpers Ferry, on the opposite shore of the Potomac, a giant upthrust rocky prominence called Maryland Heights rises thirteen hundred feet above the town. In Virginia, on the eastern shore of the Shenandoah, stands the sheer face of another mountain of almost equal size called Loudoun Heights. The lower town of Harpers Ferry rises up a rocky slope to Bolivar Heights, more a hill than a mountain and gentle enough to carry wagon traffic, and on its plateau was built the neighboring town of Bolivar. In the nineteenth century a pike, eight miles long, carried travelers to Charles Town, the seat of Jefferson County, and in between emerged the village of Halltown.[3] The road was only the beginning of a pike that by 1859 stretched up through Winchester, Strasburg, Mount Jackson, New Market, Harrisonburg, and Staunton, a route much traveled by the likes of Stonewall Jackson, Jubal Early, Nathaniel P. Banks, Philip H. Sheridan, and thousands of road-weary soldiers dressed in dusty blue or tattered butternut. To the east and stretching south, deep into North Carolina, lay the Blue Ridge Mountains with befuddling passes that could hide whole armies.

In 1780, Harper built a stone house partway up the hill to Bo-

2. Joseph Barry, *The Strange Story of Harper's Ferry* (3rd ed.; Shepherdstown, W.Va., 1969), 12–13. In the town's early years its name was written "Harper's Ferry."

3. *Ibid.*, 7–8.

livar Heights to escape the floods that visited the lower settlement almost annually. Having no children, he left his property to his niece, Sarah, who married a Philadelphian named Wager. Sarah never settled in Harpers Ferry, but other Wagers came to town, and one of them attached the family name to the town's first large hotel.[4]

In 1794, George Washington, a substantial property owner himself, looked at the powerful flow of water skirting both sides of the Ferry and chose the town as the site for his new national armory. Two years later, machine shops, an arsenal, and a canal sprang up along the south shore of the Potomac River. In 1819 John H. Hall, a native of Maine, invented a breech-loading rifle and headed the town's new factory, Hall's Rifle Works, located on upper Virginius Island, where he used the waters of the Shenandoah to power his machinery. New industry attracted skilled mechanics from the North, and Germans with names like Allstadt, Wager, Herr, and Kitzmiller moved to the growing town. Housing crept along the rivers and up the hill towards Bolivar Heights. North Potomac Street ran along the canal powering the national armory. Shenandoah Street followed the river of its name from the lower town to Hall's Rifle Works. High and Clay Streets climbed the hill to form Washington Street and connected the town to Bolivar. Ridge and Fillmore Streets paralleled Washington Street, the latter ascending to Camp Hill and containing mostly tenement homes for government employees. By 1859 the former ferry crossing had grown to a town of more than two thousand residents. The neighboring town of Bolivar claimed eleven hundred citizens, and most of them walked down the hill each day to work in Harpers Ferry.[5]

Contributing to the burgeoning prosperity of the town was the building of the Chesapeake and Ohio Canal, which skirted Maryland Heights and disappeared up the Potomac. In 1834 the Baltimore and Ohio Railroad came up the gorge as far as Sandy Hook, two miles below the Ferry, and waited on the Maryland side for a bridge to carry the line into Virginia. Two years later a magnificent S-shaped structure, nine hundred feet long, with six spans set on

4. *Ibid.*, 13.

5. *Ibid.*, 14, 21; Harpers Ferry National Historical Park, 1859 Base Map, National Parks Service, HFA; Annie P. Marmion, "Under Fire" (manuscript), 6, File HFB-206, HFA.

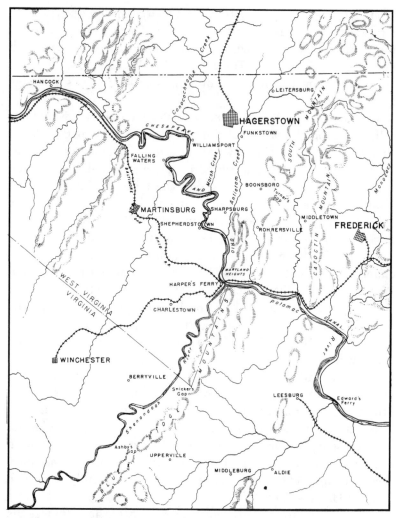

Harpers Ferry area
*From* Civil War Atlas to Accompany Steele's American Campaigns *(West Point, N.Y., 1941)*

massive piers, gave passage to trains, wagons, horsemen, and pe-
destrians. With the crossing of the Baltimore and Ohio came the
thirty-two-mile-long Winchester and Potomac spur, which connected Baltimore and Washington to the granary of the lower
Shenandoah Valley. Fontaine Beckham, Harpers Ferry's future
mayor, became the agent for the two railroads and worked in an

office next to the Wager House. Passengers entering town could step off the train and walk directly into either the Wager House or the Potomac Restaurant. The Gault House Saloon, located on the Winchester and Potomac spur, offered a variety of intoxicants to passengers not wanting to cross the tracks for plusher accommodations at the Wager House.[6]

The bridge spanning the Potomac brought more prosperity to the town. In 1852 the Baltimore and Ohio completed its line to Wheeling, laying 513 miles of track. The railroad passed through Martinsburg and Cumberland, zigzagging back and forth into Maryland and Virginia. By 1861 thousands of tons of coal passed through Harpers Ferry monthly en route to eastern seaports, and thousands of passengers rode the rails, stopping at the Wager House for a hot meal or a cold beer. On the eve of the Civil War, the Baltimore and Ohio, proud that it had grown up with the nation, boasted 236 locomotives, 128 passenger cars, and 3,451 freight cars. An investment of $30 million made the line one of the costliest roads in the country. No wonder John W. Garrett, the railroad's banker-president, devised a scheme early in the war to offer the line to both sides as a neutral public utility.[7] Harpers Ferry and the Baltimore and Ohio shared a similar indisposition— they were joined together by an important bridge and became the target of constant depredations.

For more than sixty years the U.S. Armory built weapons and continued to expand. Twenty-five buildings lay on the grounds along the Potomac River with the tracks of the Baltimore and Ohio in between. Two arsenal buildings and housing for armory officials accounted for another dozen buildings scattered about the town. In 1860, 265 armory workers produced 15,468 muskets, most of them rifled. Hall's Rifle Works, consisting of nine buildings located on the Shenandoah Canal below Virginius Island, turned out 3,000 percussion rifles a year.[8] No arms producer south of the Mason-Dixon Line could match the output of the Harpers Ferry armories.

6. Edward Hungerford, *The Story of the Baltimore and Ohio Railroad* (2 vols.; New York, 1928), I, 146, 149–50.

7. *Ibid.*, I, 323; Baltimore and Ohio Railroad Company, *Thirty-Sixth Annual Report* (Baltimore, 1864), 167, 172.

8. Merritt Roe Smith, *Harpers Ferry Armory and the New Technology* (Ithaca, N.Y., 1977), Tables I and II.

By the summer of 1859, sectional differences in the Deep South began to worry the once ambivalent citizens of Harpers Ferry. Equally divided in sentiment, townsfolk argued quietly on the streets and vehemently in the Gault House Saloon. Bounty hunters passing through town fueled the growing debate by drinking heavily and castigating northern abolitionists. About seven hundred slaves lived in the area, and every so often one disappeared. But the average family knew their comfort depended upon the armory, the railroad, Abraham Herr's mill, and all the small businesses that flourished because government money kept the town employed. Political ranting in Washington caught their attention, but war seldom entered their discussions.

In early July a tall, sinewy man with a full silver beard rode into town on a small one-horse wagon. He walked into the post office and asked if there was any mail for Isaac Smith. The curious old chap said little to the postmaster, but neither did dozens of other itinerants who stopped on occasion for mail. Smith suffered from malarial fevers, and he stopped briefly at the office of Dr. Nicholas Marmion for medicine before crossing back to the Maryland side.[9]

Nobody paid much attention to the old man whose fierce obsession was about to ignite the flames of hell in a border town called Harpers Ferry. The town's wartime history is written in campaigns of the Army of the Potomac and the Army of Northern Virginia, but it all started when John Brown, alias Isaac Smith, came from Kansas to free the slaves.

9. Brown to Kagi, June 30, 1859, in Franklin B. Sanborn, *The Life and Letters of John Brown* (Boston, 1885), 526–27; Marmion, "Under Fire," 23, HFA.

# 1

## A Shadow over the Valley

John Brown arrived at Harpers Ferry on July 3, 1859. He wore black, much like a preacher, and with him were three men—his sons, Owen and Oliver, and a man named Jeremiah Anderson, who had joined him in Kansas to become his bodyguard. Brown, because he was wanted in Kansas for murder, had grown a flowing beard as a disguise, but perhaps he had another reason, one more consistent with his image of himself. He lived by the Old Testament, and when he first rattled across the bridge spanning the Potomac and rolled his wagon into the Ferry, he could have stepped out of the Book of Judges, as he had come "to make this land of liberty and equality shake to the centre."[1]

At fifty-nine years of age, John Brown could have passed for a weary prospector or an old farmer weathered by the elements. The years had been harsh and business failures many, and for a man who liberally chastised others for their transgressions against God, he came to the Ferry with the blood of five Kansas settlers on his gnarled and calloused hands. Yet, to look into his gray-blue eyes, eyes filled with righteousness and honesty, was to many of his disciples a simple vindication of the old man's ways. He could

1. Oswald Garrison Villard, *John Brown, 1800–1859: A Biography Fifty Years After* (Boston, 1910), 408, 682.

delude the rich men of the East who financed his schemes, as well
as the young lads who followed him, because neither could find a
cause to support greater than the one John Brown brought to the
bustling little industrial town of Harpers Ferry. His men called
him "Captain," a title no more official than his incursion into
Jefferson County, Virginia. But in a secret convention held in
Chatham, Ontario, on May 8, 1858, the Captain authored a new
constitution and established the Provisional Government of the
United States to deal with the slave issue. With a few strokes of
the pen, followed by a quick election, Captain John Brown rose to
the post of commander in chief of the Provisional Army. This
army, scattered from New England and New York to Canada and
Kansas, was about to answer the commander's call to arms.[2]

Brown visited the Ferry on July 3 to confer briefly with John
Cook, a confederate sent to infiltrate the town in the summer of
1858. Cook not only ingratiated himself with the townspeople; he
made love to a plump blonde maiden named Mary Virginia Kennedy, whom he impregnated and married a few months before she
bore him a son. Having established himself as a solid citizen with
a full-time job on the Chesapeake and Ohio Canal—and with a
part-time job as a wandering bookseller—Cook made rough
sketches of the armory, arsenal, and rifle works. Brown took the
drawings, tucked them in his leather pouch, and left town after
urging Cook to begin enlisting local blacks for the Provisional
Army. Knowing Cook's talkative nature, Brown may have confused the young man with cross-signals by warning him at the
same time to keep his mouth shut and his eyes open.[3]

Brown wanted to be near the Ferry but insulated from nosy
neighbors who might ask too many questions. He rented an empty
and dilapidated two-story farmhouse on the Boonsboro road in
Maryland, about six miles from the bridge to Harpers Ferry. The
old dwelling, owned by the heirs of Dr. Booth Kennedy, was
known around the countryside as the Kennedy farm. The home
suited Brown, as it lay set back from the road running to Hagerstown, Maryland, and Chambersburg, Pennsylvania. His presence
baffled the few neighbors who traveled the road, as he claimed to

2. James Redpath, *The Public Life of Capt. John Brown* (Boston, 1860), 232–33.
The complete text of this constitution is in Richard J. Hinton, *John Brown and
His Men* (New York, 1894), 619–37.
3. Hinton, *John Brown and His Men*, 240. See also Cook's confession, 700–14.

be a farmer from New York State, but when his wagon rattled over the road with crates full of military supplies, he let the meddlesome natives think the boxes contained mining implements. Even Henry Kyd Douglas of Shepherdstown, who later became the youngest member of General Thomas J. "Stonewall" Jackson's staff, once helped old Brown transport a wagonload of "tools" to the farmhouse.[4]

Prior to his arrival at the Ferry, Brown established an outpost at Chambersburg, where John Henry Kagi, his secretary of war, operated Isaac Smith & Sons under the name of J. Henrie, an alias as fictitious as the business itself. Kagi was an important link in Brown's conspiracy. Fifteen boxes containing 198 Sharps rifles and 200 Maynard revolvers arrived from Ohio, sent by John Brown, Jr. Kagi loaded them on carts driven by Owen and Oliver Brown and forwarded them to the Kennedy farm. Later he received 950 pikes from Connecticut and sent them clattering down the Boonsboro road. Brown, believing slaves were incapable of using firearms without extensive training, envisioned a pike in the hand of every black recruit.

Kagi's presence at Chambersburg performed another important task. All of Brown's carefully disguised correspondence to his backers and volunteers emanated from the Pennsylvania office. Once he established his headquarters at the Kennedy farm, he ordered War Secretary Kagi to summon the troops. Kagi penned nearly a hundred letters, and the wait began.[5]

Brown's vision of an army began to diminish as recruits dribbled into Chambersburg. There they waited at widow Mary A. Ritner's boardinghouse until Owen or Oliver brought the wagon to pick up another load of "tools." Four Kansas raiders arrived at about the same time, Provisional Army Captains Aaron D. Stevens and Charles Plummer Tidd, and Lieutenants William H. Leeman and Albert Hazlett. From North Elba, New York, came Captain Watson Brown, who left his wife and newborn child to fight his father's war. He brought two of his brothers-in-law, William and Dauphin Thompson, who disliked living in the harsh climate of the Adirondacks and joined the Provisional Army because they

4. Boyd B. Stutler, *Capt. John Brown and Harper's Ferry* (Harpers Ferry, 1926), 19; Henry Kyd Douglas, *I Rode with Stonewall* (Chapel Hill, N.C., 1940), 2.

5. John Brown to John Kagi (J. Henrie), July 12, 1859, and Brown to John Brown, Jr., August [?], 1859, both in Sanborn, *Life and Letters*, 532–36.

had nothing better to do. From Springdale, Iowa, came two young Quakers, Barclay and Edwin Coppoc, who had forsaken their vows to not carry arms. Brown had persuaded them that God granted redemption to those who brought weapons of deliverance against the evils of slavery.

Kagi's call to Canada produced two black recruits, Stewart Taylor, a spiritualist, and Osborn P. Anderson, a printer who left his girlfriend behind because old Brown declared that freeing his brethren was more important than the woman who loved him. Two more blacks—John A. Copeland and his uncle, Lewis Leary—made their way from Oberlin, Ohio. Leary kissed his wife and baby good-bye, promising to return as soon as the Virginia business was finished. Copeland and Leary reached the Kennedy farm on October 15. Neither would ever see Oberlin again.

Two freed slaves joined the Provisional Army and squeezed their bodies into the cramped attic of the Kennedy home. Shields Green had come to Chambersburg with Frederick Douglass, whom Brown wanted at his side as he knifed deep into the South. Douglass called the mission insane and returned to Rochester. His fight was with words, not with guns. Green stayed, drawn into the scheme by Brown's intensity. Cook recruited Dangerfield Newby, a man desperate to free his enslaved wife, Harriet, and their eight children. Her master needed money and threatened to sell part of the family to a planter in Louisiana. Newby, the oldest of the recruits, begged to be included, and Brown promised to rescue the wife and children as soon as he emptied the Federal arsenal and armed his volunteers.[6]

As the farmhouse filled to capacity, the men began to lose confidence in their commander. By October, Brown was short of money and out of time. Neighbors noticed inexplicable activity at the Kennedy farm—blacks had been seen in the house—so they alerted the sheriff. Brown's men spotted mysterious hoofprints in the field behind the farmhouse. Locals began to speculate that Isaac Smith was neither farmer nor miner, but a sneaky abolitionist setting up a transfer point for the Underground Railroad between the Maryland line and Chambersburg. Brown made another discovery that delayed his attack, one he tried to hide from

6. Sanborn, *Life and Letters*, 546. Villard, *John Brown*, provides biographical data on all of Brown's men in the appendix.

the others. For his two hundred revolvers he had purchased the wrong percussion caps. Half his arsenal was useless.

Brown believed in signs and omens, and whenever his life reached a new setback, the Lord had always provided. Six days before the raid on Harpers Ferry, God delivered Francis J. Meriam to the farmhouse on the Boonsboro road. Meriam had been on Brown's trail since early 1858, tracking him to Kansas but never finding him. With guidance from the commander's eastern backers, he reached the farmhouse on October 10 with six hundred dollars in gold—enough to buy percussion caps and lay in fresh provisions. Meriam had one eye and a frail body. He was emotionally unbalanced, perhaps mentally retarded, but Brown could not allow incapacities to interfere with his desperate need of men and money. Of the fifty lads he had hoped to attract to his noble cause, Meriam became the twenty-first—and the last.[7]

On Sunday morning, October 16, Brown gathered his men in two large rooms to explain his plan. He believed the Sabbath was a good day to begin the work of God, to strike the first blow against the evils of slavery. As at the meetings held around the smoky campfires on the bloody plains of Kansas, he conducted a worship service, invoking the Lord's blessing. Sixteen whites sprawled on the floor to hear their chieftain speak. Clustered together in the back of the room, five blacks leaned against the wall, many hearing for the first time the old man's intentions. Cook had sent his wife to Chambersburg, and he sat attentively at the front with the other officers. Before leaving the Ferry, he had reconnoitered the armory one last time and reported no Federal troops there.

A light rain beat against the stained windowpanes. Fog rolled across the valley, shrouding the landscape in a cloak of impenetrable white. The time had come to strike.

Brown's voice filled the room—a metallic voice, not harsh but firm and fervent, ringing like the strike of the hammer that chiseled the Ten Commandments on stubborn blocks of stone. He spread out his war charts and issued assignments to his captains. Kagi, Tidd, Cook, and Stevens would follow him into the Ferry and disperse—some to the arsenal, some to the rifle works—while others spread through the countryside to call the slaves to arms. The commander, with a small force, would occupy the ar-

7. Sanborn, *Life and Letters*, 548–49.

mory. Watson Brown would hold the bridge across the Potomac, Oliver the bridge across the Shenandoah. Owen, because of his withered arm, would remain at the farmhouse with one-eyed Meriam and Barclay Coppoc, a boy too frail to endure the hardships of warfare. The trio would move to the schoolhouse on the road to the Ferry, arm the slaves from Maryland with pikes, and, as more volunteers reported for duty, supply them with guns, ammunition, and instructions. Some of the men harbored silent misgivings. Others who had fought with the old man in Kansas envisioned a frolic and a little plunder. None expected to die.

Late that afternoon the men ate in silence, packed their supplies, and loaded their revolvers. As darkness fell Brown voiced a few final instructions. He wanted no bloodshed, but the men must defend themselves, even if it meant killing to preserve their own lives. He promised a glorious struggle, and if some must die, he offered redemption: "We have here only one life to live, and once to die; and if we lose our lives it will perhaps do more for the cause than our lives would be worth in any other way."

At 8 P.M. Brown went to the door and looked outside. A drizzle beat upon the tin roof of the farmhouse. Fog lay heavy in the gloom of early darkness. A chill pervaded the moonless landscape. Whatever his doubts, he kept them to himself. He stepped back into the house and donned his Kansas cap with the floppy earflaps. "Men, get on your arms," he said. "We will proceed to the Ferry." The raiders slung their Sharps rifles over their shoulders and slipped into heavy gray shawls. Owen Brown, Meriam, and Barclay Coppoc loaded the wagon with pikes and tools. The commander in chief took the reins and headed down the road. Eighteen men followed. Owen wondered if he would ever see his father again.[8]

The six-mile march to the bridge over the Potomac proceeded quietly, the men slogging through puddles behind the creaking wagon. Pikes rattled in crates as the wagon bumped down the muddy road. Most of the men knew nothing of the Ferry but what old Brown had told them, and as they approached the bridge they could see the eerie lights of town dimly glowing through the fog. At Brown's command, Cook and Tidd fell out of line and cut the

8. *Ibid.*, 552–53; Hinton, *John Brown and His Men*, 708; Osborn P. Anderson, *A Voice from Harper's Ferry* (Boston, 1861), 27–32.

telegraph lines to Baltimore. Stevens and Kagi double-quicked into the covered bridge ahead of the wagon and captured William Williams, the night watchman. Williams recognized Cook and the man called Isaac Smith. At first he thought the whole affair a joke worth a hearty laugh, but the wind caught in his throat when he noticed rifles pointed at his belly. Taylor and Watson Brown remained behind to guard the bridge. The others proceeded across the river.[9]

At 10:30 p.m. Brown steered into the Baltimore and Ohio covered way, passing first the Potomac Restaurant and then the Wager House, which served as a combination hotel and railroad station. All was quiet inside. Turning into the Ferry Lot, he stopped outside the armory, his men converging at the gate. Daniel Whelan, the armory watchman, stepped out of the guardhouse to investigate the noise. Brown jiggled the gate and found it locked.

"Open the gate!" he ordered sharply.

"I couldn't if I was stuck," Whelan replied.

Brown's men began climbing the fence. Another grabbed Whelan by his coat, pulling him hard against the fence. Muzzles from a half-dozen Sharps jabbed him in the ribs.

"We haven't got time to bother with a key," said Stevens, and with a crowbar twisted against the chain, he snapped open the gate.

Brown led the wagon into the yard, glaring hard into the frightened watchman's face. "I have come here from Kansas," he said sternly, "and this is a slave State; I want to free all the negroes in this State; I have possession now of the United States armory, and if the citizens interfere with me I must only burn the town and have blood."[10]

Brown posted guards at the armory and led the others to the arsenal, located a short distance down Shenandoah Street. He captured a few souls strolling the street and hustled them over to the guardhouse with Whelan. Leaving Edwin Coppoc and Hazlett to hold the arsenal, Brown continued down Shenandoah Street, sending Oliver to the Shenandoah bridge and leaving Kagi, Copeland,

9. Sanborn, *Life and Letters*, 553.

10. U.S. Senate, Mason Committee, *Report on the Invasion of Harpers Ferry*, 36th Cong., 1st Sess., Vol. 1, Rpt. 278 (Washington, D.C., 1860), see Whelan's testimony, II, 22, hereinafter cited as Mason Report; Anderson, *A Voice from Harpers Ferry*, 32.

and Leary at the rifle works. Satisfied he had both bridges and all the town's weapons under his control, Brown returned to the armory and dispatched Stevens and Cook with a squad of six men into the Virginia countryside to take hostages and free slaves.

So far the raid had worked perfectly. Brown controlled the armory while most of the townsfolk lay snug in their beds, unaware that the wrath of God had descended in the night to lay siege to their futures.

Stevens led the wagon down the Charles Town pike, hurrying the men along. The Baltimore express was expected from Wheeling, and he wanted to be back before it pulled up to the platform at the Wager House. Stevens worried that Brown had spread the men too thin. He kept one ear cocked for the distant whistle of the train, but he heard nothing but the steady clop of the horse and the muffled voices of the men following the wagon. Anxious to reach his destination, the home of Colonel Lewis W. Washington, he quickened the pace. Brown wanted the distinguished colonel, a prosperous planter and great-grandnephew of the Republic's first president, as a hostage and his slaves as enlistees in God's army of freedom fighters.

At midnight Patrick Higgins strolled to his post on the bridge to relieve Williams, but the watchman was not there. Thinking Williams had gone down the tracks, Higgins picked up a lantern and started after him, calling as he went. When he reached the halfway point, Watson Brown stepped out of the shadows and grabbed Higgins by the coat. The watchman lurched to the side, threw Watson off balance, and ran back down the bridge. Fearing Higgins would spread the alarm, Watson took aim and fired. The ball creased the watchman's head. Higgins accelerated his pace and dodged into the Wager House, blood running down his forehead. When he tried to explain to the night clerk what had happened, he sounded incoherent. The clerk accused Higgins of overindulging in bad whiskey, but the watchman hotly disagreed. No, he said. Somebody down the bridge hollered "Halt." "I didn't know what 'Halt' mint then," he blustered, "any more than a hog knows about a holiday." The clerk ignored the remark. He blamed the incident on a band of armory workers who had been discussing a strike.[11]

11. Higgins' statement in the Baltimore *American and Commercial Advertiser*, October 19, 1859.

Brown, hovering near the armory gate, heard the hollow report of Watson's gun echo through the covered bridge and into town. He wondered who fired the shot and why, and whether anybody else had heard it. But all remained quiet, except for the distant clatter of hoofbeats coming closer. He looked towards the sound of the noise and observed a large four-horse wagon filled with men rounding into the Ferry Lot, and behind it his own horse-drawn wagon. Stevens was back with three hostages—Colonel Washington, John Allstadt, and Allstadt's eighteen-year-old son—and a half-dozen slaves.

Washington bounded off the wagon, walked over to the grizzled man in the Kansas cap, and demanded an explanation. Brown greeted his prime hostage with due deference. "You will find a fire in here," he said, motioning towards the guardhouse. "It is rather cold this morning." Brown paused to admire the colonel's four-horse wagon. Then he ordered Cook and Tidd to take the wagon across the bridge, gather more hostages, and bring all the volunteers they could enlist to the armory. He needed to consolidate his army now, for he needed help to carry the captured arms and supplies deeper into the South.

After seeing the wagon off, Brown stepped into the guardhouse and spoke to Washington. "I shall be very attentive to you, sir, for I may get the worst of it in my first encounter, and if so, your life is worth as much as mine. My particular reason for taking you first was that, as the aid to the Governor of Virginia, I knew you would endeavor to do your duty, and perhaps you would have been a troublesome customer to me; and apart from that, I wanted you particularly for the moral effect it would give our cause having one of your name, as a prisoner."[12]

The mysterious shot from the bridge continued to worry Brown. He returned to the armory gate just as the 1:25 A.M. express slowly passed the armory and came to a stop at the Wager House. Conductor A. J. Phelps stepped off the train and sauntered into the lobby of the hotel. Higgins, dabbing his head with a bloody cloth, reported that he had been attacked on the bridge by men with guns and that Bill Williams was missing.

Shephard Hayward, the night baggage handler, had been dozing

12. Washington's testimony, Mason Report, II, 30–36. See also John H. Allstadt's testimony, *ibid.*, 40–42.

when the train pulled to the loading dock. Doubting Higgins'
story, he lifted his heavy body to an upright position, went out
the door, and clambered down the tracks to find Williams. A voice
from the dark ordered him to halt. Hayward whirled about and
started running back to the hotel. Watson Brown fired. Hayward
lurched forward, stumbled painfully back to the loading platform,
and fell mortally wounded in a pool of blood. Ironically, the first
fatality in Brown's crusade was a free black who lived and worked
in Harpers Ferry.[13]

The gunfire at the bridge and the commotion at the Wager
House attracted a few late drinkers at the Gault House. They wandered over to the Wager House and stared curiously at the dying
baggage handler. Another townsman, Dr. John D. Starry, heard the
shot from his bedroom window, dressed, and hurried to the hotel.
Conductor Phelps, after finding the telegraph out of order, walked
down the trestle with the engineer to inspect the tracks. Spying
two guards standing behind a simple barricade, they returned to
the hotel to hear Starry pronounce Hayward beyond medical help.

Suspicion now centered on unusual activity at the armory. The
doctor and the conductor walked across the lot, and Brown met
them at the gate. They talked briefly. Brown did not want the train
in town and told Phelps to proceed to Baltimore. Stevens protested, warning that Phelps would spread the alarm at the next
stop, but Brown planned to be deep in the Blue Ridge Mountains
before the government had time to organize a force against him.

Brown, thinking Starry was a passenger, released both men. The
doctor acted quickly, sending messengers to Charles Town, Shepherdstown, and Martinsburg to raise the militia. Recruiting every
able-bodied man at the Gault House, he asked them to circulate
through town and warn the public. At daylight townspeople
armed with knives, old rusty cutlasses, squirrel guns, and a few
ancient muskets gathered near the saloon.[14]

When bells began to toll in Harpers Ferry, Brown knew his raid
had been discovered. His volunteers began to fidget. He looked

13. Thomas Drew, comp., *The John Brown Invasion: An Authentic History of
the Harper's Ferry Tragedy* (Boston, 1859), 69; New York *Herald*, October 19, 24,
1859. Shephard Hayward is also known as Hayward Shepherd and by several other
variations of the same name.

14. Phelps's and Dr. John D. Starry's testimony, Mason Report, II, 13–26, 69–
70; Baltimore *American and Commercial Advertiser*, October 17, 1859.

longingly across the river. Where was Cook? Where was the army of slaves? Cook had promised there would be dozens, maybe even hundreds, all joining in the march south.

Workers began to report at the armory. James Darrell, the bell ringer, came to the gate and was captured. Others followed, including George W. Cutshaw, who had just escorted a lady across the river to a canal packet boat. Then firing erupted, some at street corners and some from the second-story windows opposite the armory on North Potomac Street.

Irish grocer Thomas Boerley, the local strongman, loaded his gun and walked to the corner of Shenandoah and High Streets. Taking aim, he fired into the midst of several raiders standing outside the enginehouse. The shot went astray, but one of Brown's men leveled a Sharps on the Irishman's big body and pulled the trigger. Boerley slumped to the ground, blood gushing from his groin. He died a few hours later, the first white male killed by the raiders.[15]

Once the train reached the Maryland side of the river, the engineer gave it full throttle and screeched into Monocacy in a cloud of steam. Conductor Phelps raced to the telegraph office and wired an urgent message to William Prescott Smith, master of transportation for the railroad, reporting "armed Abolitionists" in possession of the Federal armory and arsenal and stating that no further trains would be permitted to pass through Harpers Ferry. At the next stop, Ellicott Mills, Phelps received a reply. Smith scoffed at the message, calling Phelps's dispatch "exaggerated and written under excitement." Besides, he asked, why would abolitionists want Harpers Ferry? Phelps was furious. He had talked to Brown and heard the chieftain's plans. "My dispatch is not exaggerated," he replied. "I have not made it half as bad as it is. The captain expects a reinforcement of 1500 men to liberate the slaves." Smith, second in command of the Baltimore and Ohio, informed John W. Garrett, the railroad's president, who on learning the details telegraphed President James Buchanan. Garrett believed Phelps and warned Buchanan, "This is a moment of greatest peril."[16]

15. Baltimore *Weekly American,* November 5, 1859.
16. Quoted in Jules Abels, *Man on Fire: John Brown and the Cause of Liberty* (New York, 1971), 274.

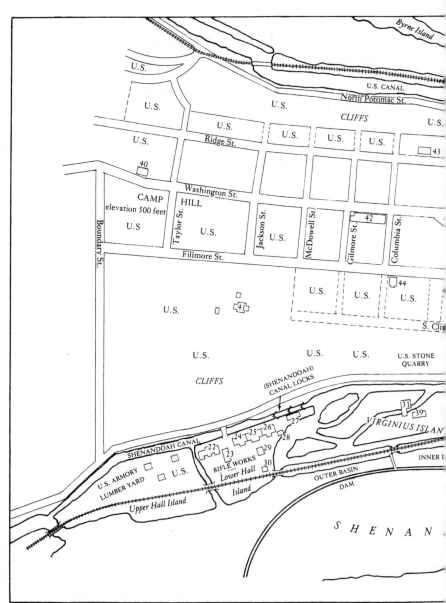

Harpers Ferry in 1859

*Reprinted from Merritt Roe Smith,* Harpers Ferry Armory and the New
Technology: The Challenge of Change. *Copyright © 1977 by Cornell University.
Used by permission of the publisher, Cornell University Press.*

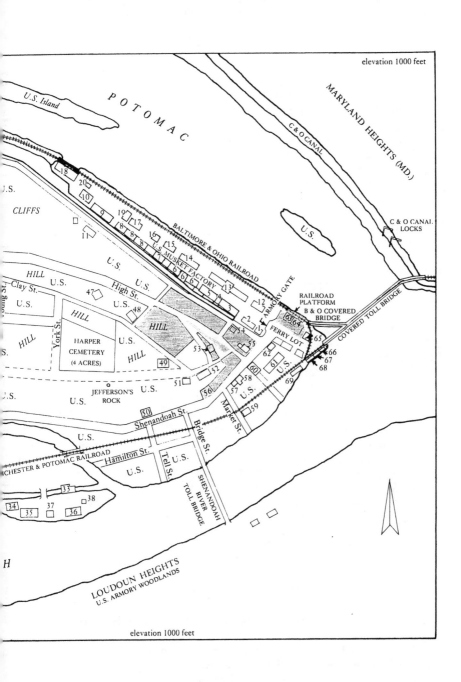

elevation 1000 feet

U.S. Island

P O T O M A C

MARYLAND HEIGHTS (MD.)

C & O CANAL

C & O CANAL.
LOCKS

U.S.

CLIFFS

U.S.

18

20

10

9   19   17

8   16

11   8   8

15

BALTIMORE & OHIO RAILROAD

U.S. MUSKET FACTORY

14

HILL

U.S.

U.S.

High St.

Clay St.

U.S.   47

U.S.   48

York St.

HILL

HILL

HARPER
CEMETERY
(4 ACRES)

U.S.

HILL

49

JEFFERSON'S
ROCK

U.S.

U.S.

6   6   6

13

5   4

3

ARMORY GATE

12

2

1

54

55

53

52

51

56

57

58

60   61

62

59

50

RAILROAD
PLATFORM
B & O COVERED
BRIDGE

63 64

FERRY LOT

65

COVERED TOLL BRIDGE

66
67
68

69

Shenandoah St.

Market St.

U.S.

U.S.

Bridge St.

WINCHESTER & POTOMAC RAILROAD

Hamilton St.

U.S.

Tell St.

U.S.

SHENANDOAH
RIVER
TOLL BRIDGE

33

34   37   38

35   36

H

LOUDOUN HEIGHTS
U.S. ARMORY WOODLANDS

elevation 1000 feet

Key to Map 2

UNITED STATES ARMORY BUILDINGS
 1. Enginehouse (site of John Brown's capture)
 2. Armory offices
 3. "Bell" of finishing shop
 4. Polishing shop and washhouse
 5. Boring mill
 6. Stocking and machine shop
 7. Millwright shop
 8. Grinding mill, sawmill, and carpenter's shop
 9. Tilt-hammer and barrel-forging shop
10. Lumber house and coal bin
11. New stock and storehouse
12. Warehouse
13. Smith and forging shop
14. Annealing shop and brass foundry
15. Proof house
16. Charcoal house
17. Old stock storehouse
18. Rolling mill
19. Limehouse (exact location unknown)
20. Icehouse (exact location unknown)
21. Armory magazine

RIFLE WORKS ON LOWER HALL ISLAND
22. Finishing and machine shop
23. Filing shop
24. Machine shop
25. Barrel-drilling and finishing shop
26. Tilt-hammer and forging shop
27. Annealing furnace and proof house
28. Coal house
29. Stockhouse
30. Proof house

BUILDINGS ON VIRGINIUS ISLAND
31. Iron foundry
32. Island Flour Mill, owned and operated by Abraham H. Herr and
    James S. Welch
33. Sawmill and lumberyard owned by Lewis Wernwag
34. Machine shop operated by John Wernwag
35. Cotton mill destroyed by the 1852 flood
36. Cotton factory operated by Abraham H. Herr
37. Smith shop
38. Lewis Wernwag's sawmill and lumberyard office
39. Chopping mill

OTHER BUILDINGS AT HARPERS FERRY

40. Lutheran church on Camp Hill
41. Armory superintendent quarters and grounds
42. Firehouse and public square on Camp Hill
43. Female Seminary on Camp Hill
44. Armory paymaster's clerk house
45. Armory superintendent's clerk house
46. Armory paymaster quarters and grounds
47. Methodist Protestant church
48. Methodist-Episcopal church
49. St. John's Protestant Episcopal Church
50. Presbyterian church
51. Catholic church
52. St. Peter's Roman Catholic Church
53. Harper-Wager House (*ca.* 1775/1782)
54. Tavern and store
55. Dry goods store
56. Small shops
57. Old master armorer's house
58. New master armorer's house
59. Market house
60. Small U.S. arsenal
61. Large U.S. arsenal
62. Old superintendent's office
63. Potomac Restaurant (on original Ferry Lot)
64. Wager House Hotel (on original Ferry Lot)
65. Baltimore and Ohio Railroad office
66. Tollhouse for covered bridge
67. Baltimore and Ohio Railroad office
68. Gault House Saloon
69. Winchester and Potomac Railroad depot

At 10 A.M. Buchanan dispatched a rider to Arlington to locate Brevet Colonel Robert E. Lee of the 2nd U.S. Cavalry and bring him to Washington. Lee, in civilian clothes, arrived at noon with Lieutenant James Ewell Brown "Jeb" Stuart, who volunteered to act as Lee's aide. Because the rest of the army was stationed in the West, Buchanan called at the Navy Yard to ask whether Lieutenant Israel Green could muster a few marines for immediate duty. Green reported ninety men available, and Buchanan turned them over to Lee. Taking two small howitzers and all his men, Green departed for Sandy Hook at 3 P.M., but Lee and Stuart missed the train. Buchanan nervously wired Garrett, who put a special car on the rails to pick up the two stranded officers.[17]

In the meantime, Brown's men at the armory, along with his now numerous hostages, listened to bullets pellet the engine-house and ricochet with a lethal whine off the armory fence. Cook had taken a hostage on the Boonsboro road, Terrence Byrne, and ordered Willie Leeman and Will Thompson to deliver him to Brown. Leeman crossed the bridge with Byrne, dodged through a hail of shot, and entered the watchhouse. Brown asked how many slaves had been armed. Leeman said there were none but promised they would come. Brown wanted to send Leeman back to hurry Cook, but before he could the raiders lost control of both bridges.[18]

The situation for the guards on the bridges had become untenable. Oliver Brown made a dash for the armory yard and scrambled inside, bullets nipping at his heels. Leary thought his chances were better with Kagi and sought refuge at the rifle works. Watson Brown and William Thompson stole down the covered way and double-quicked into the enginehouse.

Dangerfield Newby followed Watson as far as the Ferry Lot and decided he had seen enough of old Brown's planning. He made a furtive effort to blend back into the town's society but neglected to throw away his rifle. A sharpshooter hidden in a house at the foot of High Street loaded his rifle with a rail spike and shot Newby in the head. Townsfolk dragged the body into an alley and took their revenge. They cut off his genitals, slit his throat, and rammed sticks into his wounds. Another knife wielder trimmed off Newby's ears and put them in his pocket. When the crowd

17. Shepherdstown *Register*, February 5, 1886.
18. Baltimore *Weekly Sun*, November 12, December 3, 1859.

tired of their sport, they pushed the remains into a gutter, and the town's hogs finished off the body. A few spectators temporarily lost their appetite for pork.[19]

By midmorning, word of the raid reached Frederick and Winchester, and from there spread rapidly. From New York City to Topeka, Kansas, headlines blazed: "Negro Insurrection at Harper's Ferry!" and "Fire and Rapine on the Virginia Border!" In Kansas, the name "Osawatomie" Brown rang with familiarity, and pro-slavery elements who lived in Douglas and Miami Counties perhaps whispered to their friends—"So the devil has gone to Virginia!"[20]

Stevens, the only member of Brown's force with military experience, and Secretary of War Kagi, perhaps the brightest of his captains, both pleaded with their commander to recall the men and withdraw to the Maryland side. Kagi had two men at the rifle works, and two were still hidden on the second floor of the arsenal. All the rest of the raiders were either in the enginehouse or stranded in Maryland. Brown was about to learn a lesson the Union army also failed to discover until the morning of September 15, 1862—Harpers Ferry was easy to attack but almost impossible to defend.

Late Monday morning Brown was stunned to find his force surrounded and attacked from all sides. The Jefferson Guards arrived from Charles Town, crossed in skiffs to the Maryland side, and took possession of the Potomac bridge. Two militia companies from Shepherdstown and three from Frederick occupied the Shenandoah bridge. Others swarmed behind the railroad trestle overlooking the armory. A company of railroaders from Martinsburg hooked two cars to an engine, sped to the Ferry, and took positions inside the armory. Osborn Anderson thought the old man looked wistful and somewhat "puzzled" by the unexpected turn of events.[21]

But Brown had not gone to the trouble of taking important hostages like Colonel Washington without good reason, and when men reported to work at the armory he grabbed Archibald Kitz-

19. Alexander R. Boteler, "Recollections of the John Brown Raid," *Century Monthly*, XXVI (July, 1883), 399–411.

20. New York *Tribune*, October 18, 19, 1859; Topeka *Tribune*, October 21, 1859.

21. Anderson, *A Voice from Harper's Ferry*, 36; Barry, *Harper's Ferry*, 64–65.

miller, acting superintendent, Benjamin Mills, master armorer, Armistead Ball, master machinist, and John E. P. Dangerfield, armory clerk. A less important hostage, Rezin Cross, agreed to speak with the militia on behalf of Brown, who promised to release the hostages in exchange for safe passage of his army to Maryland. He sent Will Thompson, carrying a flag of truce tied to a ramrod, across the Ferry Lot with negotiator Cross at his side. Militia had been whetting their thirst outside the Gault House and paid no attention to white flags. They freed Cross and captured Thompson, confining him to a second-floor room in the Wager House.[22]

An hour passed and Brown could not learn what had happened to his two emissaries. Acting armory superintendent Kitzmiller offered to investigate the matter and promised to return promptly. Brown agreed, but sent along Stevens and his son Watson under another flag of truce. At a time when nobody but Brown gave any thought to the rules of war, the trio got as far as the Ferry Lot when Kitzmiller's friends beckoned him aside. Shots from the second-story window of the Gault House Saloon brought down Watson and Stevens. Militia grabbed Stevens and hauled him to the Wager House. Watson crawled back to the enginehouse, a bullet in his bowels, and was pulled inside by his brother.[23] Brown was appalled by the attack on his son, feeling that his Provisional Government, although insurrectionists, deserved the same consideration as any recognized country at war. His détente towards civilians ended.

George W. Turner, a graduate of West Point, had come to town on business. He made the mistake of walking down High Street and coming into view as he crossed Shenandoah Street. A bullet from a Sharps rifle opened a gaping hole in his chest, and Turner died instantly.

Fontaine Beckham, the town's kindly old mayor, had attempted to remove himself from the fighting on the street by confining himself to the Baltimore and Ohio ticket office, where he worked as agent for the railroad. Townspeople demanded he take mayoral action to quell the disorder before the threatened slave multitude ravished the town. In his official capacity, Beckham climbed the trestle and peeked around the town water tower. A Sharps barked

---

22. Drew, comp., *The John Brown Invasion*, 76.
23. *Ibid.*, 75, 79, 80.

from behind a crack in the enginehouse door. Beckham slumped to the ground, a bullet in his head, shot by Edwin Coppoc, the Quaker boy from Iowa who had promised his mother to not bear arms.[24]

If Brown's raid had not already spawned enough ironies, Beckham's death produced another. No person in Harpers Ferry had been a better friend to the blacks than the mayor. He owned a family of slaves, which he treated well, and had looked after the welfare of Shephard Hayward, now dead on the loading platform. In his will, Beckham had provided for the liberation of his slaves. Coppoc's shot, fired by a man who knew little about firearms, emancipated Isaac Gilbert, his wife, and their three children.[25]

Word of the mayor's death enraged the town, especially militiaman Harry Hunter, who was drinking at the saloon when he learned Uncle Fontaine had just been killed. With George W. Chambers, the saloonkeeper, in tow, Hunter mounted the stairs of the Wager House and, over the objections of Christine Foulke, sister of the proprietor, dragged Will Thompson outside. "Mr. Beckham's life," Hunter snarled at her, "is worth ten thousand of these vile abolitionists." A crowd followed Hunter onto the Potomac bridge, where he stopped above the river, shot Thompson in the head, and pushed him through the trestle. "Before he had reached the ground," Hunter later admitted, "some four or five shots had been fired into his body." Thompson landed on the bed of the river. For fifteen minutes the men on the bridge enjoyed a little useless target practice.[26]

While Hunter performed his grisly work on the bridge, a sniper on the railroad trestle above the armory took careful aim on the heavy door of the enginehouse. He noticed that it cracked open from time to time, followed by one or two shots from a Sharps rifle before closing again. The next time it opened, he fired. Oliver Brown lurched backwards and fell at his father's feet, shot, like his brother, in the bowels.[27]

24. Baltimore *Weekly American*, November 5, 1859; Villard, *John Brown*, 441; George W. Chambers' testimony, Mason Report, II, 29.

25. Mayor Beckham's Will Book, JCCR.

26. Barry, *Harper's Ferry*, 60; Harry Hunter's testimony, New York *Tribune*, October 29, 1859, and New York *Herald*, October 31, 1859.

27. Statement of John T. Allstadt to K. Mayo, April 15, 1909, quoted in Villard, *John Brown*, 441.

Brown needed to contact Cook and Tidd, but he had no way of communicating with his men on the opposite side of the Potomac. He believed that by now Cook would have raised a black army on the Maryland side. It was time for them to counterattack. Twenty-year-old Leeman, anxious to make his escape from the clutches of the old man, agreed to cross the river and locate Cook. Leeman could not swim, but the water was low and Brown agreed to let him try. From the armory yard Leeman dropped down a culvert and plunged into the river. Militia spotted him and opened fire. Wounded, Leeman drifted downriver and pulled himself onto a rock. George A. Schoppert, a visitor from Richmond, waded into the river and, to keep his powder dry, brandished a revolver above his head. Leeman hollered, "Don't shoot! I surrender!" Schoppert smiled and shot the boy's face off. Men followed Schoppert to the rock and fired into Leeman's remains. Slugs jolted the body off the rock. It slipped into the current and floated downriver. The militia returned to the bridge. They remembered Stevens, lying under guard at the Wager House, and decided to get him, too.[28]

Captain Thomas Sinn of the Frederick militia, disdaining any flag of truce, sauntered over to the armory and asked to speak with Isaac Smith. Brown came to the door, cracked it open, and complained about his men being "shot down like dogs while bearing a flag of truce." Sinn replied that they got what they deserved. Brown said "he knew what he had to undergo when he came there. He had weighed the responsibility and would not shirk from it. He had full possession of the town and could have massacred all the inhabitants had he thought proper to do so, but, as he had not, he considered himself entitled to some terms." Brown added that they had not knowingly shot at anyone unless shot at themselves. Sinn disagreed. The unarmed mayor had been killed. Brown shook his head apologetically and replied, "I fight only those who fight me."

Sinn finished his conversation with Brown and returned to the Wager House, where he found a group of men badgering Stevens. "Get out," Sinn barked. "If that man had a toy gun, you would jump out the window." Because of Sinn, Stevens was spared, but only temporarily.[29]

28. Baltimore *American Weekly*, November 5, 1859; Hinton, *John Brown and His Men*, 535; Villard, *John Brown*, 440.

29. Drew, comp., *The John Brown Invasion*, 40; New York *Tribune*, October 31, 1859.

At midafternoon Captain E. G. Alburtis of the Martinsburg militia attacked the enginehouse from the rear, releasing a few prisoners still confined in the guardhouse. Brown had portholes cut through the bricks in the enginehouse and his men repulsed the attack, killing one and wounding two.[30]

While the action ebbed and flowed all afternoon at the armory, another fatal encounter occurred on upper Shenandoah Street at Hall's Rifle Works. When men reported to work in the morning, they found the main building occupied by three of Brown's raiders—John Kagi and two blacks, John Copeland and Lewis Leary. Dr. Starry led the militia to the rifle works, diverting some across the Shenandoah bridge to take positions on the opposite shore. Kagi, observing he was about to be surrounded, slipped out the back of the building and attempted to escape down the roadbed of the Winchester and Potomac Railroad. Seeing armed men approaching from the front, he waded into the Shenandoah. Caught in a crossfire from both sides of the river, Kagi never felt the ball that entered his head and killed him instantly.

Leary and Copeland waded the river further upstream, but with no better luck. A ball struck Leary in the back, knocking him face first into the current. Copeland grabbed him by the shawl and helped him onto a rock in the center of the river. Copeland stood quietly, watching as James H. Holt waded towards him, a revolver in his hand and a murderous gleam in his eyes. Holt shoved the gun in Copeland's face and pulled the trigger. With the powder dampened, the gun misfired. Holt clubbed Copeland with the weapon and dragged him to shore. Leary survived his wound until late in the night, his groans growing feebler, his words rasping as he muttered, "I am ready to die."[31]

Late in the afternoon Cook looked down upon the Ferry from the Maryland side of the river. He had no army of liberated blacks to rescue the old man. He listened to the firing and knew the raid had failed. To some extent he blamed himself, for he had not delivered on his promise. In a final desperate act of frustration, he climbed a tree and leveled his Sharps on the men firing from the Baltimore and Ohio roadbed. Congressman Alexander R. Boteler, who was standing among the men as an observer, heard a bullet

30. Baltimore *Weekly Sun*, October 22, 1859; Boteler, "Recollections of the John Brown Raid," 407.

31. Boteler, "Recollections of the John Brown Raid," 407; Mason Report, II, 27.

whiz by his ear and looked across the river. He spied Cook and pointed him out to the others. A barrage opened from the roadbed. One ball broke the limb supporting Cook, and he tumbled twenty feet to the ground. Stunned, Cook brushed himself off and limped back up the road to the schoolhouse. The time had come to flee. He would get Owen, Tidd, Barclay Coppoc, and Meriam and retreat to Chambersburg, where his wife waited for him at the widow Ritner's home.[32]

As night fell, the gunfire subsided. Osborn Anderson and Albert Hazlett had spent the day hiding on the second floor of the arsenal. They had witnessed the shooting and waited for the streets to quiet before attempting an escape. Slipping through a back window, they edged down to the river, found a boat lying alongshore, and poled towards the Maryland side. The current drifted them downriver. When they came ashore at 10 P.M. they could hear a locomotive snuffling at Sandy Hook. Had they gone downriver a little further, they might have seen a handsome man with graying hair addressing a group of men dressed in blue naval uniforms.[33]

Robert E. Lee had arrived. In his haste to reach the Ferry, he had not found time to change from civilian clothing. He had hurried from Arlington to capture Isaac Smith, an invader from the North. Lee could not have guessed how soon would come nearly two million more.

32. Hinton, *John Brown and His Men*, 710–11.
33. Anderson, *A Voice from Harper's Ferry*, 47–55.

# 2

## Sowing the Wind

At 11 P.M., Monday, October 17, Robert E. Lee entered Harpers
Ferry with Lieutenants Stuart and Green and a company of ninety
armed marines. Having been warned by Buchanan to expect more
than five hundred insurgents, Lee was relieved to find the number
cut back to a few armed ruffians holed up in the enginehouse and
under the command of a Kansas raider known as Osawatomie
Brown. Lee closed the saloons and deployed the marines around
the armory yard with orders to keep the raiders contained until
daylight as he did not want the hostages hurt, one being his cousin
Lewis Washington. The marines entered through the back gate,
replacing the volunteers and militia already within the grounds.[1]

Dampness and cold penetrated the grim darkness of the enginehouse. The sleepless old man pattered about the brick floor. He
had neither eaten nor slept for nearly two days. Two sons, Oliver
and Watson, lay dying on the floor. Oliver groaned and called for
his father. "Shoot me," he begged. "I cannot stand the pain."
Brown turned away, saying, "If you must die, die like a man." The
hostages thought the words harsh, and someone uttered a rebuke.
Brown, who understood pain and suffering, turned sorrowfully

1. Israel Green, "The Capture of John Brown," *North American Review*, CXLI
(December, 1885), 564–69.

and answered, "Gentlemen, if you knew of my past history you would not blame me for being here. I went to Kansas a peaceable man, and the proslavery people hunted me down like a wolf. I lost one of my sons there." He did not mention the five bodies his men had dismembered on the moonlit banks of the bloodied Pottawatomie. Oliver had been there, too, with a stained broadsword clutched in his hands. Brown spoke softly to his son but there was no answer. "I guess he is dead," Brown sighed, and then he resumed his pacing.[2]

In the gray gloom of dawn, fog lay heavy over the valley of the Potomac, wetting the Ferry in a dismal mist. Brown peered through loopholes cut through the brick wall and observed a company of marines, armed with muskets, bayonets, and sledgehammers, formed in front of the enginehouse. To their side was a gray-haired man in civilian clothes, and to the rear, two thousand spectators who had gathered to see the raiders killed. Brown counted his men: Shields Green, Edwin Coppoc, Jeremiah Anderson, and Dauphin Thompson. Watson still lived, but he could not raise his rifle. Green slipped his Sharps through a loophole and took aim on the gray-haired gentleman talking to a cavalry officer.

"Don't fire," Brown said curtly. "The man is unarmed."

Brown slung a rope across the inside of the heavy enginehouse doors, just loose enough so they would give slightly—but not break when struck. He ordered the men to load their rifles and encouraged them "to sell their lives as dearly as they could." Then he sat down beside Watson. With one hand he felt his son's pulse, the other held his weapon.

Instead of attacking, Lee sent Stuart to the enginehouse under a flag of truce. Brown went to the door, cracked it open, thrust the muzzle of his Sharps into the lieutenant's face, and snatched from his hand a note written by Lee. The message demanded Brown's surrender but gave assurances he would be protected from harm and turned over to civil authorities. Brown rejected the offer and reminded Stuart he had hostages. He would release them only in exchange for his and his followers' freedom. Stuart had no authority to negotiate, but Lewis Washington suggested that Lee come to the door and speak with Brown. Stuart replied that Lee

2. Villard, *John Brown,* 448.

would agree to no other terms. He stepped back from the door and with a flourish of his hat signaled Green to attack.[3]

The marines, aligned in two rows of twelve each, rushed forward, the first row with sledges, the second with muskets and bayonets. With the crowd cheering in the rear, Green led the charge and stood by as his men beat on the sturdy oak doors. When the doors failed to split, a detail brought a heavy ladder and, using it as a battering ram, broke through two or three planks. Green, a small man, slipped into the enginehouse and stood atop the fire engine, shouting, "Where's Brown!" More marines crawled inside and were confronted by a blistering fire from the raiders.

Washington pointed to Brown, who was kneeling by his son with a cocked rifle, and said, "This is Osawatomie."

Green drew his dress sword, leaped from the fire engine, and knocked Brown over before the old man could fire. Green's flimsy sword struck bone and buckled. He tried to finish the job by pouncing on the old man and beating him on the head with the butt of his sword. With blood oozing though his silver beard Brown slumped to the floor, and Green, breathing hard, thought him dead.

As the smoke cleared, Green, gasping for breath and badly shaken, looked around the room. He saw one of the raiders, Jeremiah Anderson, pinned to the wall with a bayonet through his chest. Another, Dauphin Thompson, lay in pool of blood under the fire engine where he had been impaled repeatedly by a bayonet. Edwin Coppoc and Shields Green lurked in the rear and were taken outside under guard. But a young marine, blue-eyed and blond-haired Luke Quinn, lay dead on the floor of the enginehouse, and another, Private Rupert, whose upper teeth had been knocked out, leaned against the wall and dabbed at a flesh wound.[4]

Lee glanced at his watch. The attack had taken three minutes. He ordered the enginehouse cleared and the bodies moved to the Ferry Lot and laid on the ground. The hostages, who had huddled against the back of the building during the attack, filed out to the cheers of the crowd. Washington exited last. He did not want to appear in public before covering his soiled hands with a clean pair

3. H. B. McClellan, *The Life and Campaigns of Major General J. E. B. Stuart* (Boston, 1885), 28–29.

4. Green, "Capture of John Brown," 565–69; Mason Report, II, Appendix, 29–43; Shepherdstown *Register*, February 5, 1886; Villard, *John Brown*, 451–55.

of kid gloves. Being quite hungry, the hostages joined friends and relatives for a hot breakfast at the Potomac Restaurant.

A doctor from the Frederick militia examined Brown and his son Watson and pronounced them both mortally wounded. Watson died a few hours later, but Brown recovered consciousness and seemed surprised to be alive. For a man who believed in signs and omens, he attributed his return to earthly substance as a special gift from God. Time had been divinely granted for him to complete his mission. Lee moved Brown and Stevens to the paymaster's office to protect them from a hostile mob who pressed against the thin line of marines holding them back.

John C. Unseld, a farmer who knew Brown as Isaac Smith, rode into the Ferry and, finding Lee in charge, suggested that Brown's headquarters be searched. With Unseld acting as guide, Lee dispatched Stuart with a detachment from the Baltimore Grays. Mounted on borrowed horses, they first stopped at the schoolhouse. Stuart found crates filled with rifles and revolvers, enough arms to give credence to Brown's claim of instigating a slave revolt. When they arrived at the farmhouse they discovered a tattered carpetbag filled with Brown's private papers. Stuart thumbed through maps, letters, and documents, enough to incriminate old Osawatomie and implicate a group known as the Secret Six, Brown's abolitionist backers. Stuart returned with the evidence and deposited it with Lee.[5]

While Stuart was at the Kennedy home, Governor Henry A. Wise stepped off the Baltimore and Ohio with Senator James M. Mason of Virginia, Congressman Clement L. Vallandigham of Ohio, and a swarm of reporters. The townsfolk cheered Wise, who responded to the attention by reopening the saloons. The party strolled over to the paymaster's office to question Brown, whose vitality recovered when he observed the presence of a dozen prying reporters with notepads. Knowing that whatever he said would be published in every newspaper from New York to Kansas, the wounded raider's running commentary of righteous justification for his acts impressed everybody in the room but Wise, Mason, and Vallandigham. After three hours of interrogation, Wise walked back to the hotel, muttering, "He is the gamest man I ever

5. McClellan, *Life and Campaigns of J. E. B. Stuart*, 29–30; Lee's Report in Mason Report, Appendix, II, 40–44; Baltimore *Weekly Sun*, October 22, 1859.

saw." A Baltimore reporter who observed the session wrote: "In the midst of his enemies, whose home he had invaded; wounded, and a prisoner; surrounded by a small army of angry men; and with the gallows staring him full in the face, he lay on the floor, and, in reply to every question, gave answers that betokened the spirit that animated him."[6]

Wise, Mason, and Vallandigham returned to the Wager House, where the carpetbag awaited their inspection. They spread the contents on the table, focusing special interest on Brown's constitution and Provisional Government, which they condemned as blatant acts of treason against the United States. They fished through Brown's accounts and found letters from his backers, men like wealthy New York State landowner Gerrit Smith and Boston businessman George Luther Stearns. Senator Mason wanted Brown tried in a Federal court for crimes against the country, claiming jurisdiction because the U.S. Armory had been raided. But for a better reason, he wanted Frederick Douglass and the pestiferous abolitionists exposed for their roles in the raid. But Wise claimed the trial must be held in Virginia, arguing that her citizens had been murdered. If the state could not hang John Brown, the Federal government could have him.[7]

For the trial and protection of Brown, Stevens, Edwin Coppoc, John Copeland, and Shields Green, Lee escorted the raiders to the jail at Charles Town, the county seat of Jefferson County. Copeland and Green, being black, shared the same cell. A few days later the prisoners were joined by Cook and Hazlett, both of whom had been captured in Pennsylvania, Cook near Chambersburg and Hazlett a few miles from Carlisle. Five men escaped: Owen Brown, Charles Tidd, Barclay Coppoc, Francis Meriam, and Osborn Anderson. The first four named were nearby when Cook, acting recklessly in an effort to see his wife, was apprehended on his way to Mrs. Ritner's boardinghouse by Daniel Loganon.[8]

6. A number of newspapers covered the interview, including the Baltimore *Weekly Sun*, October 22, 1859; Baltimore *American and Commercial Advertiser*, October 21, 1859; *National Intelligencer*, October 25, 1859; New York *Tribune*, October 22, 1859; and New York *Herald*, October 22, 1859.

7. Governor Wise's speech, Richmond *Enquirer*, October 25, 1859.

8. Ralph Keeler, "Owen Brown's Escape from Harper's Ferry," *Atlantic Monthly*, XXXIII (March, 1874), 344–47; *National Intelligencer*, October 25, 27, 1859; Villard, *John Brown*, 444; Hinton, *John Brown and His Men*, 476–78.

Governor Wise followed the procession escorting Brown to Charles Town for trial. He refused to return to Richmond until a guard of eighty men had been posted at the jail and a pair of howitzers emplaced near the street. As the Jefferson County Circuit Court was scheduled to commence its fall session on October 20, the wheels of justice moved with uncommon speed. Wise informed the press that Judge Richard Parker, of Winchester, would not waste time bringing the murderers to justice.[9]

At 10:30 A.M. on October 25, Sheriff James W. Campbell assembled a detail to conduct the raiders across the street to the courthouse. Two rows of militia formed a lane to hold back the crowd. Brown, manacled to Edwin Coppoc, wobbled with help into the courtroom. Stevens, flushed with fever, hung onto the arm of a guard. Both men complained of weakness. The sheriff charged the accused with "treason and murder," after which Charles B. Harding, the state's attorney, asked Brown if he had provided for counsel. Brown had none, but replied:

> Virginians: I did not ask for any quarter at the time I was taken. I did not ask to have myself spared. The Governor . . . tendered me his assurance that I should have a fair trial; and under no circumstances whatever will I be able to attend a trial. If you seek my blood you can have it at any moment without the mockery of a trial. I have had no counsel. I have not been able to advise with one. I know nothing about the feelings of my fellow-prisoners, and am utterly unable to attend in any way to my own defence. My memory don't serve me. My health is insufficient, although improving. There are mitigating circumstances, if a fair trial is to be allowed us, that I would urge in our favor. But if we are to be forced, with the mere form of a trial, to execution, you might spare yourselves that trouble. I am ready for my fate. I do not ask for a trial. I plead for no mockery of a trial—no insult—nothing but that which conscience gives or cowardice would drive you to practice. . . . I do not know what the design of this examination is. I do not know what is to be the benefit to the Commonwealth. I have now little to ask other than that I be not publicly insulted as cowardly barbarians insult those who fall into their hands.[10]

The court appointed Charles J. Faulkner and Lawson Botts as counsel for the prisoners, neither of whom Brown wanted. With

9. Richmond *Enquirer*, October 25, 1859.
10. *National Intelligencer*, October 27, 1859.

the eyes of the public upon him, he wished to speak for himself. "I do not care anything about counsel," he said to the court. "It is unnecessary to trouble any gentleman with that duty." Because Faulkner had been at Harpers Ferry during the raid and observed the mayhem, he withdrew as counsel and was replaced by Thomas C. Green, the mayor of Charles Town, who perhaps expected to accumulate a little political capital by giving a good performance.

Although Harding acted as the prosecuting attorney for Jefferson County, Andrew Hunter, a skillful local lawyer, joined him as counsel for the Commonwealth. The governor refused to let Harding, well known as a heavy drinker, prosecute the trial without help, as dozens of reporters had squeezed into the courtroom to watch every move and record every word of an event promising to capture center-stage interest across the nation.

The trial commenced on October 26 and proceeded along the lines of the testimony given in magistrates' court. Brown, still feeble from his wounds, attended the hearing on a cot covered by a blanket. Colonel Washington testified first, relating how Stevens and his accomplices broke into his home, forced their way into his bedroom, stole his guns and the Sword of Frederick (a relic bestowed upon Great-Uncle George by Frederick the Great), and then with his blacks and his four-horse wagon conveyed him hostage to the armory. Washington recalled Brown bragging he "had arms enough for two thousand men, and could get enough for five thousand if wanted."

John Allstadt, whose home Stevens had invaded next, castigated the raiders for battering down his door and kidnapping him and his son. While confined to the enginehouse with his slaves, who had been armed with pikes, he claimed he had observed Brown fire "several times" at townspeople. He identified all the accused except Copeland, the "yellow man" who had been at Hall's Rifle Works.

Armistead Ball, the armory's master machinist, testified to being captured when he reported for work. He recalled Brown saying "that his object was not to make war against the people, and they would not be injured if they remained quiet; his object was to place the United States' arms in the hands of the black men, and he proposed then to free all the slaves in the vicinity."

William Johnson, who participated in the assault on the rifle works, identified Copeland, "who was attempting to escape across the river; he was armed with a spear and rifle, and was arrested in the middle of the Shenandoah." Johnson failed to mention that Copeland was on trial only because James Holt, intent on taking no prisoners, got his powder wet, causing his pistol to misfire.

Joseph A. Brua of Harpers Ferry testified that on several occasions Brown had attempted but failed to communicate with the militia under a flag of truce. He admitted, however, to observing Edwin Coppoc shoot Mayor Beckham, and he remembered seeing Brown watch, saying afterward, "That man is down."[11]

Alexander Kelly, another witness from the Ferry, described the death of his friend, Thomas Boerley. Contrary to the testimony of an earlier witness, Kelly admitted that Boerley was armed and had fired at the raiders first.

Albert Grist explained how he and his son were returning home from a prayer meeting when they were seized on the Shenandoah bridge by two men with rifles. Conducted to the armory, they met with Brown, who related how he intended to free the slaves, warning that as long as "we were peaceable we would not be hurt; if not, the town would be laid to ashes." Brown then released the Grists, who remained at Harpers Ferry and in the morning conveyed Brown's message to Mayor Beckham.

Archibald Kitzmiller, the armory's acting superintendent, denied he had escorted Stevens and Watson Brown across the Ferry Lot to negotiate terms. He claimed he had simply taken his handkerchief out of his pocket to wave at the rifle company on the bridge. He admitted asking Stevens and Brown to wait a few steps behind him, and that he later observed both of them fall after being hit by gunfire. At this point, Brown called out from his cot, "Describe the circumstances connected with the death of [William] Thompson." Kitzmiller claimed he did not see Thompson taken to the bridge and killed. He only remembered the murder of Mayor Beckham.

Brown persisted from his cot, demanding that the manner of Thompson's death be entered into the record. Prosecutor Hunter asked the court to rule the evidence inadmissible, as his son, Henry, had instigated the execution. When Brown accused the court of denying him a fair trial, Judge Parker allowed the testimony. Henry Hunter took the stand and proudly described the

11. *Ibid.*, October 27, 29, 1859.

grisly details. "We carried him to the bridge," Henry bragged, "and two of us levelled our guns, and at this moment of wild exasperation . . . a dozen balls were buried in him." His father could not listen and looked away, his face pale and distressed.[12]

Before the trial began, Brown had written his friends, asking that they arrange to provide him with a good defense attorney. His backers in the East sent George H. Hoyt, a young and inexperienced lawyer who arrived on the third day of the trial with a secret plan for Brown's escape. On the fourth day Hiram Griswold arrived from Cleveland and Samuel Chilton from Boston, both capable defense lawyers. They asked the court for time to review the evidence, but Parker had other commitments and accepted a motion from the prosecution to continue the trial without delay. The court excused Botts and Green, whom Brown accused of failing to follow his instructions during cross-examination.

Aware that some eastern newspapers had begun to glorify the raid, while others had softened their tone, Brown now believed his "noble cause" could only be sustained by martyring his life on the gallows. He relished the idea, wishing to be neither rescued nor acquitted. He dallied for time—time to express his convictions to every American who would listen—and as he cross-examined each witness for the prosecution he began to alter the attitudes of the spectators in the courtroom from outright hostility to cautious sympathy.

Brown provided the court with a list of witnesses for the defense, but most of them left the county before subpoenas could be served—warned off, Brown claimed, by Sheriff Campbell. John Dangerfield testified that Brown had made two efforts under a flag of truce to speak with town officials, but his men were shot down. Brown had promised all hostages they would not be harmed, and Dangerfield admitted the old man's threat to reduce the town to ashes was only a threat and never intended to be carried out. Dangerfield also testified that when the marines attacked, Brown did not want the hostages harmed by mistake and "cried out to surrender, but he was not heard."

Benjamin Mills, master armorer, corroborated Dangerfield's account, adding that before the firing started Brown attempted to release the hostages in exchange for the raiders' freedom before

12. *Ibid.*, November 5, 1859.

anybody got hurt. In response to a question from Brown, Mills admitted the raiders fired mostly in defense.

Hoyt protested that without the other witnesses, the defense would not be able to prove the absence of malicious intent on behalf of his clients, which was precisely what Hunter and Harding wanted to prevent at the time the trial began. Griswold and Chilton asked once more for a delay, begging time to familiarize themselves with the case and prepare a proper defense. Parker again rejected the request. This pleased Harding, who attempted to present the closing argument for the prosecution. Harding had been drinking and "dwelt for some time on the absurdity of the claim . . . of the prisoner that he should have been treated according to the rules of honorable warfare." Halfway through the summation, Harding started to argue against himself, and Hunter forced him to sit down. A reporter for the *National Intelligencer* noted that Harding "seemed to have lost sight of the fact that [Brown] was in command of a band of murderers and thieves and had forfeited all title to protection of any kind." Judge Parker, also puzzled by Harding's remarks, interrupted the summation and adjourned the session.[13]

When the trial resumed on Monday, October 31, Griswold argued that Brown could not be guilty of treason, as he was not a citizen of the Commonwealth; also, having never sworn allegiance to Virginia, he could not be a rebel against her authority. He had not warred against the state, but had merely resisted authority. Chilton added that while Brown may have forcibly entered the armory, the property fell under the jurisdiction of the Federal government and not the Commonwealth. As to inciting a slave insurrection, no evidence existed as no insurrection occurred, and the deaths of several townspeople resulted from the attempts of Brown's men to defend themselves while being shot at by a drunk, disorderly, and undisciplined mob. The identity of the person who shot Shephard Hayward remained unknown, argued Griswold, and as Brown himself said, "Why would we shoot a Negro?"

Prosecutor Hunter made the closing remarks for the Commonwealth, defining treason as an act respecting no boundaries, as "the Constitution of the United States provides that citizens of

13. *Ibid.*, November 1, 1859.

each State shall be entitled to all the privileges of citizens in the several States." Therefore, by warring against the Commonwealth of Virginia, Brown committed treason upon the country. Hunter also set aside the death of Hayward, stating that even if he had been killed by mistake, the same could not be said for the murder of Mayor Beckham.

Parker ordered a half-hour recess to allow time for the jury to deliberate. When court reconvened, the jury returned. Brown sat on his cot to hear the verdict: "The jury find the prisoner guilty of treason in advising and conspiring with slaves and others to rebel, and of murder in the first degree."[14]

With John Brown convicted, the trial of four of his men concluded at light speed. On November 2, Judge Parker sentenced Brown "to be hung in public on Friday, the 2nd of December." Parker ordered Edwin Coppoc, John Cook, John Copeland, and Shields Green executed in the same manner on December 16. In keeping with segregation, the judge provided for the two blacks to be hung together, but not with Coppoc and Cook. Albert Hazlett and Aaron Stevens came to trial later, dying together on the gallows on March 16, 1860.[15]

Brown had not expected to be endowed with a thirty-day extension of life. Once sentenced, he expected to be summarily hauled off to the gallows and hanged. He used his final days in jail to stir the abolitionist movement into a raging frenzy. He attracted thousands of sympathizers through the use of the press. Even his jailer, John Avis, succumbed to the old man's hypnotic methods, but not so much as to turn him loose. On the day of his death, Brown shook hands with the jailer and slipped a final message into the hands of one of the guards: "I John Brown am now quite *certain* that the crimes of this *guilty, land: will* never be purged *away;* but with Blood. I had, *as I now think:* vainly flattered myself that without *very much* bloodshed; it might be done."[16]

For Governor Wise, hanging John Brown required an official ceremony, but the event also demanded the presence of the militia. Rumors circulated from unknown sources that a rescue had been instigated by Brown's friends. Local farmers reported hun-

14. *Ibid.,* November 3, 1859.
15. Baltimore *Weekly Sun,* November 5, 1859; *National Intelligencer,* November 15, 1859.
16. John Brown Papers, CHS; Villard, *John Brown,* 554.

dreds of strangers prowling the countryside. Barns had been burned, stock stolen, and imaginary Kansas raiders spotted filtering into Harpers Ferry to spring the condemned murderer on the day the sheriff conducted him to the execution site.

At the governor's request, Buchanan ordered Colonel Lee to the Ferry to keep order. Because the execution was a Commonwealth affair, Lee's role was to safeguard government property, not John Brown, but the president was taking no chances and sent Lee with four companies, including 264 artillerymen from Fort Monroe, to guard the bridges and line the Potomac shore with pickets during the period of the execution. With Lee covering the Ferry, Wise dispatched Major General William B. Taliaferro to Charles Town, placing him in charge of a thousand militia, warning that if necessary, he would "call out the whole available force of the State to carry into effect the sentence of our laws" to hang Brown and his bloody insurrectionists. Wise, again responding to rumors, believed "an attempt will be made to rescue the prisoners, and if that fails, then to seize the citizens of this State as hostages and victims in case of execution." The governor had listened closely to the rumors, as a plot had been hatched and discarded by Brown's friends in Boston to kidnap Wise, hold him at sea on a yacht, and ransom him in exchange for the raiders' freedom.[17]

Wise also wired the Virginia Military Institute and ordered Professor Thomas J. Jackson to load up a company of cadets and a pair of howitzers and bring them by train to Charles Town to maintain order. This may have been Jackson's first trip to the area, but it would not be his last.[18]

On December 2, the day of execution, the morning sun broke over the hills of northern Virginia and set the landscape aglow with the colors of late fall. Turkey buzzards soared above the gibbet, built in an open field on Rebecca Hunter's farm located on the southeastern outskirts of Charles Town, and the smell of fresh-cut lumber still hung in the air. Fifteen hundred militia and cavalry in full military regalia formed along the road leading from the jail to the gibbet. Spectators were restrained by bayonet. For a moment, Brown stood on the steps of the jail, wearing white

17. Robert E. Lee, Jr., *Recollections and Letters of General Robert E. Lee* (New York, 1909), 22–23; Thomas Wentworth Higginson, *Cheerful Yesterdays* (Boston, 1898), 165–66; Villard, *John Brown*, 515–16.
18. Villard, *John Brown*, 522–23.

socks and an old pair of red slippers, a black broad-brimmed hat, a tattered black frock coat, and a loose pair of black pantaloons that flapped in the breeze. Struck by the pomp and ceremony, he remarked, "I had no idea that Gov. Wise considered my execution so important."[19]

Sheriff Campbell looped a rope around Brown's arms, pinioned them behind his back, and marched him to the roadside where a wagon waited. With help from jailer Avis, attendants lifted Brown's frail body onto the wagon and set him atop a black walnut coffin encased in poplar. As the wagon, driven by undertaker George Sadler, started down South George Street, the militia formed in the rear and followed to the beat of a drum. Brown paid little attention to his escorts. He stared off into the countryside, his eyes fastened on the Blue Ridge Mountains, the hills he had hoped to conquer as his black army pushed southward. "This is beautiful country," he remarked, drawing deeply from the fresh air blowing across vast fertile fields. "I never had the pleasure of seeing it before."[20]

Brown mounted the platform and stepped upon the trap without a trace of concern. He hesitated for a moment. Looking down he spied prosecutor Hunter and Mayor Green among the front-row officials and said, "Gentlemen, goodbye."[21]

Professor Jackson, a deeply religious man, watched from his post by the gibbet where he could see the old man's face and hear every spoken word. He thought Brown uncommonly cheerful, as if death meant nothing—a moment of final triumph. After reaching the top, Brown shook hands with his executioners. The sheriff placed the rope gently around the old man's neck, put a white hood over his head, and asked kindly if Brown wished to give the signal for cutting the rope that dropped the trap. Brown replied it made no difference as long as he was not kept waiting. Ten minutes passed while militia companies fumbled about the field to take their positions in the ordered formation. Cavalry surrounded the squares formed by the militia. On a snow-white horse, Captain Turner Ashby cantered back and forth behind the lines. A

19. Mary Anna Jackson, ed., *Memoirs of Stonewall Jackson* (Louisville, 1895), 130–32; William Fellows to the New York *Sun*, February 13, 1898.

20. New York *Herald*, December 3, 1859; Richmond *Enquirer*, December 6, 1859.

21. Richmond *Enquirer*, December 6, 1859.

dark-eyed private in the Richmond Grays stared hypnotically at the ragged figure on the gibbet. John Wilkes Booth had made a special effort to witness the execution. While waiting for the fatal day to come, he amused the troubled community of Charles Town by performing dramatic readings from Shakespeare at the Episcopal Lecture Room located on the corner of Liberty and Lawrence Streets.[22]

At 11:15 A.M. Colonel Francis N. Smith, an officer in Taliaferro's retinue, signaled Sheriff Campbell and shouted, "All ready." A hush pervaded the crowded field. The sheriff hesitated, as if he had not heard, and Smith repeated the order. Campbell nodded and swung the axe. The rope snapped, the trap fell, and the body of John Brown dropped through the opening. His pinioned arms jerked upwards as the body descended; his hands clenched and twitched for several minutes and, in a final spasm, fell limp across his back. Colonel John T. L. Preston of the Virginia Military Institute broke the silence by calling out, "So perish all such enemies of Virginia! All such enemies of the Union! All such foes of the human race!"[23]

For thirty-five minutes the body swung back and forth in the breeze, pulse still beating. John Brown was a hard man to kill. Jackson watched in a transitive state. Before the hanging he had sent up a petition to save the old man's life—he did not know why. It was an intuitive act he could not explain. "I hope that he was prepared to die," Jackson wrote his wife, "but I am doubtful. He refused to have a minister with him."[24]

A bodyguard of fifteen civilians conducted Brown's body to Harpers Ferry, where his wife, Mary, waited sorrowfully in the Wager House for her husband's remains. Philadelphia lawyer Hector Tyndale, who had accompanied Mrs. Brown to Harpers Ferry, insisted upon opening the coffin to make sure the body had not been substituted for a look-alike. At the time, Tyndale did not

22. Jackson, *Memoirs of Stonewall Jackson*, 130–32; Millard K. Bushong, *Historic Jefferson County* (Boyce, Va., 1972), 197; Richmond *Enquirer*, November 28, 1859.

23. Boyd B. Stutler, "The Hanging of John Brown," *American Heritage*, VI (February, 1955), 8–9; Richmond *Enquirer*, December 6, 1859; Jackson, *Memoirs of Stonewall Jackson*, 132; Elizabeth Preston Allan, *Life and Letters of Margaret Junkin Preston* (Boston, 1903), 115–17.

24. Jackson, *Memoirs of Stonewall Jackson*, 131.

know he would return to the Ferry two years later as a major in the 28th Pennsylvania Infantry. As a kindness to the Brown family, several townsmen attempted to locate the bodies of her sons Oliver and Watson, but the latter's remains had been sent to the Winchester Medical College for preservation as an anatomical specimen, and Mrs. Brown could not steel herself to the task of identifying Oliver. A detail gathered up the bodies of the raiders killed at the Ferry, placed them in two large boxes, and buried them on the shores of the Shenandoah. Their blood would not be the last to color the placid flow of Virginia's famous river.[25]

As Brown's body traveled to his home near Lake Placid, the North eulogized him, and the South tried to forget him. But John Brown would not be forgotten, and eighteen months later most of the men who witnessed his execution would become the wearers of the gray. Most of all, Brown would not be forgotten by the citizens of Harpers Ferry. He had come to steal their slaves, and for his insolence he gave his life. The specter of John Brown, an old man who still ranks among the villains and heroes of nineteenth-century history, cast its shadow on a little town in Virginia and set the country on fire.

As Longfellow aptly prophesied on the day John Brown mounted the gibbet, "This will be a great day in our history; the date of a new Revolution—quite as much needed as the old one. Even now as I write, they are leading old John Brown to execution in Virginia for attempting to rescue slaves! This is sowing the wind to reap the whirlwind, which will come soon."[26]

Professor Jackson had felt it too on the day he watched the old man hang. In plaintive words he wrote his wife, "And soon the wind blew his lifeless body to and fro." Was Jackson able to see more than the body of a convicted murderer swinging on the gallows? Was he able to see the winds blowing—not an old man's lifeless body but his living spirit springing to and fro over the land long after the body was mouldering in the grave?[27]

The whirlwind came, howling across the South, raging down the valleys of the Potomac and Shenandoah, and burst in a clash of arms upon the country—and on a once quiet town called Harpers Ferry.

25. Villard, *John Brown*, 558–59.

26. Samuel Longfellow, ed., *Life of Henry W. Longfellow* (3 vols.; Boston, 1891), II, 347.

27. Jackson, *Memoirs of Stonewall Jackson*, 132.

# 3

## War Clouds Rising

During the six-week interval between October 18, the day of Brown's capture, and December 2, the day of his execution, Harpers Ferry remained a town in distress. Rumors persisted. Some said a large abolitionist army lay poised on the Pennsylvania border. Farmers reported armed bands of fugitive slaves roaming the mountains. Governor Wise feared more attacks and kept a few companies of militia and cavalry camped in town. They had no place to stay and quartered themselves in the armory.

On October 19, with Brown and his men safely ensconced in the Charles Town jail, acting superintendent Archibald Kitzmiller reported to the armory and rang the bell at the usual hour. Men dribbled in to work, not knowing what to expect. They had not been permitted inside the buildings since the raid. The exceptions were Benjamin Mills, master armorer, Armistead Ball, master machinist, and a few others who with Kitzmiller had been hostages. The experience had shattered their nerves. Too exhausted emotionally to work, employees wandered through the buildings, kicking aside glass from broken windows, picking up tools, and making room for troops who preferred camping in the armory to sleeping outside in tents. Mills, having resigned before the raid, now wasted no time departing.

Armory superintendent Alfred M. Barbour, who had been in Hartford, Connecticut, visiting Samuel Colt during the raid, returned on October 21 and found the armory at a standstill. Damage was slight, but repairs had not been started. Employees straggled about as if waiting for an aftershock. Slaves turned up missing, and many armory workers remained at home to protect their families from the rumored insurrection. A week passed before workers returned to their machines to make rifled muskets and percussion rifles.[1]

When Lee's regulars and the Virginia militia vacated Harpers Ferry, they left the town much as they had found it, quietly producing arms for the Federal arsenal. For several weeks one company of infantry remained behind. Their first sergeant, a man named McGrath, drilled volunteer mechanics on the finer points of warfare. After he departed people slept better, but not for long. Most of the townsfolk were moderate in their sentiments towards the slave issue, but they now found themselves in the geographic center of a sectional crisis percolating in Congress. With the militia gone and raids a constant threat, the town raised four militia companies. Fully armed and uniformed, they paraded up and down Shenandoah Street the first Saturday of each month. By January, 1860, every able-bodied man had joined the local guard. Joseph Barry, a chronicler of the town, remembered bundling up that winter for many midnight trampings over muddy streets. When his turn came to "watch out for prowling abolitionists," he carried an old Hall's rifle on his shoulder. He especially enjoyed the company of Dan O'Keefe. They made an extra effort to keep watch on Dan's house, as he always had a "corpulent flask" stashed in a cupboard near his door.[2]

While most of the citizens of Jefferson County claimed fidelity to the South, workers at the town's two armories had migrated from the North. John Brown had lived among them for almost four months, and John Cook, spy for the Provisional Army, walked among them for more than eighteen months and married a local girl. Slave owners and staunch disunionists worried that more abolitionist sympathizers had infiltrated their quiet valley and were

1. Letters of Colonel Henry K. Craig, October 18, and Kitzmiller to Craig, October 19, 1859, cited in Smith, *Harpers Ferry Armory*, 307.

2. Barry, *Harper's Ferry*, 67; Barton H. Wise, *The Life of Henry A. Wise of Virginia, 1806–1876* (New York, 1899), 256–57.

secretly plotting another attack. Yankees had never been popular in Harpers Ferry, and townsfolk began to watch neighbors of northern antecedents with more than a passive interest.

Brown's Harpers Ferry raid worried so many Virginia legislators that the assembly passed a bill on January 21, 1860, to reopen Richmond's old Virginia Manufactory of Arms, a publicly owned enterprise closed since 1822. Virginia wanted to shed her dependence on the Federal government for weapons to arm her growing militia. The state assembly appropriated $500,000 for the project, with $320,000 going to the remechanization of the Richmond armory. Rather than wait for the first gun to come off the line, they designated the remaining $180,000 to be spent "without delay" for the purchase of munitions and artillery. John Letcher, Virginia's new governor, appointed a three-man Armory Commission—consisting of George W. Randolph, Colonel Francis N. Smith, and Philip St. George Cocke, all prominent men with prior military service—to superintend the project. Smith eagerly accepted the post. On the day of Brown's execution, Smith had stood before the gibbet and shouted the order to spring the trap. The commissioners wasted no time assessing the requirements for reopening the factory. They had a talented man in mind, Armistead Ball, but the master armorer would not leave Harpers Ferry. The committee settled for another northerner, Salmon Adams of the Springfield, Massachusetts, armory.[3]

In private, the commissioners discussed a plan to confiscate the Federal government's machinery at Harpers Ferry. In the meantime, the armory continued to produce rifled muskets, and Abraham Lincoln became the Republican party's nominee for president.

Citizens of the Ferry, a Democratic stronghold since the 1830s, faced the uncomfortable dilemma of casting their vote for one of two Democratic candidates: Stephen A. Douglas, who advocated popular sovereignty, and John C. Breckinridge, protector of "southern rights." A third candidate, John Bell of the Constitutional Union party, won Jefferson County, but the vote in Harpers Ferry went to Douglas—Breckinridge running a distant second. Abe Lincoln, the scorned "Black Republican," received no votes

3. Smith, *Harpers Ferry Armory*, 310–11.

at all. Thereafter, Virginia girded for the inauguration and watched her southern sisters amble down the dangerous path to secession.[4]

Harpers Ferrians knew their livelihoods depended upon the continuance of gunmaking. They listened to the heated arguments of secessionists, but in the national election they voted against them by favoring Douglas. Three days before South Carolina passed her Secession Ordinance, concerned citizens attended a public meeting in the same courthouse where John Brown received his death sentence. The issue involved a resolution to support or reject decisions reached during a state convention slated to begin on February 13, 1861. Because the issue of secession stood high on the list of matters to be debated, Jefferson County residents argued over the selection of their delegates. Should they be for separation, or against it? Jefferson County, led by votes from Harpers Ferry, elected two pro-Union men to attend the convention: Alfred Barbour, the armory's new superintendent, and Logan Osburn, a Union Conservative candidate. States' rights advocates Andrew Hunter, who had prosecuted Brown, and William Lucas lost by large margins. Barbour applied to Washington for permission to attend the convention, and he found his Federal employers, knowing how he intended to vote, quite receptive.[5]

During the convention Barbour and Osburn sent home encouraging reports, but after two weeks of inconclusive debate the discussions became sectionally deadlocked. Western Virginia argued against secession, but the Piedmont and Tidewater regions felt differently. For a while pro-Union delegates retained an imposing majority. Of 152 delegates, 80 percent opposed secession at that time, and about half of those opposed it at any time. The staunchist Union delegates came from the Trans-Allegheny and Ohio Valley areas. The moderates comprised the largest group and, like those who lived in Harpers Ferry, came from the counties drained by the Shenandoah and Potomac Rivers.

When the debate reached the fourth week, the fire-eaters, finding Barbour more pliable than Osburn, exerted enormous pressure on him to change camps. Because he worked for the Federal government, they branded him a "submissionist." Fierce pressure came from friends and associates. Continuous heckling of lobby-

4. Bushong, *Historic Jefferson County*, 143.
5. Smith, *Harpers Ferry Armory*, 314; *Virginia Free Press*, December 20, 1860, February 7, 1861.

ists up from South Carolina, Mississippi, and Georgia meddled with his mind and compromised his loyalty. Barbour's resistance began to crack. Without giving an explanation, he wrote the Ordnance Department on March 21 requesting that all Federal troops stationed at Harpers Ferry be removed. The following day he resigned as armory superintendent. Ordnance chief Colonel Henry K. Craig held the resignation, giving Barbour time to reconsider, but the goose was out of the sack. Nonetheless, on April 4, eight days before South Carolina militia unleashed the first salvo on Fort Sumter, Barbour and Osburn joined with a majority of Virginia delegates to reject the Commonwealth's Secession Ordinance by a vote of 85 to 45.[6]

Word reached Richmond of Lincoln's decision to relieve Fort Sumter while delegates to the convention were still in the city. They reconvened to await the outcome of events at Charleston harbor. On April 12 they learned that Brigadier General Pierre G. T. Beauregard's artillery had opened on Fort Sumter. Thirty-four hours and four thousand shells later, the small Union garrison under southern-born Major Robert Anderson surrendered. As Union troops evacuated the harbor, Lincoln issued a call for 75,000 volunteers to suppress the rebellion. The following day, April 16, Governor Letcher refused to send Virginia's quota of troops. His reply amounted to a declaration of war.[7]

Delegates reconvened and on April 17 adopted Virginia's Secession Ordinance by a vote of 88 to 55. Osburn, true to his oath, voted against secession. Barbour did not vote during the session but later signed the Ordinance. He had engaged in a conspiracy with former governor Wise and was on a special mission to Harpers Ferry.

Passage of the Ordinance required ratification by the voters of the Commonwealth, who went to the polls on May 23. With mixed emotions, Jefferson County approved the Ordinance by a vote of 813 to 365. Although strongly attached to the Union, Virginians could not fight against their own people. States' rights ran deep in their blood. They could not accept the thought of Union

6. Charles H. Ambler, *West Virginia, the Mountain State* (New York, 1940), 313–14, 317; Wise, *Life of Henry A. Wise*, 269–73; Henry T. Shanks, *The Secession Movement in Virginia, 1847–1861* (Richmond, 1934), 160–78.

7. F. N. Boney, *John Letcher of Virginia: The Story of Virginia's War Governor* (University, Ala., 1966), 112.

forces invading their land and suppressing their individual and collective freedoms. Voter participation in the ratification process was unexpectedly small. Fighting men, young and old, had already left their homes to join the Confederate army.[8]

For the townsfolk of Harpers Ferry there was a mixture of celebration, skepticism, and tears. No doubt the Gault House Saloon did a thriving business that day, along with the Potomac Restaurant and the tavern and store across from the armory on North Potomac Street. But change had already assailed the Ferry. The day Governor Wise came to town to seize Brown and his raiders was also the day he set eyes on the U.S. Armory and Hall's Rifle Works, the two best-equipped arms-making factories in the South. He knew if war followed in the months to come, both factories were valuable to the South and vulnerable to seizure. With Harpers Ferry on the border of Maryland, whose allegiance remained unclear, the armories lay a bridge crossing away from Union soil. Even if Maryland seceded, Pennsylvania lay but thirty miles to the north.

Squeezed between two opposing forces, citizens of Harpers Ferry felt much like their delegate, Logan Osburn, who after voting against secession said, "I regarded [ratification] as mischievous in its tendency and destructive in its consequences, to all our best interests, socially, politically, and commercially. My opposition was honestly entertained and frankly expressed. But my opinions have been overruled by a large majority of the freemen of my state. I therefor bow . . . in humble submission to their will, and acquiesce in their decision. My lot has been cast. I am a son of Virginia, and her destiny shall be mine."[9] Townsfolk shared Osburn's views, wondering each day if submissiveness was enough to insulate their lives from the ravages of a vague and uncertain war.

On April 16, one day before the Virginia Convention passed the Secession Ordinance, Wise concocted a scheme to occupy the armory before the Federal government garnered enough troops to hold it. Earlier he had advocated taking Virginia out of the Union but keeping her neutral while seizing, however, all Federal property. He drew little support for his idea, rejected neutrality as an option, and privately took matters into his own hands. Ignoring

8. Ambler, *The Mountain State*, 320; Bushong, *Historic Jefferson County*, 144–45.

9. *Virginia Free Press*, June 13, 1861.

Governor Letcher, he arranged a secret meeting at Richmond's Exchange Hotel to organize the seizure of the Harpers Ferry armory. He took Nat Tyler, editor of the Richmond *Enquirer*, into his confidence and used him to contact several militia commanders, one being Captain John Imboden. Before reaching the hotel, Imboden met Wise on the street, and Wise gave him the names of the men he wanted brought to the hotel at 7 P.M. "to confer about a military movement."[10]

The collection of conspirators meeting in the former governor's private room included Imboden, Captains Turner and Richard Ashby of Fauquier County, Captain Oliver R. Funsten of Clarke County, Captain John A. Harman of Staunton, and armory superintendent Barbour. Had a register been signed by witnesses to John Brown's execution, it would have contained the names of those attending Wise's private party. They all agreed the task must be done, although the decision made Barbour, who had been entrusted by his constituency to keep Jefferson County in the Union, especially nervous. Wise sent a committee of three to solicit the governor's support, but Letcher rejected the scheme as an act of treason, reminding the committee that Wise had hung a fifty-nine-year-old zealot named Brown for attempting the same tactic eighteen months earlier.

Wise, ignoring Letcher's rejection, decided to act on his own. Late that evening he called upon Colonel Edmund Fontaine, president of the Virginia Central Railroad, and John S. Barbour, president of the Orange and Alexandria and the Manassas Gap Railroads, asking their assistance in transporting troops to Harpers Ferry. They agreed providing the Secession Ordinance passed and the governor supported the attack. Sometime after midnight Wise took his committee back to the governor's home, woke him up, and explained the plan in detail. Letcher agreed to the attack only if the convention passed the Ordinance in the morning. Assuming personal responsibility for the enterprise, Wise then issued written instructions to his collaborators. Harman, Imboden, and the Ashbys left Richmond in the morning to assemble their commands. To pave the way for the enterprise, Wise sent Barbour back to the Ferry to recruit the cooperation of armory employees.

At the convention the next morning, Wise drew a pistol from

10. John D. Imboden, "Jackson at Harper's Ferry," *B&L*, I, 111.

his coat, placed it on a table beside his watch, and stretched a point by announcing that two thousand troops under the command of Major General Kenton Harper were on the road to Harpers Ferry with instructions to take possession of the armory. With half of the convention agog and the other half cheering, Wise condemned Letcher for vacillation. With Lincoln in the White House war was inevitable, Wise declared, and Virginians must not allow the Federal government to squeeze the Commonwealth into submission while the convention wasted time in debate. He told the delegates he had just learned that a Massachusetts regiment, a thousand strong, had been ordered to Harpers Ferry. If Virginians occupied the town quickly, the armory's few guards could be driven away without firing a shot. Besides, Wise argued, the town provided a gateway to the Shenandoah for a Union army; for the South—a bastion on the Potomac. Robert Y. Conrad and John B. Baldwin accused Wise of usurping the governor. With support from their fellow "cooperationists," they declared the Harpers Ferry raid "unauthorized and illegal." Members of the convention were at each other's throats when word arrived that Letcher, unable to stop the attack on the Ferry, had decided to support it. Debate came to a halt, and on the afternoon of April 17 the Secession Ordinance passed. Wise pocketed his pistol and left the convention. He had fired a shot without pulling the trigger.[11]

When Imboden, Funsten, Harman, and the Ashbys reached home the following day, thousands of people gathered at the station and demanded to know by whose authority the militia had been mobilized. Assuming the convention had by now, as it was noon, voted for secession, Imboden replied they were acting on the governor's orders. The delegates did not vote until later, but shortly after Imboden arrived at Staunton, Letcher wired General Harper to take command of the militia and proceed to the Ferry. Harper, a native of Pennsylvania and a Mexican War veteran, set out for Winchester late in the day, leaving Brigadier General William H. Harman with instructions to put the Augusta militia on trains and meet him there.[12]

Barbour reached Harpers Ferry the morning of April 18 tired,

11. *Ibid.*, 112; Wise, *Life of Henry A. Wise*, 274–81; Shanks, *Secession Movement in Virginia*, 202–205.

12. Imboden, "Jackson at Harper's Ferry," *B&L*, I, 113–14; General Kenton Harper Obituary, File HFD-587, HFA.

disheveled, and bolstered by too many drinks. With him came James A. Seddon, who later became the Confederacy's fifth secretary of war. Seddon, a capable lawyer, politician, and planter, wanted a firsthand look at the armory, but his ostensible role was to support Barbour, whom the town had sent to the Richmond convention because he had promised to keep Virginia "unconditionally" in the Union. Barbour had the awkward mission of telling his Federal employees that the armory would soon belong to Virginia. He promised the men excellent wages if they agreed to remain and work for the state, but the Unionist element revolted. Word spread through the town like fire. Men poured into the streets, castigating Barbour for misrepresentation. Someone shouted, "Treason!" Others celebrated. Fistfights erupted in the Ferry Lot. Workers from the armory rushed through the gate and mixed in the melee.

Barbour retreated from the disruption just as the morning train from Baltimore pulled up to the Wager House and deposited Captain Charles Kingsbury, the new armory superintendent, on the loading platform. Barbour hurriedly transferred responsibility for the armory to Kingsbury, extricated himself from the mob, sought refuge in a nearby building, and encountered Joseph Barry at work in a small office. Barbour thought enough of the young man's intellect to ask his advice, and Barry advised him to "hold out for the Union." A few days later Barbour stopped again at the office, but only for a minute, to say, "You were right."[13]

Kingsbury had just quieted the crowd when John Burk, a young man in a gray uniform on guard at the telegraph office, walked into the street out of sheer curiosity. His sudden appearance provoked another round of fighting. Women and children hung out second- and third-story windows on North Potomac Street and wondered why so many men were shouting and brawling. Kingsbury's superintendency became the briefest in the history of the armory, lasting less than a day.[14]

First Lieutenant Roger Jones, commanding forty-two men of the U.S. Mounted Rifles who were stationed at the armory, wired Washington for reinforcements. A ruggedly handsome man, Jones

13. Barry, *Harper's Ferry*, 97.
14. G. W. Cullum, *Biographical Register of the Officers and Graduates of the U.S. Military Academy from Its Establishment, in 1802, to 1890* (2 vols.; Boston, 1891), II, 25.

had come to the Ferry at the age of thirty-one with the credential of having graduated from West Point near the bottom of the rather undistinguished class of 1851. Since early 1860 Jones's company had been posted in one of the armory buildings to protect Federal property from further mischief.[15]

Secretary of War Simon Cameron had recently transferred a third of Jones's command to Fort Pickens in Pensacola Bay, leaving him shorthanded on the eve of a crisis. The lieutenant listened with disbelief when Barbour addressed the armory employees. He may not have known all the reasons behind the ensuing riot when he asked the local militia for assistance. They laughed in his face, and Jones looked elsewhere for help. By evening his force had grown to about sixty, including a dozen workers from the armory.

Abraham Herr, the local miller, offered to catch the morning train to Washington and carry a message to the War Department. Jones scribbled a hurried appeal, asking Cameron for reinforcements "at once and by the thousands." He handed the sealed note to Herr and urged him to not wait until morning but to catch the night train instead. Herr returned the following day, the note still in his pocket. Halfway to Washington he reconsidered. If word of his message-carrying mission leaked to local secessionists, someone might destroy his business. Herr confessed his timidity to Jones, who expected no help anyway.[16]

On the rumor that large bands of uniformed troops had been seen approaching from the south, Jones posted sentinels along the roads to the Ferry. Jeremiah Donovan, a gigantic Irishman who lived in town, offered his services, shouldered a musket, and stood guard at the armory gate. Fifty yards away, John Burk, dressed in Confederate gray, stood guard at the telegraph office. They eyed each other over the Ferry Lot, once again a no-man's-land.[17]

Midmorning on April 17, Imboden's artillerymen rolled their six guns off the train at Strasburg and started the trek down the Valley pike to Winchester. After they hauled their horseless battery three or four miles, the pace slowed to a crawl. Imboden stopped at a farm to hire horses. The farmer took one look at the rebel rabble and warned Imboden that if anybody touched his animals he would take them to court. The captain ordered a detail

15. *Ibid.*, 466–67.
16. Imboden, "Jackson at Harper's Ferry," *B&L*, I, 125.
17. Barry, *Harper's Ferry*, 97–98; Bushong, *Historic Jefferson County*, 209.

to commandeer six teams and follow the infantry. "The people generally received us very coldly," Imboden observed. "The war spirit that bore them up through four years of trial and privation had not yet been aroused." By the following afternoon the artillery reached the railroad station at Winchester, and Imboden gave up his horses. Men rolled the battery into cars waiting to transfer the unit to Halltown. Winchester was already a beehive of military activity. From sunrise to sunset, townsfolk watched ten militia units pass through town—including the West Augusta Guards, the Monticello Guards, the Albemarle Rifles, and now the Staunton Artillery. When Imboden's road-weary artillery reached Charles Town they joined Colonel William Allen's Jefferson Guards and the mounted companies of Funsten, Scott, and the Ashbys.[18]

At 9 P.M. on April 18, Jones wired Washington a message of distress. Several companies of Virginia militia had been observed forming at Halltown, four miles away. Three hundred and sixty men with four pieces of artillery were already there and waiting for the larger force coming from Charles Town. Jones expected to be attacked within the hour. In a final appeal to army headquarters, he warned, "If the Government purposes maintaining its authority here, no time should be lost in sending large bodies of troops to my assistance." In closing Jones added, "A courier has just reported the advance of troops from Halltown." Jones's message went unanswered. Perhaps nobody was awake at the War Department. If so, it would have made little difference. Ashby's cavalry stole down the Potomac at dark and cut the telegraph lines to Baltimore and Washington.[19]

Most of General Harper's militia were still on the road between Winchester and Harpers Ferry when the first of General Harman's men appeared on Bolivar Heights. They expected to be confronted by a strong regiment from Massachusetts but found only a few pickets who fled back to town. Harman noticed smoke and advanced quickly, thinking Federal troops had set fire to the town.

Jones had no malicious designs towards the town, but he gave up hope of help from Washington. At 10 P.M. he set fire to the

18. Imboden, "Jackson at Harper's Ferry," *B&L*, I, 114–15.
19. Lieutenant Roger Jones to Army Headquarters, April 18, 1861, *OR*, I, 3–4 (all citations to *OR* are from Series I unless otherwise designated); Imboden, "Jackson at Harper's Ferry," *B&L*, I, 115.

arsenal to destroy fifteen thousand muskets neatly boxed in wooden crates. Another detail stacked combustibles in the main buildings of the armory, struck matches, and set them on fire. With Virginia militia a few minutes from the outskirts of the Ferry, Jones put his men in marching order and led them across the Potomac bridge. An angry mob of secessionists, armed with squirrel guns, pursued Jones halfway across the span but lost their courage when the Federals formed a skirmish line. The throng backed out of range, and Jones resumed his retreat. Jeremiah Donovan and several volunteer pickets on Bolivar Heights did not know they had been abandoned until pressed back into the town at midnight. At 2:30 P.M. the following day, Jones's weary company straggled into Carlisle Barracks, Pennsylvania.[20]

As Jones marched across the bridge to Maryland, a keg of powder exploded in the arsenal, and then another. The sound rumbled down the valley and out across the Charles Town pike. Harman's militia heard the sound, and when they observed a reddish glow lighting the sky above the town they quickened their pace. As they came down Washington Street, the main arsenal and the carpenter shop lay engulfed in flames. Fearing the blaze would expand into town, citizens acted quickly to contain the fire. Jones had ordered powder trains spread in the armory buildings, but some of the employees followed behind the soldiers and wet them almost as fast as they were laid. After midnight Harper arrived with the main force. With the armory fire doused and the Federals gone, Harper celebrated the conquest well into the night. He had captured the armory without firing a shot.[21]

Jeremiah Donovan, however, returned to town from his post on Bolivar Heights to find Jones gone. A crowd swarmed around him, and someone slung a rope around his neck. As they hustled him over to a tree, Ashby rode among the mob and ordered the man released. Ashby wanted the armory, not Donovan, and he set the Irishman free "to move north and seek employment under the government of his choice." Joseph Barry, who witnessed the affair, thought Donovan was lucky to fall into the hands of Virginians, whom he considered more tolerant than men from the Gulf states, who, he reported, came to town a few days later and "were near

20. Jones to General Winfield Scott, April 19, and Jones to Army Headquarters, April 20, 1861, *OR*, I, 4–5.
21. Bushong, *Historic Jefferson County*, 209.

lynching Dr. Joseph E. Cleggett and Mr. Solomon V. Yantis, citizens of the town, for their union opinions."[22]

Charles Gratton, who eventually became Commissary Sergeant for the 5th Virginia Military District, arrived at Harpers Ferry in mid-April and in his *Reminiscences* wrote:

> Genl. Harper was a Major General of Militia and would be in command of all volunteer companies, as well as such of the militia of the brigades of Harman, [Gilbert S.] Meem and [James H.] Carson. When it is remembered that each of these four generals had the regulation staff and as many additional aides, adjutants, and inspector generals as he had friends, who wished to go and see a little war and yankee killing on his own account, and that [every officer] was ornamented according to his taste and ability to acquire . . . it is easily conceived what an incongruous mass it was. I do not suppose at any time before or since was there ever such a collection of variegated uniform, so much tinsel, so many nodding plumes, so long or so many sashes, cocked hats, jingling spurs and swords, or such resplendent dress as of the first week or two at Harpers Ferry. Things took care of themselves pretty much, or if there was a divinity that shaped their ends, the rough hewing had been badly done.[23]

On the morning of April 19, Barbour, Seddon, and Harper inventoried the remains of the armory and reported only moderate damage. They counted more than four thousand firearms in usable condition, and components for building several thousand more. Hall's Rifle Works had not been touched by Jones's incendiaries and continued to operate. Harper set the men to work turning out muskets from parts salvaged at the armory, but he soon encountered a work stoppage. "I am wholly unprovided with funds," he wrote in an appeal to Letcher. "I can get them at the Winchester banks, if you will give authority. You may judge of the state of things here when I say even Virginia money will procure nothing, but at an enormous discount, in the store of this place."[24]

Barbour, with help from the militia, packed up the U.S. Armory—more than 300 machines, thousands of feet of shafting and belting, and some 57,000 assorted tools—for shipment to Rich-

22. Barry, *Harper's Ferry*, 98–99.

23. Charles Gratton, "Reminiscences of Camp Life with Stonewall Jackson," 2, Civil War Times Illustrated Collection, USAMHI.

24. Harper to Letcher, April 22, 1861, *OR*, II, 775.

mond's old musket works. Crating the equipment proved to be a far easier job than transporting it to Richmond. The Baltimore and Ohio, the principal railroad servicing Harpers Ferry, operated through enemy territory. The Winchester and Potomac, a rough, lightly constructed spur operated by the Baltimore and Ohio, ran south to Winchester but ended there. The feeble little line had but two small engines and a few passenger cars. To reach Richmond, crates had to be loaded on the spur, unloaded at Winchester, and carted twenty miles up the Valley pike to Strasburg, where the Manassas Gap Railroad operated a line to Richmond.[25]

The first shipment of machinery was about to roll down the tracks to Winchester when Harper received an urgent message from the governor. Militia General George H. Steuart needed a thousand muskets delivered to Baltimore to block the passage of northern troops to Washington. Harper stopped the train and removed several dozen crates.[26] The Baltimore and Ohio, however, still served the border states and promptly delivered the weapons to Steuart.

Six weeks passed before details began stripping the rifle works. By then, Union troops under Major General Robert Patterson were forming in Maryland and threatening to attack the Ferry before the equipment could be moved. James H. Burton, superintendent at the Richmond armory, brought a crew to town and in two weeks cleaned out the rifle works. Preferring not to have the South's arms-making capability concentrated in one city, the Confederate government eventually shipped much of the machinery to Fayetteville, North Carolina. Many workers, regardless of their political sentiments, went south with their skills. Merritt Roe Smith, who provided trailblazing research on Harpers Ferry's armories, writes, "Richmond and Fayetteville formed the backbone of Confederate ordnance manufacture during the Civil War. Neither factory could have played this role without the rich human and technical resources of the Harpers Ferry armory."[27]

James Shewbridge, an employee of the armory, decided to re-

25. George Edgar Turner, *Victory Rode the Rails* (Indianapolis, 1953), 65.

26. Extract from the proceedings of the Advisory Council of the State of Virginia, April 22, 1861, quoted in Briscoe Goodhart, *History of the Independent Loudoun Virginia Rangers, 1862–65* (Washington, D.C., 1896), 15.

27. Harper to Letcher, April 22, 1861, *OR*, II, 774–75; Smith, *Harpers Ferry Armory*, 320–22.

locate his family in Kentucky rather than risk the ravages of war in Virginia. He was typical of the men who worked at the armory, and on April 23 he wrote to his brother, asking for help: "David, we are in dreadful condishon [*sic*] here. Our armory is burnt and we have no money and no nothing else. At this time there is about five thousand soldiers at this place and more coming. Our men is leaving—them that have money enough to carry them away. . . . We have two months work that we expect to lose. Most of the hands here have not a cent and I am . . . now in a suffering condishon [with] a large family, no money and no work."[28]

While the bombardment of Fort Sumter marked the beginning of the military phase of the Civil War, the capture of the Harpers Ferry armory marked the beginning of the war in Virginia, and the horrors that followed. After militia took possession of the town late on the night of April 17, a strong Confederate force under Colonel Thomas J. Jackson came to town and continued to strip the area of its industry.[29]

Many families who rented their homes from the government were forced out and at great inconvenience compelled to seek shelter elsewhere. Father Costello, the town's Catholic priest, yielded to the intruders and billeted Confederate officers in his home. Small businesses, some of them decades old, vanished with the town's main industry, replaced temporarily by occupations less permanent and not so dignified. Some families survived by baking bread and pies for whichever side occupied the town over the next four years. Sharp traders splintered wood or cut up bits of rope, selling it at hefty prices to green recruits as bona fide scraps salvaged from John Brown's gallows. A few ladies turned to prostitution, but on a small scale, as their customers reeked of filth. Whiskey smugglers made the most money but also ran greater risks, as the business was strictly forbidden by military commanders on both sides. A few citizens, both male and female, earned favors by acting as spies. At times the practice got out of hand. If a person had a grievance against his neighbor, a few words of vilification spoken to a receptive officer landed the accused in

28. James Shewbridge to David Shewbridge, April 23, 1861, Shewbridge Letters, File HFD-581, HFA.

29. Jackson to Lee, May 6, 1861, *OR*, II, 809–10.

a dirty guardhouse—"a prey to vermin," Joseph Barry observed, "and objects of insult to the rabble that guarded them."[30]

The once industrious citizens of Harpers Ferry, who worked hard for their wages and raised their families with hope for the future, witnessed their aspirations and their livelihoods turned upside down the night Virginia militia took possession of the town. Whether secessionist or Unionist, they were not ready for what happened next. The winds of destruction that had blown John Brown into their valley in the autumn of 1859 now blew from the south. His shadow was still upon the land. Old Brown would have wanted it that way. The blood of his sons had taken root in the valley—and the whirlwind was at work, sowing the seeds.

30. Captain E. D. Tracy to his wife, May 16, 1861, Tracy Letters, Civil War Times Illustrated Collection, USAMHI; Barry, *Harper's Ferry*, 101–102.

# 4

## Professor Jackson Comes to Town

By April 21 two thousand troops of the Virginia militia had filed
into the Ferry, along with three brigadier generals and a dozen
colonels, all under the command of General Harper. Because militia behaved like free spirits, Harper admitted he could not provide an accurate count "on account of imperfectness in the returns." Nor could he predict the number of troops still on their
way, because the governor, on the afternoon of April 18, had sent
telegrams to militia units all over the state. To those who asked
for returns, Harper simply expressed "embarrassment." He had no
written orders and no control over the men who swarmed into the
Ferry without guns, ammunition, or credentials and demanded
food, firearms, and pay. Admitting bewilderment, Harper waited
for someone else to take charge of the situation, promising in the
meantime to "trust in God and keep my powder dry."[1]

President Jefferson Davis, writing from Montgomery, Alabama,
asked Governor Letcher for thirteen regiments—at least one to
be raised at Harpers Ferry. With enough troops for two regiments
already assembled in the town, the task sounded easy, but the
governor mentioned nothing to Harper, who daily asked Richmond for instructions. Feeling excluded from the governor's com-

1. Harper to Richardson, April 21, 1861, *OR*, II, 772–73.

munication loop, the general tried to conceal his anxiety by writing, "The hourly telegraphic dispatches sent in are exciting; but I feel calm, as I have taken adequate measures to guard against surprise. Some here, who do not know, no doubt think I am a little incredulous as regards their information. But trust me; I am well posted, and shall be found ready. . . . If man could have effected more, then I am willing to be condemned."[2]

If Harper sounded doubtful of his role, at least he had the presence of mind to post sentinels on Maryland Heights and picket the crossings along the Potomac, but no enemy challenged his occupation of the Ferry. After a few uneventful days passed, he learned that the Baltimore and Ohio intended to bring several trains stranded at Wheeling east to Washington. He ordered Colonel William S. H. Baylor's 5th Virginia and Imboden's artillery down the track to intercept them, but he hoped it could be done peaceably.

Imboden emplaced three horseless batteries just outside of town, and Baylor sent mounted pickets down the track, some proceeding as far as three miles, where they waited for the approach of the first engine. Shortly after midnight a nervous cavalryman heard the muffled rumbling of a distant train. As it passed he looked in the windows. The train carried a few passengers and the regular mail, but the picket thought he saw soldiers inside and fired. As the train sped towards Harpers Ferry, a rattle of musket fire followed it. Imboden heard the shooting and imagined a firefight. He ordered the artillery to open when the engine rounded a curve four hundred yards down the track. Baylor waited above, his men directly in Imboden's line of fire. Riding ahead, Baylor peered into the windows of the passing train, and when he saw no troops on board he signaled his men to stop the train. Just above the point marked by Imboden for his artillery to open, the train screeched to a halt. The conductor stepped out and asked why the train had been stopped. Baylor ignored the question and asked how many Federal troops were on board. The conductor replied, "One old fellow in uniform asleep on the mail-bags in the first car." Baylor entered the car and captured Brigadier General William S. Harney, commanding the Department of the West at St. Louis, who claimed to be on his way to Washington to resign his commission

2. Davis to Letcher, and Harper to Letcher, April 22, 1861, *ibid.*, 773, 775.

and "go to Europe rather than engage in a fratricidal war." Harney finished his slumber at Harper's headquarters and in the morning obtained his parole.

As he boarded the train for Richmond, Harney turned to Harper and asked, "Where is your army encamped, general?"

Harper's features reddened as he replied, "Excuse me from giving information."

Harney laughed and apologized. "Pardon me for asking an improper question, but I had forgotten I was a prisoner."

The two generals shook hands and parted. Harney was released at Richmond and proceeded to Washington, arriving two days later with quite a story.[3]

Several of the Ferry's citizens were subjected to harsher treatment. Militia rifled through mailbags removed from the train and collected the names of Unionists. They arrested William McCoy, an elderly man living in Bolivar, placed him in confinement, and eventually sent him packing to Ohio. A few days later soldiers tore down the "neat fence around his residence" and converted the home into a cozy barracks. "Uncle Billy," as they called him, died a short time later. Others, like Abraham Herr, owner of a large mill on Virginius Island, suffered a worse misfortune. Although Herr voted to ratify the Secession Ordinance, letters from relatives in Pennsylvania cast him under suspicion, and Harper confiscated his property.[4]

The telegraph line to Richmond went through Washington, and Harper isolated himself by having it cut. He did not know that on April 23 the governor had appointed Major General Robert E. Lee as commander in chief of Virginia's military and naval forces. He learned of the appointment three days later when Lee sent a message asking whether the unfinished muskets at the armory could be assembled there. Before Harper could respond, Letcher decided his militia at the Ferry needed stronger leadership and ordered Lee to transfer the command to Professor Jackson of the Virginia Military Institute. On April 27 Colonel Jackson started for Harpers Ferry. His instructions were simple: muster men into regiments, preferably from the same section of the state; transfer all remain-

3. Imboden, "Jackson at Harper's Ferry," *B&L*, I, 119–20; General Order No. 9, April 23, 1861, *OR*, I, 670–71.
4. Barry, *Harper's Ferry*, 103–104.

ing machinery to the Richmond Armory; and, after building as many muskets as possible, forward the parts and raw material to the interior.[5]

Jackson's eccentricities were well known on the campus of the Virginia Military Institute, where he taught physics and artillery to a group of cadets who disliked his harsh discipline and peculiar habits but respected him to his face. The boys considered him an overzealous Presbyterian and a scholarly curiosity, but mostly a dull instructor who never wavered from his written text. At age thirty-seven, Jackson stood six feet tall and weighed about 175 pounds. His most distinguishing features were his oversized feet, his broad, lined brow, and his intense pale blue eyes. Later, many of his soldiers claimed his eyes glowed in battle, giving birth to one of his many nicknames, "Old Blue Light."[6]

Jackson was no stranger to Harpers Ferry, and when news of Virginia's secession reached his home in Lexington he promptly volunteered. Letcher commissioned him colonel and on Sunday morning, April 21, ordered him to bring the Virginia Military Institute's Corps of Cadets to Richmond "immediately." Jackson made arrangements to march from Lexington at 1:00 P.M. sharp and asked Dr. William S. White to conduct a fifteen-minute prayer service at 12:45. White, anxious to get the cadets on their way, performed the service at 12:30, enabling Jackson to depart fifteen minutes early. The colonel, however, kept the men standing in formation. Soon a cadet approached Jackson and asked, "Everything is now ready. May we not set out?" Jackson pointed silently to the dial-plate of the barracks clock and did not order "Forward, march!" until the clock struck one. For a man who later built his reputation on the speed of his foot cavalry, the governor's order to depart "immediately" failed to convey enough urgency for the professor to move up his departure time. No wonder cadets, in the privacy of their barracks, disaffectionately called him "Tom Fool."[7]

Jackson spent six days in Richmond before Lee sent him to the Ferry. In the meantime, Harper ordered Imboden to Richmond with a sheath of requisitions for supplies and with verbal instruc-

5. Letcher's Order, April 23, Lee to Jackson, April 27, and Letcher to Walker, May 1, 1861, *OR*, II, 775, 774, 792.
6. Douglas Southall Freeman, *Lee's Lieutenants* (3 vols.; 1942–44), I, xlii.
7. Jackson, *Memoirs of Stonewall Jackson*, 144–46.

tions to make the governor aware of the "defenseless condition" of the militia. While there, Imboden learned that every militia officer above the rank of captain had been demoted, including himself, and a military council had been appointed to fill the vacancies. "This was a disastrous blow," Imboden declared, "to 'the pomp and circumstance of glorious war' at Harper's Ferry."

Jackson arrived at the Ferry during Imboden's absence and lost little time reorganizing the growing mass of high-ranking militia officers. "What a revolution three or four days had wrought!" Imboden observed upon his return. "I could scarcely realize the change. The militia generals were all gone, and the staff had vanished." Jackson brought one staff officer with him from the Virginia Military Institute, Major James W. Massie, assistant adjutant general, and they shared quarters in a small room on the second floor of the Wager House.[8]

Jackson neglected to address the militia after deposing their field officers, and most of the soldiers wandered about Camp Hill in a storm of protest. Nobody could answer their questions, and Jackson, who arrived in his well-worn and dingy Virginia Military Institute uniform, failed to meet their expectations of a smartly appointed military man.

As Imboden trekked up Camp Hill to rejoin his company, men from different commands stopped him with a barrage of questions. Rather than address each inquiry individually, he ordered his own Staunton Artillery into line, knowing the others would listen to whatever he said. Jackson's first order of business was to recruit from the militia at least one regiment—more if possible. Imboden explained that an army of the Confederacy was being organized to protect the South from invasion. Men were to be inducted for either twelve months or the duration of the war, which, Imboden declared, officials in Richmond believed would be swift and decisive for the South. He asked the Staunton Artillery to enlist for the war, thereby setting a good example for the others. Shouts of "For the war! For the war!" broke out, and before the lads could change their minds Imboden circulated through the ranks and collected their signatures.

With the ink barely dry on the muster list, he walked proudly back to Jackson's room and said, "There, colonel, is the roll of the

8. Imboden, "Jackson at Harper's Ferry," *B&L*, I, 120–21.

first company mustered in for the war." Jackson scanned the list and shook Imboden's hand, replying, "Thank you, captain—thank you; and please thank the men for me." Imboden cautioned that if the militia was not enlisted quickly, men might change their minds and return home with their deposed officers. Jackson agreed and sent the captain back to muster two more artillery companies. By sunset Imboden had the rolls on Jackson's desk.[9]

By mid-May Jackson had all the units organized into infantry regiments, and five companies from Jefferson County formed part of the 2nd Virginia. The Jefferson Guards mustered in as Company A, with Captain John W. Rowan as their commander, followed by the Hamtramck Guards, designated Company B, under Captain Vincent M. Butler. Both units had seen action at the Ferry in the autumn of 1859, arriving in time to prevent the raiders' escape from the enginehouse. Brown's defense attorney, Lawson W. Botts, became captain of Company G, the Botts' Greys. Company H, the Letcher Riflemen, mustered in on May 12 and elected James H. L. Hunter as captain. Company K, the Floyd Guards, joined five days later with George W. Chambers as captain and Brown's jailer, John Avis, as first lieutenant.[10] Chambers, owner of the Gault House, already had a notch or two cut into the stock of his rifle. During Brown's raid he had downed Aaron Stevens on the Ferry Lot with a slug fired from the second-story window of his saloon.[11] Of the five units, Company K came directly from Harpers Ferry, and after the battle of Bull Run they all became part of the famous Stonewall Brigade. The companies, however, did not receive their alphabetical designations until they were officially absorbed into the Confederate army.

Four more Jefferson County units enlisted later and joined the cavalry. Company A, Captain Thomas M. Isbell; Company B, Captain Robert W. Baylor; and Company D, Major John L. Knott, joined the 12th Virginia Cavalry Regiment of Brigadier General William E. "Grumble" Jones's brigade. Company F, 1st Virginia Cavalry, Captain William A. Morgan, joined Brigadier General Fitzhugh Lee's brigade. Although most of these men once belonged to an infantry company, they fancied riding to war rather

9. *Ibid.*, 121.

10. Virginia Confederate Rosters, I, 65–69, 70–74, 93–97, 98–102, 108–11, VSL; see also Wager Scrapbook, File HFD-262, HFA.

11. Drew, comp., *The John Brown Invasion*, 75.

than marching. Chew's Battery, Captain Robert Preston Chew, a nineteen-year-old from the Virginia Military Institute, became Jefferson County's lone contribution to the artillery and consisted of men from all over the Harpers Ferry area. They joined Captain Turner Ashby's battalion and later became part of Stuart's Horse Artillery. Chew and two of his men sold Ashby on the idea of carrying a battery of horse artillery. Before long, no cavalry regiment was without one, standard issue being a stubby 12-pounder howitzer, deadly at close range, a long-range English Blakely gun, and a medium-range 3-inch rifled piece.[12]

Jackson had plenty of officers to lead the newly formed companies, but he lacked experienced regimental commanders. Once the rolls filled, Letcher demoted Harper to colonel of the 5th Virginia Regiment, giving him Brigadier General Harman as lieutenant colonel and Colonel Baylor as major. The demoted officers returned to camp and observed a multitude of changes. Imboden, who had watched Jackson transform militia into a semblance of military order, wrote:

> The presence of a master mind was visible in the changed condition of the camp. Perfect order reigned everywhere. Instruction in the details of military duties occupied Jackson's whole time. He urged the officers to call upon him for information about even the minutest details of duty, often remarking that it was no discredit to a civilian to be ignorant of military matters. He was a rigid disciplinarian, and . . . the easiest man in our army to get along with pleasantly so long as one did his duty, but as inexorable as fate in exacting the performance of it.[13]

But meddling by the governor spawned another crisis when Jeb Stuart, bearded and flamboyant, appeared in camp to claim overall command of the cavalry. Ashby, who had won the confidence and loyalty of Jackson's newly organized cavalry, threatened to resign. Imboden, who had been through a similar crisis when the governor sent Colonel William A. Gordon to assume command of the artillery, calmed Ashby by assuring him the mistake would be corrected. Gordon had been transferred to an infantry command,

12. Virginia Confederate Rosters, VIII, 53–58, X, 107–14, 117–24, 139–45, XVIII, 496–99, VSL; Jennings C. Wise, *The Long Arm of Lee* (2 vols.; Lynchburg, Va., 1915), I, 163–64.

13. Imboden, "Jackson at Harper's Ferry," *B&L*, I, 121–22.

Imboden counseled, and something would be done about Stuart. Jackson solved the problem by dividing the cavalry between Stuart and Ashby, thereby creating a second regiment.[14]

Jackson needed muskets for the soldiers and horses for the artillery, but he considered sending requisitions to Richmond a waste of time. From the military stores at Lexington he ordered a thousand old-fashioned flintlocks and ten barrels of powder. He then sent his quartermaster, Major John A. Harman, into the rich farmland bordering Harpers Ferry with orders to buy or impress as many animals as were needed. Harman discovered that Quaker settlers, who were mostly Unionists, raised some of the finest horses in Virginia. Ignoring the owners' objections, he executed Jackson's orders with such energy and dispatch that the colonel later elevated the major to chief quartermaster, a post Harman held until Jackson's death.

In mid-May scouts reported Federal troops under the command of Brigadier General Benjamin F. Butler occupying a position near the Relay House, the junction on the Baltimore and Ohio where trains could be switched from the main east-west line to Washington. For some reason, Virginians suspected Butler of organizing his regiments with black troops. "We have from twelve to fourteen thousand men," Private William H. Cook wrote, "and we are so placed that we don't think thirty thousand of the *blackies* can drive us from our post." Cook had little to worry about. Butler and his "blackies" would pose no threat.[15]

Jackson took special interest in the railroad and sent Imboden's artillery, supported by infantry, eight miles downriver to guard the bridge at Point of Rocks. Details fortified only the Virginia side, as the Confederate government still hoped Maryland would secede and did not wish to irritate her citizens by an unnecessary invasion of her soil.

Jackson made a surprise visit to the camp one morning—not to test the alertness of Imboden's unit but to study the Chesapeake and Ohio Canal and familiarize himself with the roadbed of the railroad. He was especially interested in the thirty-mile section of double track running between Point of Rocks and Martinsburg.

14. *Ibid.*, 123–24.

15. William H. Cook to M. and R. Jackson, May 29, 1861, Cook Letters, File HFD-230, HFA.

With Imboden's artillery holding the eastern end of the track, he sent part of Harper's 5th Virginia up the line to Martinsburg.[16]

By 1861 the Baltimore and Ohio had become one of America's major railroads, boasting 513 miles of track, 236 locomotives, and more than 3,400 freight cars. The line connected Washington and Baltimore with the Midwest, and the rich valleys of the Potomac and Shenandoah Rivers with the East. Baltimore and Ohio track passed westward through central Maryland, crossing into Virginia at Harpers Ferry, and recrossing back into Maryland at Cumberland before taking a final jog back into Virginia for the final run to Wheeling. Both sides claimed the line, and until Jackson came to Harpers Ferry the Baltimore and Ohio continued to operate by an unwritten détente, shuttling coal in record quantities from the mines of western Virginia to the Union's supply centers on Chesapeake Bay.[17]

Jackson's interest in the double tracks running between Point of Rocks and Martinsburg emanated from the railroad's special use of the section. Outbound trains were detained between the two points while waiting for inbound trains to clear the single-tracked line. The thirty-mile stretch also contained two important features: the bridge over the Potomac at Harpers Ferry, and the huge North Valley Depot at Martinsburg. When Jackson complained to railroad officials that the continuous noise of trains passing through the Ferry at all hours of the night disturbed the sleep of his men, Baltimore and Ohio President John Garrett agreed to hold all nightly eastbound trains at Martinsburg until morning and send them through the Ferry between the hours of 11 A.M. and 1 P.M. When westbound empties continued to roar through at night, Jackson complained the noise was as bad as ever and demanded the cars be held at the eastern end of the track and sent through during the same hours. "Mr. Garrett promptly complied," Imboden observed, "and we then had, for two hours every day, the liveliest railroad in America."[18]

Jackson mentioned nothing to Lee about his plans to disrupt the railroad, although the general had, in a different context, instructed Jackson to keep his plans and operations secret. Lee authorized Jackson, however, to destroy the Baltimore and Ohio

---

16. Imboden, "Jackson at Harper's Ferry," *B&L*, I, 122.
17. Baltimore and Ohio Railroad Company, *Thirty-Sixth Annual Report*, 186.
18. Imboden, "Jackson at Harper's Ferry," *B&L*, I, 122–23.

bridge and obstruct the canal if the enemy threatened to attack Harpers Ferry.[19]

Jackson also stressed the importance of holding the Ferry, warning Lee that "the fall of this place would, I fear, result in the loss of the northwestern part of the State." To defend against enemy attack, Jackson began fortifying Maryland Heights. Lee reacted immediately, warning Jackson that any intrusion into Maryland was inadvisable "unless compelled by the necessities of war." With Lee's caution ringing in his ears, Jackson hesitated to mention anything about his plans for the Baltimore and Ohio but confessed placing 500 troops on the heights, claiming 2,200 Federal troops under Butler had been reported at the Relay House and another 4,000 under Major General Robert Patterson at Chambersburg. Jackson's actions unnerved Lee, who worried that the former professor was overly anxious to pick a fight. "The true policy is to act on the defensive," Lee replied curtly, "and not invite attack."[20]

Lee may have relaxed a trifle after former U.S. senator Mason of Virginia stopped at Harpers Ferry on May 13 and spent two days inspecting Jackson's defenses. Mason had witnessed the aftermath of Brown's raid on the armory and consumed much of 1860 looking for the invader's hidden conspirators, but he remembered well his visit to the town. Mason reported Jackson's formation of a good military organization and complimented him for fortifying Maryland Heights. Jackson mentioned nothing of his plan to raid the Baltimore and Ohio but convinced Mason that the line should not be permitted to operate. Jackson must have been persuasive. Mason returned to Richmond and informed Lee that Maryland "remains one of the United States, a power now foreign to Virginia, and in open and avowed hostility to us." He ended his report by suggesting the railroad be dismantled.[21]

By May 20 Jackson's force at Harpers Ferry had swelled to 7,700 volunteers, consisting of the 1st, 2nd, 3rd, 4th, and 5th Virginia, the 4th Alabama, two regiments from Mississippi, five Virginia artillery companies, four companies of cavalry, and four companies of Kentucky infantry. Joseph Barry characterized the Ken-

19. Lee to Jackson, May 1, 6, 1861, *OR*, II, 794, 806.
20. Jackson to Lee, May 7, 9, and Lee to Jackson, May 9, 10, 1861, *ibid.*, 814, 824, 822, 825.
21. James M. Mason to Lee, May 15, 1861, *ibid.*, 849.

tuckians as "rough Ohio boatsmen and low bummers." He also condemned the men from the Deep South for being too eager to lynch citizens for the crime of unionism. To keep the men from causing trouble, Jackson encamped them on the outskirts of town rather than in it. Lieutenant Colonel George Deas, inspector general, reviewed the force at Harpers Ferry, but like all of the town's official visitors, he learned nothing of Jackson's scheme to upset the railroad. Even at this early stage of the war, Jackson, who eventually earned the reputation for keeping his own counsel, excluded Lee, Mason, and Deas from his plans.[22]

Deas, however, observed that Jackson's incursions across the Potomac attracted several hundred recruits from the Maryland Guards, the Baltimore City Guards, the Independent Grays, and the Law Grays, who trickled across the Harpers Ferry bridge and offered their services. Deas mustered them in as six companies, added two companies mustered at Point of Rocks, and eventually formed a ninth, the 1st Maryland Infantry under the command of Colonel Arnold Elzey.[23]

For a day or two Jackson, perhaps waiting for Deas to leave, allowed trains to string out over the double-tracked section between Point of Rocks and Martinsburg. At night scouts patrolled the stretch, counting the rolling stock. Satisfied his ruse had worked, Jackson put his plan into operation on the morning of May 22. At 11 A.M. Imboden crossed into Maryland and tore up four hundred yards of track on the eastbound side, allowing the westbound to pass unmolested. Harper dismantled the westbound track at Martinsburg, allowing the eastbound trains to pass. By 1 P.M. Jackson had more than four hundred locomotives and cars stranded between Point of Rocks and Martinsburg. Expecting Federal troops at Chambersburg and the Relay Station to make an effort to recover the rolling stock, Jackson switched four light engines and all the cars they could haul to the Winchester and Potomac spur. For several days the town of Harpers Ferry listened to the endless clatter of details shuttling engines and freight cars back and forth in an effort to get them on the spur. When the racket finally ended, the old ticket office where Mayor Beckham

22. Barry, *Harper's Ferry*, 99; Deas to Garnett, May 21, 1861, *OR*, II, 861.
23. W. W. Goldsborough, *The Maryland Line in the Confederate Army* (Baltimore, 1900), 10–11.

once worked closed its doors, another casualty of the coming war.[24]

Captured engines were still chuffing down the Winchester spur when Brigadier General Joseph E. Johnston arrived at Harpers Ferry looking for Jackson. On May 15 the Confederate government, still operating out of Montgomery, chose to send a senior military officer to the important command at the Ferry and selected Johnston for the job. The change came as some relief to Lee, who considered Jackson too pugnacious, too secretive, and too unpredictable, but he shared with President Davis the utmost confidence in Johnston. With Virginia now ensconced in the Confederacy, Johnston's job was to integrate Jackson's force into the Confederate army.[25]

An hour after his arrival, Johnston located Jackson and attempted to take command. Lee had failed to notify Jackson of the change, and the colonel refused to step aside without authorization from Richmond. Johnston, somewhat abashed, returned to his saddlebags to dig for the letter establishing his authority. An autocratic and petulant man, Johnston would never tolerate this kind of abuse from a subordinate, but under the circumstances he credited Jackson with following military protocol. When he returned with the document, Jackson saluted and offered his services. He knew Johnston only by reputation but considered him a competent professional soldier.[26]

Neither Johnston nor Jackson, or for that matter Lee, shared the popular belief that Harpers Ferry was a veritable fortress worth defending. After Jackson familiarized Johnston with the topography, the latter concluded that a strong force of the enemy could cross the Potomac above the town, readily invest it from Bolivar Heights, and, by occupying Maryland Heights and Loudoun Heights, cut off any hope of escape for its defenders. Johnston praised Jackson's deployments but added that fifteen or twenty thousand men could not prevent his flanks from being turned, as

24. Festus P. Summers, *The Baltimore and Ohio in the Civil War* (New York, 1939), 65–67; Imboden, "Jackson at Harper's Ferry," *B&L*, I, 123.

25. Cooper to Johnston, May 15, 1861, *OR*, II, 844–45.

26. Johnston's Orders, May 24, Jackson to Johnston, May 24, and Jackson to Garnett, May 25, 1861, *ibid.*, 871, 872, 877; Joseph E. Johnston, *Narrative of Military Operations* (New York, 1874), 14–15; Jackson, *Memoirs of Stonewall Jackson*, 157.

the command was strung out over thirty miles of river. He claimed the Valley could be better defended by withdrawing from the town and deploying troops where they could maneuver and respond to attack. Lee agreed but warned that a precipitant abandonment of Harpers Ferry would "be depressing to the cause of the South." If withdrawal became necessary, he added, "destroy all facilities for the approach or shelter of the enemy." That Lee intended to destroy the town is unlikely, but his reference to "facilities for the . . . shelter of the enemy" could have been interpreted to mean every dwelling in Harpers Ferry.[27]

After Johnston familiarized himself with Jackson's military organization, he brigaded the force, giving Jackson the Virginia regiments. Jackson's brigade consisted of the 2nd, 4th, 5th, 27th, and 33rd Virginia Infantry. Every man was a volunteer, drawn mostly from the Shenandoah Valley. Jackson furnished each soldier with a musket and forty rounds of ammunition, drilling them, company by company, until they dropped.[28] Unlike Johnston, who later mastered the art of strategic retreat, Jackson looked for a fight.

From his outpost at Shepherdstown, Captain Robert L. Doyle of the 3rd Virginia warned Johnston that a force of "twenty or twenty-five thousand men" was about to invade Virginia at the upper Potomac fords. Informants reported Federal units engaging boats and scows to effect a crossing at three points upriver. Doyle asked permission to destroy the boats, but Johnston envisaged a more serious problem. He disliked Harpers Ferry as a defensive stronghold and worried about being attacked and overwhelmed by superior numbers.[29]

In the meantime, Jefferson Davis moved the government to Richmond and began to involve himself in all military matters. He vetoed any suggestion of a withdrawal from Harpers Ferry. "The evacuation," Lee warned Johnston, "would interrupt our communication with Maryland, and injure our cause in the State." As Davis soon learned, whenever Johnston set his mind to making a move, nothing could stop him but a direct order, and often even that was insufficient.[30]

27. Johnston to Garnett, May 26, and Lee to Johnston, May 31, 1861, *OR*, II, 881, 897, 901.

28. Jackson, *Memoirs of Stonewall Jackson*, 168.

29. Doyle to Johnston, June 4, 1861, *OR*, II, 905.

30. Lee to Johnston, June 7, 1861, *ibid.*, 910.

Dr. Hunter McGuire of Jefferson County, who knew many of the men in the 2nd Virginia, took a special interest in the unit. One day he joined Johnston during the daily drill and said proudly, "If these men of the Second Virginia will not fight, you have no troops that will."

"I would not give one company of regulars for the whole regiment," Johnston replied sarcastically.

McGuire recoiled from the snub and confided it to Jackson. "Did he say that?" the colonel asked in disbelief. "And of those splendid men?" Jackson shook his head disapprovingly and added, "The patriot volunteer, fighting for country and his rights, makes the most reliable soldier on earth." Jackson would not have to wait long to prove his point.[31]

A few days later the situation changed when a large force of Union troops began to congregate in camps outside Alexandria. Confederate spies in Washington reported a movement afoot. Davis considered striking first with General Beauregard's force, but he worried about the threat to Harpers Ferry. The president bent, encouraging Johnston to hold the Ferry but to not allow himself to be trapped. If he must retire, Davis wanted Johnston's force accessible to Beauregard and ordered the general to Winchester, or, if that route was blocked, to Manassas.[32]

On June 14 the first units of sixty-nine-year-old Major General Robert Patterson's Union militia crossed the Potomac at Williamsport. Patterson held views quite opposite to Johnston's. He believed that the first great battle of the war would be fought at Harpers Ferry and that the result would be decisive. He considered the town a formidable position that, if strongly entrenched, could not be taken without great sacrifice of life. Victory at Harpers Ferry was so crucial to the Union cause, Patterson declared, that he could not sleep without thinking about it. A month later he was still thinking about it—and perhaps not sleeping well—when he asked headquarters with less assertiveness, "Shall I reoccupy permanently Harper's Ferry or withdraw entirely?"[33]

31. Hunter McGuire and George L. Christian, *The Confederate Cause and Conduct in the War Between the States* (Richmond, 1907), 207.

32. Cooper to Johnston, June 13, 1861, *OR*, II, 923–35.

33. Patterson to Cameron, June 10, and Patterson to Townsend, July 17, 1861, *ibid.*, 672, 167.

Wars were no stranger to Patterson. At the age of twenty he fought in the War of 1812, rising to the rank of colonel in the Pennsylvania militia, and in 1815 he mustered out as captain of the 32nd U.S. Infantry. He started a wholesale business in eastern Pennsylvania, became a power in the state's politics, served in the Mexican War as major general of volunteers, and eventually won high praise from Major General Winfield Scott by distinguishing himself at Cerro Gordo and Jalapa. Although still erect and energetic, age had caught up with the old warrior, and on the eve of the first major battle of the Civil War he manifested signs of bewilderment.[34]

Johnston, relieved to be on open ground where he could maneuver, moved part of his force to the main road running between Hagerstown and Winchester. He left Jackson at Harpers Ferry to instruct his brigade in the fine art of demolition. At 4 A.M. a gigantic explosion shattered the slumber of the town's residents as the high road and Baltimore and Ohio bridges toppled into the river. Within an hour the historic structures lay in charred ruins on the bed of the Potomac. Jackson's men then went to work on the long span that connected the Winchester and Potomac spur to the main line of the Baltimore and Ohio. The last train to steam to Winchester carried four prominent citizens of the Ferry—Edmond H. Chambers, Hezekiah Roderick, Nathaniel O. Allison, and Adam Ruhlman—all prisoners of the state to be lodged in the town jail for "inveterate unionism." A detail then pushed a large locomotive, too heavy for the flimsy Winchester bed, off the bridge and into the river. After demolishing the bridges, they cut down water towers, smashed gondolas, and blocked traffic on the Chesapeake and Ohio by shoving the debris into the canal. Another detachment marched down Shenandoah Street with axes and powder and set Hall's Rifle Works on fire. For two days another demolition team emptied the armory and destroyed nineteen of the Federal government's twenty-five buildings. By ironic coincidence, the only structure left untouched by the wreckers was John Brown's fort, the armory's old brick enginehouse. On June 18 all of Jackson's brigade but a company posted as guards marched out of the town and joined Johnston's force at Bunker

34. *HTI*, 561–62.

Hill. By the time Jackson departed, he left the town without bridges, without industry, and without hope for the future.[35]

With Jackson's brigade gone, roving marauders made an unauthorized visit to the town. The guard drove them away, but in their haste to depart the looters squabbled over spoils and murdered one of their comrades, leaving him dead in the street.[36]

Johnston halted four miles south of Martinsburg and set up twelve batteries. Patterson kept his force curiously divided by the Potomac River, placing some units at Falling Waters and the others at Hagerstown. With Patterson encamped about seven miles north of Martinsburg and with Johnston south of the town, neither general showed interest in occupying the railroad center. Then Jackson arrived.[37]

Johnston sent Jackson's brigade with Jeb Stuart's cavalry towards Martinsburg, but each with a different mission. While Stuart reconnoitered the enemy, Jackson destroyed railroad property. The brigade fanned out along the roadbed, ripping up track, scattering cars, and setting fire to those filled with coal. Weeks later, inspectors passing down the line found cars red-hot and with the coal inside still burning. Jackson disliked the detail. The South desperately needed rolling stock. "It was a sad work," he wrote his wife, "but I had my orders and my duty was to obey." Another detachment marched to Shepherdstown and destroyed the multi-spanned highway bridge across the Potomac.[38]

On June 20 Jackson entered Martinsburg and made a quick survey of the North Valley Depot's machine shops and enginehouses. He counted fourteen locomotives and tenders, a large quantity of cars, and another nine engines in the yard waiting for repair. His orders emphasized "destruction," but he despaired over wrecking good locomotives and valuable machinery. He understood the scarcity of materials better than the politicians who expected a short war. Most of the engines were still in good condition. If the rolling stock sent from Harpers Ferry to Winchester could be

35. Hungerford, *Baltimore and Ohio Railroad*, II, 28; Barry, *Harper's Ferry*, 105; Chester G. Hearn, "The Great Locomotive March: Jackson's Railroad Campaign," *Civil War Times Illustrated*, XXV (December, 1986), 23, 28.

36. Barry, *Harper's Ferry*, 105.

37. Johnston to Cooper, June 17, 18, 1861, *OR*, II, 934, 937; Jackson, *Memoirs of Stonewall Jackson*, 160–61.

38. Jackson, *Memoirs of Stonewall Jackson*, 167.

hauled over the road by teams to Strasburg, the same could be done from Martinsburg, although the distance was double.[39]

Jackson spent more than a week gathering teams and enlisting volunteers to tug the engines south, but on the morning of July 2 Stuart sent a courier to Jackson—Patterson had crossed the river and was advancing towards Martinsburg. When Johnston ordered Jackson to avoid an engagement, the colonel still needed another few days to finish his work at the yard, but he also wanted to bloody his brigade, to give them a taste of fighting, and he sent Harper's 5th Virginia to Falling Waters. Jackson went with the regiment and witnessed a sharp little fight, but he found the Federals too strong. Patterson advanced cautiously, slowed by Captain William N. Pendleton's spirited Confederate artillerists. Jackson hurried back to Martinsburg and demolished the stock left in the yard.[40] With clouds of black smoke from the wreckage curling skyward, he turned his back on Martinsburg and joined Johnston at Winchester.

The Baltimore and Ohio summed up the damage in their *Annual Report* of 1861 to stockholders: "Forty-two locomotives and tenders, 386 cars, chiefly coal, 23 bridges embracing 127 spans, and a total length 4,713 feet, were also destroyed or damaged to a great extent by fire, and numerous engines and cars were thrown into the Potomac, the Opequon and other streams. Thirty-six and a half miles of track were torn up, and the iron and track fixtures removed for use on Southern roads."[41] Jackson caused most of the damage in June along the section of track lying between Point of Rocks and Martinsburg.

On July 3 Jackson learned he had been elevated to brigadier general. "May your advancement increase your usefulness to the State," Lee wrote.[42] Two weeks later the freshman general and his brigade won immortality near a small stream by the name of Bull Run.

After Jackson's departure from Harpers Ferry, a lull pervaded the town. The 9th New York took possession of the Maryland side

39. Hungerford, *Baltimore and Ohio Railroad*, II, 10–12; Hearn, "The Great Locomotive March," 28.

40. Jackson, *Memoirs of Stonewall Jackson*, 165–66, 167; Jackson to E. K. Smith, July 3, and Johnston to Cooper, October 14, 1861, *OR*, II, 185–86, 472–73.

41. Baltimore and Ohio Railroad Company, *Thirty-Sixth Annual Report*, 7–8.

42. Jackson, *Memoirs of Stonewall Jackson*, 166.

and lobbed wild shots at Confederate scouts nosing through the lower town. John "Ginger" Chambers, a man strongly attached to the Union, picked up a musket and fell in with the New Yorkers. Not all the citizens of Harpers Ferry fought for Virginia.

On the morning of July 4 a dozen New Yorkers climbed into a pair of skiffs and rowed across the river to Harpers Ferry. From the opposite shore they had seen the Stars and Bars, accompanied by the state flag of Virginia, fluttering from the flagstaff at the armory. Private Edwin Butler of Company C, 9th New York, climbed the pole, tore down both flags, ripped them into equal parts, and shared the souvenirs among his comrades. As they rowed back across the river, Captain John Henderson's cavalry company from Charles Town jogged to the shore, swung down from their saddles, and for a half hour exchanged shots with pickets on the Maryland shore. One New Yorker was killed and three wounded on the Maryland side, and a Harpers Ferry shoemaker named Harding was shot, Barry claimed, by a ball from the rifle of "Ginger" Chambers.[43]

After Henderson withdrew, German-born Unionist F. A. Roeder invited Joseph Barry to his house for a friendly cup of schnapps. During the conversation Roeder remarked, "Well, we have got rid of that lot and have escaped at least with our lives, but what will the next party that comes do with us?"

Later, Roeder left his home to take a little air and walked down to the battered railroad office. While he sauntered about, a shot echoed from across the river, and Roeder slumped to the loading platform, mortally wounded. He died thirty minutes later. The target had been Ambrose Cross, who was also near the river and peering at the destroyed bridge. An old bummer straggling back to his regiment, the 1st Pennsylvania, fired the shot after getting drunk during a Fourth of July celebration at Sandy Hook. Having missed the earlier action, he swore he would kill "some damned rebel anyway." The shot missed Cross, struck the end of the Wager House, and ricocheted into Roeder's groin. War is filled with little ironies. Barry knew both men, Cross as "one of the sternest Union men in the whole land" and Roeder as "one of the first men in the

43. Stone to Townsend, July 5, 1861, *OR*, II, 121; Barry, *Harper's Ferry*, 106–107.

State of Virginia who dared to express sympathy with the Republican party."[44]

On July 17 General Patterson moved his headquarters to Harpers Ferry. He found the lower town in shambles and assigned details to begin repairs. Lieutenant Orville E. Babcock of the Engineer Corps took a detachment downriver to Sandy Hook. The damage seemed insurmountable, but the general expressed optimism. "Babcock has been at Sandy Hook," Patterson wrote headquarters, "trying to get the canal in operation, preparing the entrance to the ford, putting in operation a ferry, and reconstructing the bridge." The vast resources of the Union were hard at work. Harpers Ferry still had hope.[45]

But the town had not seen the last of Stonewall Jackson.

44. Barry, *Harper's Ferry*, 107–108.
45. Patterson to Townsend, July 18, 1861, *OR*, II, 170.

# 5

# The Owls' Mournful Hoots

Patterson seemed oblivious to Johnston's withdrawal from Winchester until the Confederate division showed up at Bull Run with Jackson's brigade. Hope for a short war diminished after Beauregard and Johnston routed Brigadier General Irwin McDowell's Union army near the small town of Manassas.[1]

The townsfolk of Harpers Ferry reacted with mixed feelings. Some cheered. Others prayed the foolish killing would stop. After looting government buildings, a few opportunists turned to raiding abandoned homes. At any hour of the day or night women and children could be seen freighting wheelbarrows filled with household goods from a fine home on the hill to an obscure dwelling somewhere up Shenandoah Street. "In many instances their shamelessness was astounding," Joseph Barry wrote, "and it appeared as if they considered that a state of war gave unlimited privilege for plunder." Ownership rested with the current possessor. Citizens attempting to recover stolen property were abused and beaten. Spies propagated faster than mosquitoes, and many "carried water on both shoulders"—acting as double agents.[2]

1. The Battle of Bull Run, or First Manassas. Also called First Bull Run, as a second battle occurred in the same area thirteen months later.
2. Barry, *Harper's Ferry*, 109.

Patterson's tenure at the Ferry lasted until July 27, when his three-month tour of duty expired. Union General in Chief Winfield Scott, enfeebled by age and gout, blamed the defeat at Manassas partly on Patterson for "doing nothing" and cheered his departure. To accusations that Johnston had stolen a march on him, Patterson replied indignantly, "The enemy has stolen no march upon me. I have kept him actively employed, and by threats and reconnaissances . . . caused him to be re-enforced." Patterson's intelligence was as faulty as his reply. Johnston slipped out of Winchester on July 18, leaving behind 2,500 men to screen his departure and defend the Valley. Months later Patterson, although honorably discharged, was still trying to understand how Johnston eluded him. Another Union general, Irwin McDowell, was also commiserating over his defeat, and the same orders cut on July 19 shifting Major General Nathaniel P. Banks to Harpers Ferry brought George B. McClellan to Washington to form the Army of the Potomac.[3]

If anybody in the War Department had been watching, he might have noticed that Banks consumed six days moving his staff from Baltimore to Harpers Ferry—seventy miles by rail. Most of Patterson's volunteers, with their ninety-day enlistments expiring, left town before Banks arrived. Three regiments "without shoes and without pants" agreed to stay an extra ten days. To leave they needed clothes, but Harpers Ferry had been stripped so thoroughly of pants, shirts, and underwear that washerwomen refused to hang their laundry out to dry without posting a guard. "They cannot march," Patterson wrote Washington, "and unless a paymaster goes to them, they will be indecently clad."[4]

Banks arrived at Harpers Ferry on July 25 to relieve Patterson and found the department destitute of manpower. One lone regiment, the 24th Pennsylvania, had remained behind to protect their general. Patterson packed his bags and vanished across the Potomac with the Pennsylvanians. Every private toted a tiny bundle of loot culled from the vacant homes of Harpers Ferry, and a few of them carried off the town's last chickens. Joseph Barry

3. Scott to McClellan, July 18, Patterson to Townsend, July 18, and General Order No. 46, July 19, 1861, *OR*, II, 743, 168, 171.

4. Patterson to War Department, July 19, 20, 21, and Thomas to Patterson, July 21, 1861, *ibid.*, 170, 171, 172.

watched them go, baffled by what the soldiers wanted with a tombstone from the Methodist cemetery.[5]

Banks disliked the notion of establishing permanent headquarters in an isolated Virginia town with no bridge at his back. When the last of the ninety-day volunteers departed from the Ferry, he moved across the river and into the home of Jacob Miller, near Sandy Hook, leaving a small force in Harpers Ferry to picket the roads. His lack of a military education did not effect his powers of observation. In his first message to Scott he asked for twenty thousand troops, warning, "There are three points that must be held—Loudoun Heights, Maryland Heights, and the plateau beyond the village of Bolivar that commands the road to Winchester. If the enemy has possession of either one, it will command the town." Scott agreed to beef up Banks's division and suggested that the general fortify Maryland Heights. For the next several days, Banks imagined an overpowering force in his front and hurried a few batteries to the summits of Loudoun and Maryland Heights.[6]

For about eight weeks Banks's reinforced division camped in Pleasant Valley, near the Chesapeake and Ohio Canal on the Maryland shore, and provided nearby residents with the same kind of "felicity" felt by Harpers Ferrians during Jackson's visit. While at Sandy Hook, Banks earned the reputation for "being a thorough gentleman," a quality that complemented his decency but diluted his efficacy as a military commander.[7]

From 1853 to 1857 Banks had served as a prominent congressman from Massachusetts, and from 1858 to 1861 as governor. As a young adult, he rose from poverty to become a self-made man. By the age of forty-five he had developed exquisite social graces and wielded considerable political influence. Neither qualified him for command, but like so many Union generals, his political muscle netted him two stars. Unlike Patterson, Banks cut a fine figure with his boldly handsome features, his dark, abundant hair, and his taut, athletic physique. He displayed youthful energy on the fine horses he rode, and he always appeared in public dressed in a carefully brushed gold-braided uniform. But life on the shores of the Potomac, although picturesque, isolated him from easy ac-

5. Barry, *Harper's Ferry*, 110.

6. Banks to Army Headquarters, July 26, 29, and Scott to Banks, July 27, 1861, *OR*, II, 764, 767–68, 765.

7. Barry, *Harper's Ferry*, 110–11.

cess to Washington. In mid-August he moved his division not to Maryland Heights but twenty miles downriver to Darnestown, Maryland, leaving a few regiments along the upper Potomac to guard the canal, picket the crossings, and enjoy the last weeks of summer among the stately, forested heights and the clear, sparkling waters of the Valley.[8]

Banks's withdrawal of his regiments from the Ferry disheartened a large number of the town's ladies, who found the Union soldiers less disorderly and much better company than Patterson's chicken thieves. On July 31 they expressed their appreciation by presenting the 2nd Massachusetts with a skillfully stitched Union flag, complete with thirteen stripes and thirty-three stars, and in a brief ceremony voiced their fidelity to the Federal government. Now the men were gone, and so was their flag. For security they depended on the 13th Massachusetts, Colonel Samuel H. Leonard, which Banks posted across the river at Sandy Hook to guard the canal and the stem of the railroad.[9]

With Banks comfortably situated in Maryland, Ashby jogged into town and posted sentinels along the Potomac to keep watch on the Massachusetts volunteers. Not a day passed in late August without the crackle of musket fire. Townsfolk stayed away from the river, even on wash day. Union snipers were "uncommonly zealous" in shooting at rebels as long as the Potomac kept them separated from direct contact. Squads took turns lurking under the buttresses of the ruined bridge or crouching in the dry bed of the canal as they watched for a target to pop up within range of their muskets. Some climbed partway up Maryland Heights and sheltered themselves among the rocks and thickets. Firing was sporadic but constant. "Everything that moved about the streets they shot at vindictively," Joseph Barry recalled. "The appearance of even a mullein leaf swaying in the wind elicited a volley . . . and it was lucky for the place that they were indifferent marksmen, else [the town] would have been totally depopulated."[10]

One night a detachment from the 13th Massachusetts crossed

8. *HTI*, 38; Scott to Banks, August 13, and Banks to Army Headquarters, August 15, 1861, *OR*, V, 560, 562, 578.

9. Frank Moore, ed., *The Rebellion Record: A Diary of American Events* (12 vols.; New York, 1977), II, *Documents*, 40; Williams to Leonard, August 21, 1861, *OR*, V, 578.

10. Barry, *Harper's Ferry*, 111–12.

in skiffs, crept through town, and started filing up the hill. Confederate pickets posted in the cemetery on the hill met the intruders with scattered fire. Barry heard the rattle of muskets and came into the street in time to observe a Union officer, bedecked in a red sash and a fine jacket, making a headlong sprint towards the river. The officer jumped into the Shenandoah and took refuge behind a stone wall built to protect the Winchester and Potomac roadbed from the strong current of the river. Losing his hold, he washed downriver. The brilliant red sash around his waist permanently stained his fine jacket, which was loaded down with medals and badges of merit earned in the Crimean campaign. A skiff picked him up and toted him, drenching wet, to safety. Barry went back to bed, wondering by what method the Union army selected its officers. A few days later he learned that the mysterious skedaddling officer had "lost caste with his regiment" and would be court-martialed.[11]

Exaggerated reports of Confederate movements kept Banks occupied shifting units to imagined pressure points ranging from the mouth of the Monocacy all the way to Williamsport. Ashby caused the confusion by roaming the shores of the Potomac and popping up at Sharpsburg one day and at Harpers Ferry the next. By August 20 Banks's command had grown to fourteen thousand men, whom he moved about like a novice playing his first game of chess. One of the moves involved Colonel John W. Geary, who brought his 28th Pennsylvania to Sandy Hook in mid-September and took command of various companies left behind by the 13th Massachusetts, the 3rd Wisconsin, and a battery from the 9th New York.[12]

Forty-one-year-old John White Geary of Pennsylvania was one of those rare individuals equally comfortable in both politics and the military. After settling on a career in law, he enlisted as a volunteer in the Mexican War and won praise as colonel of the 2nd Pennsylvania Infantry. In 1856 he served as territorial governor of Kansas, arriving there four months after John Brown massacred five settlers who lived along Pottawatomie Creek. Geary now found himself at Harpers Ferry fighting a war Brown started in Kansas and brought to Virginia. When the Civil War began, he

11. *Ibid.*, 112–13.
12. Banks to Cameron, September 4, and Geary to Williams, September 14, 1861, *OR*, V, 583–84, 600.

issued a call for troops, and because of his fine reputation, sixty-eight companies responded. Overwhelmed by numbers, Geary selected fifteen of the best units and organized the oversized 28th Pennsylvania Infantry. The regiment had just settled into their new camp when informants in Harpers Ferry warned that Ashby, with three thousand infantry, intended to pay the town a visit.[13]

Geary doubted the rumor but kept a sharp eye on the Ferry. For several days detachments from his command skirmished with small parties of Confederate cavalry ranging along the railroad. Other fights broke out at the base of Loudoun Heights, another on the summit. Firing from Bolivar Heights harassed Union soldiers guarding the canal locks across the river. Geary advanced two pieces artillery to drive away the snipers, but at no time did he cross the river to reoccupy the town. After three days of sporadic fighting he reported four casualties. His sole prisoner, Second Lieutenant William S. Engles of Company K, 2nd Virginia, had his home in Harpers Ferry.[14]

In early October, Abraham Herr, proprietor of the mill on Virginius Island, invited Geary across the river to remove twenty thousand bushels of wheat before Ashby appropriated the summer harvest. Herr still remembered the day Virginia militia came to town, arrested him as a Unionist, and shipped him off to Richmond for questioning. Paroled, Herr returned a few days later and minded his own business. When the Federals evacuated the Ferry in August, Banks ordered the mill disabled to deny the Confederacy its use. Herr, being a Union man at heart, held no grudge against Banks, but when he learned that James L. Ranson, the Confederate agent for conscription and supply in Jefferson County, was working towards the Ferry with Ashby, the miller invited Geary to come and take the wheat.

Geary assigned the transfer of grain to Major J. Parker Gould, who obtained a large barge, floated it up the Shenandoah, and on October 8 crossed with three companies of the 13th Massachusetts. The grain lay in loose piles on the mill floor and cascaded off army shovels like sand. Gould, unable to collect and bag the grain without help, asked headquarters for reinforcements. While waiting he brought three companies of the 3rd Wisconsin and a

13. *HTI*, 302; Geary to Williams, September 14, 1861, *OR*, V, 600.
14. Geary's Report, September 17, 1861, *OR*, V, 198.

section of the 1st Rhode Island Light Artillery across the river to speed up the loading.

A few days later Union scouts reported three companies of Ashby's cavalry reconnoitering across from Pleasant Valley. When news of Herr's generosity reached the Confederate camp, Ashby proposed to capture the grain for the South. Most of the wheat still lay at the mill, and Geary refused to be forced out of town without it. He sent four companies of the 28th Pennsylvania across the river to check Ashby, who had also sent for reinforcements. Another detail marched through town impressing able-bodied men to relieve the shovelers at the mill, as Geary now needed his soldiers on the firing line. Barry got caught in the dragnet and for several days toted grain under the eye of a grim Wisconsin sergeant. "We were promised a liberal per diem," he wrote, "but that, like many other good promises and intentions, forms a part of the pavement of a certain region where it never freezes."[15]

Ranson discovered he could not get into Harpers Ferry and became quite distressed over losing the wheat. After urging Ashby to attack the invaders, Ranson picked up his pen and reported the situation, with embellishments, to President Davis:

> The enemy crossed the Potomac at Harper's Ferry last week, and in considerable numbers . . . and have been arriving ever since, pillaging and ravaging as they advanced. The farmers below this place are being robbed of slaves, horses and everything the enemy can use.
>
> Last night a lady swam the Shenandoah to let us know that the enemy were being re-enforced, and the first aim would be to destroy our woolen factories along the Shenandoah; also our large flouring mills. . . . The delay heretofore has been caused by the shipping of some 20,000 bushels of wheat seized at Harper's Ferry.[16]

At nightfall on October 15, with Herr's mill swept clean, Geary recalled the grain detail, ordering them back to camp in the morning. But at daylight on October 16, the second anniversary of the Brown raid, musket fire erupted on Bolivar Heights. With a demoniac yell, Ashby's Confederate horsemen charged out of the woods. Supported by three hundred Virginia militia armed with

15. Geary to Copeland, October 18, 1861, *ibid.*, 239–40; Barry, *Harper's Ferry*, 114.

16. Ranson to Davis, October 15, 1861, *OR*, V, 898–99.

flintlocks, Ashby attacked in three columns from the west, covering a two-and-a-half-mile front from the Potomac to the Shenandoah. Geary's Pennsylvania pickets scattered in confusion. Some fell back on the 3rd Wisconsin, posted on the left; the others scrambled into the ranks of the 13th Massachusetts, which moved into a defensive position on the outskirts of Bolivar. Ashby, followed by infantry, charged Bolivar Heights. Lieutenant Chew's Confederate horse artillery, posted near the Charles Town road, opened with shot, shell, and grape.

Geary had only half his command at Harpers Ferry. The other half, about 450 men, remained on the Maryland side. When four pieces of Confederate artillery and a company of sharpshooters opened from Loudoun Heights on the grain ferry, Geary detached a company from the 13th Massachusetts to defend the fords and safeguard the vessel. The New Englanders fanned out along the Shenandoah, taking cover in Hall's Rifle Works and Herr's mill. With no bridge at his back, Geary recognized the situation as serious. He must fight Ashby.

Four companies of the 28th Pennsylvania (A, D, F, and G), supported mainly by the 3rd Wisconsin, checked Ashby's first charge on the outskirts of Bolivar. As part of the 13th Massachusetts came up, Geary moved Companies A and G to his right, where they met and repulsed Ashby's second attack. Regrouping for a third try, this time on Geary's left, Ashby met a storm of fire from the 3rd Wisconsin. As he fell back, Geary sent Companies A and G around the Confederate left flank, driving them off the heights directly above the Potomac. Lieutenant J. W. Martin, commanding a battery of the 9th New York (also called the 6th) on Maryland Heights, opened a well-directed fire on Ashby's artillery. Captain John A. Thompkins of the 1st Rhode Island Light Artillery opened from the Maryland side and silenced the guns on Loudoun Heights. With Ashby's left flank collapsing, Geary ordered a charge. Joined by Major Hector Tyndale and five fresh companies of the 28th Pennsylvania, the men counterattacked en masse and recaptured Bolivar Heights. Ashby retreated to Halltown, and Geary, having no cavalry to follow up his advantage, left him there. Tyndale planted the regimental colors on Bolivar Heights and sent a detachment to drive off a nest of Confederate snipers infesting the banks of the Shenandoah at the base of Loudoun Mountain.[17]

17. Geary to Copeland, October 18, 1861, *ibid.*, 239–41.

For Ashby, the defeat represented a mild disaster. He lost a fine 24-pounder columbiad and its ammunition wagon. Another gun, a 4-pounder, one of its wheels splintered by fire from Martin's battery, was dragged off the field by the cannoneers. Ashby made the attack at a considerable disadvantage, but he had been watching the enemy "committing depredations in the vicinity of their camp" for several days and believed he could flush them back across the river or force their surrender. He had two companies of cavalry and about three hundred militia armed with the Virginia Military Institute's old flintlocks. Before the attack, he borrowed three companies of cavalry from Colonel Angus W. McDonald, but many of the men were unmounted and most of them carried the cumbersome flintlocks.

Ashby's cavalry drove the strongly picketed Union line into lower Bolivar before being stopped by Geary's infantry. When the 28th Pennsylvania attacked his left flank, the militia fired one round from their ancient flintlocks and retreated to the rear. Confederate gunners posted on Loudoun Heights failed to get high enough on the mountain for their shells to reach the Union infantry at Bolivar, and Geary's artillery on Maryland Heights drove them away. A company of sharpshooters firing from the base of Loudoun Mountain failed to prevent Tyndale from reinforcing Geary and soon exhausted their ammunition. After four hours of fighting without any hope of winning, Ashby retired to Schoolhouse Hill to await Geary's assault. When no attack came, he pulled his force back to Halltown.[18]

Casualty claims made interesting reading. Geary reported Ashby's losses "to be about 150" in killed and wounded, which he claimed were carried off the field in wagons and on horses. Union soldiers captured four prisoners, among them Reverend Nathaniel Green North, Ashby's chaplain. Geary recorded his casualties as four killed, seven wounded, and two captured. Ashby's report came closer to the truth. He believed the enemy lost about twenty-five killed with an undetermined number wounded, but reported his own loss at only one killed and thirteen wounded. With roughly eleven hundred men involved in a skirmish lasting four hours, where total casualties added up to five killed and

18. Ashby to Benjamin, October 17, 1861, *ibid.*, 247–48.

twenty wounded, enough cannot be said about poor marksman-ship.[19]

In the aftermath of the fight, however, Geary recovered his four dead and to his dismay found them "stabbed through the body, stripped of all their clothing . . . and left in perfect nudity." One was laid in the form of a crucifixion, with his hands spread out and cut through the palms with a dull knife. "This inhuman treat-ment incensed my troops exceedingly, and I fear," Geary pre-dicted, "its consequences may be shown in retaliatory acts here-after."[20]

When the skirmish ended both sides claimed victory, but nei-ther commander showed any interest in holding the contested ground. Geary returned to the Maryland shore with Herr's grain, and Ashby licked his wounds at Charles Town. Two men from the neighborhood of Harpers Ferry received wounds, Privates John W. Rider of Halltown and John Yates Beall of the 2nd Virginia Infantry. Beall was at home recovering from a wound when Ashby rode into town. He picked up his musket and joined the attack. His second wound was worse than his first, disabling him from active service. When he mended, Beall joined a conspiracy to free Confederate officers imprisoned on Johnson's Island in Lake Erie. The scheme might have worked had they not been betrayed by a woman jilted by one of the conspirators. Beall spent the balance of his career spying for the Confederacy. Caught in civilian clothes outside Buffalo, New York, he was tried and hung on February 24, 1865.[21]

In the aftermath of the skirmish, a detail from the 28th Penn-sylvania arrested Patrick Hagan and several others for allegedly harboring the enemy in their homes and permitting them to shoot Union soldiers from behind drawn curtains. Hagan, known as one of the most "peaceable men" of the area, was jostled over to Sandy Hook without so much as his coat and confined for several months in a Federal prison. Hagan, like many others, became an innocent victim of the war.

Herr's mill suffered next, this time at the hands of the Confed-

19. Geary to Copeland, October 18, and Ashby to Benjamin, October 17, 1861, *ibid.*, 241–42, 247–48.

20. Geary to Copeland, October 18, 1861, *ibid.*, 242.

21. D. B. Lucas, *Memoir of John Yates Beall* (Montreal, 1865), 11–29, 50–57, 81.

erate cavalry. Ashby decided to put Herr permanently out of business and sent a detachment to the Ferry to burn the mill. The firebrands rode to Virginius Island and found Herr repairing his machinery. In his memoirs, written in 1903, Joseph Barry said, "The shattered and toppling walls are still to be seen, a monument of vandalism and a reproach to civilized warriors."[22]

Charles Town resident Alexander R. Boteler voiced his own complaint as depredations began to spread across the countryside: "The condition of our border is becoming more alarming every day. No night passes without some infamous outrage upon our loyal citizens." Boteler suggested elevating Ashby, whose cavalry had just destroyed the Ferry's only mill, to full colonel, thereby entitling him to a full regiment. Then, Boteler promised, "a better state of things will exist up here."[23] Ashby obtained his promotion a short time later, but the situation in Jefferson County remained the same. Union soldiers received much of the blame for damage done by vagrants.

On the eve of winter Harpers Ferry became a no-man's-land, visited regularly by scouts from both sides. At night people in homes facing Maryland Heights lived in darkness, fearful some trigger-happy Union sniper would find a twinkle of light too irresistible a target. Residents living along the Shenandoah shared similar fears from equally mischievous Confederate scouts. Eight-year-old Annie P. Marmion remembered her childhood years during the war: "The great objects in life were to procure something to eat and to keep yourself out of sight by day, and your lamps . . . hidden by night, lights of every kind being regarded as signals to the Rebels were usually greeted by a Volley of guns."[24]

When word spread that recruiter Ranson intended to make a pass through Harpers Ferry, six young men with strong Union sentiments decided the time had come to leave town. As Confederate conscriptors worked down Washington Street, Alexander Kelly, John Kelly, J. Miller Brown, G. S. Collis, Lafayette Davis, and Joseph Barry climbed into a small, leaky skiff and crossed to the Maryland shore. A sentinel met them along the bank and refused to let them land. After several appeals from the skiff, a Union officer arrested the sextet and marched them over to the 28th Pennsylvania headquarters. Major Tyndale considered them spies,

22. Barry, *Harper's Ferry*, 116.
23. Boteler to Hunter, October 24, 1861, *OR*, V, 919.
24. Marmion, "Under Fire," 7, HFA.

searched them for incriminating evidence, and interrogated each man separately. Finding nothing incriminating, he detained them under guard and quartered them with a few suspicious prisoners sharing rooms at Eader's Hotel in Sandy Hook. Barry promised the Irish guard a bottle of whiskey in exchange for a half hour's freedom—time enough to purchase cheese, crackers, and sausage for his friends and "a very corpulent bottle" of Sandy Hook's potent "tangle foot" for the guard. Tyndale eventually released the men, but Barry, who had concealed a book of romantic verses written to certain ladies of Harpers Ferry, was banished to a distance of ten miles "from the lines of the army for his unholy poetry."[25]

By the end of 1861 the Ferry had become little more than a ghost town, occupied mainly by people too old and feeble to be driven away or by transients who took up temporary lodgings abandoned by once prosperous residents. "Imagine a town filled with houses enough to accommodate over 2,000 people," wrote Annie Marmion, "and more than nine tenths of them empty." Men young and old joined the army, their only means of employment. Some went north, but most went south, joining regiments already formed, filling vacancies left by the dead and wounded. By then most of the town had been abandoned and every scrap of metal scavenged by looters. "Not a door in all these houses had locks and bolts of any kind," Annie Marmion recalled. "The Owls enjoyed the Open House System and joined their mournful hoots to the general slamming of doors to emphasize the silence and loneliness. No one entered the Town except some Messenger of Ill, sent always . . . at night and by water from the Blockading party, always the Northern Army."[26]

When both combatants went into winter camp, a few people returned to the Ferry. They looked at the remains of their town and convinced themselves that neither side would ever find a strategic reason to return. With the railroad gone, the bridges destroyed, the armory gutted, the rifle works demolished, and Herr's mill torched, nothing of value remained for either side to want.

With tender hope, a few families returned to their homes. They prayed that war had paid its final visit, but they forgot the prophecy of old John Brown.

25. Barry, *Harper's Ferry*, 116–19.
26. Marmion, "Under Fire," 6, HFA.

# 6

## Frightful Days in the Valley

Throughout the winter of 1861–1862, Captain Robert W. Baylor's Confederate cavalry kept a close watch on Jefferson County, taking special interest in Harpers Ferry. Townsfolk practiced neutrality but some chose sides, and Baylor administered depredations on anyone accused of unionism. Baylor's spies reported increased enemy activity along the Maryland shore, and as dawn broke on February 7 a morning patrol encountered two scouts in the lower town.

Two Unionists from Harpers Ferry, men named Rohr and Rice, had crossed from the Maryland side during the night to gather information from friends. They were shoving off in their skiff when sighted by Baylor's patrol, who had been watching for them. As the skiff slid into the current, Rohr and Rice exchanged fire with the riders. Bullets splashed around the boat. Rohr slumped over the gunwale dead, and Rice jumped into the icy river. Shielding himself behind the skiff, he floated with the current and when safely downriver climbed on board and made it back to camp in a state of numbness.

The town had nothing to do with shooting Rohr, but the act invited Union retaliation. Colonel Geary, enraged at the loss of his favorite scout, sent a detachment to destroy several buildings at the foot of Shenandoah Street, a shelter for snipers firing at Union soldiers on the Maryland side. The demolition squad, led by Major Tyndale, arrived in force. They set fire to the Wager House, the Potomac Restaurant, and all the buildings near the ruins of the railroad bridge. As the structures burned, Tyndale may have recalled the afternoon of December 2, 1859—the moment when he opened John Brown's coffin and, turning to Mrs. Brown, asked if she wished to identify the body. She replied "No," and looked away. At the time, neither the major nor the widow knew of Brown's prophecy of destruction. If Tyndale recalled the martyr's words, he left no record of it as he struck a match to the lower town.[1]

By early February Banks's division had swelled to more than eighteen thousand troops scattered from the outskirts of Washington to the western extremity of Maryland.[2] On February 23 he divided Geary's 28th Pennsylvania, leaving part of the regiment on Maryland Heights and sending the remainder across the river to occupy Loudoun Heights. Captain James C. Duane, U.S. Engineers, brought pontoons up from Washington, and on February 26 two hundred pioneers began placing them just above the piers of the ruined railroad bridge.

Laying a pontoon bridge in high water required skill and courage. Rice, the local ferryman who had survived a dip in the icy Potomac a few weeks earlier, now led five men from the 28th Pennsylvania across the river in a skiff. With them went James Stedman, another local resident who scouted for Geary. Rice intended to help the pioneers set pontoon boats from the Virginia side, but the night was black and stormy, with high winds whipping down the gorges of the valley. Either in a burst of wind or by mismanagement of the skiff, the boat overturned and dumped all seven men into the icy river. Rice swam to one of the bridge buttresses, but Stedman and the others drowned, their bodies never recovered. There is no record of whether anybody else ever risked riding with Rice in a skiff. After two close calls with death, the scout survived the war and became a railroad engineer. One day he fell out of his cab and was cut to pieces by the engine. Had Rice landed in water, he would surely have swum to safety.[3]

1. Villard, *John Brown*, 558; Barry, *Harper's Ferry*, 119–20.

2. Banks's Returns, February 6, 1862, *OR*, V, 719.

3. David Nichol to his father, February 26, 1862, Nichol Papers, Harrisburg Civil War Round Table Collection, USAMHI; Barry, *Harper's Ferry*, 121.

Private Warren Lee Goss, Company A, U.S. Engineers, worked with the crew setting the scows, clamping joists, fixing a flooring of planks, and cleating the floating structure into place. He complained about the work and the weather, but in the end Goss took pride in building "the first boat-bridge thrown out in active service of the army of the United States." In an idle moment he fished through the armory buildings collecting mementos of historic interest. He knocked a brick loose from "the old engine-house where John Brown so coolly fought" and slipped it into his knapsack. When he returned to the bridge he was greeted by "a slight, short man, with sandy hair" who wore a blue uniform with two stars on each shoulder. Major General George B. McClellan had come to town.[4]

Sergeant David Nichol of Battery E, Pennsylvania Light Artillery, was among the first gunners to cross into Harpers Ferry. Sharing bright prospects with a friend at home, he wrote, "General McClellan and staff is here, as also Genl Banks. The greatest joy prevails among the troops on arriving in the Land of Dixie. It is well seen the Secesh has been here—nearly every house is deserted and there [is] not a young man in the place. Our soldiers are all quartered in the houses and seem to like the style."[5]

The 15th Massachusetts crossed with the Pennsylvania Light Artillery and settled into the remaining buildings. Sitting by a warm fireside, Walter A. Eanes penned a note to his wife: "The streets are thronged with troops constantly arriving. There is so much confusion that I cannot write much. . . . When I have time, I will write and give you some description . . . of this ruined town with its burned and shattered buildings. It is a romantic place with its rushing rivers [and] its precipitous mountains." Two days later he sauntered through the town and found it "entirely deserted by its former inhabitants, [but] before its destruction," he added, "[it] must have been very beautiful."[6]

A few days later Eanes discovered a dozen families holed up in their homes along Washington and Shenandoah Streets. Most of

4. Warren Lee Goss, *Recollections of a Private: A Story of the Army of the Potomac* (New York, 1890), 19–21.

5. David Nichol to friend, February 27, 1862, Nichol Papers, Harrisburg Civil War Round Table Collection, USAMHI.

6. Walter Eanes to his wife, February 27, March 1, 1862, Eanes Letter Book, 130, 132, USAMHI.

them were a sorrowful-looking lot whose sole purpose was to guard their possessions. They had good reason, for as Eanes admitted to his father, "We have searched the town and brought in tables, chairs, etc. so that the rooms are pretty well furnished, but still we lie on the floor and eat raw pork so we will not forget we are soldiers. . . . I [enclose] this bit of wood cut from the door of the engine house that was the scene of John Brown's fight."[7]

Eanes was not to be the last of the army's souvenir collectors, though few of the tiny treasures sold contained an ounce of authenticity. Wily hucksters lured the soldiers into buying worthless scraps of junk. In one instance, even Eanes succumbed to the scam. On March 16 he wrote his father, "Enclosed find a bit of wood. At the time of the execution of John Brown, he made a speech standing on a stump from which this chip was cut. Gov. Wise stepped from his carriage and mounting the same stump also addressed the assembled people. The stump, or what is left of it, is now enclosed by a railing. It has nearly all been cut off and carried away." At the time of the alleged incident, Brown was surrounded by guards and lay critically wounded in a room at the paymaster's office.[8]

With the army came numerous reporters and sightseers, among them Nathaniel Hawthorne, who gained a rather dismal impression of Harpers Ferry. He wandered through the armory, skirted piles of broken bricks, and declared it "a waste of shapeless demolition" with heat-bent gun barrels "in heaps of hundreds together"—all rusting in the rain. "The brightest sunshine," Hawthorne declared, "could not have made the scene cheerful, nor taken away the gloom from the dilapidated town . . . it has an inexpressible forlornness."[9]

McClellan, the army's new commander in chief, arrived at Sandy Hook on February 26, just in time to watch 8,500 infantry with eighteen guns and two squadrons of cavalry march across the river and into Harpers Ferry. A few days later Brigadier General William H. Burns's brigade, another 8,000 strong, stomped across the pontoons carting more guns and bringing another regiment of cavalry through the town. With no more empty buildings for lodg-

7. Walter Eanes to his father, March 3, 1862, *ibid.*, 134–35.
8. Walter Eanes to his father, March 16, 1862, *ibid.*, 139–40.
9. Extract from Nathaniel Hawthorne, "The Conflict of Convictions," File HFB-216, HFA.

ing, latecomers pitched their tents on the wintry slopes of Camp Hill. The town became so congested that the 1st New York Light Artillery spent their first days at Sandy Hook. Lieutenant Thomas Hodgkins of Battery M finally bedded down in an abandoned dwelling with several refugees from Harpers Ferry. They were anxious to return to their homes, but Hodgkins could offer them no assurances. At McClellan's request, however, Banks picketed a strong force west of Bolivar Heights, leaving residents with the impression that he had come to stay.[10]

McClellan had ranked second in the West Point class of 1846 and won two brevets for distinguished service in the Mexican War. He also claimed the distinction of registering two victories in northwestern Virginia on the eve of the Union army's defeat at Bull Run, and this success led to his command of the Army of the Potomac and the ousting of ancient and ailing Winfield Scott as general in chief. His admirers called the thirty-five-year-old general "the Young Napoleon," and during his brief visit to Harpers Ferry he encouraged Banks to continue the practice of organizing and drilling his command.[11]

A few days later Brigadier General James Shields crossed into Virginia with eleven thousand Federal troops and marched to Winchester. He sounded anxious for a fight, writing on March 13, "Rumors among [Winchester] citizens have it that the rebels mean to concentrate all their disposable strength and give us one grand battle between here and Richmond."[12] Shields soon discovered he would not have to travel far from his Winchester headquarters to taste the mettle of Stonewall Jackson's "disposable strength."

Irish-born James Shields came to the United States in 1826 and settled in Illinois, where he became a lawyer, a judge, and an active Democrat—so active, in fact, that he once challenged Abraham Lincoln, then a Whig, to a duel. The pair settled their differences amicably and became good friends. Shields served in the Black Hawk War and the Mexican War, earning in the latter the brevet of major general. In August, 1861, he applied to Lincoln for

10. Thomas Hodgkins to his sisters and brothers, March 3, 1862, Hodgkins Letters, Civil War Times Illustrated Collection, USAMHI; Banks to Marcy, February 23, and McClellan to Stanton, February 26, 1862, *OR*, V, 726–27.

11. *HTI*, 456.

12. Shields to Williams, March 13, 1862, *OR*, V, 749.

a commission, and now, at the age of fifty-one, he commanded the 2nd Division of Banks's corps.[13]

When Banks took command of the V Army Corps on March 20, he transferred his own 1st Division to fifty-one-year-old Brigadier General Alpheus S. "Old Pap" Williams, another lawyer and judge who fought in the Mexican War but as a general from Connecticut.[14] Both Shields and Williams had far more military experience than Banks, most of their regiments had been bloodied, and all appeared to be in good condition and eager for a fight. With Shields occupying Winchester, Williams camped a few miles to the north at Bunker Hill. For a few weeks Banks remained at Harpers Ferry, holding two brigades in reserve and posting a strong garrison on the heights.

On March 4 engineers went to work rebuilding the Potomac bridge. Two construction crews, one at each end, worked towards the center through days of cold, rainy weather. They repaired the masonry on the piers, laid new stringers, capped it with flooring, and, after two weeks of ceaseless labor, laid track and reopened the bridge. A crew from the Baltimore and Ohio moved into town and resumed operations on the Winchester and Potomac spur. On the night of March 16 the first locomotive chuffed across the bridge and deposited a load of supplies with the army quartermaster. Another crew repaired the roadbed and culverts to Martinsburg. By March 29 the Baltimore and Ohio ran once again from Wheeling to Washington, and on the following day 3,800 freight cars passed through Harpers Ferry. Passenger service resumed, and travelers noted that the town's new station flew the Stars and Stripes, signifying to all observers that the railroad was at long last an exclusive Union enterprise.[15]

Private Stanley Hamer of the 54th Pennsylvania Infantry passed through Harpers Ferry on the second train to Martinsburg. He stopped at the Ferry long enough to stretch his legs. After a short jaunt along North Potomac Street he returned to the train and wrote his brother, "Harpers Ferry looks as though it has been sick

13. *HTI*, 683–84.

14. Summary of Principal Events, *OR*, V, 1; Mark M. Boatner III, *The Civil War Dictionary* (New York, 1959), 926–27.

15. Banks to Marcy, March 4, 13, 1862, *OR*, V, 734, 746; Summers, *Baltimore and Ohio*, 115–17; Walter Eanes to his father, March 17, 1862, Eanes Letter Book, 141, USAMHI.

for a long time; a great many houses are burned and a great deal of property destroyed." But sickness struck more than towns. Nine months later, Hamer died of typhoid fever.[16]

Townsfolk began to return to their homes to reconstruct their lives, but they found most of their possessions carried off or destroyed. Besides soldiers, they discovered heavily perfumed invaders in their homes. Walter Eanes wrote his brother, "Quite a number of prostitutes have made their appearance here . . . and when they get fairly started in business we shall find plenty of victims for the Guard House"—John Brown's fort. "What a pity," Eanes added, "that so beautiful a spot should be ruined by the ravages of war."[17]

In a moment of leisure, Private Goss of the Engineers climbed the hill to Jefferson Rock and scanned the ruins of the charred armory and the town in general. He observed puffs of smoke from musket fire on Loudoun Heights and could see Geary's men climbing the summit to chase away enemy scouts. Noise from the streets below filtered up to the Rock. Goss recalled that "the murmur of many voices, the mellow, abrupt call of negro drivers to their mules, the glistening arms of infantry reflected in the sunlight, [and] the dull rumble of artillery wheels and baggage-wagons" combined to offer a picture of "war's wrinkled front." Geary's men returned with several prisoners who presented a shabby and unmilitary appearance, but as the war wore on Goss learned to respect their "unmusical yell and dauntless front."[18]

Within a week the town became both an armed camp and the supply base for Union operations in the Valley. Civilians visiting relatives in the army flowed into the crowded town. Former residents returned, expecting never to be torn from their homes again, but first they had to evict soldiers and vagrants squatting on their properties. Within weeks, hundreds of jobs became available for those willing to work. With greenbacks in town and the bleak, leafless hills showing signs of sweet spring, whiskey sales and prostitution revived with the same vigor as trade in fresh-

16. Samuel Hamer to John Hamer, April 1, 1862, Hamer Letters, Harrisburg Civil War Round Table Collection, USAMHI.

17. Walter Eanes to his brother, March 4, and to his wife, March 6, 1862, Eanes Letter Book, 135, 136–37, USAMHI.

18. Goss, *Recollections of a Private*, 20–21.

baked bread and fruit pies. For a clever opportunist a small fortune could be pocketed if the war would only last a little longer.

Soon supplies and reinforcements flowed over the old Winchester and Potomac roadbed to Shields's division encamped thirty miles up the Valley. For Banks, this spur could not come soon enough. Allen Pinkerton had rattled the general's nerves by erroneously reporting Jackson's force at 13,000.[19]

At the time, Jackson had about 3,100 infantry and 300 cavalry, but they were troops seasoned by hard marching and accustomed to fighting. His division contained the Stonewall Brigade, mustered in at Harpers Ferry and bloodied at Bull Run. Turner Ashby, now a brigadier general, led the hard-riding but undisciplined cavalry, which contained Chew's Jefferson County mounted battery of light guns. Shields's division, supported from the Ferry, had grown to 11,000 men, with 8,000 in the vicinity of Winchester. When Jackson attacked Shields at Kernstown on March 23, he struck with enough energy to convince the Union general he had been hit by a division of 15,000 veterans. Shields repulsed Jackson's disjointed attack and claimed the Confederates had been driven out of the Valley. But the general suffered a wound, forcing him to temporarily transfer the division to Colonel Nathan Kimball. Shields's claims of Jackson's strength coincided with Pinkerton's guesswork and convinced the strategists in Washington that Banks's force must not be diluted to support McClellan's Peninsula campaign.[20]

Keeping the Union army nearby suited the civilians at Harpers Ferry, but after Shields's engagement at Kernstown, Banks moved the rest of his corps to Winchester. He left a detachment in town to guard the railroad and on March 29 placed them under the command of Colonel Dixon S. Miles, a gray and grizzled regular army man who liked his whiskey.[21]

Banks intended to throw his entire force at Jackson and drive him out of the Valley. McClellan, on the eve of launching his "On to Richmond" campaign, wanted Jackson destroyed so Banks

19. Pinkerton to McClellan, March 8, and McClellan to Stanton, March 14, 1862, *OR*, V, 736, 755.

20. Shields to Williams, March 23, and Jackson's Report, April 9, 1862, *ibid.*, Pt. 1, pp. 335, 383; Nathan Kimball, "Fighting Jackson at Kernstown," *B&L*, II, 302–309.

21. Special Order No. 95, March 29, 1862, *OR*, XII, Pt. 3, pp. 30–31.

could move east and cooperate with the Army of the Potomac. Banks emptied the Ferry of artillery and supplies, moving everything by rail to Winchester. Teamsters unloaded the cars and filled hundreds of regimental wagons. Soldiers stocked up on supplies and ammunition for the march south. Morale soared. The boys in blue trundled up the Valley with high expectations. They planned to be home by summer.

After Johnston evacuated the Manassas line and moved his force to Richmond, Jackson's role changed, although he still hoped to reclaim northwestern Virginia and impair the operation of the Baltimore and Ohio. Richmond reinforced Jackson, raising his division to 6,000 men, and then asked the general to annoy Banks—just enough to keep more than 19,000 Union troops from crossing the Blue Ridge Mountains and turning the Confederate flank.

Jackson fell back from Winchester—first through Strasburg, then up the Manassas Gap Railroad to Mount Jackson—forcing Banks to extend his line for miles along the narrow Valley pike. On April 21 Banks reached Harrisonburg, fifty-five miles south of Strasburg, twenty-five miles north of Staunton, and within striking distance of the important Virginia Central Railroad. Banks, however, had diluted his force as he progressed up the Valley, posting Shields's division at Strasburg and leaving detachments behind to occupy captured territory. If he intended to flank Johnston, he was in position to do it by moving swiftly through Brown's Gap or by detaching Shields from Strasburg, but Banks was after Jackson.

The Union supply line, which had started at Harpers Ferry, now shifted to the Manassas Gap Railroad, which crossed westerly to Strasburg and ended at Mount Jackson. To reach Harrisonburg, the Union quartermaster resorted to wagons. After luring Banks far up the Valley and more than twenty-five miles from the nearest railroad, Jackson launched a campaign so bold in concept and effective in execution that it remains to this day a classic in military tactics.[22]

Jackson viewed Banks's extended supply line as an opportunity to drive him out of the Valley by cutting the Manassas Gap Railroad at Front Royal, which lay to the east of Strasburg and near

22. For a well-researched and readable contemporary work, see Robert G. Tanner, *Stonewall in the Valley* (Garden City, N.Y., 1976).

the northeastern base of Massanutten Mountain. While Banks moved his extended line along the valley to the west of the Massanuttens, Jackson faced about and began a forced march down the narrower valley to the east, using the mountains to screen his movement. Banks, unaware of Jackson's advance, reversed his line of march when Shields received orders from Washington to join McDowell at Fredericksburg. Jackson waited until Shields departed from the Valley before springing his attack on Banks, who had returned to Strasburg and set his men to work digging massive earthworks.[23]

Major General John C. Fremont's force of 16,000 men lay at Franklin, about thirty-five miles west of New Market. Banks had no authority over Fremont's command and miscalculated Jackson's intentions when he agreed to detach Shields. By scattering the commands of Banks, Fremont, McDowell, and Shields, the Union War Office committed a serious military blunder at a time when Jackson was being reinforced. Banks seemed oblivious to the threat, depended upon Fremont for support, and confidently notified Secretary of War Edwin M. Stanton that he would defeat Jackson "upon anything like equal ground."[24] Stonewall grasped the tactical advantage and struck Banks first.

Jackson started his sprint on May 19, picking up reinforcements as he marched. Three days passed before Banks sensed Jackson's approach. The Union force at Strasburg had been reduced to about 5,000 infantry, 1,800 cavalry, and 16 pieces of artillery. Jackson, with 20,000 men on the move, targeted most of them on Banks. On the morning of May 23 Confederate cavalry cut the Manassas Gap Railroad east of Strasburg. Early in the afternoon Jackson struck Colonel John R. Kenly's 1st Maryland at Front Royal and drove them back to Winchester.[25]

The combined attack broke the Union supply line, and with Jackson on his flank, Banks abandoned his freshly dug entrenchments at Strasburg and began a hurried retreat. He had a vague notion that Jackson was still somewhere up the Valley pike, and

23. Jackson to Ewell, May 13, 14, 1862, *OR*, XII, Pt. 3, pp. 888–89; Munford to Ewell, May 16, 1862, *ibid.*, Pt. 1, p. 502.

24. Fremont to Stanton, May 24, and Banks to Stanton, May 22, 1862, *ibid.*, Pt. 1, pp. 642, 524.

25. Kenly to Wilkins, May 31, 1862, *ibid.*, 555–58.

at dawn, May 24, Banks started his infantry and wagons for Winchester.[26]

For a few hours Jackson lost sight of Banks's command, but when a courier reported the Union army in full retreat, Stonewall divided his force, putting himself on the pike and Major General Richard S. Ewell's division on the Middletown-Winchester road. Banks had a head start, but Jackson put his two divisions on a forced march to cut the blueclads off at Winchester. Confederate cavalry pounced on the wagon train, strewing equipment along the road for miles, but the action only accelerated the Union retreat. Banks reached Winchester first and deployed to meet the expected attack, but "secessionists, Union men, refugees, fugitives and prisoners" convinced the Union commander that Jackson had more than 25,000 men. Banks attempted a weak resistance to cover his withdrawal. Jackson's main force had been delayed moving down the pike by a clutter of wagons, unhitched teams, sutlers' stores, and personal belongings that littered the road for eight miles. Ewell reached Winchester unimpeded and hit Banks with just enough force to contain him on the outskirts of town.[27]

Banks was so confused by Jackson's tactics that he sent the 1st Maine Cavalry from Harpers Ferry to Martinsburg to act as railroad guards. Private Charles E. Gardner, a member of the unit, commented that the Ferry "was not much like a Northern town." He disliked Martinsburg even more, where fewer of the townsfolk had been displaced. "The women and the young ladies gave us some terrible tongue lashings," Gardner recalled, "and some even spit in our faces. We had to watch them closely as there were many spies."[28]

With Fremont's division supposedly on the way from Franklin, Banks attempted to hold Winchester and on May 25 fought Jackson with unexpected stubbornness. A flanking movement drove Banks through the town and sent him fleeing down the road towards Martinsburg. Jackson, unable to locate Ashby's cavalry, sent his men in pursuit. Banks never stopped for a breather, leaving behind 3,500 men (half his force), 9,000 small arms, 2 pieces of artillery, tons

26. Banks to Stanton, June [?], 1862, *ibid.*, 546–47.

27. Ewell to Dabney, June 4, 1862, *ibid.*, 778–80; Douglas, *I Rode with Stonewall*, 55.

28. Charles E. Gardner, "Three Years Experience in the First Maine Cavalry," 2, Civil War Times Illustrated Collection, USAMHI.

of food, droves of cattle and sheep, and, according to Quartermaster Harman, "more medical stores than you ever heard of."[29]

With the Army of the Potomac isolated on the Peninsula and McDowell's force anchored at Fredericksburg, Lincoln and Stanton had visions of Jackson moving through Harpers Ferry to Frederick, Baltimore, or Washington. The Ferry had been stripped of most of its men and much of its artillery, leaving Colonel Miles with his miscellaneous companies of railroad guards. Stanton detached Brigadier General Rufus Saxton from Washington and sent him to Harpers Ferry with the 78th New York, 109th Pennsylvania, four companies of the 5th New York Cavalry, and a naval battery of Dahlgren guns.[30]

On the night of May 24, the 111th Pennsylvania reached Harpers Ferry by train from Baltimore, and at dawn the adjutant, looking to soothe his nerves, initiated a conversation with Major John A. Boyle. "Major," he said, "you seem to be wrestling with some profound problem this morning."

"Yes, I am," the major replied absently. "I was just trying to determine whether that mountain yonder comes down to the river, or whether the river comes up to it."

"Well," said the adjutant as he buckled on his sword belt, "one thing is certain. *We* have come to the seat of war."

And so it seemed to the 111th Pennsylvania. As the sun rose that morning, all the bustle of a military post filled the town with the clatter of horses and equipment. Batteries frowned down from the heights, flags streamed in the morning breeze, army wagons rolled up the streets, and marching squads kicked up clouds of dust. Trains chuffed, waiting to be unloaded, and from everywhere came the sounds of mules braying, drums beating, and bugles blaring among the city of white tents flecking the surrounding hillsides. "And into these initial scenes of war," the regimental historian wrote, "the One Hundred and Eleventh [Pennsylvania] plunged, not to emerge again for three fateful years."[31]

29. Banks reported losses of 2,019 (*OR*, XII, Pt. 1, pp. 553–54); see also Jackson Letter Book, 1862, May 26, 1862, Hotchkiss Papers, LC; Jackson's Report, May 23, 1862, *OR*, XII, Pt. 1, pp. 701–709. For Banks's Report see *ibid.*, 545–52.

30. Stanton to Saxton, May 24, 25, and Saxton to Stanton, May 25, June 2, 1862, *OR*, XII, Pt. 1, pp. 626, 627, 639.

31. John Richards Boyle, *Soldiers True: The Story of the 111th Pennsylvania Veteran Volunteer Infantry* (New York, 1903), 27–28.

Saxton arrived the following morning. As he stepped off the train, Miles greeted him with the news that Banks was retreating from Winchester. Saxton doubted the information, blaming it on the enemy's meddling with the telegraph, but by noon he had the 109th Pennsylvania en route to Charles Town, supported by cavalry from the 5th New York. Just prior to Saxton's arrival, Miles, on reports of heavy firing to the south, put the 111th Pennsylvania and three companies of the 1st District of Columbia infantry on cars and shipped them to Winchester. They returned midafternoon, giving lurid stories of Banks's retreat and their own narrow escape. Saxton put them back on the train with orders to join the 109th Pennsylvania posted outside Charles Town. He then issued orders to five companies of the 1st Maryland Cavalry and told them to ride up the line until they made contact with Banks. The troopers, part of Miles's railroad guard, lost a day waiting for saddles and horseshoes. By the time Saxton got the Marylanders in the saddle, Banks had removed himself from the action.[32]

Saxton now knew the truth and wired Stanton, "General Banks' army is disorganized and in full retreat to Martinsburg. The enemy is in full pursuit. It may be necessary for us to fight the enemy with the river in our rear." Saxton expected no help from Banks if Jackson attacked Harpers Ferry, which he considered likely, and pleaded for more men and artillery.[33]

In the aftermath of the Union retreat from Winchester, Jackson sent Brigadier General Charles S. Winder's brigade of four regiments and ten guns to Charles Town to drive the rest of the bluecoats out of Virginia. On May 28 Winder struck the Pennsylvania regiments on a rise called Potato Hill, flanked them, and in twenty minutes drove them back towards Bolivar Heights. In a brisk fight Winder had the services of Captain Chew, who knew all the roads and byways between Charles Town and Harpers Ferry. Saxton had never seen the area before, but his military training at West Point came in handy at a critical moment. He posted most of his infantry on Bolivar Heights, now reinforced by the 3rd Delaware and a few pieces of light artillery, and swung the heavy naval guns on Maryland Heights to play upon Winder's advance. When the Pennsylvanians fell back, a strong line was waiting to support them,

32. Saxton to Stanton, May 25, 1862, OR, XII, Pt. 1, pp. 627, 630.
33. Ibid., 628.

and the men scrambled into defensive positions on Camp Hill.[34]

Saxton's force had grown almost overnight to seven thousand men and was more than a match for Winder's small brigade. After probing the Union line, Winder pulled back to Charles Town, and at midnight Jackson arrived with the Valley army. He rested his footsore troops for a day and waited for developments while his cavalry overspread Jefferson and Loudoun Counties.[35]

Before Jackson left Winchester, he learned that Shields had turned about and was marching back to Front Royal. An exhausted elderly citizen returning from Culpepper claimed he had stayed on the road for twelve hours just to bring the information to the general. Jackson hoped his informant was correct, but he distrusted civilians and needed confirmation from his own scouts. While waiting he decided to keep pressure on Banks and Saxton, knowing the anxiety his presence would create in Washington.[36]

Banks crossed the Potomac with the remnants of his splintered corps on May 25 and established headquarters at Williamsport. With nerves shattered, he wired Washington that Jackson's force had been strengthened and would enter Maryland at two points, Harpers Ferry and Williamsport. After being routed from Winchester, Banks's flight had been pressed by little more than an infantry brigade and two regiments of Ashby's cavalry. Banks entered some of Patterson's old fortifications and notified Washington that he had heard nothing from the detachment at Harpers Ferry and feared the worst.[37]

On May 30 Winder again probed Saxton's position and found it too strong, but the attack terrified Colonel William P. Maulsby's 1st Maryland Potomac Home Brigade. The men abandoned their positions and fled across the bridge to the Maryland side, leaving behind three hundred tons of powder, the arsenal's commissary, and all the quartermaster's stores. Maulsby chased after his command but reported "he could not bring them back to duty." Saxton, however, lost none of the supplies. Peter H. Watson, Stanton's

34. Winder to Dabney, June 15, and Saxton's Report, June 2, 1862, *OR*, XII, Pt. 1, pp. 738–39, 639.

35. Saxton to Lincoln, May 26, and Winder to Dabney, June 15, 1862, *ibid.*, 632, 738–39.

36. John Harman to his brother, May 29, 1862, Hotchkiss Papers, LC; Douglas, *I Rode with Stonewall*, 63.

37. Banks to Stanton, May 25, 1862, *OR*, XII, Pt. 1, p. 529.

assistant secretary of war, arrived at Harpers Ferry in time to witness the stampede of the Marylanders. He asked officers and men alike why they were running, as he saw no enemy in sight. Back to Maryland, one of them replied, as they had no intention of fighting in Virginia. In his evening report to Stanton, Watson suggested the 1st Maryland be dismissed in disgrace, as their hasty retreat "came near to causing a panic." Saxton blamed the behavior of the regiment on Maulsby, whom, he claimed, made little effort to hold his men in their assigned positions.[38]

The scare induced Saxton to pull his entire force back from Bolivar Heights and consolidate them on Camp Hill, a rise just above the Ferry with less area to defend and better protection against a flanking movement. Saxton believed Jackson's whole army was converging on his front, and in a drenching rain lasting well into the night, mixed with lightning, thunder, and the crash of artillery, Union defenders maintained a constant fire on any object moving across their field of vision. Jackson held most of his force at Charles Town and sent only Colonel James W. Allen's 2nd Virginia to seize Loudoun Heights, and the brigades of Brigadier General Arnold Elzey and Winder against Saxton's flanks, hoping that fear, rather than force, would drive the enemy across the river.[39]

Signal lights flashing from the surrounding hillsides convinced Saxton he was in serious trouble. In a steady downpour he circulated through the ranks to calm the men. When morning came, reconnoitering cavalry reported the enemy gone.[40]

Late at night Jackson's scouts returned from the Valley with bad news, some of it erroneous. Believing Banks had been reinforced, and hearing that a second blue column was on the road to Front Royal and only a few miles behind Shields, Jackson issued marching orders and put the Valley army back on the pike before dawn. Saxton pushed his infantry as far as Charles Town, where reports circulated that Jackson had withdrawn through town with a force ranging from 18,000 to 25,000. Saxton felt relieved, but he also felt quite proud. He believed he had repulsed the celebrated Stonewall Jackson with "not more than 7,000 effective men, [who]

38. Saxton to Stanton, May 27, 31, 1862, *ibid.*, 633, 636; Watson to Stanton, May 30, 1862, *ibid.*, Pt. 3, pp. 296–97, 304.
39. Hotchkiss Diary, May 30, 1862, Hotchkiss Papers, LC.
40. Saxton to Stanton, June 1, 1862, *OR*, XII, Pt. 1, p. 637.

being completely worn out by fatigue and exposure, I deem it not prudent to advance, at least until the men rested."[41] Had Saxton advanced fast enough to catch the retiring enemy, he would have found 1,337 of Winder's haggard infantry lagging far behind the main column.

Busting up the divisions of Fremont and Shields became Jackson's next objective. He had no intention of getting trapped by four converging Union divisions in the lower Shenandoah. By noon he had his force spread for fifteen miles along the pike. As Jackson marched up the Valley, Saxton ordered his weary regiments back to Harpers Ferry.

On June 17, Secretary of War Stanton expressed his thanks to Saxton. Jackson had not crossed the river. Washington was safe. In 1893 Saxton received the Medal of Honor for his defense of Harpers Ferry, but for the balance of the war he served with the Department of the South, where he commanded various districts under Union occupation.[42]

On June 1, as Jackson began to bring a climactic end to his Valley campaign, Stanton ordered Major General Franz Sigel to the Ferry and, by adding several fresh regiments, bloated the command to 10,000 troops. For three days the Baltimore and Ohio, operating around the clock, steamed reinforcements and supplies into the town. Banks crept south from Williamsport, reaching Winchester the morning of June 5. He expected to find Sigel there with 6,000 fresh troops. Banks, still nervous, claimed the German could not be found. Next he learned that the Winchester spur had been disabled by Ashby's cavalry. Banks may not have been truthful with Stanton, as Sigel arrived at Winchester on the repaired spur with most of his command at noon on June 4, a full day before Banks arrived. One of the two generals falsified his reports by at least a day. Banks estimated Jackson's force at 40,000 (about twice its actual size), and he began to fidget as rumors of Confederate activities filtered into headquarters.[43]

Banks's nervousness can also be traced to natural causes. The

41. Hotchkiss Diary, May 30, 1862, Hotchkiss Papers, LC; Saxton to Stanton, June 2, 1862, *OR*, XII, Pt. 1, pp. 639–41.

42. Stanton to Saxton, June 17, 1862, *OR*, XII, Pt. 1, p. 641; Boatner, *Civil War Dictionary*, 722–23.

43. Stanton to Banks, June 1, Banks to Stanton, June 3, 4, 6, and Sigel to Stanton, June 4, 1862, *OR*, XII, Pt. 1, pp. 538, 539, 540, 541, 813.

skies opened over the Potomac and washed away the general's communications. "The river, higher than for ten years, has divided my command," Banks moaned, "and separated me from all my supplies and transportation. I am here [at Winchester] . . . unable to move." Floodwaters ripped the planking off the Harpers Ferry bridge, necessitating the use of a steam ferry to haul supplies across the river. With both of his familiar escape routes blocked by high water, Banks hunkered into the entrenchments at Winchester and hoped Jackson would strike elsewhere.[44]

On June 8 Banks received orders from Stanton to move up the Valley and support Fremont at Front Royal. With well-practiced political deception, Banks replied that he did not wish to leave Winchester until the arrival of Sigel, who, he claimed, was not expected for another "few days." Sigel, however, was already there and had dispatched scouting parties to Front Royal and Strasburg. Neither Banks nor Sigel was certain of Jackson's movements, but on June 9 President Lincoln stepped into the picture and ordered his dallying political general to move his main force to Front Royal as soon as possible.[45]

In frail compliance with presidential orders, Banks dispatched to Front Royal only two regiments, whose commanders probably felt like sheep being forced to the slaughter as they marched timorously up the Valley. On June 11 Banks finally admitted Sigel had arrived, probably because he now had reason to avoid Front Royal. A message from Fremont had just arrived. Shields had been defeated by Jackson, who Fremont claimed had been reinforced with 30,000 to 35,000 men from the commands of Major General James Longstreet and Brigadier General Gustavus W. Smith. Banks declared moving from Winchester with his force so weak imprudent.[46]

Stanton, sensing another retreat brewing, advised Banks that Jackson could not have been reinforced by more than two regiments and demanded that both Front Royal and Winchester be held. Banks promised to "not fall back an inch" and on June 16 began a slow advance up the Valley. By the time he reached Front

44. Banks to Fremont, June 6, 1862, *ibid.*, 32.

45. Thomas to Banks, June 8, and Lincoln to Banks, June 9, 1862, *ibid.*, 541–42.

46. Banks to Stanton, June 9, 12, 1862, *ibid.*, 542, 543–44.

Royal, Jackson was gone, leaving nothing behind but broken bridges and three shattered Union armies.[47]

Banks moved his headquarters to Middletown, where on June 26 he learned the War Department had reconstituted his force as the II Army Corps and attached it to Major General John Pope's Army of Virginia. On June 29 Sigel replaced Fremont and took command of the I Army Corps—also part of Pope's army. By the end of July both corps left the Valley and moved east of the Blue Ridge.[48]

On June 4, when Sigel departed from Harpers Ferry, he placed Colonel Miles in charge of the garrison and left him with eighteen companies of infantry, including Maulsby's Maryland dissidents and the naval battery on Maryland Heights. What Jackson failed to accomplish with his night attack on May 30, the flooded Potomac took care of on the night of June 5 by washing out the rebuilt Baltimore and Ohio bridge and sweeping away a trestle on the Shenandoah serving the Winchester spur. Miles had sixty thousand rations at the Ferry and no way to move them, and, he added, "the river is still rising."[49]

Miles commanded about fifteen hundred infantry, cavalry, and artillery in and around Harpers Ferry, along with several small companies strung along the river between Point of Rocks and Martinsburg.[50] He understood his two primary responsibilities: to defend Harpers Ferry and to protect the Baltimore and Ohio Railroad. The colonel could easily manage his small command, but he was a man seeking to redeem himself. He would get his chance, but under circumstances neither he nor the War Department ever suspected.

47. Banks to Stanton, June 12, 16, 1862, *ibid.*, 544–45.
48. Lincoln to Banks *et al.*, June 26, General Orders, August 12, Ruggles to Sigel, June 29, and Sigel to Pope, June 29, 1862, *ibid.*, XII, Pt. 3, pp. 435, 568, 444.
49. Miles to Stanton, June 2, 5, 1862, *ibid.*, 323–24, 342.
50. Miles to Stanton, June 12, 1862, *ibid.*, 378.

# 7

## Colonel Miles Takes Command

At the outbreak of the Civil War, Colonel Dixon S. Miles, a forty-year veteran, was among the top-ranking officers in the Union army. At the age of fifteen he had entered West Point. He had struggled with his studies and in 1824 graduated twenty-seventh in a class of thirty-one. Aside from the Mexican War, where he achieved an element of distinction, Miles spent most of his life performing garrison duty and fighting Indians in military outposts ranging from Florida to New Mexico. At some point during his long career he developed an appetite for whiskey, a penchant for irritating his superiors, and a reputation for badgering his subordinates. But on January 19, 1859, he received at long last promotion to full colonel, becoming one of only twenty-two on the roster of the nation's 13,000-man regular army. On the eve of the Civil War he commanded the 2nd U.S. Infantry at Fort Leavenworth, Kansas, one of only eight infantry regiments comprising the U.S. Army. Despite his irascible disposition, Miles now had an opportunity to chart a brilliant military career.[1]

When General Patterson took command of the Department of Pennsylvania in April, 1861, he asked for Miles and his regiment. Patterson wanted a veteran to command one of his brigades, but

1. Cullum, *Biographical Register*, I, 344–45.

he also wanted a Marylander committed to the Union, and Miles met both requirements. The colonel took his time coming east and did not reach Patterson's department until after Jackson had destroyed the bridge at Harpers Ferry. Soon after arriving at Williamsport, Miles received new orders, joined McDowell's army at Arlington, and took command of the 5th Division's 6,000 soldiers.[2] For the first time in forty years, fifty-seven-year-old Dixon Miles had an opportunity to become a general.

Suffering from a bout of heavy drinking, Miles fell ill a few days before the Battle of Bull Run (First Manassas). To bolster the colonel's constitution for the expected fight, his doctor prescribed small but frequent drams of brandy. Relegated to a reserve position, Miles rode back and forth from the battlefield, nipping at his flask. He stopped frequently to criticize subordinates for their troop dispositions and punctuated his comments with choice profanity. At a critical moment for McDowell's army, a staff officer approached Miles and suggested that he deploy his division on the flank to shore up the collapsing Federal right. Heavily intoxicated, Miles replied, "I have something else to attend to." McDowell ordered Miles relieved and replaced him with Colonel Israel B. Richardson. Miles ignored the order. Richardson was an old enemy from frontier days, and Miles threatened to arrest him.[3]

On July 26 Richardson preferred charges against Miles for drunkenness. In a fight as bloody as First Bull Run, the 5th Division reported only six killed and eighteen wounded, testifying to Miles's confused mental state in managing his troops. A court of inquiry let Miles down easily and blamed his condition not on drunkenness but on the doctor who prescribed brandy. Senior members of the court considered proceeding to court-martial inappropriate and time-consuming, but they also wanted to avoid the publicity of resurrecting an embarrassing Union defeat by trying Miles.[4]

No longer did Washington trust the gray-haired colonel with

2. General Order No. 12, April 27, Patterson to Townsend, June 3, Patterson to Townsend, June 17, and Department of Northeastern Virginia Returns, July 16, 17, 1861, *OR*, II, 607, 661, 697, 309.

3. Miles's Report, July 24, and Richardson's Report, July 25, 1861, *ibid.*, 374–76, 423–26; *HTI*, 493.

4. Return of casualties in the Fifth Division, and Decision of Miles's Court of Inquiry, November 6, 1861, *OR*, II, 426, 438–39.

an important infantry division. The War Department sent him to
Harpers Ferry with little more than a regiment to guard the tracks
of the Baltimore and Ohio Railroad. But by April, 1862, the Railroad Brigade, comprised mostly of militia and green troops with
short enlistments, had swelled to about 3,600 men. Miles's task
was to prevent enemy bushwhackers from disrupting service on
the line, and whoever recommended him for the role probably
thought the old Indian fighter the right man for the job. Stanton
lacked confidence in Miles—otherwise he would not have sent
thirty-seven-year-old General Saxton, a man young enough to be
the colonel's son, to Harpers Ferry at a time of crisis. Miles resented the intrusion. But in June, 1862, when Banks, Shields, Saxton, and Sigel moved to other fields, Miles, now fifty-eight and
looking much older, resumed his role as ranking officer at Harpers
Ferry and set up headquarters in a building next to the former
Gault House Saloon. The saloon, however, was closed, and since
his trial the colonel had diligently refrained from touching so
much as a glass of champagne at a party given on July 4 for the
officers' ladies.[5]

Miles had enough routine work to keep him busy without resorting to the bottle. The bridge rebuilt in March washed out
twice in the spring, and work crews spent part of July and most
of August reinforcing the flimsy structure with cables and girders.
Work never went smoothly because of nightly raids along the railroad by guerrillas and uniformed cavalry, who were seldom seen
and rarely caught.[6]

Although discredited by the War Department, Miles found a
friend in seventy-eight-year-old Major General John Wool, who
on June 1 took command of the Union Army's Baltimore-based
Middle Department. Prior to the war, Wool had been the ranking
brigadier general in the army, and he expected a commanding role
in the coming conflict. Instead, he was relegated to the Department of Virginia and grimly watched as the post he wanted went
to McClellan. Wool had little use for the political and militia officers overrunning the military and put his faith in old regular
army men like Colonel Miles. When Wool assumed his new post,
he was somewhat chagrined to find Miles the sole regular army

5. Organization of the Army of the Potomac, April, 1862, *ibid.*, V, 22; Investigation of Harper's Ferry, *ibid.*, XIX, Pt. 1, p. 761.
6. Hungerford, *Baltimore and Ohio Railroad*, II, 21.

officer assigned to the department and quickly praised him as being "very zealous" and the best officer he had.[7]

When the Army of the Potomac moved to the Peninsula, Wool demanded reinforcements for Harpers Ferry. Four regiments of infantry and a company from the 5th New York Artillery arrived in June. On August 8, Wool placed all the troops at Williamsport, Hagerstown, and Frederick under Miles. Later in the month he detached the 2nd Maryland Eastern Shore Volunteer Infantry to help Miles construct a blockhouse on Maryland Heights. With the Baltimore and Ohio bridge reaching completion and the Chesapeake and Ohio Canal back in service, Wool wanted those structures protected at all costs, and he trusted Miles to keep them safe from attack.[8]

As fresh troops poured into the Ferry, Wool made a remarkable observation. "I have examined Harper's Ferry," he wrote Stanton, "and find it in a very indefensible position." After admitting the area was difficult to defend, he argued for four more regiments and additional artillery. On the matter of indefensibility, three Confederate generals—Lee, Johnston, and Jackson—would have agreed.[9]

Once again Harpers Ferry became an armed camp of thousands, and once again civilians returned to the town to rebuild their lives by providing a variety of services to the military. The availability of bootlegged whiskey reached new heights, and Miles, a former heavy drinker, ignored the problem. With Wool in command of the department, Miles felt comfortable resorting to some of his old habits.

By mid-August a nervousness pervaded the Harpers Ferry garrison. On August 7 an engagement had been fought at Cedar Mountain, and ten days later another at Clark Mountain. Confederate forces edged north, and cavalry in gray showed increased activity around Leesburg and Winchester, but neither Wool nor Miles anticipated a serious threat to their corner of northern Virginia. All the battles remained to the south, and the two old friends expected the fighting to stay there.

On August 23 a detachment from the 12th Virginia Cavalry—

7. Wool to Stanton, June 1, 1862, *OR*, XII, Pt. 3, p. 320; Investigation of Harper's Ferry, *ibid.*, XIX, Pt. 1, p. 792; *HTI*, 842.

8. Investigation of Harper's Ferry, *OR*, XIX, Pt. 1, pp. 788–89.

9. Wool to Stanton, June 15, 1862, *ibid.*, XII, Pt. 3, p. 394.

thirty volunteers under two lieutenants from Jefferson County, George Baylor and Milton Rouss—slipped by Union pickets at Winchester and jogged towards Harpers Ferry. They followed the tracks of the Winchester and Potomac and seized upon a plan to stop the next train. Miles maintained a company of guards at Summit Point and Wade's Depot. Each company patrolled the four-mile section, but neither showed enthusiasm for walking the rails at night. At the midpoint between the two stations Baylor and Rouss placed obstructions on the tracks and stopped the next train from Harpers Ferry. The robbery progressed in fine style. The raiders captured $4,000 in greenbacks, eight soldiers on their way to Winchester, and several dispatches from Pope to Brigadier General Julius White, the new commander at Winchester. Before burning the cars, the cavalry helped themselves to several bottles of champagne and a few boxes of fruit. Not knowing what to do with the train, they detached the engine, filled the fire box, opened the throttle, and sent it racing towards Winchester with no one on board. The engine ran out of steam before completing its trip and stopped three miles short of town. The raiders then cut telegraph lines and dislodged a few sections of track before returning to camp.[10]

Cavalry raids grew more frequent, and four days later an informant reported a band of Confederate guerrillas in the vicinity of the pro-Union Quaker community of Waterford, about sixteen miles from the Ferry. Miles dispatched Captain Henry A. Cole, 1st Maryland Cavalry of the Potomac Home Brigade, and the Loudoun Rangers, an independent Virginia company under Captain Samuel C. Means, to investigate. The two companies separated, and instead of guerrillas, Means's Rangers collided with Captain Elijah V. White's 35th Battalion Virginia Cavalry from Munford's command. White charged, scattering the Rangers and driving twenty-three of them into a nearby church. The Confederate horsemen wanted Means, who had a price on his head of $1,000. They despised the Virginian, for Means had recruited a company of cavalry from Loudoun County and forsaken the South. When he joined the Union army, Richmond authorities designated him a traitor. After exhausting their ammunition, the Loudoun Rang-

10. George Baylor, *Bull Run to Bull Run; or, Four Years in the Army of Virginia* (Richmond, 1900), 55–67; Watson to Garrett, and White to Pope and Halleck, August 24, 1862, *OR*, XII, Pt. 3, pp. 650–51, 652.

ers surrendered with one killed and seven wounded, losing thirty
horses and all their arms. But Means, the target of White's attack,
was at home asleep. White paroled the survivors, who got a taste
of hiking on foot as they trundled into Point of Rocks to report
their misfortunes. Means greeted them with amusement. Paroles
or not, he put them back in the saddle in less than a week.[11]

Two days later the Confederate army surprised Pope at Manassas, and on August 30 Jackson and Longstreet sent the Union
Army of Virginia reeling back towards Washington. With Pope's
army crushed and the Army of the Potomac divided, Lee seized
an unexpected opportunity. Maryland lay open for invasion. Lee
knew the Valley well, but Jackson knew it better. The handiest
crossings into Maryland lay at White's Ford, the home of Elijah
White, and Point of Rocks, a scant nine miles downriver from
Harpers Ferry.

Hesitant to act on his own, Lee on September 3 wrote the first
of several letters to Davis outlining his plans. He would occupy
Frederick, the largest city in western Maryland, where he hoped
to build his force by enticing loyal southerners to join the Confederate fight. Lee, however, had misgivings about venturing too
far north. He needed ammunition, his transportation consisted of
nothing but old, rickety wagons, the men were down to their last
clothes, and thousands had no shoes. "Still," Lee declared, "we
cannot afford to be idle, and though weaker than our opponents
in men and military equipments, we must endeavor to harass if
we cannot destroy them."[12]

Lee moved his army up to Leesburg, but hearing nothing from
Davis, wrote, "I am more fully persuaded of the benefit that will
result from an expedition into Maryland, and I shall proceed to
make the movement at once, unless you . . . signify your disap-
probation."[13] Lee waited a day before moving. He used the delay
to assess the degree of confusion rampaging through the Union
ranks and decided there would never be a better opportunity to

11. Miles to Halleck, August 27, 1862, *OR*, XII, Pt. 3, p. 705; see also Goodhart,
*Loudoun Virginia Rangers*, 29–40; Frank Myers, *The Comanches: A Study of
White's Battalion, Virginia Cavalry, Laurel Brigade, Hampton's Division, Army
of Northern Virginia, C.S.A.* (Baltimore, 1895), 97–101.

12. Lee to Davis, September 3, 1862, *OR*, XIX, Pt. 2, pp. 590–91. White's Ford
was named after and adjoined the family farm of Elijah White.

13. Lee to Davis, September 4, 1862, *ibid.*, 591–92.

carry the war north. Pope had retreated to the fortifications encircling Washington, leaving no force to contest a Confederate advance into Maryland.

Major General Henry W. "Old Brains" Halleck, Stanton's newly appointed general in chief, admitted having no idea where Lee would strike. With transport vessels steaming McClellan's army back from the Peninsula, and with Pope's remnants scattered around the capital, Halleck had the job of sorting through a messy situation and reshaping the Army of the Potomac. He also had the complicated task of divining Lee's intentions. With Pope relieved on September 5 and McClellan back in command of a unified Army of the Potomac, Halleck began probing for information. When intelligence reached the War Department that part of Lee's force had been seen near Leesburg, Halleck expected trouble along the Potomac and wired Wool to watch the upper fords, warning that Lee might attempt to cut off Harpers Ferry.[14]

Wool alerted Miles, who promptly dispatched Cole's Marylanders and Means's Loudoun Rangers to reconnoiter the crossings between Point of Rocks and Leesburg. On the previous day, September 2, Cole and Means had been patrolling the Leesburg area when Confederate cavalry attacked in force and cut them to pieces. Miles reported that Means "broke and ran," but failed to mention that Cole had done the same. Miles and Means had little use for each other, but the animosity emanated from Means's tendency to act independently because he considered himself under orders from Stanton.[15] Miles, however, looked upon Means as a spy sent by the War Department to monitor his drinking problem.

Miles distanced himself from Means by keeping him at Point of Rocks, but on September 3 he sent him on another reconnaissance to Leesburg. Means rode to the top of a mountain a mile from town and, using his glass, counted forty regiments and about sixty pieces of artillery encamped in the countryside. He led his men back to headquarters and reported his observations to Miles, who replied sharply, "It is a damned no such thing." Means, feeling undeservedly rebuked, suggested the colonel send someone "who could see better than I could." The scout thought Miles had

14. Halleck to Wool, September 3, 1862, *ibid.*, 173.
15. Wool to Stanton, September 3, 1862, *ibid.*, 174; Civil War Centennial Commission, County of Loudoun, Commonwealth of Virginia, *Loudoun County in the Civil War* (1961), 41.

been drinking a trifle and felt justified exercising a little insubordination.

Miles, turning to another of his scouts, replied, "Here is a man who is right from there, and he says everything is quiet."

"Colonel," Means retorted, "that man lives 13 miles from Leesburg, and there is a large mountain between him and Leesburg, and he must see clear through that mountain to see better than I did with my glass."

Means turned to the other scout and asked, "Mr. Hough, when were you in Leesburg?"

"I have not been there at all," Hough replied, "[and] I have not heard anything."

Miles dismissed Means and sent him back to Point of Rocks without orders. Later in the evening he advised Halleck that a division of twelve thousand men had been observed at Leesburg, but he credited the report to "a paroled prisoner from Leesburg" and gave Means no credit for an accurate piece of scouting.[16]

Colonel Henry B. Banning occupied Point of Rocks with the 87th Ohio and sent Means downriver with a squad of cavalry to locate a missing company of pickets. Means found evidence of a fight. Banning reported the pickets captured, wired the information to Miles, and requested reinforcements.

On September 4 Means went back downriver with a squad of cavalry, posted vedettes, and continued to scout. Late in the afternoon he was well above Noland's Ferry when the first of Lee's main army came into view. "I suppose 10,000 crossed over that night," Means declared, "and the first good place they came to, they just laid right down."[17]

Means's low count can be excused by darkness and distance, as Lee's main army began crossing about 5 P.M. at Noland's Ferry, White's Ford, and Cheek's Ford, all near the mouth of the Monocacy River. Of the three fords, Noland's lay about three miles downriver from Point of Rocks and a dozen miles from Harpers Ferry. Lee advertised his crossing, and bands played chorus after chorus of "Maryland, My Maryland" as each regiment waded the gently flowing Potomac.[18]

16. Investigation of Harpers Ferry, *OR*, XIX, Pt. 1, pp. 754–55; Miles to Halleck, September 3, 1862, *ibid.*, Pt. 2, p. 174.
17. Investigation of Harpers Ferry, *ibid.*, Pt. 1, p. 755.
18. Henry Kyd Douglas, "Stonewall Jackson in Maryland," *B&L*, II, 620.

Miles, however, inexplicably rescinded his previous report and erroneously advised Wool and Halleck that earlier accounts of enemy infantry at Leesburg were "without foundation of truth," having been originated by skittish paroled prisoners. Means was neither skittish nor a paroled prisoner, but Miles decided to ignore him anyway. But Banning, having received a courier from one of Means's patrols, wired headquarters warning that thirty thousand of the enemy were crossing at the lower fords and advancing up the Potomac. He asked again for reinforcements. When he heard nothing back from the colonel, he sent Means to Harpers Ferry for orders. The cavalry officer confronted Miles at headquarters and reaffirmed Lee's crossing. Miles appeared to be neither confused nor excited, but "stubborn," Means said. "In the fix he was in then, he would not believe anything you would tell him." Miles, perhaps in an attempt to protect his credibility, held the information until 8:20 P.M., when he finally advised Halleck and Wool of the situation. He could easily have been confused by Cole, whose reconnaissance in Loudoun County earlier in the day had failed to flush a single rebel. Two hours later Banning abandoned Point of Rocks and began withdrawing to Harpers Ferry.[19]

Miles ordered Banning to halt his retreat and obstruct the road, promising reinforcements. Wool, receiving Miles's message after he had gone to bed, wired back, "You will re-enforce Colonel Banning if it can be done without danger to your position, and," he added with perhaps some doubt, "if it be true that the enemy is advancing on him."[20]

Miles also went to bed and did not read Wool's message until morning. By 9 A.M. he finally concurred with all of Means's scouting reports, admitting that the enemy, identified as General Ambrose P. Hill's division, had crossed at Noland's Ferry and cut the canal. No reinforcements sent to Banning from Harpers Ferry could possibly stop the enemy, Miles reported. Furthermore, he added, an enemy force had been reported at Charles Town, and he now had intelligence that three brigades were in the Valley and threatening "to attack this place and Martinsburg."[21]

Because of the flow of contradictory messages from Harpers

19. Miles to Halleck and Wool, September 4, September 4 (10:00 P.M.), 1862, OR, XIX, Pt. 2, pp. 180, 181; Investigation of Harpers Ferry, ibid., Pt. 1, p. 755.

20. Wool to Miles, September 4, 1862, ibid., Pt. 1, p. 522.

21. Miles to Wool, September 5, 1862, ibid., 522.

Ferry, Wool might have begun to wonder if Miles had restocked his liquor cabinet. From other sources, however, he learned on September 5 that Lee's main army had crossed into Maryland. From Baltimore, Wool dispatched a detachment under Colonel Thomas J. Cram to scout enemy activity along the Potomac. Cram went as far as Point of Rocks but found no enemy. This puzzled Wool even more, as Miles had reported the Confederate horde advancing towards Harpers Ferry. Leaving nothing to chance, Wool renewed his orders to Miles—if Point of Rocks is attacked, Banning's 87th Ohio must be reinforced. "Be energetic and active," Wool demanded, "and defend all places to the last extremity. There must be no abandoning of a post, and shoot the first man that thinks of it, whether officer or soldier."[22]

Despite Wool's directives, Banning withdrew from Point of Rocks, probably on September 5, and moved downriver to Berlin (Brunswick), shelling a few Confederate horsemen as he retreated. With only two howitzers from Captain John H. Graham's 5th New York Artillery in support, Banning continued his withdrawal, first to Knoxville and finally to Sandy Hook, where he joined Maulsby's 1st Maryland Potomac Home Brigade. Miles evidently sanctioned the withdrawal, as he met Banning at Sandy Hook and put the 87th Ohio into line. His messages to Wool, however, spoke of Banning fighting "superior numbers" at Berlin and of facing an enemy "in large force" at Knoxville. Banning's retreat from Point of Rocks was premature and probably unnecessary, as a detail sent back to Berlin to recover an abandoned limber and a supply of ammunition encountered no opposition. Miles puzzled over the disappearance of Lee's army, and when Confederates cut the telegraph lines to Baltimore and Washington he felt alone and deserted. He discovered that messages could be routed through Wheeling via Pittsburgh, but on September 6 the first telegram rattling into Harpers Ferry headquarters read, "How are you, General Pope? General Jackson's army." Up to this point, nothing had been heard from Jackson's corps. Miles naturally assumed that Stonewall was with Lee.[23]

When Wool had expanded Miles's command earlier in the summer, he included a company of the 1st Maryland Potomac Home

22. Wool to Miles, September 5, 1862, *ibid.*, 523; Wool to Halleck, September 5, 1862, *ibid.*, Pt. 2, pp. 188–89.

23. Binney's Report, September 18, 1862, *ibid.*, Pt. 1, pp. 533–34.

Brigade, Captain William T. Faithful, whose sole mission was to guard quartermaster stores and medical supplies at Frederick. On September 5, when Miles learned that Lee intended to occupy the town, he ordered Faithful to destroy all stores and join Colonel Maulsby at Sandy Hook. Faithful ignored Miles's orders, commandeered all the cars in Frederick, packed them with supplies, and shipped everything he could to Baltimore. He then pressed wagons and horses into service, loaded them with hospital stores and 275 convalescents, and sent them to Gettysburg. What little remained he burned. The next day he marched his company to Sandy Hook and reported to Maulsby. Miles could have profited by paying more attention to the example Faithful set by his commendable evacuation of Frederick, but the colonel chose to ignore it.[24]

On September 7 Miles still expected to be attacked by a large force from below, although Faithful had just passed through the area unmolested. He sent Major William L. Markell with a squadron of the 8th New York Cavalry and Lieutenant Hanson T. C. Green with a detachment of Cole's Marylanders on a reconnaissance. He asked them to not return until they "felt the enemy and ascertained something definite." Markell probed Berlin and returned, reporting no enemy in sight. Green pushed further eastward but found nothing in his front until he reached the outskirts of Frederick, where he drove in a few pickets and captured some prisoners. A messenger from Green jogged back to Harpers Ferry and reported that Lee went north.[25]

But in Martinsburg, sixteen miles northwest of the Ferry, reports of heavy enemy cavalry activity drifted into Wool's headquarters at Baltimore. Colonel Arno Voss, 12th Illinois Cavalry, met the attack and captured several prisoners. They admitted being from the advance of a column that came through Manassas Gap and had been at Winchester. Miles interpreted the information as meaning that the point of attack would not be Harpers Ferry but Martinsburg.[26]

Miles ignored requests from Martinsburg for reinforcements, but Wool, still blinded by Miles's confusing reports, wired General

24. William T. Faithful's Report, September 8, 1862, *ibid.*, LI, Pt. 1, pp. 136–37.

25. Binney's Report, September 18, 1862, *ibid.*, XIX, Pt. 1, p. 534; White to Wool, September 7, 1862, *ibid.*, Pt. 2, p. 205.

26. White to Wool, September 7, 1862, *ibid.*, Pt. 2, pp. 205–206.

White, who was then at Martinsburg, "If 20,000 men should attack you, you will, of course, fall back. Harper's Ferry would be
the best I could recommend."[27] The instruction sounded like orders to hold out against any force less than 20,000, and to do it
with less than 3,000 railroad guards.

Lee's army had vanished into Wool's department, but nobody
in his command knew where. General McClellan, still in the dark
regarding Lee's intentions, asked Halleck, "Have you anything
from Colonel Miles today? . . . I would recommend that [he] be
required to report at least twice every day." At 5 P.M. Lincoln
asked McClellan, "How does it look now?" McClellan referred
the question to Halleck, who replied, "Nothing from Colonel
Miles." The Confederate cavalry screen kept McClellan guessing
and Miles jittery. Only one senior officer in Wool's department
felt imminently threatened, but nobody would listen to him. Brigadier General Julius White was not a regular army man but a pa-
tronage general and a friend of the president—a man, in Wool's
opinion, not qualified by training or experience to assess a military situation.[28]

Precious hours ticked slowly away, but Miles remained oblivious to the trap closing around his Valley empire.

27. Wool to White, September 7, 1862, *ibid.*, Pt. 1, p. 791.
28. McClellan to Halleck, Lincoln to McClellan, and Halleck to McClellan,
September 8, 1862, *ibid.*, 210.

John Brown, as he appeared in 1855
*Courtesy Kansas State Historical
Society*

John Brown, as he appeared in 1859
*Courtesy U.S. Army Military History
Institute*

Drawing of the fight at the enginehouse on October 16, 1859
*From* Frank Leslie's Illustrated Paper, *October, 1859*

Drawing of Robert E. Lee's marine detachment storming the
enginehouse, October 17, 1859

*From* Frank Leslie's Illustrated Paper, *November, 1859*

General Robert E. Lee during the
Civil War years

*Courtesy U.S. Army Military History
Institute*

Colonel Roger Jones, the lieutenant responsible for guarding
the U.S. Armory when attacked
by the Virginia militia on April
18, 1861

*From* Battles and Leaders of the Civil
War

General Thomas J. "Stonewall" Jackson, who, as a colonel of militia, commanded the troops at Harpers Ferry after the secession of Virginia
*Courtesy U.S. Army Military History Institute*

General Joseph E. Johnston, whose Civil War career started with his first command at Harpers Ferry on May 24, 1861
*Courtesy U.S. Army Military History Institute*

Brigadier General John D. Imboden, whose artillery company was among the first to reach Harpers Ferry in April, 1861
*Courtesy U.S. Army Military History Institute*

Major General Robert Patterson, who established headquarters at Harpers Ferry on July 21, 1863, and was relieved two days later
*Courtesy U.S. Army Military History Institute*

Colonel Turner Ashby, whose Confederate cavalry occupied Harpers Ferry after the withdrawal of Union forces on August 21, 1861
*From* Battles and Leaders of the Civil War

Brigadier General John W. Geary, who recaptured Harpers Ferry on September 17, 1861, and withdrew voluntarily on October 18
*From* Battles and Leaders of the Civil War

Major General Nathaniel P. Banks, who reoccupied Harpers Ferry on February 24, 1862, using the town as a supply center for the Department of the Shenandoah
*Courtesy U.S. Army Military History Institute*

Colonel Dixon S. Miles, who commanded the Harpers Ferry garrison periodically from March 29, 1862, until his mortal wound on September 15, 1862

*Courtesy U.S. Army Military History Institute*

# 8

## Girding for Battle

Forty-six-year-old Julius White abandoned his lucrative Lincoln-
ian appointment as Chicago's collector of customs when news of
the first Union defeat at Manassas hit the streets in the Windy
City. He organized the 37th Illinois (Fremont Rifles) and in September, 1861, became the regiment's colonel. White had no previous military training, but he had a bright mind and worked hard
at his new profession. Assigned to Fremont's department at St.
Louis, he fought in several skirmishes in southwestern Missouri,
notably against Major General Sterling Price's Confederates, and
in March, 1862, distinguished himself in the hotly contested Battle of Pea Ridge, Arkansas. For gallant conduct, White won his
first star. When Lincoln brought Halleck and Pope east in the summer of 1862, White came with them and took command of the
Army of Virginia's brigade of three thousand men garrisoning Winchester.[1]

Many veteran officers from the regular army felt hostility towards the new brand of volunteers infesting the ranks, who they
felt had obtained unmerited and lofty commissions. Wool and
Miles snubbed men like that. But when White took command of

1. *HTI*, 820–21; James Grant Wilson, *Biographical Sketches of Illinois Officers
Engaged in the War Against the Rebellion of 1861* (Chicago, 1862–1863), 77.

Winchester, young Captain Edward H. Ripley of the 9th Vermont hailed the change favorably. "Gen. [Abraham Sanders] Piatt has been superseded by Gen. Julius White, a Volunteer," Ripley wrote, "and a pretty able man we begin to think. He is prompt, precise and energetic, and knows what he is about."[2]

After Pope's defeat at Second Manassas, Halleck began to worry about White's inexperience and the exposed garrison at Winchester. He sent Brigadier General George W. Cullum to the town to confer with White and prepare a strategy for withdrawal if attacked. Cullum returned to Washington convinced that White's small garrison could be easily stampeded out of Winchester, and on September 2 Halleck ordered White to send off the artillery and "withdraw your whole force to Harper's Ferry." Halleck also notified Miles but failed to mention whether White, a general, would supersede the colonel.[3]

White estimated a Confederate force of twenty thousand within twenty miles of Winchester and approaching at a fast pace. His brigade had stockpiled about eighty thousand rations, a large amount of ammunition, and a heavy complement of artillery. With little time left to evacuate, the brigade accomplished the herculean task of loading everything on cars but a few emplaced 32-pounders, which, White claimed, would have required an extra day to remove. Twenty-four hours later White and his brigade rolled safely into Harpers Ferry.[4]

White arrived late afternoon on September 3, the same day Means reported the Confederate army at Leesburg. With White at Harpers Ferry, the potential for command conflict ripened. Miles still smarted over Saxton's usurpation of his command. Expecting similar treatment from White, he began to erect roadblocks. He notified Wool there was no enemy infantry in the Valley, only rumors spawned by paroled prisoners, leaving Wool to question why White abandoned Winchester. Wool, consistent with his prejudice against volunteer generals, assured Miles he would retain command of the Ferry and promised to have White reassigned to the Army of the Potomac. White's brigade, however, would remain at the Ferry and report directly to Miles. A few hours later,

2. E. H. Ripley, *Vermont General*, ed. Otto Eisenschiml (New York, 1960), 11.
3. Halleck to White and to Miles, September 2, 1862, *OR*, XII, Pt. 2, p. 767; S. B. Pettengill, *The College Cavaliers* (Chicago, 1883), 51–52.
4. White to Halleck, September 2, 3, 1862, *OR*, XII, Pt. 2, p. 768.

Wool changed his mind and ordered White to Martinsburg to take command of the town's railroad guards. After stripping White of his brigade and dismissing him to a post where no one expected trouble, Wool nonetheless told White to exert "the most sleepless energy."[5]

On September 5, White, not wishing to defy a superior officer, said good-bye to his brigade and departed for Martinsburg. But the general was not happy and lodged a complaint with Halleck, recounting his shabby treatment. "I respectfully ask to be restored to my command," he wrote, "if consistent with the public interests." Cullum, Halleck's chief of staff, replied, "No order from General Halleck has been given to you to go to Martinsburg," but Cullum left White in limbo as to Halleck's wishes. Hearing nothing more on the matter, White wrote Halleck directly, asking to be relieved and reassigned to duty at the front. Halleck admitted that by moving to Harpers Ferry, White had put himself under Wool's jurisdiction, but he promised a different assignment "as early as possible."[6] During the next few days White would find himself about as close to the front as one could get.

Captain Henry Curtis, Jr., White's aide from the 37th Illinois, wrote his mother somewhat despairingly, "I don't like it. Have no heart for anything. What is the matter I cannot say, but that there is a screw loose somewhere is very evident."[7]

At this time both Stanton and Halleck were deeply involved in reorganizing the Army of the Potomac and searching for Lee. Neither considered White's predicament a priority, nor did intelligence suggest that Lee had designs on Martinsburg. Halleck may have felt more comfortable leaving command of Harpers Ferry with Miles, a regular army officer who had been on site for several months, than with White, who knew nothing about the area of the Potomac Valley. Wool may have influenced Halleck's decision to keep White at Martinsburg, as Wool's mind had already been

5. Miles to Wool, and Wool to Miles, September 4, 1862, *ibid.*, 180, 181; Wool to White, September 4, 1862, *ibid.*, Pt. 1, p. 522; Wool to Miles, September 4, 1862, *ibid.*, Pt. 2, p. 181.

6. White to Cullum, and Cullum to White, September 6, White to Halleck, and Halleck to White, September 8, 1862, *ibid.*, Pt. 2, pp. 198, 199, 218.

7. Captain Henry Curtis, Jr., to his mother, September 4, 1862, Curtis Letters, USAMHI.

poisoned by Miles's innuendoes regarding White's supposed abandonment of Winchester.

On September 7, without advising White of his decision, Halleck wired Miles, "It is important that Harper's Ferry be held to the latest moment. The Government has the utmost confidence in you, and is ready to give you full credit for the defense it expects you to make." Miles replied, "Thanks for the confidence. Will do my best. Enemy advancing on Winchester."[8] With White out of the way, Miles was now ready to admit the presence of the enemy at Winchester, and with the information fed by Miles to army headquarters, Halleck had more reason to expect an attack at Harpers Ferry than at Martinsburg.

Miles's force, combined with White's, numbered about 13,000 men, including 1,500 cavalry. Miles divided the command concentrated at Harpers Ferry into four brigades and made daily adjustments to their dispositions. He ignored White, whom Wool had sequestered at Martinsburg. By then, word filtered into camp that Jackson's corps was not with Lee's army, but nobody knew where it was.[9] If this bit of intelligence worried Halleck, it made no visible impression on Miles.

Most of the Harpers Ferry garrison had not been tested in battle, and Miles's decision to organize them into four brigades made sense. Using the terrain to best advantage, he posted the brigades at three strategic points—Bolivar Heights, Maryland Heights, and Camp Hill. He ignored Loudoun Heights, convinced that nothing but a company of apes could climb the mountain and drag artillery to the top.

The 1st Brigade, under Colonel Frederick G. D'Utassy, consisted of his own 39th New York, the 111th New York under Colonel Jesse Segoine, the 115th New York under Colonel Simeon Sammon, and Captain John C. H. Von Sehlen's 15th Battery, Indiana Light Artillery. Miles posted the brigade to the right on Bolivar Heights, a ridge about two miles west of the Ferry stretching from the southern bank of the Potomac to a position about halfway to the Charles Town pike.[10] Geometrically, Bolivar Heights

8. Halleck to Miles, September 7, and Miles to Halleck, September 8, 1862, *OR*, XII, Pt. 1, p. 757.

9. Wool's Report, September 28, and Binney's Report, September 18, 1862, *ibid.*, 519, 534–36.

10. Binney's Report, September 18, 1862, *ibid.*, 533.

formed the base of a triangle elevated about two hundred feet above Harpers Ferry. The town, buried in the Valley, formed the apex.

D'Utassy, an Austrian, commanded the 39th New York (Garibaldi Guards) at Bull Run. During Miles's court of inquiry for drunkenness he had come to the colonel's defense, and Miles repaid the favor by putting the Austrian in charge of a brigade. Although D'Utassy claimed prior military experience, he demonstrated little understanding of tactics. His colonelcy emanated directly from his ability to raise a regiment composed of Italians, Germans, Frenchmen, and Hungarians living in New York City. He outfitted them in fancy French trousers, Hungarian hussar jackets trimmed with gold, and black felt Italian hats adorned with long, dangling green cock feathers. Although D'Utassy was a small man with a pitted face, his fluency in several languages proved to be crucial in recruiting European immigrants. He kept his men well fed and well clad, but in matters of discipline one of his own officers admitted "he was practically useless."[11]

Miles posted the 2nd Brigade, Colonel William H. Trimble, to the left of D'Utassy, but only as far as the Charles Town pike, leaving a gap of about a mile between the pike and the Shenandoah River. Trimble's brigade consisted of his own 60th Ohio, the 126th New York under Colonel Eliakim Sherrill, the 9th Vermont under Colonel George J. Stannard, and Captain Silas F. Rigby's Indiana Battery. The exposed left flank of Trimble's brigade invited attack.[12]

Fifty-one-year-old William Trimble owed his colonelcy to the political influence of his father, a former governor of Ohio; to his brother, a congressman; and to some degree to himself, as he had been a state legislator from Highland County, Ohio, where he helped to recruit the 60th Ohio. Trimble failed to achieve his political expectations and at the outbreak of war sought redemption by raising a regiment. He was not an assertive man, but one who followed orders. He had been under fire before, but not enough to have seasoned to fighting. Miles's choice of Trimble for brigade

11. G. E. Waring, "The Garibaldi Guard," in *The First Book of the Author's Club* (New York, 1893), 568–72.

12. Binney's Report, September 18, and White's Report, September 22, 1862, *OR*, XIX, Pt. 1, pp. 527, 533.

command is baffling because Stannard of the 9th Vermont was probably the best soldier at Harpers Ferry.

Trimble had enough sense to confer with Stannard on deploying the brigade, and together they examined the undefended left flank. Much of the terrain was wooded, and the steep bank above the Shenandoah was snarled with brush and vines, but a field of head-high corn and a woods about a half mile from the left of the line offered ideal cover for the enemy. Stannard suggested slashing the woods and cutting the corn, and Trimble carried the recommendation to headquarters. On September 9 Miles ambled through Trimble's sector and without explanation vetoed the request. Startled by the colonel's curt reply, Stannard huddled with Trimble to find another way to secure the flank. Trimble then asked Miles for enough men to entrench and set rows of abatis in the gap between the pike and the Shenandoah. At this stage of the war the use of entrenchments had not become a popular defensive measure among old army men accustomed to fighting Indians. Miles, adhering to conventional regular army wisdom, considered the idea unsound. He claimed the artillery posted on Bolivar Heights would enfilade any infantry attack and declared the ravines running up from the river impassable.[13]

Miles's refusal to listen to advice from subordinates recalled similar problems at Bull Run. Even farm boys fighting in the 9th Vermont grew critical of the commander's indifference to obvious defensive measures. Staring into the exposed left flank, one of Stannard's junior officers remarked, "Now was the time when we would have been glad to dig day and night; but in spite of all the pressure put upon him by the officers of higher rank, Colonel Miles would not allow it, ridiculing the anxieties of the garrison. The dullest soldier . . . could foresee the inevitable result. Bitter criticism and growing distrust of [Miles's] loyalty were to be heard on all sides."[14]

Miles placed the 3rd Brigade, commanded by Colonel Thomas H. Ford of the 32nd Ohio, on Maryland Heights. On this strategic prominence Miles deployed his weakest brigade and some of the least reliable units in his command. In addition to the 32nd Ohio, the brigade included 1st Maryland Potomac Home Brigade under

13. Investigation of Harper's Ferry, *ibid.*, 535, 743, 756.
14. Ripley, *Vermont General*, 27–28.

Major John A. Steiner, the 5th New York Heavy Artillery, Company F, under Captain Eugene McGrath, the 1st Maryland Cavalry under Captain Charles H. Russell, and the 7th Squadron, Rhode Island Cavalry, under Captain Augustus W. Corliss, the latter being ninety-day volunteers. McGrath commanded the battery of heavy naval guns emplaced halfway up the bluffs. Miles assigned Russell's and Corliss' cavalry companies to Ford for reconnaissance, intending that neither of them be counted upon for anything else.[15]

At forty-seven years of age, Attorney Thomas Ford organized the 32nd Ohio in his hometown of Mansfield and, like Trimble, his fellow Ohioan, became its colonel. Ford enjoyed more success in politics than Trimble, becoming lieutenant governor under Salmon P. Chase. However, he did not follow Chase into the Republican party and fell quickly out of favor. Like Trimble, Ford supplanted frustrated political ambitions by using his influence to organize a regiment. Unlike Trimble, Ford had raised a company for service in the Mexican War and served under Zachary Taylor's Army of the Rio Grande. Although his primary duty had been to guard wagon trains, he received a wound and tasted a little gunpowder. Miles, then a captain, had served under Taylor at the same time, and it is possible the two men rubbed elbows in 1846 and formed a common bond when they met at Harpers Ferry.[16]

Ford, now a year older but no smarter on military matters, held the keystone to a balanced defense of Harpers Ferry. Steiner's Potomac Home Guards, however, had not distinguished themselves, being part of the Maryland command refusing to fight in Virginia. For infantry Ford had to rely upon his own regiment, the 32nd Ohio. They had seen action in western Virginia and been bloodied by Jackson at Cross Keys and Port Republic, but Ford missed most of the fight in the Valley. He had a fistula removed from his buttocks, an ailment more common to a horse's withers, and because of inflammation and swelling he had spent most of a sixty-day leave in bed. When Ford took command of the 3rd Brigade, he was still in pain and barely ambulatory.[17]

Miles assigned the 4th Brigade to Colonel William Greene

15. Binney's Report, September 18, 1862, *OR*, XIX, Pt. 1, p. 533.
16. Paul R. Teetor, *A Matter of Hours: Treason at Harper's Ferry* (Rutherford, N.J., 1982), 65–68.
17. Investigation of Harper's Ferry, *OR*, XIX, Pt. 1, p. 576.

Ward, whose claim to fame included such distinguished Revolutionary relatives as General Nathaniel Greene, perhaps Washington's best field general, and Colonel Samuel Ward, another Revolutionary patriot and son of Rhode Island's royal governor. Ward's uncle, another Samuel, was closely connected with William H. Seward, former governor of New York and currently Lincoln's secretary of state. Young Ward, who enjoyed close political ties in his home state of New York, came to Harpers Ferry in command of the 12th New York State Militia, another ninety-day regiment. The genetic pool for military genius had been badly diluted in the generations between Nathaniel Greene and young William. Ward received an excellent education at Columbia College, but the school offered no courses in military training. The formation of the regiment (and Ward's colonelcy) cost the Ward family about $10,000, a sum they could easily afford.

Ward manifested all the trimmings of a pampered aristocrat, and his famous cousin, Julia Ward, married Dr. Samuel Gridley Howe, one of John Brown's Boston backers in the Secret Six. Julia, a poetess and staunch reformer, rewrote the words to the song "John Brown's Body," converting the lyrics into the beautiful "Battle Hymn of the Republic." Such was the elegant social atmosphere that produced Colonel William Ward, who in his mid-twenties found himself in timorous command of the 4th Brigade.[18]

With Ward's brigade composed mostly of untrained militia, Miles posted it on Camp Hill, providing a second line of defense should the two brigades on Bolivar Heights be forced to fall back. In addition to Ward's own 12th New York, the brigade included the 87th Ohio under Colonel Henry B. Banning, the 5th New York Heavy Artillery, Company A, under Captain John H. Graham, and the 32nd Ohio, Company F Artillery, under Captain Benjamin F. Potts.[19]

Before Ward arrived at the Ferry, Confederate and Union forces had taken turns digging shallow rifle pits and fortifying Camp Hill, and the colonel considered most of the hard work done. Unlike Bolivar Heights, Camp Hill lay on a gentle slope just above the town. The crest, about a mile wide, lay between the two rivers flowing together at the Ferry. With both flanks protected by high,

18. Teetor, *A Matter of Hours*, 78–79.
19. Binney's Report, September 18, 1862, *OR*, XIX, Pt. 1, p. 533.

steep banks, Camp Hill offered an ideal defensive position. For some reason Miles planned to make his stand on Bolivar Heights, spreading two brigades thinly over a span of three miles and leaving the left flank in the air and the right flank weak. Ward's brigade became the inner defense line, which by itself was weakest, but because the line was composed of ninety-day militia, Miles distrusted the firmness of the unit. However, had he examined General Saxton's dispositions four months earlier, he might have observed that Camp Hill offered a more defensible position than Bolivar Heights. Miles, however, displayed a capacity for ignoring the obvious if the thought did not emanate from his own archive of personal wisdom. His subordinates aptly referred to this troubling ailment as "plain stubbornness."[20]

Miles retained a number of independent commands under his own purview, including part of the 1st Maryland Potomac Home Brigade under Colonel Maulsby and the brigade's 1st Maryland Cavalry under Captain Cole, all of whom had been stationed throughout the summer at Sandy Hook. The 8th New York Cavalry, Lieutenant Colonel Benjamin F. "Grimes" Davis, also remained at the Ferry and represented one of the best units in the command. Miles failed to utilize advantageously Davis' cavalry, whose veterans had arrived late on August 30. Instead of using the unit's reconnaissance skills, he dispatched it as a screen of vedettes between Summit Point and Kearneysville. Davis found it difficult to communicate with Miles, who tended to ignore the cavalry commander and left the unit comfortably encamped on Hall's Island with little to do.[21]

The ability of the 1st, 2nd, and 4th Brigades to repulse an enemy attack depended heavily upon McGrath's battery of naval guns, 9-inch Dahlgrens emplaced halfway up Maryland Heights. Miles believed that those guns, well served, could enfilade any force attempting to breach Ward's line on Camp Hill. Dahlgrens, however, were smoothbore shell guns, and the brigades on Bolivar Heights were barely in range. McGrath's gunners warned that shots aimed at the heights could fall haphazardly on D'Utassy's line. The warning had no effect on Miles's deployment. Had he

20. Investigation of Harpers Ferry, *ibid.*, 743; Moore, ed., *The Rebellion Record,* VI, 159–60.

21. Binney's Report, September 18, 1862, *OR,* XIX, Pt. 1, p. 533; Binney to Davis, August 31, 1862, *ibid.,* LI, Pt. 1, p. 772.

worried about the instability of his forward brigades, he had a simple and viable solution. By posting all three brigades on Camp Hill he would have strengthened his defensive line, covered his left flank, and enabled McGrath's battery to properly support the infantry. His refusal to listen to the suggestions of his officers eventually led to disaster.

The successful defense of Harpers Ferry depended upon holding Maryland Heights, and Ford, ailing fistula and all, needed to inspire his men with courage and by example. The best way to keep green troops from running was to give them protection, and Ford, up on Maryland Heights, had more than his share of greenhorns. Earlier in the summer Miles had sent McGrath and Steiner to survey the approaches to the Heights for the purpose of fortifying them against attack. The pair found the bluffs too steep along the river, but by following Elk Ridge about six miles north they came to Solomon's Gap, the first saddle in the ridge. McGrath and Steiner reported Maryland Heights vulnerable from the rear and recommended that artillery with infantry support be placed on the northern slope of Elk Ridge. They also suggested fortifying Solomon's Gap, as an enemy attack would likely start from there. Miles informed McGrath that he had requisitioned four 32-pounders and two 24-pounders from Washington and requested from Wool another company from the 5th New York Artillery. McGrath made arrangements to emplace the guns but never got them.[22]

In mid-August Wool made a perfunctory visit to Harpers Ferry. The general was not familiar with the area but was responsible for the heavily manned garrison and the enormous quantity of supplies stored there. His visit also prompted Miles to reorganize his command into brigades because the colonel, at the time, had virtually every military unit reporting to himself. Putting organizational structure aside, Wool thought Miles had not given enough thought to defending the town from attack and ordered Bolivar Heights entrenched, Camp Hill abatised, and a sturdy blockhouse built on top of Maryland Heights. Despite Wool's order to entrench Bolivar Heights, and Stannard's and Trimble's request to do so, Miles seemed to be intent on following no one's suggestions but his own. In order to expedite the completion of

22. Investigation of Harpers Ferry, *ibid.*, XIX, Pt. 1, pp. 693–94.

the blockhouse, however, Wool detailed Major Robert S. Rodgers from the Engineer Corps and on August 28 ordered him to Harpers Ferry to hurry the work. Despite the availability of building materials, Miles provided Rodgers with no help and no encouragement. Instead, when he needed a few dispatches delivered to Washington, he sent Rodgers. After the major completed his courier mission, he returned to Baltimore and reported Miles's odd behavior. By then Wool could not question Miles's inattention to orders, as the telegraph had been cut by roving Confederate cavalry.[23]

While inspecting the Ferry, Wool also observed that the only means of escape for the three brigades posted on Bolivar Heights and Camp Hill was a rapid retrograde movement through the town, across the pontoon bridge, and up Maryland Heights. Wool ordered Miles to place a battery of six guns in the lower town to cover the road to the bridge in the event of a retreat. Miles agreed to do it but failed to comply. "He seemed to be very zealous at the time," Wool recalled later, "and determined to do everything [I asked], but I am inclined to think he was overwhelmed with his duties."[24] If Miles, however, did not have guns to defend Solomon's Gap, he may not have had guns to cover the bridge. If Wool ever received any of the colonel's alleged requisitions, the matter never came up in the general's subsequent testimony.

General McClellan, who once visited Harpers Ferry, formed a better perspective of the strategic situation than either Wool or Miles. When Lee crossed the Potomac and marched to Frederick in early September, McClellan needed every man he could muster to meet the threat. He did not know Lee's intentions, but he knew that Wool, who commanded a separate department, had more than ten thousand men at the Ferry. In a late-night session with Seward, Halleck, and Stanton, McClellan asked Halleck to issue orders for Miles to either abandon the Ferry and unite with the Army of the Potomac or to remove the entire garrison from the town, post it on Maryland Heights, and hold out until relieved.[25]

Halleck declined sending either order to Miles. At the time,

23. Wool's Report, September 27, Binney's Report, September 18, 1862, and Investigation of Harpers Ferry, *ibid.*, 519, 535, 789, 791, 793; Garrett to Stanton, September 7, 1862, *ibid.*, Pt. 2, p. 209.

24. Investigation of Harpers Ferry, *ibid.*, Pt. 1, p. 791.

25. George B. McClellan, *McClellan's Own Story* (New York, 1886), 549–50.

Lee's legions lay outside Frederick, and Halleck preferred to wait until Lee showed signs of movement. If the situation changed, he believed Miles had enough men in strong defensive positions to slow Lee down until McClellan caught up with him. Halleck's official report gave other reasons for keeping Miles at the Ferry, but on the night he met with McClellan he privately hoped Lee would waste time in a futile effort to capture the garrison's supplies.[26]

On September 5 Halleck withdrew his resistance to one of McClellan's suggestions and wired Wool that he had no personal knowledge of the Harpers Ferry area but approved the withdrawal of the command to Maryland Heights. Wool disagreed with the dispatch, holding to the belief that Miles should make every effort to defend the town. The dispute fell through a crack in the chain of command when McClellan soon afterwards took control of Wool's troops and neglected to issue the order to Miles.[27]

Captain Curtis, who on September 4 declared "there is a screw loose somewhere," believed he had discovered its source when a week later he wrote his wife, "By ill luck [we] got into Wool's hands, who left Col. Miles (of Bull Run fame) in command at Harper's Ferry with 12,000 men and shoves us out [to Martinsburg] with 2500 short. Miles is, as everybody knows, a ——— fool and won't help us. So we keep ourselves as far as possible."[28]

If during his visit to Harpers Ferry Wool had doubts of Miles's capacity to command, nothing should have stopped him from moving his headquarters there or recalling White from Martinsburg. But the seventy-eight-year-old general did neither, as his quarters in Baltimore were undoubtedly better suited to his comfort and more accessible to Washington.

During Wool's inspection neither he nor Miles made mention of Loudoun Heights, the twelve-hundred-foot eminence rising high above the Ferry from across the Shenandoah. Because of the difficulty involved in scaling the mountain, at least from the western face, Miles believed guns could not be raised to the summit. He considered the task of fortifying Loudoun Heights hopeless and

26. *Ibid.*, 550.
27. Halleck to Wool, September 5, 1862, Investigation of Harpers Ferry, *OR*, XIX, Pt. 1, p. 793; Halleck's Report, November 25, 1862, *ibid.*, 4.
28. Captain Henry Curtis, Jr., to his wife, September 11, 1862, Curtis Letters, USAMHI. Curtis was later captured and paroled at Harpers Ferry.

assumed the enemy shared his convictions. As a consequence, he did nothing. Had he climbed the mountain and looked down upon Camp Hill he may have felt differently. Any gun brought to the summit bore directly on the rear of the greenhorns manning rifle pits on Camp Hill.

By September 8 Miles had his four brigades placed to his satisfaction. He shored up Trimble's left on Bolivar Heights with Potts's light artillery, but he diluted Ford's firepower on Maryland Heights by taking a battery from the 32nd Ohio. D'Utassy's right flank remained weak and in danger of being shelled by the naval guns halfway up Maryland Heights. Ward's ninety-day militia on Camp Hill were thinly scattered in shallow pits and exposed to artillery fire from Loudoun Heights. The key to the position, Maryland Heights, had no guns on the summit, and Colonel Ford, with little more than seven hundred infantry, lived with the knowledge that in his rear lay Elk Ridge, whose fourteen-mile perimeter could not be defended without a battery of heavy guns at Solomon's Gap. When two Parrotts arrived, Miles placed them with the Dahlgrens overlooking the Ferry. Despite Wool's orders to hold Maryland Heights at all costs, Miles sent no guns to Elk Ridge, although emplacements had been built to receive them.[29]

On September 7, however, the War Department received word that Lee had left Frederick, bypassing Harpers Ferry. For the moment, at least, Miles had been spared. One of the puzzles became the reported disappearance of Jackson's command, but even that vital piece of intelligence could not be verified. With the exception of a few brushes with nosy Confederate cavalry, Harpers Ferry lay peaceful and quiet in the late-summer sun.

Miles did not know he had but nine days to live.

29. Investigation of Harpers Ferry, John Joliffe's Report, October 27, 1862, *OR*, XIX, Pt. 1, pp. 778–79.

# 9

## Jackson Springs the Trap

On September 5, when Lee began crossing into Maryland, he hoped to provide "the people of that State an opportunity of liberating themselves." At the time, he had no specific plan for going beyond Frederick. He intended the incursion to be a raid, something to further shatter the nerves of Lincoln's war machine. He did not think of the drive as an invasion for the purpose of grasping a foothold on northern soil, but he hoped to replenish his thinned ranks with Marylanders and his commissary from the countryside's abundant harvest.[1]

The following day he heard artillery fire in the vicinity of Point of Rocks and, turning to Longstreet, asked his opinion as to whether a force should be sent to capture Harpers Ferry. The firing had come from two howitzers of Banning's 87th Ohio when a few Confederate horsemen probed the position. Being in enemy territory, Longstreet discouraged the notion of dividing the army. The men were already fatigued from marching on short rations, he said, and with the enemy nearby, any detachment from the main army would be observed, isolated by a stronger force, and attacked. Lee made no reply, and Longstreet considered the matter settled.[2]

1. Lee to Davis, September 5, 1862, *OR*, XIX, Pt. 2, pp. 593–94.
2. Binney's Report, September 18, 1862, *ibid.*, Pt. 1, p. 534; Longstreet to D. H.

Two days later Longstreet discovered Lee in a private conference with Jackson. Invited to join, he was surprised to hear the two generals discussing an attack on Harpers Ferry and "both heartily approving it." Longstreet again argued against dividing the army, but Lee and Jackson had reached agreement and nothing Longstreet said could change their minds.

Lee, the master of operations planning, and Jackson, the magnificent executioner, believed the Confederacy could survive only if the North was steadily pressed by effective countermeasures. Unlike Longstreet, both men felt inclined to take the offensive, and the following day, September 9, Lee issued Special Order No. 191, outlining to a select number of his generals the planned movements of the army. Lee made his decision while suffering considerable physical pain, as he had recently fallen from his horse and broken both of his wrists.[3]

The plan required audacious and carefully timed implementation. The entire force would march on Wednesday morning, September 10, taking the Hagerstown road (now Alternate Route 40) and passing through South Mountain to the western side of the Blue Ridge. Jackson's force would lead the march, splitting into three divisions, with Stonewall commanding one and Major Generals Lafayette McLaws and John G. Walker the others. Jackson planned to cross the Potomac at a ford in the vicinity of Sharpsburg and by Friday morning, September 12, take possession of the Baltimore and Ohio Railroad, capture the garrison at Martinsburg, and collect any soldiers attempting to escape from Harpers Ferry. At the same time, McLaws, on reaching Middletown, would detach from Longstreet's command and with Major General Richard A. Anderson's division occupy Maryland Heights and invest Harpers Ferry from the Maryland side. Walker, traveling by another route, would cross the Potomac at Cheek's Ford, march to Lovettsville, ascend Loudoun Heights, and force the retreating enemy into Jackson's hands. Nothing in Lee's orders specified that Jackson was to go on to Harpers Ferry after capturing Martinsburg. Lee expected the threatened Union garrison to evacuate the town. The

---

Hill, February 22, 1883, Hill Papers, VSL; James Longstreet, "The Invasion of Maryland," *B&L*, II, 663.

3. Douglas Southall Freeman, *R. E. Lee: A Biography* (4 vols., New York, 1947), II, 153.

entire affair, coming from three different directions and occupying three different points of attack simultaneously, required complex coordination. Jackson had the longest march and Walker the shortest, as the latter was already at Monocacy demolishing the locks of the Chesapeake and Ohio Canal. None of the marches was easy, and each mission had to be completed in two days. Because of the risks involved in dividing his command, Lee distributed only seven copies of Special Order No. 191.[4]

Why Lee, after his chat with Longstreet, changed his mind and decided to attack Harpers Ferry and Martinsburg concerned matters of logistics. Lee had expected the two garrisons, which were now cut off from the Army of the Potomac, to evacuate, but they had not moved. Jackson, who knew every inch of the Valley, encouraged the attack, said it could be done, and considered it an opportunity to capture an enormous quantity of supplies, ordnance, and horses. If the Army of Northern Virginia moved westward and threatened Pennsylvania, Lee would need to shift his line of supply to the Shenandoah Valley, and by moving towards Hagerstown he would not be dependent on the risky route through Manassas, which he expected to be interrupted by the enemy. Supplies could be carted to Shepherdstown by routing them through Staunton, Harrisonburg, and Winchester, and from there delivered to the Confederate army in either Maryland or Pennsylvania. Lee had no choice. To do this necessitated the elimination of the garrisons at Harpers Ferry and Martinsburg.

Lee had hoped the Union War Department would erroneously assume that Harpers Ferry had been his primary objective and order its evacuation. If so, he could steal a march on McClellan, take his army north, attack Harrisburg, burn the Pennsylvania Railroad bridge over the Susquehanna, and perhaps move as far east as Philadelphia.[5]

To make quick work of the Harpers Ferry mission, Lee might have sent his entire army as Longstreet suggested, but a curious meeting between Colonel Miles and Lieutenant Milton Rouss, a Confederate prisoner from the 12th Virginia Cavalry, may have

---

4. Longstreet, "The Invasion of Maryland," *B&L*, II, 663; James Longstreet, *From Manassas to Appomattox* (Bloomington, Ind., 1960), 202; Special Order No. 191, September 9, 1862, *OR*, XIX, Pt. 2, pp. 603–604; John G. Walker, "Jackson's Capture of Harper's Ferry," *B&L*, II, 604.

5. Walker, "Jackson's Capture of Harper's Ferry," 605.

changed his mind. Rouss's company had recently hijacked the Winchester train, but on September 5 Colonel Davis' 8th New York Cavalry captured Rouss and brought him to Harpers Ferry.[6] Rouss claimed he was wounded and on his way to Summit Point, where his father lived, but nobody inspected the prisoner's thigh to determine whether he was telling the truth. Colonel Davis took him to headquarters for questioning and waited for Miles's arrival. Rouss groaned frequently and complained of his wound, and Davis, tired of waiting, sent him to the base hospital with the surgeon. Rouss, showing visible signs of pain, lagged behind with his team. The surgeon rode ahead, and when he reached the hospital he discovered that his prisoner had skedaddled. The doctor reported the escape to Miles, and by morning the 8th New Yorkers had Rouss back at headquarters. Davis asked the prisoner how he managed to slip through the lines, and Rouss replied with a laugh that "he [had] flanked us with his team."

Lieutenant Henry M. Binney, the colonel's ubiquitous aide-de-camp from the 10th Maine Infantry, heard part of the questioning and claimed Miles "did everything he could to worm out of him [Rouss] the position of the enemy and what their plans were," but was unable to get much information. Binney, however, heard only a small portion of the private conversation and later remembered the interview being exceptionally long.

Rouss, claiming to be a man of honor and a gentleman, pleaded for his parole, promising not to take up arms until properly exchanged. Miles cheerfully agreed, and Binney escorted him outside of the lines. When word leaked that Rouss had been released, Binney informed Miles the camp disapproved of it. The colonel shrugged, replying that nearly three hundred Union prisoners paroled at Manassas had passed through the Ferry and that Rouss was entitled to the same consideration.

Binney put the matter out of his mind, but an incident occurring about nine days later led him to believe that Rouss went directly to Lee's camp to give a detailed description of Miles's dispositions. At the time, Binney was a prisoner of A. P. Hill's division, and he was surprised to spot Rouss back in command of a company of cavalry. He, like other Union prisoners, remembered

6. Hervert Enderton, comp., *The Private Journal of Abraham Joseph Warner* (San Diego, 1973), 180.

the lengthy meeting between Miles and Rouss. They all began to suspect that during that conference Miles, a loyal Marylander, agreed to surrender the Ferry after a weak display of resistance. The allegation will never be proven, but the colonel's behavior during the Confederate envelopment of the town must speak for itself. Lee, however, made his decision to attack Harpers Ferry on September 8, which would have given Rouss just enough time to get back to the Confederate camp and make his report.[7]

Assuming Miles made no secret pact with his prisoner, Rouss probably observed enough of the colonel's deployments to provide Jackson with an accurate picture of the garrison's weakness. Jackson's own familiarity with the area was enough to fill any voids. He knew Maryland Heights was the key to capturing the town, and any good scout could have told him that Loudoun Heights was undefended. To prevent the enemy from escaping through Bolivar to Shepherdstown, it became important for Jackson to move his own force from Martinsburg to Shepherdstown to collect the Union units he expected to find fleeing from McLaws.

Jackson, however, did not intend to bring his force all the way to Harpers Ferry. He believed Miles would surrender once McLaws captured Maryland Heights, but for good measure he wanted Walker on Loudoun Heights to make sure he did. McLaws and Walker could not support each other, as they were on opposite sides of the river, and this in itself suggests that Jackson expected only a weak resistance. Lee's Special Order No. 191 specified that McLaws' seizure of Maryland Heights would be the catalyst to the garrison's surrender. In view of Miles's failure to improve the defenses along Elk Ridge, Special Order No. 191 read like a script for a mock battle coauthored by Jackson and Miles.[8]

Jackson's division departed from Frederick at 5 A.M. on Wednesday, September 10, and by evening the first of his regiments passed through Boonsboro and settled into camp on the western outskirts of town. On September 8 Wool had wired Martinsburg asking White to send a cavalry detachment from Lieutenant Colonel Stephen W. Downey's 3rd Maryland towards Hagerstown to determine whether a rumored force of Confederates was actually in the area. Downey, operating out of Kearneysville with twenty men,

7. Investigation of Harpers Ferry, *OR*, XIX, Pt. 1, pp. 737–38.
8. Special Order No. 191, *ibid.*, Pt. 2, pp. 603–604.

scouted the road between Sharpsburg and Boonsboro and on Wednesday evening struck Lieutenant Alexander D. Payne's squadron of Black Horse Cavalry a few miles south of Boonsboro. Revolvers flashed briefly before Payne changed course and galloped back towards the Confederate camp. Downey's troopers pressed forward, firing as they advanced and knocking Lieutenant Henry Kyd Douglas' newly plumed hat off his head. Payne's retreating cavalry came upon a solitary officer, Stonewall Jackson, who was leading his horse in the direction of the firing. Arriving just in time to save Jackson from the embarrassment of capture, a company of the 1st Virginia Cavalry joined Payne and stampeded the Marylanders back down the road. For Downey's insolence a bullet grazed his scalp, but at 9 P.M. he returned to Kearneysville, wired White at Martinsburg, and reported the enemy in force. Downey could not ascertain whether Jackson was taking his command to Hagerstown or to Martinsburg, but Stonewall's division had now been located.[9] Two hours after Downey wired White, Thomas Noakes, another scout, arrived at Martinsburg and reported not less than fifteen thousand, "at least twelve regiments of infantry," passing through Boonsboro. "Probable destination," Noakes declared, "Hagerstown."[10]

Downey also sent a copy of the message to Miles, adding the warning that he had spoken to a local and loyal citizen who learned from Jackson's soldiers that a strong (but exaggerated) force of "70,000 men" intended to strike Harpers Ferry. Miles replied the enemy intended no such thing and chastised Downey for recklessly exposing his command. The colonel refuted Downey's report, claiming the scouts had intercepted nothing but a foraging party. "I cannot learn [that the enemy] has any disposition to advance this way," Miles declared. After condemning Downey's good piece of scouting and discarding the probability of an attack on the Ferry, Miles added a curious comment to the rest of his message. If an effort would be made to capture Harpers Ferry, Miles declared, "it will be through Soloman's [sic] Gap or

9. Wool to White, September 8, 1862 *ibid.*, Pt. 1, p. 520; White to Wool, September 10, 1862, *ibid.*, Pt. 2, p. 249; Douglas, *I Rode with Stonewall*, 153–54.

10. White to Wool, September 10, 1862 (11:00 P.M.), *OR*, XIX, Pt. 2, p. 249. Thomas Noakes lived in Martinsburg, and a month earlier he had captured Belle Boyd, a widely sought Confederate spy.

across the Potomac. If the former, you will *soon* know it by the report of the heavy battery on Maryland Heights."[11]

Downey thought the colonel seemed confused, as the battery faced in the opposite direction and could not play upon an attack from Solomon's Gap. What is interesting is Miles's prediction of the attack coming *soon* from the same gap he had refused to fortify.[12]

If Miles doubted Downey's report, he had an opportunity a few hours later to question Captain Charles H. Russell, whose 1st Maryland Cavalry had just returned from a scout and reported to Ford that the enemy's line was twenty miles long and "there were 20,000 yet to pass Boonsborough [*sic*]." Ford asked Miles, "Have you any news? What has become of General White?"[13]

Hearing nothing from Miles, Ford sent scouts down Elk Ridge, and when Miles visited Maryland Heights on the morning of September 11, Ford reported a large enemy force breaching Solomon's Gap. Scouts also reported enemy advancing into Pleasant Valley, along the eastern slope of Maryland Heights. Miles ordered out more pickets, and Ford sent the 32nd Ohio, Captain Jefferson J. Hibbets, and two companies of the Potomac Home Brigade to the summit. Two hours later Miles and Ford heard scattered artillery fire. Couriers returned on the run to report enemy also working through Brownsville Gap. Accompanied by Major Henry B. Mc-Ilvaine, Miles's artillery chief from the 5th New York, McGrath and Steiner climbed to the top of Maryland Heights and through a softly falling rain observed McLaws' troops coming down South Mountain and into Pleasant Valley. As night approached rain fell heavily and the firing ceased, perhaps leaving the Ferry commander with the impression that the action had been nothing but a feint.[14]

Late that morning Jackson began crossing the Potomac below Williamsport and started his descent to Martinsburg. Running behind schedule, Jackson's infantry pushed on, scattering Union cavalry. Hill's Light Division took the direct turnpike. Jackson,

---

11. Miles to Downey, September 11, 1862, *ibid.*, LI, Pt. 1, p. 820.
12. Investigation of Harpers Ferry, *ibid.*, XIX, Pt. 1, p. 622.
13. Ford to Miles, September 11, 1862, *ibid.*, LI, Pt. 1, pp. 820–21.
14. Investigation of Harpers Ferry, Ford's Report, September [?], 1862, and Binney's Report, September 18, 1862, *ibid.*, XIX, Pt. 1, pp. 691, 542, 536.

with the rest of his command, took a side road, enabling him to approach Martinsburg from the west. If White withdrew, he wanted to force the garrison towards Harpers Ferry, where he could trap all of them at once. Jackson could not afford to lose more time, as Lee had gambled half of his force on the enterprise.[15]

White, with 3,000 men, observed the movement of the enemy with growing apprehension. He ordered Colonel Daniel Cameron's 65th Illinois, supported by every able-bodied soldier in the Martinsburg garrison, to probe Jackson's intentions. Stopped at all points by 12,000 Confederate infantry, Cameron's reconnaissance in force collapsed, and he fell back to town in good order. Towards evening White wired Miles, "As near as I can learn I am being surrounded, and shall make immediate preparations to move towards you." He asked for cars to move baggage and supplies to the Ferry and for infantry support at Kearneysville. "I shall march before daylight," White added. "Don't fail me."[16]

Until Jackson crossed back into Virginia, Stanton and Halleck feared an invasion of Pennsylvania. Confederate pickets had been observed as far north as Greencastle, a small border town filling with dozens of refugees from Hagerstown. Each brought along a wagon loaded with personal belongings and a full plate of rumors, undoubtedly planted by Jackson's cavalry. When word reached Washington that Jackson had veered to the south and reentered Virginia, Pennsylvania Governor Andrew D. Curtin expressed relief, but with all the telegraph lines to Frederick cut, McClellan believed Jackson intended to double back and attack Harpers Ferry.[17]

On September 11 McClellan asked Halleck to evacuate Harpers Ferry and order the garrison to Rockville, Maryland. He believed Miles would be swallowed up by Jackson's superior force and be of little use unless heavily reinforced. Halleck hesitated. He wanted positive intelligence of Jackson's objective before acting. By the following evening every telegraph line serving the Ferry had been cut. "If Harper's Ferry is still in our possession, I think

15. Douglas, "Stonewall Jackson in Maryland," *B&L*, II, 623.

16. Investigation of Harpers Ferry, *OR*, XIX, Pt. 1, p. 636; White to Miles, September 11, 1862 (7:30 P.M.), *ibid.*, LI, Pt. 1, pp. 819, 820.

17. Andrew D. Curtin to Lincoln and to McClellan, September 11, 1862, *ibid.*, XIX, Pt. 2, pp. 268, 269.

I can save the garrison," McClellan advised Lincoln, adding perceptively, "if they fight at all."[18]

McClellan had good reason to be skeptical. Miles's last message to Halleck, written late on September 11, sounded fatalistically cheerful: "My eastern front is threatened. My pickets at Solomon's Gap shelled out. The ball will open tomorrow morning. Force opposing me is estimated at ten regiments of infantry with proportionate artillery . . . others have come to camp since. General White will abandon Martinsburg sometime to-night, and I expect this will be the last you hear from me until this affair is over. All are cheerful and hopeful. Good-bye."[19]

When Miles wired Halleck, he knew nothing of the Confederate force advancing on Loudoun Heights. On September 11 Walker moved his brigade up the Potomac and crossed to the Virginia side at Point of Rocks. With heavy rain falling intermittently, Walker camped for the night and marched to Hillsboro the next day. The following morning he reached the southern foot of Loudoun Mountain. By then he could hear firing on Maryland Heights.[20]

On September 12, Wool, having been out of communication with Miles for several days, gave Halleck approval to transfer the troops at Harpers Ferry and Martinsburg to McClellan. Wool had lost complete track of the garrison and could not even recall the number of troops in his command. Unfortunately, Wool's decision came a day late, as nobody could reach Harpers Ferry by wire.[21]

So on the eve of Jackson's envelopment of Harpers Ferry, Miles remained completely isolated and on his own with only White's command at Martinsburg to reinforce him. Yet, for some inexplicable reason, he remained "cheerful and hopeful."

18. McClellan to Halleck, September 11, and to Lincoln, September 12, 1862, *ibid.*, 254, 272.

19. Miles to Halleck, September 11, 1862, *ibid.*, LI, Pt. 1, p. 819.

20. Walker, "Jackson's Capture of Harper's Ferry," *B&L*, II, 607–608; Walker's Report, October 7, 1862, *OR*, XIX, Pt. 1, p. 913.

21. Wool to Halleck, September 12, 1862, *OR*, XIX, Pt. 2, p. 275.

# 10

## Mayhem on Maryland Heights

Jackson may have had the longest march, but forty-one-year-old Major General Lafayette McLaws drew the toughest assignment of the three Confederate units sent to capture Harpers Ferry. Of sixty-two graduates in the West Point class of 1842, McLaws stood forty-eighth, beating out his current corps commander and fellow Georgian, James Longstreet, who graduated fifty-fourth. McLaws was medium height, stocky, and wore an full beard, and he had seen action in all the major battles from the Peninsula to Second Manassas. When Lee agreed to cut Jackson loose to open the Shenandoah supply line, he detached McLaws from Longstreet's corps but kept part of the division in close contact with the main army.[1]

McLaws brought eight brigades to the affair. Brigadier General James L. Kershaw, commanding his own brigade, and Brigadier General William Barksdale's Mississippi brigade provided the principal punch. On September 12 Kershaw led his brigades through Solomon's Gap and up Elk Ridge. He put his own brigade on the ridge and kept Barksdale's on the partially masked eastern face. Lower down on Elk Ridge the brigades of Thomas R. R. Cobb and Lewis A. Armistead moved south, keeping in contact with Barksdale above and the brigades of Paul J. Semmes and William

1. *HTI*, 464.

Mahone below, the latter commanded by Colonel William A. Parham. Semmes and Parham advanced along Pleasant Valley, occupying Crampton's Gap and Brownsville Gap, thereby sealing off an attack from the rear. Roger A. Pryor's brigade followed Cobb's, and late in the afternoon Pryor advanced to the village of Weverton, about a mile below Sandy Hook. Brigadier General Ambrose R. Wright's brigade climbed South Mountain at Brownsville Gap and moved south, parallel to Elk Ridge and to a point overlooking Weverton. By nightfall Pryor occupied Weverton, and Wright, with two pieces of artillery emplaced on the hill above the town, effectively blocked any Union attempt to withdraw downriver. Cobb and Armistead moved down Pleasant Valley with little opposition and halted for the night outside Sandy Hook, where Maulsby had part of his Potomac Home Brigade drawn up in line. With all eight brigades in contact with each other along their line of advance, McLaws moved into Pleasant Valley with the rest of his force and headed towards the Potomac River.[2]

Early in the afternoon Maulsby reported artillery above Weverton and a strong force in his front. Miles ordered him to withdraw and re-form at the base of Maryland Heights near the Harpers Ferry bridge. Jackson's effort to compress Miles's command into the Ferry had begun.[3]

On Elk Ridge Kershaw's advance regiments met weak resistance from Ford's pickets. Miles had failed to provide Ford with artillery at Solomon's Gap, and a few dozen skirmishers from the 7th Rhode Island Cavalry (ninety-day men) and 32nd Ohio Infantry were no match for Kershaw's veterans. After a few shells exploded in their midst, the Union pickets fled up the ridge. Ford sent the balance of the 32nd Ohio forward to slow Kershaw's advance. They fired a few rounds at the rebels and scrambled back up the mountain. Unimpeded, Kershaw continued up the ridge.[4]

At 6 P.M., Confederate skirmishers led by Major J. M. Bradley's Mississippians met strong resistance at a small abatis flanked on either side by a ledge of precipitous rocks about a mile from the summit. The defenders consisted of six companies from the 39th New York, Major Hugo Hildebrandt, and two companies from

2. McLaws' Report, October 18, Kershaw's Report, September 25, 1862, *OR*, XIX, Pt. 1, pp. 853–54, 862–63.

3. Miles to Maulsby, September 12, 1862, *ibid.*, 557.

4. Kershaw's Report, September 25, 1862, *ibid.*, 862–63.

Colonel Sammon's 115th New York—reinforcements Miles had sent from Bolivar Heights late Thursday evening and early Friday morning. Ford scattered most of the men along Elk Ridge and later dispatched two companies from the Potomac Home Brigade to reinforce the 32nd Ohio at the small abatis.[5]

A quarter of a mile behind the first abatis lay a heavier abatis, and behind that a cribbed log structure or breastwork standing fifteen to twenty feet high and known as "the Lookout," as sentinels perched on it could see for miles in every direction. The first abatis lay about two miles from McGrath's batteries, which were emplaced on the side of the mountain and close to Ford's headquarters. When Ford reported enemy infantry ascending Elk Ridge, Miles promised to send up the 126th New York. The decision baffled Ford. He could not understand why Miles would send the least experienced regiment to defend the most critical sector on Maryland Heights. Colonel Sherrill, a forty-nine-year-old farmer, tanner, and politician, had no military experience, and his men had never been under fire. The regiment had just received their issue of Springfield rifles, and when they arrived at the Ferry on August 28 not a round had been fired. Nonetheless, Miles ordered the six-hundred-man regiment to take one day's rations and eighty rounds of ammunition and to march to Ford's headquarters at sunrise for orders. Sherrill started across the bridge on the morning of September 12 but was recalled by Miles and sent back to Bolivar Heights.[6]

Ford, expecting Sherrill's regiment but not getting it, stopped the retreat of the 39th New York skirmishers and sent them back to defend the small abatis. About 3 P.M., when it appeared as though Miles had the 126th New York headed back towards Maryland Heights, Major Sylvester M. Hewitt, Ford's executive officer, inexplicably recalled the 39th New York, leaving the 32nd Ohio and a few companies from the 115th New York, the 7th Rhode Island, and the Potomac Home Brigade to defend the crest. Ford, troubled by his ailing fistula surgery, did not return to the crest

5. *Ibid.*; Investigation of Harpers Ferry, *OR*, XIX, Pt. 1, p. 601; Pettengill, *The College Cavaliers*, 77.

6. A. M. Willson, *Disaster, Struggle, Triumph: The Adventures of 1,000 "Boys in Blue"* (Albany, N.Y., 1870), 50, 343; Investigation of Harpers Ferry, *OR*, XIX, Pt. 1, p. 727.

and left matters in the hands of Hewitt—a man uncertain of his authority.[7]

Until late afternoon when Sherrill came up, the odd mixture of Union companies checked Kershaw at the abatis. Later, Ford sent up Russell's cavalry and a few other units to support his Ohioans, but the reinforcements were mostly random companies drawn from other regiments. Ford, however, distrusted Sherrill's untested New Yorkers. Referring to the greenhorns, he told Russell, "I would rather do what fighting I have got to do here with the little handful of men which I have confidence in, for I believe they [126th New York] would do me more harm than good." Russell, who had been ordered up the mountain with his cavalry to perform reconnaissance, found the task impossible and agreed to dismount his cavalry and take the men with their carbines to the summit at dawn.[8]

As night fell on Elk Ridge, Kershaw retired his skirmishers and moved up four regiments, posting the 7th South Carolina, Colonel D. Wyatt Aiken, on the right, with the 2nd South Carolina, Colonel John D. Kennedy, a hundred yards in reserve. On the left he posted Colonel John W. Henagan's 8th South Carolina with Colonel James D. Nance's 3rd South Carolina in support. His total brigade of 1,041 was no larger than a full regiment. He placed Barksdale's brigade of 960 Mississippians in reserve behind Kennedy's and Nance's regiments. Darkness and steady rain put an end to the skirmishing, and Kershaw's men rested on their arms a few hundred yards from the small abatis.[9]

Behind the abatis Ford posted the 32nd Ohio, 126th New York, and two companies of the 39th New York's Garibaldi Guards. Before daybreak, September 13, four more companies from the 39th New York and Russell's 1st Maryland Cavalry joined the command on the crest. Ford, anguishing over his surgery, returned down the hill to his headquarters. He placed Major Hewitt in nominal charge of the summit but failed to communicate his wishes to the other units. Ford departed from the crest without clearly designating an overall commander. He also left a mess. Colonel

7. Investigation of Harpers Ferry, *OR*, XIX, Pt. 1, p. 601.

8. *Ibid.*, 727.

9. Kershaw's Report, September 25, 1862, and McLaws' Returns, *OR*, XIX, Pt. 1, pp. 862–63, 860–61.

Sherrill outranked Hewitt, and the major felt incapable of asserting himself under such circumstances.

A hundred yards in front of the abatis, Hewitt deployed skirmishers from the dismounted 1st Maryland Cavalry and two companies of the 126th New York. With the first golden rays of early morning, the jittery command listened to the muffled sounds of Kershaw's veterans rattling canteens and camp equipment as they prepared to attack.[10]

On Friday afternoon, September 12, Miles had ascended the mountain and ordered explosives and bundles of combustibles placed on the southeastern face. The purpose, he explained, was to ignite it as a signal to the artillery if Ford was forced off the summit. Once the defenders cleared the crest, Miles intended to use the artillery on Bolivar Heights, Camp Hill, and Maryland Heights to check the advance of the enemy.[11] Miles, of course, had no inkling of Walker's ascent on Loudoun Heights, but his order made little sense for a different reason. Batteries from all three locations would be forced to fire from lower elevations. Gunners would not be able to see the effect of their fire and make accurate adjustments. More importantly, Miles may have weakened the resolve of the defenders on Maryland Heights by suggesting that artillery could repulse the enemy when only a stiff resistance by Ford's infantry could save the Heights. A man of Miles's military experience should have known this, which adds credence to the theory that the colonel never intended to hold the Heights.

Two separate incidents occurred on Friday night, the day prior to Kershaw's attack. The first involved McGrath, who commanded the artillery on Maryland Heights. He spoke with Miles the day before the battle and promised to serve his guns until overrun by the enemy. Miles replied, "Captain, if we are compelled to leave, if they come in force, we will have to spike these guns," but as an afterthought added, "damn 'em, they sha'nt have 'em." During this brief conversation, McGrath thought the colonel behaved indecisively, as if his mind could not focus on any one problem. Having expected the colonel to reply "Fight those guns to the end, Captain!," McGrath found Miles's demeanor tim-

10. Investigation of Harpers Ferry, *ibid.*, 570, 601, 727.
11. *Ibid.*, 566.

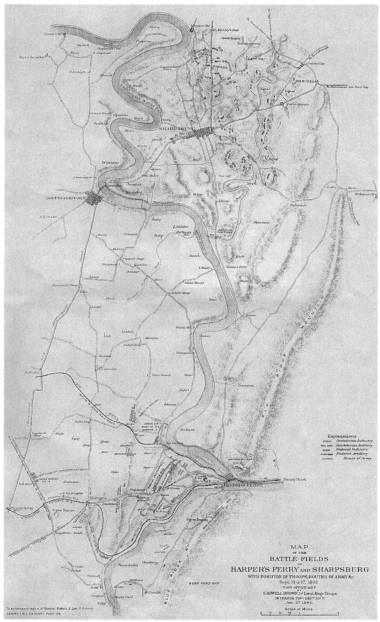

The battlefield of Harpers Ferry, September 13–17, 1862, during the invasion of Maryland by General Robert E. Lee

*From* Atlas to Accompany the Official Records, *courtesy HFA*

orous and artificially brusque, as if he expected the situation on the crest would inevitably become hopeless.[12]

The second incident involved Hewitt, who came to Miles's headquarters late Friday night, got the colonel out of bed, and demanded reinforcements. Before awakening the commander, Hewitt spoke with Ford, who declared, "To-morrow one of two things have got to be done; we have either got to drive them from that hill or they are going to drive us from it." Ford encouraged Hewitt to ride into town and speak with Miles. The colonel rubbed the sleep from his eyes and replied that he had spoken to Ford earlier in the evening and was assured by him that "he could hold that place [Maryland Heights] against all hell. . . . What in hell does he want more men for? I cannot jeopardize any force in front [of Harpers Ferry]." Hewitt prevailed, and Miles finally promised to send over two regiments at dawn with two pieces of artillery. He also promised to send a third regiment up the western side of the mountain to flank the Confederate force at the abatis. Miles did neither, although a few scattered companies reported to Hewitt late in the morning. This behavior is particularly puzzling because White's force of about 2,500 had arrived at noon from Martinsburg with Downey's 3rd Maryland Potomac Home Brigade.[13]

White's arrival sparked speculation throughout the garrison as to who would be in command. After placing the Martinsburg garrison in a bivouac area behind Bolivar Heights, Miles avoided a meeting with White until late evening. The exact conversation between the two commanders is unknown, but White later told Trimble that Miles refused to step down. Since Wool had explicitly placed Miles in command of the Ferry, and since no means of communication to the outside existed, White hesitated. Without authority from Washington, he would not supersede the colonel.[14]

White, however, withheld his decision until morning. He wanted more time to assess Miles's defensive strategy, how the troops had been deployed, and what provision had been made for withdrawal. Earlier in the day he had spoken with D'Utassy, who had been up on Maryland Heights with a topographical engineer and believed the ridge impregnable if properly defended. White

12. *Ibid.*, 693.
13. *Ibid.*, 568, 764.
14. *Ibid.*, 746; Ripley, *Vermont General*, 26.

discussed this with Miles, who thought the Confederate force on the Heights was small and that the main attack would come from the south. White agreed, as he believed Jackson would come down the Potomac and invest the town from Bolivar Heights. He argued that the entire garrison should be withdrawn over the pontoon bridge to defend Maryland Heights. With the pontoons removed, White explained, Jackson could not cross the river, and McLaws' advance would be checked. The defense of Maryland Heights, White argued, would buy time for McClellan to roll up McLaws from the rear. "As a matter of course," Miles agreed, "it is the only choice we have." The colonel then went to bed but issued no orders, leaving further decisions for morning.[15]

When Miles lost communication with the outside world, he became like a caterpillar wrapped inside its dark cocoon to await the moment of some wonderful metamorphosis. He knew his lines had been cut and his outposts driven in, and that Martinsburg was occupied by Jackson. He had more than fifteen hundred cavalry camped on Hall's Island and stretched along the Chesapeake and Ohio Canal, but he made no effort to use them to contact Wool or Halleck. White's last communication with Halleck and Wool occurred near midnight on September 10. Miles's last message to Halleck left the Ferry shortly after noon on September 11, belatedly reporting "40,000 to 60,000" of the enemy at Boonsboro. Thereafter, communication ended. On September 12 Halleck wired Miles to "obey such orders as General McClellan may give you. You will endeavor to open communication with him and unite your forces to his at the earliest possible moment." Miles never got the message.[16]

McClellan finally had the Army of the Potomac in motion and marched them to Frederick. Halleck exuded optimism. He saw an opportunity to trap Lee in Maryland and bring the war to an end. Midday on September 12 he wired McClellan, "Is it not possible to open communications with Harper's Ferry, so that Colonel Miles' forces can co-operate with you?"[17]

McClellan already had cavalry probing towards Point of Rocks

15. Investigation of Harpers Ferry, OR, XIX, Pt. 1, p. 596.

16. White to Halleck and to Wool, September 10, and Miles to Halleck, September 11, 1862, ibid., Pt. 2, pp. 249, 266; Halleck to Miles, September 12, 1862, ibid., Pt. 1, p. 521.

17. Halleck to McClellan, September 12, 1862, ibid., Pt. 2, p. 271.

in an effort to contact the garrison's outposts. He sent several squadrons across the fords at Monocacy, but none of them broke through the cordon Jackson had built around his envelopment of the Ferry. Failing to make contact with any of Miles's scouts, McClellan suspected the worst may already have happened when he advised Halleck, "If Harper's Ferry is still in our possession, I think I can save their garrison, if they fight at all."[18]

Another puzzling piece of the communications dilemma involved Captain Louis R. Fortesque of the Signal Corps. In early September he had established a signal station on the summit of Maryland Heights. From there, signals could be exchanged with a station at Point of Rocks, passing from point to point downriver to Washington. On the night of September 12, Lieutenant J. H. Fralick of the Signal Corps mounted Point of Rocks and with red lights and rockets attempted to attract Fortesque's attention at the station on Maryland Heights. Fortesque, however, believed that after Confederate cavalry chased Banning away from Point of Rocks on September 5, no one would be there to receive his signals. Having no specific orders to remain at Harpers Ferry, he abandoned the station some time prior to September 12 and made his way back to the Army of the Potomac.[19] Fortesque left his station with the approval of Miles, who probably agreed with the signal officer that without a comrade at Point of Rocks he was no longer needed. By releasing Fortesque and not using his cavalry to locate McClellan, Miles sealed Harpers Ferry as effectively from the inside as Jackson did from the outside.

Information, however, was getting to the outside—but to the wrong camp. Whether by intention or stupidity, Miles continued the questionable policy of paroling Confederate prisoners. He released sixteen of them on September 12, two being in civilian clothes, and put them on the road to Winchester. Some dallied about the town before departing on September 14. Angry pickets refused to let the parolees pass, and Miles had to escort the prisoners in civilian clothes through the lines himself.[20]

18. McClellan to Halleck and to Lincoln, September 12, 1862, *ibid.*, 271–72.

19. Major Albert J. Myer's Report, October 6, 1862, *ibid.*, Pt. 1, p. 119; see also J. W. Brown, *The Signal Corps, U.S.A., in the War of the Rebellion* (New York, 1974), 227–28.

20. Investigation of Harpers Ferry, and David Hunter's Report, November 3, 1862, *OR*, XIX, Pt. 1, pp. 739, 797, 800.

The parolees could not have gotten far before encountering cavalry from Jackson's force at Martinsburg. Although most of them departed from the area blindfolded, they were familiar with the topography of the area and had heard and seen much during their detention. Whatever intelligence they conveyed to Jackson had little to do with the action about to take place on Maryland Heights.

As daylight filtered through the clouds gripping the summit of Maryland Heights on Saturday morning, September 13, a wetness hung in the chilled atmosphere. A quiet pervaded the woods, except for the muffled stirring of men preparing a frugal morning meal. Kershaw's regiments, with a brigade in reserve, lay about a hundred yards in front of the first and smallest of two abatises on Maryland Heights. Hewitt hoped to make his stand at the second and heavier abatis, falling back upon the cribbed earthen breastwork only as a last resort. McGrath's battery and Ford's headquarters lay about two miles down from the breastwork and two miles opposite the entrenchments above Harpers Ferry. Ford commanded all the troops on the Heights, but this day he failed to leave the comfort of his headquarters to direct the engagement. Worse, he failed to place anyone in overall command of the action about to begin near the summit.[21]

At about 9 A.M. Kershaw moved his brigade forward. Henagan's 8th South Carolina, a regiment of only 126 men, butted into a ledge of rock that cut them out of the early action. Aiken's 7th South Carolina, with 526 men, led the charge and in twenty minutes drove the 126th New York and the 32nd Ohio back four hundred yards to the large abatis. Kershaw noticed firing coming from his left flank, Russell's dismounted 1st Maryland Cavalry, and extended his line by moving Barksdale's brigade down the eastern face of the ridge and posting it to the left of the 7th South Carolina. He then ordered Barksdale to advance his regiments below the brow of the ridge and come in on the flank of the cribbed breastwork in the enemy's rear. The Mississippians had a rough assignment, as the slope was steep and tangled with brush. With Barksdale moving below the ridge, Kershaw advanced the 7th and 8th South Carolina against the second abatis. Finding resistance a

21. Investigation of Harpers Ferry, *ibid.*, 734.

little stiffer, he ordered up Nance's 3rd South Carolina of 371 men in support.

Kershaw found himself checked at the second abatis, but word came from Barksdale that some of his men, after a backbreaking climb, were in position to attack. Barksdale reported he was in the rear of the enemy, but if he came over the ridge his men would come under fire from the South Carolinians. Kershaw, hoping to snare all the enemy in one charge, ordered his brigade to withhold fire, thereby enabling Barksdale to make his attack. Before word got back to Barksdale, Lieutenant Colonel John C. Fiser's 17th Mississippi fired into a body of enemy sharpshooters lodged in the rocks above them and startled about half a company of greenhorns into a full-blown rout. At about 2 P.M. the Union line began to give way, and most of it disappeared down the mountainside. For another hour or two, Union defenders tried to make a stand with the 32nd Ohio, Russell's dismounted cavalry, remnants of the Garibaldi Guards, and Downey's 3rd Maryland Potomac Home Brigade. As the retreat swept by Ford's headquarters, McGrath spiked his guns and joined the colonel in a race across the pontoon bridge to Harpers Ferry. Kershaw later found Ford's bastion on Maryland Heights much as Ford had left it, with commissary stores, ammunition, and tents all undisturbed.[22]

Kershaw's morning attack fell upon Sherrill's 126th New York, Hewitt's 32nd Ohio, three companies from the 39th New York (Garibaldi Guards), and Russell's dismounted 1st Maryland Cavalry, then totaling about two thousand defenders. From the strong breastwork behind the large abatis, Hewitt and Sherrill should have been able to check Kershaw's advance had the 126th New York held fast. The regiment had been mustered into the service on August 22. Without so much as one day's training, they were conveyed from New York's Finger Lakes country to Harpers Ferry, where they arrived on August 28. Miles sent them to Maryland Heights late on the afternoon of the September 12 and, over Ford's objections, ordered them posted on Maryland Heights. None of the recruits, including the officers, had ever been fired upon, and many of them, having had no time to drill, knew little about the idiosyncrasies of their brand-new Springfield rifles.[23]

22. Kershaw's Report, September 25, 1862, and Investigation of Harpers Ferry, *ibid.*, 863, 570–72.

23. Willson, *"Boys in Blue,"* 19, 21, 25.

When Kershaw attacked the small abatis at about 9 A.M., the 126th New York broke at the first fire, forcing the 32nd Ohio and the Garibaldi Guards to hold the line long enough to retire, in order, to the second abatis. Russell deployed his dismounted 1st Maryland Cavalry as skirmishers in support of the Union right flank. Hewitt re-formed the 32nd Ohio at the second abatis, but most of the 126th New York refused to come out from behind the cribbed breastwork in the rear. When Kershaw resumed his attack, a lieutenant from the 1st Maryland Cavalry fell and spooked the New Yorkers, who broke again, and those still at the abatis joined their comrades at the breastwork. "A goodly number of them fled out of sight," Russell reported. "I do not know where they stopped."[24] The Finger Lakes boys received another shock less than an hour into the action when Colonel Sherrill, attempting to rally the lads in front of the breastwork, was struck by a ball that mangled his tongue, mutilated his face, and disabled his speech.[25]

Miles made a perfunctory visit to Maryland Heights about an hour before Kershaw's attack. He inspected the cribbed breastwork near the summit and returned to town after a brief consultation with Ford. About the time Miles reached Harpers Ferry, Sherrill's New Yorkers came streaming down the mountainside and congregated outside Ford's headquarters. The colonel sent a courier galloping into the Ferry to report that his regiments "won't fight, and he cannot hold the heights." Miles replied laconically, "Since leaving your position on Maryland Heights and coming to this side, I can see that your position is much more defensible than it appears at your station, covered as it is by the guns of Camp Hill. You can hold on and must hold on until the cows' tails drop off."[26]

From about 10 A.M. until 2 P.M., the remnants from four Union regiments checked Kershaw at the cribbed breastwork. For four hours Hewitt waited for the three regiments Miles had promised

24. Investigation of Harpers Ferry, *OR,* XIX, Pt. 1, pp. 602, 727.

25. *Ibid.,* 570, 571; Willson, *"Boys in Blue,"* 68. See also Richard Bassett's Papers in the Ontario County Historical Society, Canandaigua, New York. Bassett leaves a colorful account of the 126th New York's first battle and the wounding of Colonel Sherrill.

26. Binney's Report, September 18, and Miles to Ford, September 13, 1862, *OR,* XIX, Pt. 1, p. 537.

to send first thing in the morning. Lieutenant John Pearce of the 32nd Ohio went down to the Ferry shortly after the fighting started to bring them up. Pearce explained the situation to Miles, who argued that "there was nobody on Maryland Heights but skirmishers," but that an attack should be expected from the Rohrersville road. Pearce replied that he had been four miles out on the road and found nothing but pickets. He pointed to the Heights and declared angrily that he had counted at least two enemy brigades on the mountain. Miles rejected the information as false and sent Pearce back to the Heights with orders for Ford to watch the Rohrersville road.[27]

Just before Kershaw's second attack at 10 A.M., Colonel Downey's 3rd Maryland Potomac Home Brigade reached the summit and joined the defenders behind the breastworks, adding about six hundred veterans to Hewitt's collapsing line. Downey later testified that Miles had threatened to put him under arrest for disobeying orders he had never been given. Miles claimed he had ordered Downey to the Heights on Friday. Downey disclaimed receiving orders until Saturday, and not until after volunteering to go there himself. He found Miles mentally confused. "On the morning I marched with my regiment [to] Maryland Heights," Downey declared, "Colonel Miles' verbal orders were, 'I desire you to report to Colonel Hall, on Maryland Heights.' He named over some three or four names. At last I said, 'You mean Colonel Ford.' 'Yes, sir,' said he, and from that conversation I came to the conclusion that Colonel Miles was not in a condition to command."[28]

For almost four hours, Hewitt, Downey, and Russell checked three attacks on their front and a few weak attempts on their flanks. They expected reinforcements momentarily. They were in a tight spot but felt fairly secure behind the breastwork. Ford had plenty of ammunition below. All they needed was a fighting regiment or three or four determined companies to keep the enemy confined to the ridge. Russell felt certain the position could be held, but he noticed a mounted officer (Lieutenant Adam Carnes of the 32nd Ohio) in the rear "waving his hat and motioning us back." Russell double-quicked to the rear to ask what he wanted.

27. Investigation of Harpers Ferry, *ibid.,* 707.
28. *Ibid.,* 621–22.

The lieutenant said he had orders from the colonel to fall back. Russell looked for Hewitt but could not find him. Moments later, defenders started to dribble down the mountain.[29]

At the time of the retreat, Hewitt was not on the field but partway down the mountain "endeavoring to rally" the 126th New York or any other unit within reach. He had been gone from the field quite a while and did not know the fight on the summit had stabilized when he dispatched Carnes with orders to withdraw. Hewitt acted entirely on his own but claimed he had been instructed by Miles on the preceding day "to fall back, if . . . overpowered." Hewitt could not produce an order from Miles and later admitted that the order may not have applied to the moment in question.[30]

Russell's version of the withdrawal coincides with Downey's. Carnes also rode over to Downey and said, "The order is to retreat."

Downey considered the order incredulous. He turned to Carnes and asked, "Who gives that order?"

"Colonel Ford."

"Sir, there can be no order to retreat," Downey replied. Then turning to his men and fellow officers for confirmation, he added, "There certainly cannot be an order to retreat from this position. If we lose this position, we lose everything; we can hold this position unless the enemy press heavier than they do now."

Another messenger then rode to the ridge and said, "The order is to retreat."

Men huddling about the couriers began to slink to the rear. Downey shouted, "For God's sake, don't fall back; we must hold this position." But, he lamented, the men commenced the withdrawal, and nobody could stop them. Downey and Russell rallied about 350 men and continued to check Kershaw at the breastwork.[31]

Hewitt acted independently, as no absolute order to withdraw came from either Miles or Ford. The only standing order was issued by Miles the previous day and concerned the placement of combustibles on Maryland Heights. These were to be ignited as a signal to the gunners on Bolivar Heights to open fire on the enemy

29. *Ibid.*, 728.
30. *Ibid.*, 734–36.
31. *Ibid.*, 819, 772.

if, Hewitt declared, "we were pressed too hard" and forced to fall back.[32]

If Miles had given Hewitt the impression that an artillery barrage from Bolivar Heights could check the enemy, Hewitt lacked the military savvy to understand the foolishness of the notion. Miles must have given Hewitt the impression that withdrawal from the Heights was inevitable. More than likely, Hewitt panicked when a few sharpshooters from Barksdale's brigade made an unexpected appearance in the rear, where the major may have been standing at the time. Barksdale's attack could not have been in force because of the difficulty in scaling the crest, and a few well-placed Union defenders could have driven off the Mississippians with heavy casualties. Evidence, however, simply suggests that Hewitt panicked, and in his retreat down the mountain he failed to carry out Miles's order to light the combustibles.[33]

General White clearly understood the importance of holding Maryland Heights but failed to assert himself. On several occasions he probed the colonel's resolve to defend the mountain and received steadfast assurances that the Heights would be held "even if the entire force at his disposal should be required for its defense." Miles, however, spoke out of both sides of his mouth, as he privately believed his orders compelled him to hold the town. He doubted whether defending Maryland Heights would mean the same to his superiors as holding Harpers Ferry. But the presence of White confounded his reasoning. He feared losing command of the garrison if he could not convince White of his commitment to defend the Heights. Miles exercised a little deceit and lied to White.[34]

On Saturday morning, September 13, White renounced his right to command and tendered "my services and those of the officers of my staff to render any aid in our power in the defense of the position." By "position" White meant Maryland Heights. Miles responded by jubilantly circulating general orders to clarify the temporary command confusion and wrote, "This act of high-

32. *Ibid.*, 566–67.

33. William H. Nichols, "The Siege and Capture of Harper's Ferry," *Personal Narratives of Events in the War of the Rebellion,* Ser. 4, No. 2 (Providence, R.I., 1889), 21; Investigation of Harpers Ferry, *OR,* XIX, Pt. 1, pp. 568–69.

34. Investigation of Harpers Ferry, *OR,* XIX, Pt. 1, pp. 686–87, 775; Moore, ed., *The Rebellion Record,* VI, 220.

toned chivalric generosity, of which there are but few precedents in our army, overwhelms me with the greatest gratitude."[35]

Miles's euphoria collapsed moments later when he confronted a situation even more overwhelming. A courier reported enemy batteries on the Charles Town pike with a force of undetermined size advancing from the south. From headquarters Miles could hear the firing and started towards Bolivar Heights with two of his aides. As they ascended to higher ground, Lieutenant Binney directed the colonel's attention to turmoil on Maryland Heights. Miles halted his horse, got out his glass, and looked across the river. "My God," he gasped, "Colonel Ford is evacuating his position. We must stop it!" Sylvester W. Clemens, chaplain of the 115th New York, stood nearby and heard Miles shout loudly, "God Almighty; what does this mean? They are coming down! Hell and damnation!"[36]

With lieutenants John Willmon and Binney at his side, Miles jogged back down High Street, crossed the pontoon bridge, and started up the serpentine road to Maryland Heights. He observed men running in every direction, some lurking behind trees and bushes, some hiding behind rocks, but all in wild confusion as they tumbled down the mountain.[37]

Miles stopped a company of the 126th New York and asked, "Boys, what are you doing here?"

"We have been ordered to fall back."

"By whom?" Miles demanded.

"By some major," a spokesman replied.

"There has been no order to give orders to fall back," Miles said angrily. "I have given no order to fall back and no major could get one unless he got it from me."

The colonel turned to his aide and said, "Mr. Binney, bring those men up."[38]

Miles continued up the mountain with Willmon, and upon reaching McGrath's battery he found dozens of stragglers milling about in disorder. "What are you men doing here?" he asked.

"We have been ordered to fall back," one replied.

35. White to Miles, September 13, and General Order No. 42, September 13, 1862, *OR*, XIX, Pt. 1, p. 525.

36. Investigation of Harpers Ferry, *ibid.*, 537, 576.

37. *Ibid.*, 707.

38. *Ibid.*, 645.

"There has been no order to fall back," Miles shouted, then turning to Willmon said, "Go up on the hill and reform the One hundred and twenty-sixth, and try to get it to the front; and tell every officer and man you see that there is no order to fall back, but the order is to go to the front immediately and do his duty there to the last."

Willmon went nearly to the top, finding about five hundred men from the 126th New York scattered about, but the fight had gone out of them. He could still hear firing on the crest, so he corralled a few unwilling volunteers and started towards the summit. Willmon found no one in overall command and gave orders to the adjutant of the 126th New York to march the stragglers to the front and keep them there.

"Well, damn them, they will run," the officer replied. "Just what I thought they would do."

Willmon looked about for officers and found four lieutenants milling well below the breastwork but up near the summit.

"Who commands you?" Willmon asked.

"Our major commands," someone from the 32nd Ohio replied.

"Where is your major?"

"He has got away from us. We don't know where he is."

"Well, what has become of your captains?" Willmon asked.

One replied, "I don't know what has become of them. They must have run away from us."

Willmon ordered the major arrested by anybody in the command who could find him, but by then Miles considered the situation hopelessly out of control. McGrath's guns had already been spiked and some of them pushed over the mountainside. Miles felt devastated and with Binney and Willmon rode back down the hill, calling every skulker he passed a "damned scoundrel."[39]

On this day scoundrels came in all shapes and sizes, and from privates to colonels. Neither Miles nor Ford thought the fight on the summit important enough to go up and direct it himself. Perhaps a secret meeting between Miles and Ford explains why.

Ford, bothered by his surgery, stayed close to his headquarters at the Unsell house, located about halfway up the mountain. Mrs. Elizabeth Brown, whose husband was a captain in the 1st Maryland Potomac Home Brigade, looked after the home and per-

39. *Ibid.*, 537, 627, 645–46.

formed household chores. About noon Miles and Ford met in a downstairs room and ordered the staff outside. Thinking their conversation private, they did not know Mrs. Brown had her ear to a stovepipe hole covered by a tin in an upper room. She distinctly heard Miles tell Ford he would have to fall back to Harpers Ferry and that he could not hold Maryland Heights. Mrs. Brown heard Ford rise to his feet, swearing he could "hold it" providing he received reinforcements. When Miles refused to listen, Ford said "it was a shame that the men should have to give up."[40]

This conversation took place at a time when Kershaw's advance had been checked by about half the defenders originally sent to the summit, and at a time when Colonel Sammon's 115th New York with nine hundred reinforcements were passing McGrath's battery on their way to the top. Sammon was detained at the battery and received no instructions until 3 or 4 P.M., when he was ordered to retire. During that time he saw "none of the Federal forces, where they were stationed, and but few of the enemy, very few, indeed." There was no question in Sammon's mind who issued the order to retire. It was signed by Colonel Ford and carried by Major Steiner.[41]

Roughly four hours elapsed between the time Miles left Ford's headquarters and when the order for withdrawal reached Sammon, who stood with his regiment a short distance from McGrath's spiked battery. This suggests Ford made an attempt to hold the Heights in defiance of Miles's order, but he never threw the 115th New York into the action because he had no authority over Sammon. At one point Downey dropped down the mountain to gather up a few scattered companies. He met Hewitt and asked if he had given the order for the withdrawal. Hewitt admitted both he and Steiner had so ordered. Downey then took command of all the troops on the Heights and hoped Sammon would come up. Downey, with no more than four hundred men, held the summit until Ford's midafternoon order forced his withdrawal. Downey's ammunition was nearly exhausted, and his request for more went unanswered.[42]

In the face of the evidence, one can conclude that neither Miles nor Ford had any idea of how to defend the Heights. Ford had no

40. *Ibid.*, 719–20.
41. *Ibid.*, 625–26.
42. *Ibid.*, 580, 615–17.

tactical training, and Miles, who had been interrupted from his intended visit to Bolivar Heights, may have been troubled by the sound of enemy artillery fire from the direction of Halltown and preparing to pull his command back to the indefensible Ferry for a final stand.

When Miles returned to headquarters, White asked him if he had given an order to evacuate Maryland Heights. The colonel answered with an emphatic "No!" White considered it unlikely Ford would order a retreat without an order, especially since Miles had just come from there. He challenged Miles, asking, "Have you had any conversation with [Ford] in relation to it; was there any discretionary power?" Miles again said "no" but explained he had authorized Ford to "spike the guns and pitch [them] down the mountain" if evacuation became necessary. White asked if those instructions did not imply discretionary approval. Miles replied "Of course," and walked away.[43]

The conversation between White and Miles occurred early in the afternoon, and perhaps early enough for White to assume command and reinforce Maryland Heights, but Miles undoubtedly left the general with the impression that the summit had been abandoned, contrary to his instructions, by Ford. White did not have the benefit of eavesdropping through the stovepipe hole in the Unsell home when Miles and Ford held their secret conference. If he doubted Miles's veracity, he did nothing to change the situation.

Binney later estimated Ford's total force at 4,600 men, with 3,000 of them assigned to the summit. Kershaw's two brigades totaled 2,000. Confederate casualties were very light, with 37 killed and 178 wounded. Union casualties were even lighter but have been commingled with returns from the following day and cannot be isolated for the fight on Maryland Heights.[44]

By late afternoon, the artillery duel on the Charles Town pike faded to a few sporadic shots, but towards evening McLaws advanced two guns from Sandy Hook and hurled a few shots into Harpers Ferry. Most of the shells landed in town and perforated residential rooftops. Miles dispatched two guns to the railroad bed above Sandy Hook and replied in kind.[45]

43. *Ibid.*, 714–15.
44. *Ibid.*, 549, 860–61.
45. *Ibid.*, 537–38.

By dusk all firing stopped. Night fell and everything became quiet. Confederate campfires on Maryland Heights and at Sandy Hook testified to McLaws' presence. Walker's brigade reached the summit of Loudoun Heights unopposed but remained silent. His long-range Parrotts were still some distance down the mountain, and he did not believe Jackson had come up. Jackson, however, camped about three miles south of Bolivar Heights, near Halltown, was in position but awaiting the arrival of Walker. The Harpers Ferry garrison was surrounded on all three sides, but realization of the danger had not yet penetrated the Union command center.[46]

After dark Miles held a meeting with White, Ford, and "Grimes" Davis of the 8th New York Cavalry for the purpose of making contact with McClellan. After some discussion, he asked Russell, who knew the surrounding area better than most, if he thought he could get a message to the Union army. Russell replied he "was willing to try." Miles asked him to select a few men and attempt to "get to any general of the United States Army, or to any telegraph station, or, if possible, get to General McClellan . . . to report that he thought he could hold out forty-eight hours; that he had subsistence for forty-eight hours, but if he was not relieved in that time he would have to surrender the place."

Russell got through the lines and reached Army of the Potomac headquarters at 9 A.M. Sunday, September 14. McClellan listened to the message and assured Russell that Major General Franklin's VI Corps was on its way and would relieve the garrison shortly. McClellan gave Russell a dispatch instructing Franklin to move faster, and the cavalry officer delivered the message at 3 P.M. Sunday afternoon. According to Miles's timetable, Franklin still had at least a day and a half to relieve Harpers Ferry. The VI Corps had a marvelous opportunity to roll up McLaws' flank if Franklin moved fast enough, but much depended upon Miles's determination to check Jackson's advance.[47]

Two hours after Russell left on his nocturnal mission to find the Union army, Miles dispatched a second messenger, Captain Henry Cole of the 1st Maryland Cavalry Potomac Home Brigade.

---

46. Walker, "Jackson's Capture of Harper's Ferry," B&L, II, 608–609; Henry Kyd Douglas, "Stonewall Jackson's Intentions at Harper's Ferry," ibid., 617.
    47. Investigation of Harpers Ferry, OR, XIX, Pt. 1, pp. 720–21.

Cole reached McClellan's headquarters about three hours behind Russell. Unlike Russell, who carried McClellan's hurry-up directive to Franklin, Cole agreed to take the general's message back to Miles. McClellan explained the situation, assured Miles the garrison would be relieved, and urged him to "hold out to the last extremity." He also encouraged the colonel to "reoccupy Maryland Heights with your whole force." McClellan sent at least three couriers to the Ferry with the same message. There is no record of any of them reaching there before Walker's guns opened at 2 P.M. on Sunday afternoon.[48]

But by a curious accident, time was beginning to run out on Lee's invasion of Maryland, and with it the fate of Colonel Dixon Miles.

48. McClellan's Report, *ibid.*, 45–46; Christopher A. Newcomer, *Cole's Cavalry: or, Three Years in the Saddle in the Shenandoah Valley* (Freeport, N.Y., 1970), 44–45.

# 11

## Day of Decision

As Lee marched northwesterly from Frederick on September 10, McClellan moved the Army of the Potomac from Rockville to the abandoned Confederate campgrounds, cautiously inching after Lee's legions while providing protection for Baltimore and Washington. Two days later McClellan sent Major General Ambrose Burnside's IX Army Corps over the Catoctin Mountains in pursuit, and on the far left he sent Franklin's VI Army Corps to open communications with Harpers Ferry. Franklin had presided over the court of inquiry that a year earlier judged Miles drunk during the battle of First Manassas. By a curious coincidence, Franklin now faced a court-martial himself for failing to come to Pope's rescue at Second Manassas. Now, with Lee invading the North, McClellan convinced Halleck he needed Franklin's fighting experience "until I can see my way out of this difficulty."[1]

For McClellan, the opportunity for seeing his way "out of this difficulty" inexplicably materialized on the afternoon of September 13 when Private B. W. Mitchell of the 27th Indiana Volunteers picked up three cigars wrapped neatly in a copy of Lee's most

1. Marcy to Franklin and to Burnside, September 12, 1862, *OR*, LI, Pt. 1, pp. 822, 823; Special Order No. 223, September 5, and McClellan to Halleck, September 6, 1862, *ibid.*, XIX, Pt. 2, pp. 188, 189–90.

secret Special Order No. 191. Colonel Samuel E. Pittman recognized the signature of Lee's adjutant general, Colonel Robert H. Chilton, on the order and announced it genuine. An hour later Mc-Clellan had the Army of the Potomac on the road towards South Mountain, confident that Franklin had ample time to relieve Harpers Ferry and prevent Jackson and McLaws from rejoining Lee.[2]

Late that night when McClellan learned Harpers Ferry had been attacked, he believed the enemy had been repulsed. His information was partially correct. Kershaw had stopped at the first abatis during a rainstorm and, with darkness approaching, withheld his attack until morning. McClellan, cautiously optimistic, assured Halleck he would do everything in his power to rescue Miles "if he still holds out."[3]

At this stage of the Ferry's envelopment, if either Franklin or Burnside moved with speed he would strike McLaws' flank and rear, upset Jackson's plans, and catch Lee's force hopelessly divided. At 6:20 P.M. McClellan wired Franklin the exact details of Jackson's intentions, confirming that McLaws was already approaching the Ferry and advancing up Elk Ridge and through Pleasant Valley. He ordered Franklin to Burkittsville and Jefferson with orders to "cut off, destroy, or capture McLaws' command and relieve Colonel Miles." In an effort to alert Miles to the rescue effort, he sent a detachment from Brigadier General Alfred Pleasonton's cavalry towards the Ferry to fire a few artillery rounds from time to time "so as to let Colonel Miles . . . know our troops are near him." McClellan did not explain how Miles would differentiate friendly rounds from hostile rounds, but he counted upon the colonel to use his cavalry to find out.[4]

Franklin marched to Crampton's Gap on the morning of September 14 and at noon reached Burkittsville, where he found Confederate infantry drawn up on both sides of the road and artillery defending the approaches to the pass. Franklin pressed the enemy back, forcing the defenders up and over the mountain. By nightfall he had part of his corps in Pleasant Valley and engaging McLaws' rear regiments. Advance units approached to within three and a half miles from the summit of Maryland Heights and less than six

2. Silas Colgrove, "The Finding of Lee's Lost Order," *B&L*, II, 603.
3. McClellan to Halleck, September 13, 1862, *OR*, XIX, Pt. 1, p. 785.
4. McClellan to Franklin, September 13, 1862, *ibid.*, 45–46; Marcy to Pleasonton, September 13, 1862, *ibid.*, LI, Pt. 1, p. 829.

miles from Harpers Ferry. Had Miles not withdrawn his force from Maryland Heights, Franklin may have made a junction with Ford's defenders that night or early the next morning.[5]

Late on September 13 Lee learned that McClellan was moving with surprising speed. The Confederate chieftain did not understand the unexpected pressure from the Union army until an informant reached headquarters the following day and warned him of the lost order. Lee cautioned McLaws that Franklin's corps was on his flank and moving towards Harpers Ferry. He stressed the importance of expediting the capture of the town and ordered McLaws to withdraw and hasten to Sharpsburg if this could not be done quickly.[6]

Despite Lee's warning, McLaws inexplicably occupied the summit of Maryland Heights but made no further effort to take possession of the slope or to pursue Ford's retreating defenders. McLaws' reluctance to push forward was his awareness of Franklin's corps intervening between himself and Lee's main army. He also worried about Jackson's corps and Walker's brigade, separated by a river, becoming isolated and swallowed up by an unseen enemy advancing undetected from some other direction.

Early Sunday morning, September 14, Jackson grew impatient with McLaws and ordered him to "move forward until you get complete possession of the Maryland Heights." Unaware of Franklin's approach, Jackson's only concern was to get McLaws' batteries emplaced where they could enfilade Camp Hill and Bolivar Heights. "So soon as you get your batteries all planted, let me know," Jackson declared, "as I desire after yourself, Walker, and myself have our batteries ready to open, to send in a flag of truce, for the purpose of getting out the non-combatants, should the commanding officer refuse to surrender. Should we have to attack, let the work be done thoroughly; fire on the houses when necessary. Demolish the place if it is occupied by the enemy and does not surrender." What remained of the once industrious community of Harpers Ferry now faced total destruction.[7]

Jackson had no time to waste, but his artillery was scattered along the road and not in position, and McLaws' delay in bringing

5. McClellan's Report, October 15, 1862, *ibid.*, XIX, Pt. 1, p. 46.
6. Talcott to McLaws, September 13, 1862, *ibid.*, Pt. 2, p. 607.
7. Jackson to McLaws, September 14, 1862, *ibid.*

up his guns cost precious hours. At 10:30 A.M. Walker signaled Jackson from Loudoun Heights that he was ready to open fire. McLaws, however, was not. Heavy firing in the rear of his division gave him grave concern. Soon after receiving Jackson's order to post his artillery on Maryland Heights, McLaws received assurance from Lee that Longstreet was on the way to protect his flank. Major General Daniel H. Hill's force held the gap through South Mountain, Lee declared, and if McLaws was pressed too hard by Franklin, the gap would be kept open for him to withdraw to Sharpsburg "as soon as operations at Harper's Ferry are finished." Later, when Hill's defense collapsed, McLaws received a second message from Lee suggesting an escape route into Virginia if his division was cut off from the main army.[8]

McLaws worried about becoming isolated. With artillery fire in his rear increasing in intensity and with Jackson waiting impatiently in front of Bolivar Heights, McLaws lost time deciding what to do. He worried that Jackson was unaware of Lee's situation, but since he was under Jackson's orders, McLaws ordered his guns forward. He did not get two batteries of four guns up the mountain until late afternoon, and after the afternoon's artillery exchange he withdrew two of the guns to protect his rear, leaving Captain John P. W. Read's battery of two guns on the Heights.[9]

Shortly before noon, Jackson signaled Walker, "Harper's Ferry is now completely invested. I shall summon the commander to surrender. Should he refuse, I shall give him twenty-four hours to remove the non-combatants and then carry the place by assault. *Do not fire unless forced to.*" Walker had exchanged signals with Maryland Heights, where anxiety had been building. He could clearly hear heavy artillery fire at Crampton's Gap and signaled Jackson that the enemy was in McLaws' rear, and McClellan, no doubt, was advancing in force. Jackson, who had not yet been informed of McClellan's movement, replied laconically that the firing was no more than a cavalry skirmish between Stuart and Pleasonton.[10]

8. Walker, "Jackson's Capture of Harper's Ferry," *B&L*, II, 609; Lee to McLaws, and Chilton to McLaws, September 14, 1862, *OR*, XIX, Pt. 2, p. 608.

9. A. H. McLaws to General McLaws, September 14, 1862, *OR*, XIX, Pt. 2, p. 608; McLaws' Report, October 18, and Kershaw's Report, September 25, 1862, *ibid.*, Pt. 1, pp. 854–55, 864.

10. Walker, "Jackson's Capture of Harper's Ferry," *B&L*, II, 609.

Walker, convinced that Jackson had misread the seriousness of the situation, requested permission to open fire. He did not believe twenty-four hours could be wasted waiting for Miles to surrender. When Jackson did not reply to his signal, Walker decided to force the issue. He advanced two North Carolina regiments to the brow of Loudoun Heights to bait enemy artillery. Federal batteries on Bolivar Heights swung into action and opened on the Carolinians. Walker withdrew his men to the safe side of the mountain and answered with his Parrotts. Jackson eventually signaled both McLaws and Walker to "fire at such positions of the enemy as will be most effective," but the order does not reveal the time it was sent.[11] After Walker opened, Jackson's artillery followed, but McLaws did not have his batteries in position for another two hours.

If an agreement had been struck between Miles and parolee Rouss to surrender the Ferry without a fight, Walker's disobedience of Jackson's orders at 2 P.M. on the afternoon of September 14 changed the course of events, but in the end altered them only slightly.

Major McIlvaine, Miles's artillery chief, counted seven Confederate batteries firing from Loudoun Heights, Maryland Heights, the Charles Town pike, and the Shepherdstown road. Trimble claimed ten. McIlvaine had about forty guns, and none of them were in position to reach either McLaws or Walker. When General White attempted to concentrate fire on Jackson's artillery, McLaws moved a battery directly across the river and enfiladed the position.[12]

The concentration of Confederate artillery pounding Camp Hill and Bolivar Heights quickly demoralized the Union greenhorns. When Walker's artillery lofted a few shells among the troops on Bolivar Heights, they scurried off the plateau and ran for cover. Lieutenant Binney, evidently writing as he watched, reported, "The cannonade is now terrific. The enemy's shot and shell fall in every direction; houses are demolished and detonation among the hills is terrible."[13]

11. *Ibid.*; Jackson to McLaws and Walker, September 14, 1862, *OR*, XIX, Pt. 1, p. 959.

12. Binney's Report, September 18, McIlvaine's Report, September 19, 1862, and Investigation of Harpers Ferry, *OR*, XIX, Pt. 1, pp. 538, 548, 742.

13. Binney's Report, September 18, 1862, *ibid.*, 538.

Colonel George L. Willard's 125th New York fled into a ravine along the north shore of the Shenandoah. Willard was unable to rally the unit until late in the afternoon when Jackson's infantry attacked the 3rd Maryland Potomac Home Brigade. By coincidence, Willard's regiment reinforced the weak left flank by their chaotic dash to safety.[14]

As in most artillery duels, the noise, smoke, and dust caused little injury but created great consternation. Companies accustomed to being under fire lay in their earthworks and amused themselves by counting the little black dots arcing towards them. A few observers remarked on the inferiority of Confederate shells. Some exploded in the air, but most of them just thudded into the soft mud or tumbled about on the rocks. Green troops, spotting a falling missile, dodged from one place of cover to another, thinking every shell would drop into their haversacks. Many sought refuge in homes and, joined by frightened occupants, crowded into wet cellars.[15]

Union guns roared back, often haphazardly and at unseen targets. White observed that few shots ever reached enemy artillery posted on the Heights. Having no jurisdiction over the batteries, he looked for Miles and found the commander pacing about at headquarters. He asked the colonel to issue an order for certain batteries to cease fire, as they were "wasting ammunition to no purpose." The colonel wrote the order and dispatched it by an orderly, but supplies at some batteries had already reached critical levels.[16]

At 3 p.m. Jackson advanced Hill's division, striking the weak Union left on Bolivar Heights. Downey's 3rd Maryland Potomac Home Brigade had been placed there after withdrawing from Maryland Heights and met the attack with stiff resistance. Downey, however, realized he could not hold the position without reinforcements. He sent "eight or ten" volunteers to "hunt up" Miles, but received no answer. Trimble's brigade, posted to the right of Downey, offered no help, as it was under attack. Neither Downey nor Trimble had any authority over several units almost

14. Investigation of Harpers Ferry, *ibid.*, 560.

15. Willson, *"Boys in Blue,"* 79; W. M. Luff, "March of the Cavalry from Harper's Ferry, September 14, 1862," *Military Essays and Recollections* (Chicago, 1894), II, 37.

16. Investigation of Harpers Ferry, *OR*, XIX, Pt. 1, pp. 630, 652, 654.

within hailing distance, although none had been engaged. Willard's 125th New York, demoralized by the shelling from Loudoun Heights, lay in ravines or crouched behind rocks and refused to fight. One of Downey's couriers finally located General White, who rode over to the left and attempted to direct the action.[17]

Jackson, however, only meant for Hill to turn the Union left and be in position for the main thrust on Monday. Hill shelled the route over which he intended to move and sent two brigades under Lawrence O'B Branch and Maxcy Gregg along the Shenandoah River, as well as three brigades under William Dorsey Pender, James J. Archer, and John M. Brockenbrough to gain the crest of the hill above the river. Branch and Gregg stayed below the brow of the ravine and hacked their way to the rear of the enemy, where they lay concealed throughout the night. The other three brigades nudged Downey and Trimble back towards Camp Hill, enabling Lieutenant Colonel Reuben L. Walker to bring up his guns during the night and have them positioned to bombard the enemy earthworks at dawn Monday.[18]

Miles had posted most of his command and artillery along the northern half of Bolivar Heights, but his earthworks were flimsy. For their own protection, Union regiments cut abatis and dug a double line of rifle pits, one along the ridge and one halfway down the western slope. The fortifications were strong enough to fight off a frontal attack but were poorly constructed to meet a flank attack from the weakly defended left. Aside from Downey's 3rd Maryland Potomac Home Brigade, Miles had no force on the far left near an incline named Bull's Hill but a few skirmishers from Trimble's brigade.[19]

White could neither determine the size of the force in Downey's front nor see the Confederate flankers, but he saw enough to advise Miles to contract the lines by swinging Downey and Trimble backwards to protect the left flank by forming the short leg of an L. White explained that the shuffling would enable one side of the line to readily support the other and, if necessary, draw quickly upon reinforcements entrenched on Camp Hill. White

17. *Ibid.*, 622, 742, 745.

18. A. P. Hill's Report, February 25, and R. L. Walker's Report, March 1, 1863, *OR*, XIX, Pt. 1, pp. 980, 984.

19. Harry W. Pfanz, *Special History Report: Troop Movement Maps, 1862* (Springfield, Va., 1976), 73, 83.

also explained that the artillery on Camp Hill could not be employed effectively as long as it fired over units entrenched a few hundred yards in their front. Miles refused to make any adjustments, stating he would fight it out on Bolivar Heights "in case he was obliged to."[20]

When Pender's and Brockenbrough's brigades struck Downey's thinly manned left, the outnumbered 3rd Maryland held out long enough for White to bring up Stannard's 9th Vermont and Ford's 32nd Ohio. Archer's brigade of Tennesseeans, Georgians, and Alabamians became hopelessly entangled in snarled vines and fallen trees, from which they failed to emerge until late the following day. Downey, Stannard, and Ford, supported by accurate fire from Rigby's battery near the Charles Town pike, stopped the Confederates about sixty yards from the Union lines. At 8 P.M. Pender attempted to storm the battery, but Rigby ordered the guns double-shotted with grape and canister and repulsed the attack. James Clark of the 115th New York watched the bayonet charge on Rigby's battery and wrote, "The awful storm of iron swept like a dreadful tornado through the enemy's ranks. When the smoke of battle lifted, swaths of rebel dead and wounded lay on the ground; while their comrades, uninjured, were hurrying from the field of carnage."[21]

Pender's command withdrew in confusion and the men rested on their arms about 150 yards from Rigby's battery, but White, seizing an unexpected opportunity, made preparations for a counterattack. If he could drive Pender off Bull's Hill, and do it before dark, Jackson's attack would stall. Although White did not know that help was on the way, capturing Bull's Hill might have given Franklin more time to bring up the VI Army Corps. To oust Pender required more troops, and White called up Colonel Ward's 12th New York Militia, which lay in reserve on Camp Hill. Word of White's intentions got back to Miles, who promptly dispatched an aide to recall the regiment, declaring that Camp Hill must be held.[22]

20. Investigation of Harpers Ferry, OR, XIX, Pt. 1, pp. 606–607.

21. White's Report, September 20, 1862, Archer's Report, March 1, 1863, and Pender's Report, October 14, 1862, *ibid.*, 527, 1000, 1004; James H. Clark, *The Iron Hearted Regiment: Being an Account of the Battles, Marches, and Gallant Deeds Performed by the 115th Regiment, N.Y. Volunteers* (Albany, N.Y., 1865), 17.

22. Hill's Report, February 25, 1863, and White's Report, September 25, 1862, OR, XIX, Pt. 1, pp. 980, 531.

The recall of a tactically sound counterattack adds to the growing list of acts fortifying the theory that Miles intended to sacrifice Harpers Ferry. Miles, however, made both good and bad decisions, which is typical of a person whose competence is overstretched by uncommon circumstances. The good decisions go unrecognized, and the bad ones cost dearly. Miles's failure to force Pender off Bull's Hill became almost as serious as his evacuation of Maryland Heights. Driving Pender back would have isolated the brigades of Branch and Gregg in the rear of Bolivar Heights. In the morning Jackson would have had to reorganize his attack, and the situation developing in Lee's front may have compelled Jackson to withdraw.

Lee contacted McLaws, advising "the day has gone against us," and ordered a withdrawal to Sharpsburg. A similar message (unfound) went to Jackson, urging him to finish the business at the Ferry. Jackson advised Lee that his advance had functioned like clockwork and his losses were light, promising "complete success tomorrow."[23] Jackson wanted more than Harpers Ferry. He wanted Miles's force removed from Lee's rear and the garrison's fifteen hundred fine horses and equipage captured for Stuart's cavalry.

On Saturday evening following the evacuation of Maryland Heights, a young West Pointer, Lieutenant Colonel Benjamin F. "Grimes" Davis, commanding the 8th New York Cavalry, proposed a scheme to break out of the Ferry. He asked permission to lead the cavalry a short distance up the Shenandoah, cross to the base of Loudoun Heights, and then race down the south bank of the Potomac to Washington. After agreeing to the plan, Miles changed his mind, claiming that "the river was full of holes, and . . . impossible to cross." As White later discovered, the Shenandoah might not have been as easily crossed as Davis suggested.[24]

During the artillery bombardment Sunday afternoon, the cavalry commanders met again and unanimously agreed to break out at nightfall. Although Colonel Arno Voss of the 12th Illinois Cavalry ranked Davis, the various commanders appointed Davis as their spokesman and tested their plan on White. He agreed and joined the trek to headquarters to get Miles's approval. Davis argued the cavalry was of no use at the Ferry. If the garrison surren-

23. Chilton to McLaws, September 12, and Jackson to Chilton, September 14, 1862, *ibid.*, LI, Pt. 2, pp. 618–19, 951.

24. Investigation of Harpers Ferry, *ibid.*, XIX, Pt. 1, pp. 630, 718.

dered, the horses would represent "as great a prize as the enemy could get."[25]

Miles opposed the plan, discarding it as "impractical and involving too much risk." Davis warned he would take out whoever would follow him, with or without the colonel's consent. White pressed for approval. Miles deliberated and finally agreed—but only if "a practical route could be found."[26]

Early in the evening, while guns roared on Bolivar Heights, Miles called a meeting of cavalry leaders to discuss the best route. Davis suggested going up the western bank of the Potomac and crossing near Shepherdstown. Miles declared the route too dangerous and ordered them to cross the pontoon bridge and go up the Maryland side, taking the Harpers Ferry road along the Potomac to Antietam Furnace, Sharpsburg, and the Williamsport road. He demanded secrecy, as he did not want the infantry to learn of the cavalry's departure.[27] Miles had no way of knowing he was sending the cavalry directly towards the camp of the enemy. The decision simply provides another example of Miles's tendency to discard a subordinate's suggestion in favor of his own.

Miles ordered the cavalry to leave the Ferry at 8 p.m., but Davis and Colonel Voss, the nominal commander of the escape, waited until dark.[28] More than fifteen hundred cavalrymen, marching in columns of twos, consumed two hours crossing the pontoon bridge under the brow of McLaws' two guns on Maryland Heights. The pitch-black night masked the crossing, and sod placed on the planks of the pontoons deadened the sound of thousands of hoofbeats pounding across the river. If Confederate pickets heard the soft rumble of moving horseflesh, they said not a word to their commanders.

Thomas Noakes of Martinsburg and Michael Burkett, aided by scouts from the 1st Maryland Potomac Home Brigade and the 1st Maryland Cavalry, guided the riders through the countryside, probing ahead for Confederate patrols. They touched the fringes of the van of the enemy near Sharpsburg, skimming Lee's main army encamped at Boonsboro. Artillery opened, and a few rounds

25. *Ibid.*, 583; Pettengill, *The College Cavaliers*, 77.

26. Henry King Norton, *Deeds of Daring; or, History of the 8th New York Volunteer Cavalry* (Norwich, N.Y., 1889), 27; Luff, "March of the Cavalry," 38.

27. Investigation of Harper's Ferry, *OR*, XIX, Pt. 1, p. 584.

28. Luff, "March of the Cavalry," 39.

crashed into a nearby woods. Voss and Davis jogged on, keeping the files closed up. When they reached the Williamsport-Boonsboro road at dawn, scouts warned of a wagon train approaching from the east. The 12th Illinois Cavalry filed into the woods on the south side of the Williamsport road and waited. Colonel Davis concealed the 8th New York in the woods on the opposite side of the road near the College of St. James, and both units waited for the wagons to approach. As Longstreet's and Jackson's Reserve Artillery began to pass, the 12th Illinois and the 8th New York pounced on the train and captured about ninety-six wagons, most of them loaded with ammunition and ordnance supplies. Mistaking the dust-covered Union cavalry for their own, the teamsters remained unconcerned until their captors swung them north on the Downsville turnpike. By then it was too late. A few drivers scuttled their wagons in ditches, where they were burned, but by 9 A.M. Voss and Davis had the train across the Mason-Dixon Line and into Greencastle, Pennsylvania.[29]

For General Robert E. Lee, the loss of the ordnance wagons proved crucial during the forthcoming Battle of Antietam. After becoming aware of the unanticipated loss of ammunition, Lee dispatched Lieutenant Colonel Edward P. Alexander to Harpers Ferry to gather up all the captured ordnance and rush it to Sharpsburg. Alexander found only a little canister, which he promptly forwarded, but most of the cannon had been mounted on the wrong limbers by A. P. Hill's infantry and could not be moved. Lee depleted most of his ammunition fighting to a stalemate at Antietam, and with many of his guns disabled he had no alternative but to withdraw. Some credit for Lee's decision to retire must be given to the accidental capture of Longstreet's and Jackson's reserve ordnance. Quite by accident, Miles contributed in some

29. *Ibid.*, 39–42; Pettengill, *The College Cavaliers,* 81–83; Newcomer, *Cole's Cavalry,* 42–43; James V. Murfin covers this colorful escape in detail in *The Gleam of Bayonets: The Battle of Antietam and the Maryland Campaign of 1862* (New York, 1965), 147–54, 191–96; Francis Dawson, *Reminiscences of Confederate Service, 1861–1865* (Baton Rouge, 1980), 63–66. The actual number of wagons captured or burned may never be known, as reports ranged from forty to more than a hundred. Robert E. Lee, on September 21, 1862, advised President Davis of the loss of the ordnance train but claimed only forty-five wagons had been lost or destroyed; see *OR,* XIX, Pt. 1, p. 142.

small way to Lee's repulse by sending the cavalry along the Harpers Ferry road and not by the routes suggested by Davis and Voss.[30]

On Sunday evening, before Voss led the first units of the Union cavalry across the pontoon bridge, Cole arrived at Miles's headquarters with McClellan's message. By a separate messenger, McClellan had dispatched one of his own scouts to carry the same message to Miles. The colonel now knew McClellan was on his way and in force. "Hold out to the last extremity," McClellan ordered, and if possible, "reoccupy the Maryland Heights with your whole force." Why Miles pocketed the message and shared it with no one cannot be explained, unless those who claimed to deliver it falsified their statements. Cole returned to the Ferry just in time to join his Maryland command as they followed Davis into Pennsylvania. Had Miles met with his brigade commanders to share the good news that relief was imminent, there may have been no surrender on Monday morning. Binney, the colonel's aide who seldom strayed far from his side, claimed neither Russell nor Cole ever returned to the Ferry. On this matter the truth may never be known, as the Harper's Ferry Commission never called Cole or McClellan's courier to testify.[31]

Before the cavalry escape late Sunday night, Miles must have alluded to surrendering the garrison in the morning instead of defending it until evening, as he had promised in the messages Cole and Russell carried to McClellan. "Grimes" Davis either knew or sensed the colonel's intentions. As soon as he reached Greencastle he notified authorities that Miles would surrender in the morning.[32] Paul R. Teetor, one of many contemporary historians suspecting the colonel of treason, wrote, "When Miles was suddenly and unexpectedly faced with the prospect of relief by McClellan, his immediate reaction was to *change his own surrender schedule to beat McClellan's relief schedule.* Stonewall Jackson could have

30. Crutchfield's Report, April 16, 1863, *OR*, XIX, Pt. 1, pp. 962–63; E. P. Alexander, *Military Memoirs of a Confederate* (Boston, 1905), 272; Dawson, *Reminiscences*, 63–66, 101–105.

31. McClellan to Miles, September 14, 1862, *OR*, XIX, Pt. 1, p. 45; Newcomer, *Cole's Cavalry*, 43; Investigation of Harpers Ferry, *OR*, XIX, Pt. 1, pp. 586, 720–21; Newcomer, *Cole's Cavalry*, 43–45; Murfin, *Gleam of Bayonets*, 132–33. Aside from Russell's testimony and Newcomer's statement in *Cole's Cavalry*, there is no hard evidence that Miles ever received McClellan's letter.

32. Curtin to Stanton, September 15, 1862, *OR*, XIX, Pt. 2, p. 305.

asked for no more."³³ The good news that the Army of the Potomac was on the way may have died that night in the depths of Miles's pocket.

Others serving under Miles simply considered the colonel incompetent. But none of the senior officers bonded together with enough resolve to ask White to take command, although many thought he should, and no colonel would risk ousting Miles with a general present.³⁴

If Colonel Willard of the 125th New York had had his way, he would have withdrawn the entire force into the town, where "many old walls, stone walls, bridges and rocks" offered safe protection. Willard's statement characterized the caliber of Miles's brigade commanders as men of no military experience. Willard's green soldiers had already demonstrated an aversion to artillery fire when they sought refuge in ravines on the far left after artillery opened from Loudoun Heights.³⁵ Willard sounded like a man who had no more fight in his blood than his greenhorns.

If nothing else, Miles's resolve to surrender early Monday morning spared the town from the devastation of Jackson's artillery and Willard's ineptitude . . . but not entirely. Mrs. Jessie E. Johnson, who witnessed Jackson's first attack from her home in Bolivar, wrote, "Grandfather came home . . . during the day and had some business to transact at HF proper [and] when he started he had no idea a battle would be fought that day. He started downtown dressed in white linen which made him a good target. So they fired so upon him from the mountain he had to go [into] the old foundation of the Methodist Church. He had to stay there all day, [and] when dark came here he came . . . we had been so worried about him."³⁶

That night, while Jessie Johnson's grandfather recovered from

33. Teetor, *A Matter of Hours,* 178; see also Allan L. Tischler, *The History of the Harpers Ferry Cavalry Expedition, September 14 and 15, 1862* (Winchester, Va., 1993), which covers the entire escape and attempts to clarify the relationships between Colonels Miles, Voss, and Davis and to correct some historical inconsistencies spawned by conflicting eyewitness statements, direct testimony, and tainted official correspondence.

34. Investigation of Harpers Ferry, *OR,* XIX, Pt. 1, pp. 622–24.

35. *Ibid.,* 541, 563.

36. Johnson (Mrs. Charles Gibbs) Letters, File HFD-418, HFA. The letter appears in the file as anonymous and is dated September 15, 1862.

his expedition to the Ferry, Union troops, thinly strung out on Bolivar Heights, rested on their arms. All night they listened to the rumbling of artillery from Jackson's camp and heard the voices of the enemy as they advanced fresh batteries. Along the plateau in their front thousands of campfires dotted the countryside. Men made their peace with God. There would be hell to pay in the morning.

# 12

## Changing of the Guard

At dawn, September 15, a thick mist rolled down the Valley and lay heavy upon the Heights. Both camps stirred, waiting for the ball to open. During the night Jackson brought up five batteries from Hill's division and placed them near the Charles Town pike. Colonel Stapleton Crutchfield, Jackson's artillery chief, lugged ten guns across the Shenandoah and positioned them on Bull's Hill, where they could enfilade Rigby's and Potts's batteries. Branch and Gregg passed down the Shenandoah undetected, climbed the vine-entangled bank, and lay in the rear of the Union left. Ewell's division, led by Brigadier General Alexander Lawton, lay in the woods on Schoolhouse Hill and prepared to assault the southern sector of Bolivar Heights. Jackson, who loved his artillery almost as much as he loved his God, had over fifty guns bearing on the enemy, every one of them assigned to a specific target.[1]

With time running out on Lee, Jackson realized he must strike hard and, at whatever cost in men, overrun the two Union batteries covering the Charles Town pike. With daylight crowning the hills, he sent A. P. Hill forward, supported on the right flank by Lawton, whose brigade had hunkered down between School-

1. Jackson's Report, April 23, 1863, *OR*, XIX, Pt. 1, p. 954; Julius White, "The Surrender of Harper's Ferry," *B&L*, II, 613.

house Hill and Bolivar Heights. Hill's batteries opened at about a thousand yards, enfilading the Union left. Lawton opened from Schoolhouse Hill, concentrating fire on Rigby's and Potts's batteries. Crutchfield opened from the rear, lofting shells into enemy positions west of the pike. Two batteries played on the Union right, and from Loudoun Heights Walker's guns sent shells into the rear of the defenders on Camp Hill. McLaws fired at long range from atop Maryland Heights in the general direction of Camp Hill, but because of fog none of his artillerymen could see their targets.[2]

The heaviest fire fell among the men supporting Rigby's and Potts's batteries, who lay on the ground in forward positions awaiting Jackson's assault, but most of Miles's infantry took shelter in ravines or shallow trenches and weathered the shelling. An hour into the artillery exchange Union batteries exhausted their long-range ammunition, but they still had shrapnel and canister.[3] Gunners slowed their fire. Most batteries stopped altogether, conserving ammunition for the expected attack.

Jackson interpreted the lull as a sign that Union batteries had been disabled or withdrawn. He ordered Hill's gunners to cease fire, the prearranged signal for the infantry to storm the Federal works. Pender led the charge but double-quicked into a hail of canister from the guns of Rigby and Potts. Hill ordered up two batteries, Pegram's and Crenshaw's, and placed them about four hundred yards from the Union front. For thirty minutes a heavy fire whizzed over the heads of Pender's infantry. With only short-range ammunition, neither Rigby nor Potts could reply.[4]

Rigby's repeated calls for shot and powder went unanswered. Four of the batteries protecting Bolivar Heights reported they would have to withdraw for want of ammunition. Miles, who wandered about Bolivar Heights during much of the shelling, knew the situation had become critical for the gunners. The tour took him to the left, where he found White near the front. The general angrily asked why more ammunition had not been brought up. Binney claimed that Miles looked puzzled and said "he did not know what he should do. He did not see that he could

---

2. Jackson's Report, April 23, 1863, *OR*, XIX, Pt. 1, p. 955; Walker, "Jackson's Capture of Harper's Ferry," *B&L*, II, 610.

3. Investigation of Harpers Ferry, *OR*, XIX, Pt. 1, pp. 651, 654, 664, 684.

4. Jackson's Report, April 23, and Hill's Report, February 25, 1863, *ibid.*, 955, 980.

hold out much longer without the butchery and slaughter of his men" and asked White's advice in the matter. "White," Binney claimed, "did not seem inclined to recommend a surrender or anything of that sort."[5] Although the shelling had been heavy, White had just finished circulating through the ranks and reported casualties light.

Miles thought the time had come to surrender, but White demanded a consultation with brigade commanders before showing the white flag. At 9 A.M. the colonel called the council, but the only officers attending besides himself were White, D'Utassy, and Trimble. Each left slightly conflicting accounts of the meeting, but White's stands as the most credible as he simply admitted "the council of war was unanimous in the opinion that further resistance was useless." Trimble, with frail hope of holding the weak left, declared that "under actual existing conditions, nothing else is to be done but to surrender." Trimble admitted he could have held out longer, but as soon as the enemy attacked, his panicky men "like wild asses or colts . . . would have run into danger rather than out of it." D'Utassy, however, replied, "I will never surrender as long as I have a shot." According to D'Utassy, Miles began to curse and asked, "How many shots have you?" D'Utassy did not know and sent for his battery commanders. When they reported four rounds of long-range ammunition between them, D'Utassy admitted he could "do nothing else but surrender, particularly as you [Miles] are averse to cutting your way out."[6]

During the council Miles neglected to dig through his pockets for the message from McClellan heralding the approach of Franklin's corps. Trimble later admitted that "nothing would have led him to countenance a surrender if he thought that relief was a real possibility."[7] White, also kept in the dark, alluded to McClellan's failure to rescue the garrison as one of his compelling reasons for surrender.[8]

Miles appointed White as commissioner and sent him to the

5. Investigation of Harpers Ferry, *ibid.*, 584.

6. White to Wool, September 16, White to Whipple, September 22, White to Thomas, September 25, 1862, and Investigation of Harpers Ferry, *ibid.*, 523, 528, 529, 530–31, 598–99, 744.

7. Investigation of Harpers Ferry, *ibid.*, 744. Whether Miles ever received such a note is uncertain, as it was never found, only alleged.

8. *Ibid.*, 531.

front to arrange honorable surrender terms. If nothing else, the gesture was curious. The colonel had clutched command of Harpers Ferry with the tenacity of a tyrant, but he sent the general to face the ignominy of surrender. D'Utassy and Trimble returned to their brigades and ordered white flags hoisted along the lines.[9]

Many Union soldiers reported the rumble of distant artillery fire and swore the Army of the Potomac was on its way. Miles ignored the information. He passed among the defenders, ordering out anything white. Captain Philo Phillips of the 126th New York stopped him and grumbled, "For _____'s sake, Colonel, don't surrender us. Don't you hear the signal guns? Our forces are near us. Let us cut our way out and join them."

"Impossible!" Miles replied, "They will blow us out of this [place] in half an hour."

Phillips disagreed, replying that even a loss of a thousand men was worth fighting it out until relieved.

"Do you know who I am?" Miles asked indignantly.

"I do," Phillips replied indifferently. "You are Colonel Miles."

Phillips turned away in disgust and started back to his command when a shell exploded nearby. He looked back and saw Miles lying on the ground, his left calf shattered to the bone. "Good!" Phillips declared. He later wrote that "the rest felt it if they did not say it. It was difficult to find a man who would take [Miles] to the hospital."[10]

Men from the 9th Vermont, however, brought blankets and, with help from the 126th New York, escorted the wounded colonel to the rear. As they passed Rigby's battery, one of the guns opened on the enemy. Miles looked up and saw the colors still flying above the battery. "Why don't they haul down that Goddamned flag?" Miles shouted to Binney. "It has been the death of me." The colonel had but a day to live, and the pain he suffered was not unlike the agony felt by the men he so willingly surrendered. From field officer to private, the 9th Vermont distrusted Miles, and like every other regiment defending the Ferry, they suspected him of treachery. "God alone knows the truth of it,"

9. White, "The Surrender of Harper's Ferry," B&L, II, 614.

10. Binney's Report, September 18, 1862, OR, XIX, Pt. 1, p. 539; Willson, "Boys in Blue," 84–85.

Colonel Ripley wrote, "and will reward him for his patriotism or punish him for his treason."[11]

Colonel Benjamin W. Thompson of the 111th New York remembered the moment a little differently:

> When morning dawned we saw a line of rebel batteries on the slight elevations in front of us, not a half mile away. Of course they were supported by infantry, which we could not see. We were all expecting an order to attack this line when the Colonel commanding our brigade came riding behind our lines, requesting in a loud voice, "There will not be one shot fired. You are surrendered."
>
> If these men had been veterans instead of recruits of yesterday, there would have been trouble. I have never seen ten thousand men all terribly angry in my life but this once. After a time, the line got in motion to go back up Bolivar Heights to be surrendered. The men broke their guns against the trees as they passed them and did every ugly thing they dared. When we came up the hill we found one of our batteries firing and two or three rebel guns replying. It seems this battery had refused to surrender. . . . Col. Miles rode up in person and ordered a sergeant to put up a white flag. The sergeant refused with an oath. Col. Miles jumped from his horse, tied his white handkerchief to his sword blade and climbed on one of the guns to wave [it]. Just at that moment a shell from an enemy gun struck one of his legs and he fell to the ground.[12]

Ironically, Miles received his mortal wound ten or fifteen minutes after the first white flag showed along the Union lines. With smoke covering part of the field and mist still lingering in the mountaintops, a chance shot from Walker's gunners on Loudoun Heights probably caused Miles's death. Thirty-three years later, however, C. A. Newcomer published a history of Cole's cavalry and claimed that after the surrender Miles was shot by one of his own gunners. Evidence to support the claim is inconclusive but demonstrates the exasperation of the common soldiers towards their commander. "If he was a traitor," Newcomer wrote, "he received his just desserts."[13]

11. E. H. Ripley, "Memories of the Ninth Vermont at the Tragedy of Harper's Ferry," *Personal Recollections of the War of the Rebellion* (New York, 1909), IV, 157–58.

12. Benjamin W. Thompson, "Recollections of War Times," 22–23, Civil War Times Illustrated Collection, USAMHI.

13. Newcomer, *Cole's Cavalry*, 41. Celeste B. Newcomer, writing in 1906 from Michigan to her parents in Harpers Ferry, collected an account from a Mr. Parks,

Sometime later an account appeared in an Indiana newspaper confirming that after Miles hoisted the white flag, Captain John C. H. Von Schlen's 15th Battery, Indiana Light Artillery, continued to fire, presumably at the enemy. General Jackson stormed up to the battery, which was near the center of the line, and shouted, "Where's the captain of this battery?"

"I am the captain," Von Schlen replied.

"You or your men fired after the white flag was up."

"We are your prisoners by agreement with General White," Von Schlen replied unapologetically.

"Well, Captain," Jackson asked coldly, "what was the meaning of this firing after capitulation? I suppose you know the penalty for violating the rules of war."

"Yes, but I could not avoid it."

"Why not?"

"I got my guns so widely scattered that I could not command them all at once."

"This is preposterous," Jackson replied. "Get your battery in line in a proper manner."

"I will as soon as possible," Von Schlen replied. Then turning to a nearby artilleryman, he said, "Sergeant . . . call the men to bring them into line."[14]

Captain Benjamin Lee of the 126th New York corralled some volunteers and carried Miles from the field. On the way to the hospital another shell exploded, wounding Lee in the thigh and blowing away the colonel's hat. Lee survived the wound, but Miles suffered horrible pain until he died at 4:30 P.M. on September 16. Binney, sitting by the colonel's bedside, heard the commander's last cogent words, "I have done my duty. I am an old soldier and willing to die." He whispered only one regret—not living long enough to see his subordinates, especially General White, receive full credit for the defense of Harpers Ferry—but he condemned the government for being too slow in sending help.[15]

---

who claimed to have witnessed Phillips order "gun number three" to load a half-second shell and fire it at the back of Colonel Miles, who at the time was riding away from the battery. Celeste B. Newcomer to her parents, March 28, 1906, File HFD-338, HFA.

14. Newspaper article, n.d., Von Schlen Papers, Civil War Miscellaneous Collection, USAMHI.

15. Binney's Report, September 18, 1862, *OR*, XIX, Pt. 1, pp. 539, 540; Auburn (N.Y.) *Daily*, September 20, 1862.

General Jackson's brief visit to the Union lines gave most of the dejected defenders their first glimpse at a "rebel." They beheld a ragged assortment of raw-boned men, many without shoes. Everything about them seemed to be covered with filth but their rifles, which glistened in the morning sun. Jackson could barely be distinguished from his rabble, as he "dressed in the coarsest kind of homespun, seedy and dirty at that; wore an old hat which any Northern beggar would consider an insult to offer him, and in his general appearance was in no respect to be distinguished from the mongrel, barefooted crew who follow his fortunes."[16]

Colonel Thompson of the 111th New York spoke to Jackson directly, recalling that Stonewall was a little cleaner than his men, who had not had their clothes off for six weeks. The general wore only one button on his coat. He told Thompson that he had been forced to give the others "as souvenirs to Maryland ladies."[17]

Hill accepted the surrender of Harpers Ferry, and Jackson, finding the garrison's prized horses gone, put the rest of his corps on the road and ordered a forced march to Sharpsburg, crossing at Shepherdstown. Hill paroled 11,000 prisoners, itemizing the spoils at 13,000 stand of arms, 73 pieces of artillery, a large quantity of wagons, and commissary, quartermaster, and ordnance stores. Hill's division did not leave the Ferry until 6:30 the following morning, reaching Sharpsburg just in time to stop Burnside's corps from rolling up Lee's right flank. McIlvaine reported the loss of forty-seven guns, which may not have included those captured on the Maryland side. The difference in counts did nothing to reduce the magnitude of a disastrous Union defeat.[18]

Among the curiosities witnessed during the paroling process was the sight of Lieutenant Rouss leading a squadron of 12th Virginia Cavalry into Harpers Ferry. Over the objections of the garrison, Miles had paroled Rouss a week earlier. Knowing Rouss could not have been exchanged within the week, Lieutenant Binney complained to General Hill, who said he knew nothing about

16. Binney's Report, September 18, 1862, *OR*, XIX, Pt. 1, pp. 539, 540.

17. Thompson, "Recollections of War Times," 23, Civil War Times Illustrated Collection, USAMHI.

18. Lee's Report, August 19, 1863, Jackson's Report, April 23, 1863, Hill's Report, February 25, 1863, and McIlvaine's Report, September 19, 1862, *OR*, XIX, Pt. 1, pp. 148, 955, 980–81, 548.

it. Binney then recalled the lengthy and private conversation conducted between Miles and Rouss just prior to the latter's release.[19]

Incidents such as this gave rise to speculation that Miles had sold out the garrison to the enemy. Halleck tended to agree and on September 22 ordered White, D'Utassy, Trimble, and Ford arrested. Upon hearing of his summons, White demanded a court of inquiry, and on September 23 the Harper's Ferry Military Commission formed to try "such cases as may be brought before it." With Major General David Hunter presiding over a committee of six, the commission began hearings on October 4.[20] Twenty days later they concluded the investigation and prepared their report. Although Colonel Voss led the cavalry out of the Ferry on the night of September 14, Colonel Davis received a brevet for his role in initiating the escape and capturing Longstreet's reserve artillery train. The court censured Colonel Ford for abandoning Maryland Heights and dismissed him from the service. White, a friend of the president, retained the "approbation" of the commission, as "he appears from the evidence to have acted with decided capability and courage." With the exception of Miles, the other officers also escaped censure. The commissioners summed up Miles's performance in one paragraph:

> The Commission has approached a consideration of this officer's conduct, in connection with the surrender of Harper's Ferry, with extreme reluctance. An officer who cannot appear before any earthly tribunal to answer or explain charges gravely affecting his character, who has met with his death at the hands of the enemy, even upon the spot he disgracefully surrendered, is entitled to the tenderest care and most careful investigation. These this Commission has accorded Colonel Miles, and, in giving an opinion, only repeats what runs through our nine hundred pages of evidence, strangely unanimous upon the fact that Colonel Miles' incapacity, amounting to almost imbecility, led to the shameful surrender of this important post.[21]

Casualties resulting from the defense of Maryland Heights and Harpers Ferry were shockingly low. Despite reports by Union commanders of overwhelming odds and intense artillery fire, from

19. Investigation of Harpers Ferry, *ibid.*, 738.
20. Halleck to Thomas, September 22, 1862, Investigation of Harpers Ferry, and White to Thomas, September 22, 1862, *ibid.*, 801, 549–50, 556, 530.
21. Investigation of Harpers Ferry, *ibid.*, 794–800.

a garrison of 12,737 men, only 44 were killed and 173 wounded. The remaining 12,520 either escaped, surrendered, or were counted as missing. McLaws lost 35 killed and 178 wounded when he attacked Maryland Heights. A. P. Hill reported 3 privates killed and 66 men wounded during the investment of Harpers Ferry.[22] Returns from Walker's brigade and the two divisions Jackson brought to the Ferry are obscured in the casualty report of the Maryland campaign and the subsequent battle at Sharpsburg. From the statistics one might conclude that Ford had gotten the better of the fight on Maryland Heights, but neither he nor Miles realized it. The decision rendered by the Harper's Ferry Commission supports that view.

During the investment of the Ferry, nearly 30,000 troops at one time or another came into the town, passed through it, or had their guns pointed towards it. Despite the numbers involved and the value of the prize, no hard fighting occurred within the town. There was no loss of life and little property damage to the few residents either courageous or foolish enough to live through one occupation after another. If Miles did not hear the roar of Franklin's guns at Crampton's Gap on September 14, the townspeople of Harpers Ferry could have told him relief was on the way. With Solomon's Gap but six miles away, they listened to the fighting all day long.[23]

When Hill pulled his division out of the Ferry on the morning of September 17, a brief but quiet moratorium settled over the Valley. A small Confederate garrison remained behind to load wagons and pick the town clean of military stores and commissary supplies. Even cooking utensils still lying about the field attracted Lee's attention after the Confederate withdrawal from Sharpsburg. "Please have them carefully collected," he ordered. "We need them much at Winchester."[24]

On September 18 the Confederate guard destroyed the pontoon bridge, leaving town a few days later with the last of the spoils. For a while Confederate cavalry remained active in the area, screening Lee's retreat after the Sharpsburg affair, but the Army of Northern Virginia had no interest in holding Harpers Ferry. As

22. Union Returns, n.d., McLaws' Returns, October 20, 1862, and Hill's Returns, February 25, 1863, *ibid.*, 549, 860–61, 983.

23. Barry, *Harper's Ferry*, 125–26.

24. Lee to Munford, September 21, 1862, *OR*, XIX, Pt. 1, p. 346.

an afterthought Lee sent a detail back to the town to dislodge and disable the metal beams on the nearly rebuilt railroad bridge.[25]

Notwithstanding the indefensible nature of the town, Union Quartermaster General Montgomery C. Meigs wanted the Ferry reoccupied at the earliest possible moment "so that our supplies may be sent by railroad and canal." He asked to have the canal repaired and the bridge rebuilt.[26]

On September 22 McClellan ordered Burnside to move the IX Army Corps to Harpers Ferry, reorganize the town's defenses, and fortify both Maryland Heights and Loudoun Heights. Advance units from Burnside's corps reached the town late in the day to string a new pontoon bridge across the river. With the early arrivals came the 14th Connecticut, whose fine band struck up the new and popular air "John Brown's Body." The entire division took up the song as they crossed the river, and a few minutes later the ragged formation solemnly trudged by Brown's fort in hushed tones. By September 24, nine days after Miles's surrender, the huge Army of the Potomac began pitching their tents on Camp Hill and Bolivar Heights.[27] Albert D. Richardson, reporter for the New York *Tribune*, described the march to the Ferry:

Our army moved down the left bank of the Potomac, climbing the narrow torturous road that winds around the foot of the mountains . . . across the long, crooked ford above the blackened timbers of the railroad bridge; then up among the long, bare deserted walls of the ruined Government Armory; past the deserted engine-house which Old John Brown made historic; up the dingy, antique oriental looking town of Harper's Ferry, sadly worn, almost washed away by the ebb and flow of war; up through the village of Bolivar to these Hights [sic], where we pitched our tents.

Behind and below us rushed the gleaming river, till its dark shining surface was broken by rocks. Across it came a line of our stragglers, wading to the knees with staggering steps. Beyond it, the broad, forest-clad Maryland Hights rose gloomy and somber. Down

25. Conway to Eckert, September 19, 1862, *ibid.*, 333; Hungerford, *Baltimore and Ohio Railroad*, II, 22.

26. Ingalls to Meigs, September 21, 1862, *OR*, XIX, Pt. 2, pp. 339–40.

27. Marcy to Burnside, September 22, 1862, *ibid.*, 344, 355–56; McClellan's Report, and Marcy to Porter, September 23, 1862, *ibid.*, Pt. 1, pp. 71, 348; Frederick L. Hitchcock, *War from the Inside: The Story of the 132nd Regiment Pennsylvania Volunteer Infantry* (Philadelphia, 1904), 81–82; McClellan to Halleck, September 24, 1862, *OR*, XIX, Pt. 2, p. 353.

behind me, to the river, winding across it like a slender S, then extending for half a mile on the other side, far up the Maryland Hill, stretched a division-train of snowy wagons, standing out in strong relief from the dark background of water and mountain.[28]

Lieutenant Thomas Hodgkins, Battery M, 1st New York Light Artillery, looked down upon the Harpers Ferry area from atop Maryland Heights and on September 28 wrote, "It is a splendid sight to see these camp fires at night. It looks like a large city lit with gas." Private Schuyler McKinzer, a boy fascinated by the vast glimmer of light below, asked for leave to see the town. Hodgkins handed him a revolver, warning that it was still dangerous to travel unarmed.[29]

The citizens of Harpers Ferry, however, had good reason to rejoice. With the Army of the Potomac for protection and Lee's shattered legions in retreat, they believed the war could not last much longer. And when McClellan talked of making the Ferry his base of operations, rebuilding the double-tracked span over the Potomac, and erecting a new wagon bridge over the Shenandoah, it seemed to the town's small persevering populace that reconstruction and prosperity lay but weeks away. They happily speculated that McClellan had come to stay.

"Little Mac" may have liked it that way, because he resorted to an old habit the president derisively called "the slows." When pressed from Washington to pursue Lee, McClellan blithely replied, "It is scarcely possible to advance from Harper's Ferry, in force, and as that is clearly our true line of operations, I need not urge upon you the necessity of communications here."[30]

Why McClellan chose to remain immobile at Harpers Ferry baffled Halleck. "It seems to me that Washington is the real base of operations," he replied, "and that it should not under any circumstances be exposed."[31] But advance units of Lee's army lay near Charles Town, not at Washington, and McClellan decided to stay at Harpers Ferry and refortify the area.

Lincoln grew impatient and on October 1 paid McClellan a

---

28. Albert D. Richardson, *The Secret Service, the Field, the Dungeon, and the Escape* (Hartford, Conn., 1866), 290–91.

29. Thomas Hodgkins to his brother, September 28, 1862, Hodgkins Letters, Civil War Times Illustrated Collection, USAMHI.

30. McClellan to Halleck, September 24, 1862, *OR*, XIX, Pt. 2, pp. 354–55.

31. Halleck to McClellan, September 26, 1862, *ibid.*, 360.

visit. Dressed in his customary black frock coat and chimney-pot hat, the president stood among McClellan's gold-braided generals during a review of the troops. To reporter Richardson, Lincoln looked even thinner than usual, his bony and bearded face etched with craters of fatigue and worry. Later the president roamed the town and peeked into John Brown's fort, a lasting remnant of what was once the U.S. Armory.[32]

Soldiers cheered the president and craned their necks to get a better look at the curious rail-splitter. Private Eanes of the 15th Massachusetts had seen him once before and considered him unusually "homely." "His dress is a plain suit of black, loose fitting and rather old fashioned. His hat is worn tipped back from his forehead, and with his sharp features one would as soon take him for a closely 'calculating' Yankee trader as for his excellency."[33]

The president and the general passed within twelve feet of Private John L. Street of the 145th Pennsylvania. They looked, the private thought, just like their pictures. When Street learned of the president's Emancipation Proclamation, he wrote his parents that "the old soldiers believe the war might have been ended before this time if the slaves had been set free." Three weeks later, however, the army was still anchored at Harpers Ferry, and Street's company, like many others, amused themselves on picket duty by "milking 'Secesh' cows, getting apples, and gathering hickory nuts."[34]

McClellan, however, did not share the average soldier's enthusiasm for their president. On the day of Lincoln's departure he wrote home, "[The president's] ostensible purpose is to see the troops and the battlefield; I incline to think that the real purpose is to push on into a premature advance into Virginia. . . . The real truth is that the army is not fit to advance."[35]

Washington continued to prod McClellan, and like two mighty wrestlers, the harder Halleck pushed, the stiffer Little Mac resisted. It would be best to wait, McClellan declared defiantly, until the railroad could be opened to Winchester.[36]

32. Richardson, *The Secret Service*, 291.

33. Walter Eanes to his father, October 11, 1862, Eanes Letters, USAMHI.

34. John L. Street to his parents, October 10, 24, 30, 1862, Street Letters, CPL. Lincoln announced the Emancipation Proclamation on September 22, 1862, to take effect January 1, 1863.

35. Richard B. Irwin, "The Removal of McClellan," *B&L*, III, 103.

36. McClellan's Report, September 23, 1862, *OR*, XIX, Pt. 1, p. 73.

For the new recruits, camp life on Bolivar Heights became a pleasant routine of watching the warm autumn sun color the forests on the towering hills around them. They drilled daily, enjoyed bathing expeditions to the Shenandoah, and looked forward to "doing the quaint old town of Harper's Ferry."[37]

Officers brought their wives to town, and the ladies paraded about the streets with their servants as if peaceful days in the army had settled forever upon the old, historic town of Harpers Ferry. The only reminder of war was the wreckage around them, or the soldiers taking target practice down by the river "where the boys fired away at imaginary Confederates and filled trees full of buck and ball."[38]

While soldiers and civilians frolicked about camp, Jeb Stuart stepped into the picture and once again humiliated McClellan by leading the Confederate cavalry around the Union army.[39] On October 10 he crossed the Potomac west of the Ferry with 1,800 picked troopers, made an unexpected appearance at Chambersburg, Pennsylvania, and on October 12 recrossed into Virginia at Monocacy, losing only two stragglers. The raiders brought home 30 prisoners, paroled 300 more, seized 1,200 horses, and destroyed over $250,000 in government property. Stuart's haul of horses compensated for Jackson's lost expectations on the day Miles surrendered Harpers Ferry.[40]

McClellan should not have been surprised when a message arrived from the White House. "You remember my speaking to you of what I called your over-cautiousness," Lincoln scolded. "Are you not over-cautious when you assume that you cannot do what the enemy is constantly doing? Should you not claim to be at least his equal in prowess, and act upon the claim? . . . I certainly would be pleased for you to have the advantage of the railroad from Harper's Ferry to Winchester, but it wastes all the remainder of autumn to give it to you."[41]

McClellan, realizing he must soon put the army in motion or

37. Hitchcock, *War from the Inside*, 84.

38. St. Clair A. Mulholland, *The Story of the 116th Regiment Pennsylvania Volunteers* (Philadelphia, 1903), 12–13.

39. Stuart's first circuit around the Union army occurred during McClellan's Peninsula campaign.

40. See Freeman, *Lee's Lieutenant's*, II, 284–309, for details of the raid.

41. Lincoln to McClellan, October 13, 1862, *OR*, XIX, Pt. 1, p. 13.

suffer another embarrassing dismissal, placed Burnside in charge of the Ferry's defenses and gave him the II, IX, and XII Army Corps to keep the town secure. But Little Mac still dallied, waiting for the bridge to be finished. Burnside, a tall, fleshy man with chubby cheeks covered by a mass of bushy whiskers, moved his men to Bolivar Heights and expanded the earthworks. Joseph Barry returned to his home and at night gazed into the hills between the rivers, comparing them to "two villages . . . aglow with hundreds of watchfires. A hum of voices like that of an immense city or the hoarse murmur of the great deep arose from the valleys on either side and filled the air with a confusion of sounds." Well into the night regimental bands harmonized martial strains, sending echoes of horns and drums rolling through the valley. It was a wonderful sight, Barry recalled laconically, except for the "drunken rioting among the soldiers," and "outrage[s] on the citizens."[42]

Chaplain John H. W. Stuckenberg of the 145th Pennsylvania arrived at Harpers Ferry on October 6 and reported a different sight—water contaminated and food occupied by "living creatures . . . pork alive with skippers." To him, the town resembled a stinkhole. Everywhere he went soldiers lay about with diarrhea, dysentery, rheumatism, measles, and colds. Men made daily visits to his rain-spattered tent beseeching him to use his influence in obtaining their discharges. "If I could only be at home," they complained—or moaned, "If my mother, my wife, my sister were only here." Stuckenberg understood the men's despair—he felt no better himself. When not attending to the demands of the sick, he kept to his tent, grumbling that his only companions were "numerous flies and long legged spiders now and then running over me."[43]

But the war machine paid no attention to the woes of the chaplain's Pennsylvanians, and to satisfy General McClellan's demands, Cyrus B. Comstock, lieutenant of the Engineers, submitted a lengthy proposal to convert Harpers Ferry into an impregnable fort. The project, endorsed by the general, called for a massive parapet running from river to river across Bolivar

42. Special Order No. 280, October 13, 1862, *ibid.*, 420; Barry, *Harper's Ferry*, 126.

43. A History of the 145th Pennsylvania Volunteers," October 12, 16, 1862, Stuckenberg Collection, MLGC. Skippers are a form of maggot. The 145th were boys from Erie, Pennsylvania, who had seen death but little action.

Heights and supported by four redoubts containing a total of thirty heavy guns. For the summits of Maryland and Loudoun Heights Comstock prepared drawings showing a line of stone blockhouses and entrenchments for 3,000 men, with camps on the slopes facing the town, each with "six or eight light guns." His sketch specified a half-dozen redoubts, each with heavy artillery, on both crests. Without intending to replicate Miles's command, Comstock nonetheless suggested a garrison of 12,000 men.[44]

Halleck was unimpressed, and so was Stanton. They agreed to rebuild the railroad bridge and leave a garrison at Harpers Ferry, but they objected to the long delay, "extending into winter," before the project could be completed.[45] Halleck envisioned McClellan holing up in the Ferry and doing nothing until he had his three fortresses. In the meantime, Lee could range all over Virginia and threaten Washington.

McClellan sulked at his new quarters, as if waiting for some private soldier to come running to headquarters with another of Lee's lost orders. In the meantime he pestered the White House for more men and more horses. On October 24 Lincoln grew impatient and replied, "I have just read your dispatch about soretongued and fatigued horses. Will you pardon me for asking what the horses of your army have done since the battle of Antietam (Sharpsburg) that fatigues anything." Three days later he asked, "Is it your purpose not to go into action again until the men now being drafted in the States are incorporated into the old regiments?"[46]

On November 1 McClellan put his army in motion but left a heavy garrison at the Ferry. Even as he moved south, he moved slowly, striking the passes of the Blue Ridge and rumbling eastward through hostile territory. For too long the army had lain mobilized but inactive, and McClellan knew it. In reviewing marching orders with Major General Darius Couch, he confided dolefully, "I may not have command of the army much longer. Lincoln is down on me."[47]

On November 5 Lincoln fulfilled McClellan's prophecy. "Couch," McClellan blurted to his friend, "I am relieved from the

44. Comstock to Duane, October 17, 1862, *OR*, XIX, Pt. 2, pp. 441–42.
45. Halleck to McClellan, October 19, 1862, *ibid.*, 442–43.
46. Lincoln to McClellan, October 24 [25?], 27, 1862, *ibid.*, 485, 497.
47. Darius Couch, "Sumner's 'Right Grand Division,' " *B&L*, III, 105.

command of the army, and Burnside is my successor." "I am sorry for it," said Couch. Then he abruptly swung his horse towards the new commander and said, "General Burnside, I congratulate you."[48]

Burnside, skeptical of his ability to lead, took command of the Army of the Potomac and marched south to the fatal fields of Fredericksburg. Bloodied and battered by Lee's army on December 13 and 14, Burnside withdrew, and Lincoln began looking for another general.

When the Army of the Potomac began its march from Harpers Ferry on November 1, McClellan left Major General Henry W. Slocum and the XII Army Corps behind to defend the garrison against unknown threats. Slocum had led the 1st Division, VI Army Corps, at Antietam, and was probably pleased when on October 15 he was elevated to corps command, but he resented being left behind when McClellan marched south with the Army of the Potomac. Little Mac was generous, however, and left Slocum with 15,000 troops to bring martial comfort to the civilians who had returned to their homes. Major General George Morell commanded another 5,445 effectives spread along the upper Potomac, and the two generals earnestly chased, but seldom caught, several roving bands of guerrillas.[49]

Slocum did not much care for living in the dirty little town, and he disliked the situation more when the War Department began to send his brigades to Burnside but left him behind. Two days before the Battle of Fredericksburg, Burnside ordered Slocum to hurry on down to the Rappahannock with the balance of his corps. Slocum pulled up stakes and departed so fast there was hardly a soldier left to look after Harpers Ferry. Morell tapped his railroad guards for two infantry divisions and on December 11 sent Brigadier General John R. Kenly to Harpers Ferry to shore up the garrison. Kenly barely got settled before the War Department made another change.[50]

48. *Ibid.*, 106; Halleck to McClellan, November 5, 1862, *OR*, XIX, Pt. 2, p. 545.
49. Special Order No. 282, October 15, Army of the Potomac Returns, November 10, and Halleck to Morell, November 14, 1862, *OR*, XIX, Pt. 2, pp. 431, 569, 581.
50. Slocum to Halleck, December 11, Morell to Cullum, December 11, and Kenly to Stanton, December 17, 1862, *ibid.*, XXI, 846, 847, 863.

At Harpers Ferry townsfolk straggled back to their homes, some having packed their belongings four or five times to escape the war. They believed fighting had finally gone south for good and that nobody would disturb their town again. Unionists and secessionists shared a common affliction, bone-deep weariness, and those who resettled in their homes wanted peace. Some returned home in time to witness thirty thousand soldiers drawn up in line to hear the Emancipation Proclamation read within musket-shot of John Brown's enginehouse. Old Brown may have finally won his war against slavery, but the fighting had not stopped. To the old man's way of thinking, the land had not yet paid for its crimes against slavery.

While Harpers Ferry rested, the purging of blood continued. The town, partially in ruins, began to rebuild. Some said Bobby Lee was done for good. Nobody believed he would be back again, or pay them an unwanted call as he passed on his way to a small town in Pennsylvania called Gettysburg.

# 13

## Springtime in the Valley

On December 16, 1862, General Halleck made several command changes, thereby eradicating selections made by the deposed McClellan and stripping responsibility for Harpers Ferry from General Kenly, who had been there less than a week. The reorganization brought to town Brigadier General Benjamin F. Kelley, whose command of about sixteen thousand troops was strung along the Baltimore and Ohio Railroad from Monocacy to Cumberland. Major General Robert Milroy, "Old Gray Eagle," whose division was at Moorfield along the South Branch of the Potomac, moved his command to Winchester. Old General Wool, still watching over his string of railroad garrisons, was nudged aside by Stanton and replaced by fifty-three-year-old Major General Robert Schenck. Milroy's division became quite scattered, but Kelley concentrated much of his infantry at Harpers Ferry to protect the growing supply center.[1]

Schenck, like Wool, set up shop in Baltimore. He had no military training but plenty of political clout. His civilian achievements included four terms in the House of Representatives, two years as minister to Brazil, and national acclaim for his skill as a

---

1. Halleck to Kelley, December 16, Stanton to Wool, December 17, and Kelley to Whipple, December 24, 1862, *OR*, XXI, 860, 864, 883.

poker player. His background as a lawyer provided him with enough savvy to administer a minor military department and produce the expected mountain of correspondence.[2]

When the war began, Benjamin Kelley, a fifty-four-year-old freight agent for the Baltimore and Ohio Railroad, raised the 1st (West) Virginia Regiment of ninety-day volunteers and on May 22, 1861, became its colonel. Wounded at the Battle of Philippi on June 3, he eventually returned to duty with his first star. His rapid rise had little to do with his military acumen, coming more as a reward for his staunch pro-Union effort in western Virginia. "Old Ben," as his men called him, was of medium height and broad shouldered, with wavy brown hair flecked with gray to match his billy-goat chin whiskers. He wore a bull-like expression, set off by a prominent chin, and bore a slight facial and physical resemblance to one of his predecessors, Colonel Dixon Miles. After the war, one of his cavalrymen wrote, "This usually dependable leader was to see much action throughout the war and to draw the comment that he made less history for the amount of fighting he did than any other general officer in the service."[3]

The appointment of Kelley, who came from western Virginia, had as much to do with politics as with military matters. Since the summer of 1861, proposals had been made to form a new state from Unionist districts in western Virginia. On October 24 thirty-five counties asked for a constitutional convention and admission to the Union. Leaders of the movement devised delays, hoping to encourage counties along the Potomac to join. Lincoln was especially interested in securing Jefferson County, as the crucial Baltimore and Ohio with its spur to Winchester ran through it.[4]

Jefferson County, mostly southern in culture and sympathy since its earliest settlement, lay on the eastern edge of the proposed state, with Harpers Ferry and its bridge on the easternmost tip. Since the railroad also ran through neighboring Berkeley County, located just west of Jefferson, conventioneers discussed annexing both counties without asking the consent of the voters, but they decided against it. The vote scheduled in Jefferson and

2. HTI, 660–61.

3. Ibid., 410; John W. Elwood, Elwood's Stories of the Old Ringgold Cavalry (Coal Center, Pa., 1914), 163.

4. George E. Moore, A Banner in the Hills (New York, 1963), 129–47. Moore comprehensively covers the formation of the state of West Virginia.

Berkeley Counties for April, 1862, fell by the wayside when Jackson sprung his Valley campaign.[5]

When Kelley took command of the Ferry at the close of 1862, Union forces controlled the shore of the Potomac, and on January 5, 1863, the bridge at Harpers Ferry officially reopened. Beginning on January 6, Schenck reported, "trains will run through from Baltimore to Wheeling." With Kelley's force at the Ferry and at Martinsburg, and with Milroy's division at Winchester to fend off another Confederate intrusion, the legislature of the provisional new state of West Virginia authorized May 28, 1863, as the day for elections in Jefferson and Berkeley Counties. All the other counties comprising West Virginia had held their elections on April 16. After the returns were certified, Lincoln, on April 20, issued a proclamation declaring that sixty days later West Virginia would become a state.[6]

Jefferson and Berkeley Counties cast their ballots during the ratification election held on May 28. By then, many former residents of Harpers Ferry had reestablished their lives amid the friendly Federal garrison. Their bridges had been rebuilt, and work crews continued to add new structures to the lower town.[7]

Although both counties continued to be pestered by Confederate cavalry and guerrilla bands, residents felt safer than they had for many months. Some of the buildings in town had been burned and many remained vacant, but Kelley brought order to the Ferry, chased away vagrants and looters, and gave old residents new hope. Joseph Barry, who spent much of his time living at Jacob Leilac's hotel in Frederick, returned to his home from time to time and observed that most of the people on the streets were soldiers. But he joined with others in observing fresh signs of peace and prosperity under Lincoln's administration.[8]

Lieutenant Fred Fredrickson of the 5th New York Heavy Artillery settled into a leisurely life on Camp Hill. To his wife he wrote, "There is nothing here but desolation and magnificent scenery. Roofless houses and those that are occupied [bear] the mark of

5. *Ibid.*, 146–47; Summers, *Baltimore and Ohio*, 200.

6. Schenck to Lincoln, January 5, 1863, *OR*, XXI, 947; Moore, *Banner in the Hills*, 205.

7. Moore, *Banner in the Hills*, 205; Hungerford, *Baltimore and Ohio Railroad*, II, 24.

8. Barry, *Harper's Ferry*, 139–40.

cannon balls—then the smells are not very agreeable as there are a number of dead horses still remaining unburied." Nobody thought to bury the animals, and frequent raids by guerrillas added to the toll, leaving the landscape dotted with mouldering carcasses and the lower town encased in the stench.[9]

After the Union defeat at Chancellorsville, Kelley's railroad guards encountered increased trouble from Colonel John S. Mosby's Rangers and hard-riding bands of White's veteran Confederate cavalry. In mid-May, Brigadier Generals John Imboden and William E. Jones swept north and struck the Baltimore and Ohio to the west of Harpers Ferry, blowing up culverts and ripping up track all the way to Parkersburg. On their way back they raided farms, destroyed property, and carried off stock.[10]

The raid irritated those western Virginians who had southern sympathies. Many of them had cast their votes for independent statehood solely to obtain protection from raids by Confederate marauders. Polls opened on May 28 in Jefferson County, but only in Harpers Ferry and Shepherdstown. Civil and military order existed nowhere else in the county. With Union officials monitoring the polls, 196 Harpers Ferry residents cast their votes for admission to West Virginia. One staunch rebel refused to be intimidated and voted no. At Shepherdstown the vote went 52 to 1. In a county that produced 1,800 votes in the 1860 election, only 250 cast ballots on May 28.[11] Jubilation lasted about a week. The Army of Northern Virginia had disappeared into the Valley, and Harpers Ferry girded for another disaster.

Kelley wired Halleck for more troops. Milroy, encamped around Winchester, also asked for reinforcements. Halleck, however, thought Schenck had more than enough men to repulse an invasion of the lower Valley. "Harper's Ferry is the important place," he wired Schenck. "Winchester is of no importance other than as a lookout." He suggested Milroy withdraw to the Ferry, bringing his supplies with him.[12]

9. Fred Frederickson to his wife, May 7, 1863, Frederickson Letters, File HFD-390, HFA.

10. Imboden's Report, June 1, and Jones's Report, May 14, 1863, OR, XV, Pt. 1, pp. 98–105, 105–106.

11. Manly Wade Wellman, Harpers Ferry, Prize of War (Charlotte, N.C., 1960), 103–104.

12. Kelley to Halleck, April 30, 1863, OR, XV, Pt. 2, p. 318; Halleck to Schenck, June 11, 12, 1863, ibid., XXVII, Pt. 2, p. 50.

Milroy, however, had his own agenda and dallied at Winchester confiscating private property and ignoring women with small children who pleaded for mercy. His depredations on citizens, who had already suffered through numerous occupations, created so much indignation in Virginia that the government offered $1,000 for Milroy's capture, dead or alive. Milroy laughed at the reward, but the Confederate force advancing towards Winchester took special interest in bagging him.[13]

Forty-seven-year-old Robert Hudson Milroy held a Master of Military Science degree from Captain Partridge's Academy in Norwich, Vermont. He served during the Mexican War as captain of the 1st Indiana Volunteers. He looked slim, sullen, and sour, having stern features, a grayish beard, and the rigid composure of a man who could not be persuaded by common sense. Having raised the 9th Indiana Regiment, Milroy became a brigade commander, fought at Second Manassas, and gained promotion to major general on November 29, 1862. Now in command of the Upper Potomac Division of the VIII Corps (Schenck's Department), he ignored Halleck's suggestion and remained at Winchester.[14]

In early May, Major General Joseph Hooker, who replaced Burnside as commander of the Army of the Potomac, had been soundly drubbed at Chancellorsville by a force half his size. In the battle Lee lost Jackson, but the victory had been so decisive that the old feeling of invincibility once again pervaded the Army of Northern Virginia. Lee looked north, remembering the lush, ripening fields of Maryland and Pennsylvania. With Great Britain and France watching the tides of the American war with political interest, Lee believed he would never have a better opportunity to invade the soil of the enemy and achieve independence for the South. Knowing he must move while the Army of the Potomac lay bloodied and disorganized on the north bank of the Rappahannock, Lee routed his line of march right down the Shenandoah Valley and through Winchester.

Correspondence between Halleck and Schenck indicates that neither had a clue as to Lee's intentions. On June 8 Halleck suspected another cavalry incursion, warning that Stuart had 12,000 troopers in Culpepper County poised for a probable raid on the

13. Virgil C. Jones, *Gray Ghosts and Rebel Raiders* (New York, 1956), 144.
14. *HTI*, 495–96.

tracks and bridges of the Baltimore and Ohio.[15] At the time, Stuart was on the Rappahannock and about seventy-five miles from Winchester. The only regular cavalry in the Valley belonged to Brigadier General Alfred G. Jenkins.

The following day Schenck asked Halleck for advice—he had about 25,000 troops and wanted to know where to put them. Halleck offered no advice but sent Lieutenant Colonel Donn Piatt, his chief of staff, with Brigadier General Daniel Tyler to Winchester to assess Milroy's ability to repulse an attack. On June 11 Piatt reported that at Winchester "all looks fine. Can whip anything the rebels can fetch here." Tyler agreed, adding, "Milroy deserves credit for his fortifications; it will take all of Lee's cavalry and light artillery to whip him out." Milroy joined the chorus and declared, "I can and would hold it [Winchester], if permitted to do so, against any force the rebels can afford to bring against me."[16]

Halleck, wary of political generals, felt a nagging uneasiness and wired Schenck to order Milroy to fall back to Harpers Ferry, along with the troops at Martinsburg if they also became threatened. Schenck passed the order to Piatt, who informed Milroy to withdraw but to leave a "lookout" at Winchester. Milroy, confused by what Piatt meant by a lookout, advised Schenck that any force left behind as a lookout would "be captured in forty-eight hours. All should go or none," Milroy declared. "Please designate what portion of my forces must be left here for the enemy." Schenck replied, "You will make all the required preparations for withdrawing, but hold your position in the meantime. . . . Give me constant information." Schenck then forwarded a copy of Halleck's telegram ordering Milroy to withdraw, thereby leaving the recipient bewildered.[17]

Late on June 12, in compliance with Schenck's request for "constant information," Milroy reported a brush with Confederate cavalry at Front Royal, admitting the enemy "are probably approaching in some force," but adding, "I am entirely ready for them. I can hold this place. Please state specifically whether I am to abandon it or not." Milroy still believed he had only cavalry in his front,

15. Halleck to Schenck, June 8, 1863, *OR*, XXVII, Pt. 2, p. 159.

16. Schenck to Halleck, June 9, Piatt to Schenck, June 11, Tyler to Schenck, June 11, and Milroy to Schenck, June 11, 1863, *ibid.*, 160, 161.

17. Halleck to Schenck, June 11, Milroy to Schenck, June 11, and Schenck to Milroy, June 12, 1863, *ibid.*, 161.

writing, "Let them come," and later in the day adding, "I fear the attack is only a feint to cover the great raid." Milroy evidently still accepted the theory that only Stuart was on the march.[18]

Late in the evening on June 13 the vanguard of Ewell's II Corps drove in Milroy's outposts. Ewell, nervous-eyed and bald, had inherited Jackson's old command, regiments filled with ragged and gaunt fighters, among the fiercest of the South. In Major General Edward Johnson's division marched the remnants of the Stonewall Brigade, organized two years previous at Harpers Ferry. Their homes lay in the Valley, plundered by the likes of "Old Gray Eagle," and they looked forward to the opportunity to bleed a little retribution from the Union looters.

Milroy's skirmishers captured a few prisoners from Brigadier General Harry T. Hays's Louisiana brigade, who admitted being a part of Jackson's old corps. Schenck did not receive the wire disclosing the presence of Ewell's corps until late the following morning, but he was probably relieved when Milroy declared, "I can hold this place for five days if you can relieve me in that time." Halleck, who had been looking for Lee's army for more than a week, now found part of it in front of Milroy. He wired Schenck nervously, "If you have not executed my orders to concentrate your forces at Harper's Ferry, you will do so immediately." Lincoln, whose nose for military matters had vastly improved, also wired Schenck, "Get General Milroy from Winchester to Harper's Ferry. . . . He will be 'gobbled up' if he remains, if he is not already past salvation."[19]

With the rest of his corps coming up, Ewell deployed his brigades to envelop Milroy's command. At 6 P.M., June 14, the Confederates attacked Winchester, driving the Federals back in confusion. At dark Milroy convened a council of war and ordered a retreat for 1 A.M. Ewell anticipated the withdrawal and at 3 A.M. severed Milroy's columns, capturing about 3,800 men, 23 pieces of artillery, and more than 300 horses, and inflicting about 400 casualties. Milroy's command fled in different directions, but most of those who escaped made their way to Harpers Ferry. "Old Gray Eagle," convinced Lee's whole army had come to get him,

---

18. Milroy to Schenck and to Piatt, June 12, 1863, *ibid.,* 163, 164.

19. Milroy to Schenck, June 13, Halleck to Schenck, June 13, and Lincoln to Schenck, June 14, 1863, *ibid.,* 165, 167.

led the retreat. Accompanied by his staff and headquarters cavalry, Milroy rode swiftly through the early morning mist, leaving much of his infantry behind to be "gobbled up," as Lincoln predicted, by Early's division.[20]

As Ewell began his investment of Winchester, Major General Robert E. Rodes passed through Berryville and, with Jenkins' cavalry leading the way, took the road to Martinsburg. On June 14, Jenkins drove in Tyler's skirmishers and nudged them into the town.[21]

Earlier in the day Schenck had ordered Tyler to pull his force out of Martinsburg, send everything to Maryland Heights, and "retreat in the direction of Harper's Ferry." Colonel Benjamin F. Smith's brigade checked Jenkins' dismounted cavalry but learned from prisoners that Rodes was closing fast. Tyler hurried to the depot to secure cars, only to discover that the agent had just sent all of them to Harpers Ferry. Early in the evening, part of Rodes's artillery arrived and began shelling Smith's defenders, who had holed up in Martinsburg's cemetery. To Tyler's surprise, he noticed the 126th Ohio and the 106th New York abandoning their positions and filing into town, looking for someone to tell them which way to run. Cut off from Williamsport by Jenkins' cavalry, Tyler pointed them down the Shepherdstown road, but in the darkness some units lost their sense of direction. Tyler got them on the right road and, with most of his supplies, reached Harpers Ferry at 7 A.M. on June 15. Casualties were light, but Smith reported "about 200 men missing," which he attributed to straggling.[22]

Early chased Milroy as far as Halltown, and Rodes sent no more than a detachment from Jenkins' cavalry after Tyler. Then both turned away to follow Ewell across the Potomac at Williamsport. The scare at Harpers Ferry, however, continued. Tyler kept his wagons rolling day and night, moving supplies up Maryland Heights. Kelley, however, remained at Harpers Ferry. As Milroy's road-weary infantry arrived from Winchester, he sent them into

20. Milroy's Report, June 30, 1863, Return of Casualties, and Ewell's Report, n.d., 1863, ibid., 46–48, 53, 441–42.

21. Ewell's Report, n.d., 1863, and Rodes's Report, n.d., 1863, ibid., 442, 547–49.

22. Schenck and Piatt to Tyler, June 14, Tyler's Report, June 25, and Smith's Report, June 27, 1863, ibid., 166, 167, 16–19, 37–39.

the outer defenses on Bolivar Heights to strengthen his own force. When Schenck learned Ewell had crossed the Potomac, he sent Colonel William F. Raynolds to the Ferry to inspect the defenses. Schenck looked for the Confederates to move up Elk Ridge and attack Maryland Heights from the rear, as McLaws had done. Raynolds wanted the Heights reinforced, and Tyler sent details to fell trees and tote more guns to defend and strengthen the summit.[23]

When Tyler arrived at the Ferry he relieved Kelley, but Milroy, who held a higher grade, seemed befuddled by the decimation of his command and refused to cooperate. Kelley, upset at being relieved, departed with his staff "without leaving behind a single record of the command." In the shuffle, Schenck ordered Milroy's division to report to Tyler, who then began moving the entire force, with all quartermaster and commissary supplies, to Maryland Heights. By the morning of June 16 only a few of Kelley's old companies still occupied the entrenchments south of Harpers Ferry. When skirmishers pressed forward to feel the enemy's strength, they found nothing but small bands of roving cavalry. By late morning they realized a few enemy horsemen had kept them poised and on the alert throughout a sleepless night.[24]

Another cavalry raid jangled the nerves of Union defenders at Point of Rocks when raiders set fire to a train, but nothing came of it. Nonetheless, Tyler still prepared for eight thousand Confederates to strike his flanks.

On June 19 several deserters drifted into headquarters on Maryland Heights and claimed to be "tired of the war." Tyler listened to their stories and informed Hooker that Ewell intended to attack Washington by way of Harpers Ferry or Frederick. But the following morning he repudiated the intelligence as disingenuous and advised Hooker, "I begin to think we are not to be attacked."[25] With reports like this, Hooker remained in a perpetual state of indecision.

Tyler's scouts probed the shores of the Potomac and northward along the Boonsboro road but found no infantry until they climbed a hill south of Sharpsburg. There they spotted a large enemy force engaged in foraging, not fighting, and reported large herds of cattle and hundreds of wagons filled with plunder rolling towards Vir-

23. Raynold's Report, August 11, 1863, *ibid.*, 13–16.
24. Tyler's Report, July 1, 1863, *ibid.*, 21–22.
25. Tyler to Hooker, June 19, 20, 1863, *ibid.*, 24, 25.

ginia. Tyler lamented not having sufficient cavalry to stop them. The following day, June 22, he reported "30,000 to 40,000 troops in and around Sharpsburg," and later, "It looks as if Lee's movement is toward Hagerstown and in Pennsylvania."[26]

Tyler's scouts could be commended for a good piece of reconnaissance. Hooker had no idea where Lee had hidden his main army, but he discounted most of Tyler's reports as speculative rather than factual. Ewell bypassed Harpers Ferry, but before he crossed into Pennsylvania Tyler spotted him at Hagerstown and wrote, "On Sunday, I saw General Ewell go into the Catholic church. He is a one-legged man." On June 22, Ewell, in advance of Lee's main army, moved up to Chambersburg, and Longstreet crossed most of his corps at Shepherdstown. Tyler watched them wade the river and dutifully notified headquarters, and on June 25 he reported Hill's corps passing north through Sharpsburg.[27]

Lee, who tried to mask his moves, was irritated on at least two occasions when Tyler attempted to communicate with "two flags of truce," asking for information "as to the killed and wounded at Winchester." Tyler's scouts had better luck finding Lee than did Hooker's huge cavalry under General Pleasonton.[28] Although the Army of the Potomac seemed confused as to Lee's whereabouts, by June 25 Tyler had located Lee's three corps and kept both Hooker and Halleck routinely informed.

On June 26 Major General William H. French relieved Tyler and took command at Harpers Ferry. When Tyler returned to Schenck's command, he once again notified Hooker that Lee's main army had passed into Pennsylvania. Had Tyler stayed on the job a few days longer, the greatest battle of the Civil War might not have been fought in the small college town of Gettysburg.[29]

Soon after French reached Harpers Ferry, a message from Hooker arrived ordering that the men cook three days' rations and be ready to march "at a moment's notice." On June 27 Hooker moved towards Harpers Ferry, intent on cutting off Lee's army from the rear. He dispatched the XII Corps to join French and hold the fords where he expected Ewell, Hill, and Longstreet to recross.

26. Tyler to Hooker, June 22, 23, 1863, *ibid.*, 26, 27.

27. Tyler to Halleck, June 24, and to Hooker, June 25, 1863, *ibid.*, 28, 29, 30.

28. Tyler to Lee, June 24, 1863, *ibid.*, 29.

29. Tyler to Hooker, June 26, 1863, General Order No. 14, and Special Order No. 12, *ibid.*, 31–32.

At Harpers Ferry he found "10,000 men . . . in condition to take the field. Here," he wired Halleck, "they are of no earthly account . . . as far as Harper's Ferry is concerned, there is nothing of it."[30]

Once again Hooker ordered French to prepare to march, but his old classmate from West Point, now wise in the ways of the War Department, asked Hooker for permission to refer the matter to Halleck. Hooker agreed, and Halleck promptly replied that French was to ignore the order. Hooker wanted freedom to use French's troops as he wished, but Halleck wanted both Harpers Ferry and Washington protected from Confederate attack while at the same time demanding that Lee be defeated wherever he chose to make a stand. Halleck flatly insisted that Maryland Heights be held. Hooker replied, "I am unable to comply," and asked to be relieved. And on June 27, 1863, Major General George G. Meade took command of the Army of the Potomac.[31]

Harpers Ferry became the catalyst for propagating a bad joke on another unlucky Union commander. In the fall of 1862 Lincoln had sacked McClellan for not advancing from Harpers Ferry fast enough. Now, on the verge of the Battle of Gettysburg, he replaced Hooker for wanting to abandon the town. In both instances Lincoln had looked for an occasion to replace commanders, and both times conditions at the Ferry provided the means.

When Tyler moved his force to Maryland Heights, Joseph Barry and others like him once again left town and sought refuge elsewhere, but Ewell skirted the town and pressed into Pennsylvania.[32] Most of the residents simply stayed in their homes and rejoiced in their good luck. Lee's army had passed them by. But many wondered—would they be so lucky when Lee returned? For the answer, they had little time to wait.

In the meantime, on June 20, West Virginia entered the Union as the thirty-fifth state, and with it Jefferson County. There was no celebration or parade down Shenandoah Street to mark the occasion. The patriotic words in Governor Arthur I. Boreman's

30. Hooker to French, June 25, 1863, *ibid.*, XVII, Pt. 3, p. 317; Butterfield to Halleck, and Hooker to Halleck, June 27, 1863, *ibid.*, Pt. 1, pp. 59, 60.

31. Walter H. Hebert, *Fighting Joe Hooker* (Indianapolis, 1944), 244–46; Halleck to Hooker, Hooker to Halleck, and Halleck to Meade, June 27, 1863, *OR*, XVII, Pt. 1, pp. 59, 60, 61.

32. Barry, *Harper's Ferry*, 129.

inaugural address did not reach the war-torn town for several days. Lee had thrust his army between Jefferson and Berkeley Counties, and Harpers Ferry, as so many times before, found itself in the midst of another hair-raising military fiasco.[33]

33. Boreman's address was published in the Wheeling *Intelligencer*, June 22, 1863.

Major General John E. Wool, commander of the Middle Department, which included the Harpers Ferry garrison, in 1862

*Courtesy U.S. Army Military History Institute*

Major General Lafayette McLaws,
who led the division that attacked
Harpers Ferry from Maryland
Heights in September, 1862
*Courtesy U.S. Army Military History
Institute*

Brigadier General James A.
Walker, who led the division that
attacked Harpers Ferry from
Loudoun Heights in September,
1862
*Courtesy U.S. Army Military
History Institute*

Brigadier General Julius White,
who surrendered Harpers Ferry
to General Jackson on September
15, 1862
*Courtesy U.S. Army Military
History Institute*

Brigadier General Joseph B. Kershaw, who led the attack on Maryland Heights on September 13, 1862

*Courtesy U.S. Army Military History Institute*

Major General Ambrose P. Hill, who occupied Harpers Ferry from September 15 to 17, 1862, paroling the captured Union force

*Courtesy U.S. Army Military History Institute*

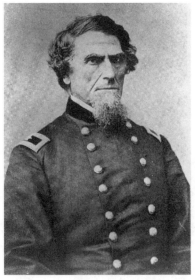

Major General Ambrose Burnside, who reoccupied the Ferry from September 22 to October 15, 1862

*Courtesy U.S. Army Military History Institute*

Brigadier General Benjamin F. Kelley, commander of Harpers Ferry from December 16, 1862, to June 15, 1863

*Courtesy U.S. Army Military History Institute*

Major General Robert C.
Schenck, who replaced General
Wool as the commander of the
Middle Department on
December 16, 1862

*Courtesy U.S. Army Military History
Institute*

Major General George B.
McClellan, who attempted to
convert the Harpers Ferry area
into a permanent fortress in the
fall of 1862

*Courtesy U.S. Army Military History
Institute*

Brigadier General Henry H.
Lockwood, commander of
Harpers Ferry from July 17 to
October 12, 1863

*Courtesy U.S. Army Military
History Institute*

Brigadier General Albion P. Howe,
commander of Harpers Ferry from
July 8 to August 6, 1864

*Courtesy U.S. Army Military
History Institute*

Brigadier General Washington L. Elliott, who received command of Harpers Ferry on June 28, 1863, and evacuated the town three days later
*Courtesy U.S. Army Military History Institute*

Brigadier General Max Weber, who took command of Harpers Ferry on April 5, 1864, and, acting under the orders of General Franz Sigel, evacuated the town unnecessarily on July 4, 1864
*Courtesy U.S. Army Military History Institute*

Major General Franz Sigel, who took command of the Department of West Virginia on March 21, 1864, and ordered General Weber's evacuation of Harpers Ferry on July 4, 1864
*Courtesy U.S. Army Military History Institute*

Major General Jubal A. Early, who forced the evacuation of Harpers Ferry during his Maryland campaign in July, 1864, by executing a feint
*Courtesy U.S. Army Military History Institute*

Brigadier General John D. Stevenson, commander of Harpers Ferry from August 15, 1864, until February 27, 1865

*Courtesy U.S. Army Military History Institute*

Major General David Hunter, who burned many fine homes in Jefferson and Berkeley Counties in 1864

*Courtesy U.S. Army Military History Institute*

Brigadier General Jeremiah C. Sullivan, commander of Harpers Ferry from October 12, 1863, to April 5, 1864

*Courtesy U.S. Army Military History Institute*

Colonel John S. Mosby, who sent his Rangers on many raids into the area supported by the Harpers Ferry garrison

*Courtesy U.S. Army Military History Institute*

Brigadier General John R. Kenly, who commanded Harpers Ferry from December 11 to December 16, 1862, and in the summer of 1864 led the wagon train that was attacked by Mosby's Rangers
*Courtesy U.S. Army Military History Institute*

Major General Winfield Scott Hancock, who took command of the Middle Military District on February 27, 1865, with head-quarters at Harpers Ferry, and remained there until June 27, 1865
*Courtesy U.S. Army Military History Institute*

Major General Philip H. Sheridan, who took command of the Middle Military District on August 6, 1864, and made Harpers Ferry his head-quarters

*Courtesy U.S. Army Military History Institute*

# 14

## Ripples from Gettysburg

On June 28, 1863, Meade took command of the militarily mismanaged Army of the Potomac. "As a soldier," he declared, "in obeying this order—an order totally unexpected and unsolicited—I have no promises or pledges to make."[1]

The new commander displayed none of the usual bravado for the job. What he needed was a little luck and time to consolidate his force before Lee advanced too far into Pennsylvania. What Halleck refused Hooker he gave to Meade, detaching French's VIII Corps from Harpers Ferry. Hooker had been right about one matter—10,000 troops at the Ferry was a "waste." Meade asked French how many troops he needed to hold Maryland Heights "against any *coup de main.*" Five thousand, replied French. On June 29 Meade issued marching orders, directing that all government property at Harpers Ferry be moved to Washington. He withdrew French's VIII Corps to Frederick and held them in reserve for possible use in Pennsylvania.[2]

French underestimated the task at Harpers Ferry and assigned Brigadier General Washington L. Elliott's brigade of 3,300 to save the supplies. Elliott claimed the transfer could not be made in less

---

1. Meade's General Order No. 67, June 28, 1863, *OR*, XXVII, Pt. 3, p. 374.
2. Williams to French, June 28, French to Williams, June 28, and Butterfield to French, June 29, 1863, *ibid.*, 378, 382, 401–402.

than ten days without leaving behind several pieces of heavy artillery and destroying much of the ammunition and quartermaster supplies. Halleck raised a fuss. "These things should not be abandoned," he declared, "but defended." Like others before him, French felt squeezed between two masters.[3]

Forty-eight-year-old William Henry French, a Marylander who graduated twenty-second in the West Point class of 1837, had seen service in the Seminole War and the Mexican War. Serving with the Army of the Potomac since its formation, French fought in all the major battles, and after commanding a division at Antietam he earned promotion to major general. A heavy-set man with a full mustache, French enjoyed a rollicking good time but, despite his grade, did not want much responsibility.[4]

When ordered to evacuate Harpers Ferry, French turned the job over to Elliott, Milroy's senior brigadier during the command's panicky flight from Winchester. Thirty-eight-year-old Washington Elliott, an 1844 graduate of West Point, had fought in the West under General Pope and came with him as the Army of Virginia's cavalry commander. He led the 3rd Division, III Corps, at Chancellorsville before joining Milroy's command at Winchester. Blue-eyed with thinning blond hair, Elliott looked more like a scholar than a general, and his undistinguished record prior to Gettysburg left him with the innocuous responsibility of demobilizing Harpers Ferry. Having little faith in Elliott's demoralized volunteers, French supplemented the force with men from Tyler's former command, bringing the total at Harpers Ferry to about five thousand defenders. On June 28, French removed the remainder of the garrison and marched them to Frederick.[5]

With no enemy infantry to pester the Union withdrawal, Elliott moved with speed and by nightfall on June 30 had most of the supplies loaded on wagons. But late that night Lieutenant Colonel Thomas B. Massie, leading the 12th Virginia Cavalry, sent a patrol of forty-two picked riders against Elliott's outpost on Bolivar Heights. The troopers, led by Lieutenants George Baylor and Samuel Hammon, knew the area intimately and worked around to the rear of the sleeping pickets, opened the attack with a piercing rebel

3. French to Halleck, and Halleck to French, June 30, 1863, *ibid.*, 428.
4. *HTI*, 292.
5. *Ibid.*, 239; French's Report, October 1, 1863, *OR*, XXVII, Pt. 1, p. 488.

yell, and struck with effect. The unexpected assault and consequent loss of twenty-one men startled Elliott. Expecting more trouble at sunrise, he recalled his pickets, blew up the remaining kegs of ammunition, and, as the last wagons crossed at dawn, sent a detail to tear up the flooring of the Potomac bridge. Massie took possession of the town in the morning and dispatched scouts to keep a close watch on Elliott.[6]

If Massie credited his cavalry for driving the Union defenders out of Harpers Ferry, he had more reason to celebrate on July 2 when Elliott abandoned Maryland Heights. The 12th Virginia Cavalry forded the Potomac, trotted down to Sandy Hook, and found a large quantity of undamaged commissary, quartermaster, and ordnance stores. Massie rounded up boats, ferried the goods across the river, commandeered wagons, and forwarded the loot to regimental headquarters.[7]

While the three-day Battle of Gettysburg raged to the north, Massie occupied the area uncontested. He knew nothing of Lee's defeat when he sent a detachment of cavalry on a raid to Frederick. The horsemen collided with Cole's Maryland Cavalry, who sent them hightailing it back to Sandy Hook. On July 6, Cole pressed Massie into Harpers Ferry and, with a gun wheeled into position on the Maryland side, checked Massie's riders while two of his Marylanders dumped several buckets of oil on the new Baltimore and Ohio bridge. A few minutes later the wooden section of the trestle burst into flames. As soon as the men cleared the structure, another detail set fire to the bridge over the canal. Cole, satisfied he had done his duty, rode triumphantly back to Frederick. Ferrians no longer kept count of how many times their bridges had been destroyed.[8]

Although Massie may have torched the bridges had Cole not done so, the destruction of the Baltimore and Ohio span proved to be a tragic mistake. Lee began his retreat from Gettysburg along the same line as his advance, intending to cross the fords well above Harpers Ferry. A strong Confederate rear guard held back Meade's feeble attempt at pursuit. While Lee waited for the swollen Potomac to recede, his force on the north bank of the river

6. Baylor, *Bull Run to Bull Run*, 150.

7. Massie's Report, July 30, 1863, *OR*, XXVII, Pt. 2, p. 766.

8. French's Report, October 1, 1863, *ibid.*, Pt. 1, p. 488; Newcomer, *Cole's Cavalry*, 54–55.

remained vulnerable, front and rear, for nearly ten days. Had the railroad bridge at the Ferry remained open, and had Meade been so inclined, he could have sent a strong force across the bridge, marched them to the Williamsport fords, and either contested Lee's crossing or harassed his flank. Meade, however, showed no inclination to do either.

On July 6 French learned that high water from recent storms had rendered the Potomac unfordable. "The enemy is sending his wounded across in flats," he reported. Lincoln read the dispatch and asked Halleck why French was allowing the enemy to get across without making an effort to stop him. Schenck collected about 18,000 troops and volunteered to take them wherever they were needed. Halleck told Schenck to stay at Baltimore, but he transferred most of Schenck's troops to French with orders to move immediately to Harpers Ferry. Elliott, who had just reached Washington with his wagons, received orders to pack back up and return to Maryland Heights. Stanton made arrangements with Garrett for hundreds of cars to move 10,000 troops with horses and batteries back to Harpers Ferry. Halleck had just completed plans to trap Lee when he received word that Cole had destroyed the Harpers Ferry bridge. No record exists of Halleck's reaction, but he lost no time by writing denunciations. Orders went directly to the Washington Navy Yard for two sets of pontoon bridges and transportation to the Ferry by way of the canal.[9]

On the morning of July 7, Kenly's Maryland Brigade drove off a weak force of Confederate skirmishers and recaptured Maryland Heights, but they could not ford the swollen river. Later in the day, Lieutenant John R. Meigs of the Engineer Corps inspected the bridge and reported the ironwork undamaged, but he asked that sharpshooters in the lower town be driven away before repair crews started work on the span.[10] Throughout the day troops poured into Sandy Hook, but none could cross the river. By July 8 tons of war material lay piled along the river below Maryland Heights.

Brigadier General Henry W. Benham arrived later in the day with his Engineer Brigade. With Meigs and a work crew, he started

9. French to Halleck, Lincoln to Halleck, Schenck to Halleck, Halleck to Schenck and to French, Heintzelman to Kelton, Garrett to Stanton, and Benham to Williams, July 6, 1863, OR, XXVII, Pt. 3, pp. 564, 567, 570–71, 574, 574–75, 564.

10. Kenly to French, and Meigs to Schenck, July 7, 1863, ibid., 585, 589.

across the bridge to assess the damage. Meade, for reasons not completely clear, did not want the bridge repaired until Lee was back across the river. Firing from the town sent two of the repair crew toppling into the river. Benham reported less than a hundred men in Harpers Ferry, but he refused to touch the span until Kenly secured the town. In the meantime, river levels began to recede upstream and Halleck pressed Meade for action: "The enemy is crossing at Williamsport. The opportunity to attack his divided forces should not be lost."[11]

While a flurry of correspondence traveled between Army of Potomac headquarters and the War Department, Lieutenant Meigs waited impatiently at Sandy Hook for instructions from Meade. With five ironclad cars for protection against musketry and small artillery, he asked Schenck for permission to start work on the bridge—stressing, however, that Meade was holding up the work. Schenck, who had no authority in the matter, replied, "You must be cautious as well as active"—advice of no help to Meigs.[12]

Command changes continued at a pace resembling the final frantic moments of musical chairs. On July 8 Meade ordered Brigadier General Henry M. Naglee to the Ferry with his brigade from the III Army Corps "to assume command of that post by virtue of his rank." Naglee arrived at Sandy Hook the following morning and tried to get an accurate count of his force. Meade seemed more interested in holding the north side of the river than in occupying Harpers Ferry. He ordered Naglee to form three brigades and send them through Rohrersville "to join the left of the army."[13] Whatever his reasons, Meade's order shuttled Naglee's force to a defensive position—not towards Lee's flanks.

Meigs detained his repair crew on the north shore of the river and waited for orders, but on July 9 he crossed the bridge and sauntered into Harpers Ferry. "I do not believe there is an armed rebel nearer than Bolivar Heights," he reported, calling attention to the fact that Lee had withdrawn all but a few pickets from the area to cover his retreat. With piles of timbers already stacked on the Maryland side to commence repairs, Meigs announced his

11. Benham to Williams, and Halleck to Meade, July 8, 1863, *ibid.*, 605.

12. Meigs to Meade and to Schenck, and Schenck to Meigs, July 8, 1863, *ibid.*, 607, 608.

13. Special Order No. 183, July 8, 1863, *ibid.*, 600; Humphreys to Naglee, July 9, 1863, *ibid.*, Pt. 1, p. 87.

crew ready to go to work "the moment General Meade orders [the bridge's] construction."[14]

Baltimore and Ohio president Garrett also manifested impatience and warned Meade that if the pontoon bridge was not laid quickly and Harpers Ferry recaptured, the enemy could do further damage to the railroad and retard the opening of the section to Martinsburg.[15]

Meade replied that he thought it best, "under the circumstances, not to attempt to repair the bridge," and ordered Naglee to send every new regiment arriving at Maryland Heights to Boonsboro. Having drained off the continuous flow of reinforcements arriving at Sandy Hook, Meade left Naglee with about 3,400 men. For several days Meigs had nothing to do, and his men roamed the countryside pilfering for provender.[16]

On July 10 Meigs crossed the Potomac in a skiff under a flag of truce to bring a child to the Maryland side. He encountered no enemy and chatted with the townspeople, who seemed oblivious to the events of the past week. They believed the Army of Northern Virginia was in Frederick and had cut off the Union force that had evacuated the Ferry on July 2. Some felt better after Meigs explained that Lee had been defeated at Gettysburg.[17]

On July 12 the swollen Potomac dropped rapidly, opening the upper fords to Lee's retreating army.[18] Meade finally began his advance, but much too late. Lee stopped him on the north side of the Potomac at Williamsport and again at Falling Waters. Almost as an afterthought, Meade realized he needed the Harpers Ferry bridge. More rain began to fall, and when the Potomac began to rise on the afternoon of July 14, Lee had his men across the river and encamped near Bunker Hill.[19]

Fearing censure for allowing Lee to escape, Meade put Major General Henry W. Slocum's XII Corps, Hays's II Corps, and French's VIII Corps on the road to Harpers Ferry. He sent another

14. Meigs to Schenck, July 9, 1863, *ibid.*, Pt. 3, p. 618.

15. Garrett to Meade, July 9, 1863, *ibid.*, 626.

16. Humphreys to Garrett, July 9, Humphreys to Naglee, July 10, and Naglee to Humphreys, July 12, 1863, *ibid.*, 633, 628, 668–69.

17. Meigs to Schenck, July 10, 1863, *ibid.*, 632.

18. MacKenzie to Warren, July 12, 1863, *ibid.*, 669.

19. Lee's Report, July 31, 1863, *ibid.*, Pt. 2, p. 310; see also John D. Imboden, "The Confederate Retreat from Gettysburg," *B&L*, III, 420–29.

four corps and the Reserve Artillery to Berlin (now Brunswick), about four miles below the Ferry. Lieutenant Colonel Ira Spaulding took charge of the bridge repair and by midafternoon, July 14, had it planked over for limited use. Naglee dispatched one of his regiments across the temporary span. They marched through the ramshackle town and into the breastworks on Bolivar Heights. Once again, Harpers Ferry belonged to the Union.[20]

Naglee sent the 1st Connecticut Cavalry with fifty men under Major Charles Farnsworth to reconnoiter the roads leading into the Ferry. At Halltown Farnsworth collided with a squad of six sabers led by Colonel Asher W. Harman of the 12th Virginia Cavalry. Harman had just returned to duty after recovering from a wound and was itching for a fight. Seeing only six men in his front, Farnsworth charged at full speed. Harman, thrown by his horse, was captured by a Connecticut rider, along with four others. Two escaped to warn their comrades on the far side of a woods. Moments later Lieutenant Colonel Massie led two hundred troopers in a screaming countercharge that ripped through the Connecticut line. After an exchange at close quarters the 1st Connecticut scattered, and before the skirmish ended Massie had collected Farnsworth, whose horse had been shot, a lieutenant, and twenty-three troopers. The 1st Connecticut returned to camp with half their number but proudly displayed their prisoners—Colonel Harman, two officers, and four privates.[21]

The following day Colonel Charles H. Smith, 1st Maine Cavalry, tried his luck. Finding no enemy at Halltown, he rode towards Charles Town. A mile down the road Smith's riders flushed a few pickets. After two hours of unproductive maneuvering, Smith returned to base with one man wounded but proudly reported, "My regiment behaved with the utmost gallantry."[22]

The 12th Virginia Cavalry continued to cover Lee's flank in Jefferson County, but they kept at a distance and merely watched as Union engineers rebuilt the bridge and laid new track. The 1st New York Cavalry under Colonel Andrew T. McReynolds kept the enemy from annoying work crews, and gradually the old road-

20. Williams' Circular, Spaulding to Benham, and Naglee to Humphreys, July 14, 1863, *OR*, XXVII, Pt. 3, pp. 695, 691, 690.

21. Naglee to Williams, July 16, Blakeslee to Naglee, July 18, and Massie to Jones, July 30, 1863, *ibid.*, pp. 204, 205, 767; Baylor, *Bull Run to Bull Run*, 151.

22. Smith's Report, August 14, 1863, *OR*, XXVII, Pt. 1, pp. 978, 980.

beds went back into service. McReynolds spread his outposts up the Potomac until he came in contact with Kelley's command, which now answered to the Department of West Virginia.[23]

Kelley's force occupied the western Potomac and consisted mostly of weakly armed railroad guards. When Lee crossed back into Virginia in mid-July, Halleck expected Kelley to do what Meade had failed to do. "Move up upon the enemy's flank and rear," Halleck ordered, "and attack and harass him wherever you can." Kelley had already started repairing track and replacing telegraph lines above Williamsport, but the order to assail Lee's army sounded unreasonable. He moved slowly enough to allow Lee to cross unmolested, and as the river rose again on July 14 he allowed his command to become conveniently stranded on the north bank of the Potomac.[24] Although Halleck was disappointed by Kelley's lethargic effort to contain Lee, his primary task was to get Meade in motion.

Meade transferred headquarters to Berlin to reorganize his army. Striking up another round of musical chairs at the Ferry, he removed Naglee and replaced him with forty-nine-year-old Brigadier General Henry H. Lockwood.[25] A graduate of the West Point class of 1836, Lockwood served briefly with the 2nd U.S. Artillery and in the Seminole War. In 1837 he resigned his commission and became a farmer. Four years later he taught at the Naval Academy, specializing in mathematics, astronomy, field artillery, and infantry tactics. At the outbreak of the Civil War he organized the 1st Delaware Infantry and became its colonel. He saw little action until Gettysburg, where he led a brigade of Slocum's XII Corps. Lockwood soon found himself fighting a different kind of war.[26]

By July 19 Meade had the Army of the Potomac back in Virginia. Chaplain Stuckenberg marched past Harpers Ferry on July 16 with the tattered remnants of the 145th Pennsylvania and "thanked God that we were not again required to stay at that

23. Special Order No. 190, July 15, and Stanton to Kelley, June 24, 1863, *ibid.*, Pt. 3, pp. 704, 299.

24. Halleck to Kelley, July 13, and Kelley to Halleck, July 14, 1863, *ibid.*, 681, 699.

25. Special Order No. 192, July 17, 1863, *ibid.*, 719–20. Naglee had fallen ill, but he recovered a few days later and took command of the VII Army Corps, Department of Virginia and North Carolina.

26. *HTI*, 442–43.

unhealthy and unpleasant place."[27] The war moved south, back to the old battlegrounds around the Rappahannock. Aside from brushes with enemy cavalry and bushwhackers, Lockwood and the few remaining townspeople enjoyed another temporary spell of peace in the Valley.

On August 1 the Baltimore and Ohio made its first regular run over the Harpers Ferry bridge since June. The sound of engines pounding down the rebuilt track drew Mosby's raiders like a magnet. Lockwood had but six companies of cavalry to cover the tracks between Point of Rocks and Martinsburg. When Mosby joined forces with White's Virginia Battalion and began disrupting the train schedules, Lockwood was forced to deploy his infantry. "Had I any cavalry here," he grumbled, "these fellows would not be so near here with impunity."[28] But the raids continued unabated.

After three months of chasing gray ghosts, Lockwood's tenure at the Ferry ended. Seven weeks later he replaced Schenck and took command of the Middle Department at Baltimore.[29] Lockwood never performed well in the field but proved to be an able administrator.

Thirty-three-year-old Brigadier General Jeremiah C. Sullivan moved his personal belongings from Clarksburg, West Virginia, and took command of the Ferry in mid-October. The young general had been a navy man and over a span of six years served as an officer on four different vessels. Before the war he practiced law, and in 1861 he helped organize the 6th Indiana Infantry. After seeing action in West Virginia and the Shenandoah Valley, Sullivan joined Grant's army in the West and fought at Iuka, Corinth, and Vicksburg. After a brief stint as Grant's inspector general, and later as Major General James P. McPherson's chief of staff, Sullivan joined his father-in-law, Benjamin Kelley, in West Virginia. The command change was remarkable for its lack of importance. Kelley assigned his son-in-law to Harpers Ferry and gave him respon-

27. Meade's Circular, July 17, 1863, *OR*, XXVII, Pt. 3, p. 718; "A History of the 145th Pennsylvania Volunteers," July 7–28, 1863, Stuckenberg Collection, MLGC.

28. Hungerford, *Baltimore and Ohio Railroad*, II, 24; Organization of the Army of the Potomac, and Lockwood to Halleck, August 1, 1863, *OR*, XXVII, Pt. 3, pp. 813, 826, 827.

29. Special Order No. 52, October 12, and No. 518, November 21, 1863, *OR*, XXIX, Pt. 2, pp. 302, 477.

sibility for the Baltimore and Ohio tracks from the Monocacy River to Sleepy Creek.[30]

As Sullivan settled into his new headquarters, another drama in the misfortunes of war entered its final act at Washington. In the aftermath of Lee's invasion of Pennsylvania, a court of inquiry convened on August 4 to investigate the evacuation of Winchester and Martinsburg in late June. Milroy and Tyler coasted through the inquiry with unabashed innocence. Tyler produced his own witnesses and presented compelling testimony in his defense. Milroy had the good sense to employ counsel and denied any wrongdoing, claiming that instead of criticism he deserved praise for retarding Lee's advance by three days or more. The court remained in session for nearly three months, exonerating Tyler with conditions but leaving many questions unanswered regarding Milroy's performance. Lincoln saw the situation for what it was, a debacle created mostly by command confusion. Neither Halleck nor Schenck had given Milroy direct orders to withdraw from Winchester, and both had sent him ambiguous if not conflicting orders prior to Ewell's attack. "No court-martial is deemed necessary or proper in the case," Lincoln ruled, as he considered neither officer "deserving of serious blame." Tyler, however, had handled his command much better than Milroy.[31]

Harpers Ferrians also chalked up their own casualties during the Gettysburg event, one of them a schoolmaster named Law. Because of his abolitionist views, Law was driven out of the Ferry shortly after John Brown's raid and narrowly escaped a coat of tar and feathers. When the war began, he attached himself to the Union army as a spy. At the time Elliott evacuated Maryland Heights, roving bushwhackers captured Law, took him to a lonely knoll on Loudoun Heights, laid him flat on his back, and tethered him to the ground. Some blamed John Mobley's gang of renegades for Law's death, as the schoolmaster was left to die of starvation if wolves, wild hogs, or turkey vultures did not find him first.[32]

But as summer passed into fall and leaves carpeted the remains of the schoolmaster's undiscovered body, an interregnum of quiet

30. HTI, 731; General Order No. 12, October 12, 1863, OR, XXIX, Pt. 2, p. 302.
31. Lincoln's Endorsement, October 27, 1863, OR, XXVII, Pt. 2, 197; the trial and conclusions are ibid., 88–201.
32. Barry, Harper's Ferry, 128–29.

returned to Harpers Ferry. The small garrison added to the exhausted town's prosperity. Some said Bobby Lee was gone for good, but there was still John Mobley's gang, Mosby's Rangers, and a cantankerous old bachelor by the name of Jubal Early who wanted to pay Washington a visit before the war ended.

# 15

## Mr. Lincoln's Germans

With Lee's army in winter quarters south of the Rappahannock, Sullivan kept his fireside well supplied with wood and settled into his office to ride out the frosty days of January. As a precaution against roaming Confederate raiders, he posted guards along the tracks and kept his cavalry saddled up and busy scouting the roads. Mosby's Rangers had been active between Leesburg and Upperville, and Sullivan, wanting no trouble, posted Cole's Maryland Cavalry on Loudoun Heights to protect the Shenandoah bridge and keep watch on the garrison's flank. Six months earlier, Cole, acting on orders from General French, had been the last to burn the Harpers Ferry bridge.

Further up the Valley, Jubal Early's corps posed a constant threat, and Sullivan kept Colonel William H. Boyd's 21st Pennsylvania Cavalry active probing the enemy's intentions. Boyd skirmished with Early's cavalry screen but reported no enemy in force. Early had come into the Valley in December to collect supplies, but he never advanced much beyond Middletown. His presence, however, sent another ripple of jitters down the Potomac to Washington.[1]

1. Boyd's Report, January 4, 1864, *OR*, XXXIII, 11–12; Millard K. Bushong, *Old Jube: A Biography of General Jubal A. Early* (Shippensburg, Pa., 1985), 166–67.

On New Year's Day, 1864, most of Cole's men huddled in tents pitched halfway up the mountain, where the thermometer nosed below zero. A squad of eighty from Company C under Captain A. N. Hunter ventured into Mosby's Confederacy, passed through Upperville, and scouted towards Rectortown. Near Middleburg, Captain William R. Smith of Mosby's command spotted Hunter near Rector's Crossroads, gathered about thirty-two Rangers, and pursued. Near Five Points the two columns collided, and when Hunter's horse went down the company panicked and fled, swimming their horses across Goose Creek. They returned to camp "nearly frozen to death," with ice rock hard in their boots. Some of the men lost their toes, others their feet, and everyone else spent the next few days in the hospital.[2]

Frank Stringfellow, one of Jeb Stuart's trusted scouts, dispatched a rider to notify Mosby that Cole's Marylanders were encamped in tents on Loudoun Heights with no infantry support. Stringfellow considered his discovery important, as Cole and his riders were high on the Confederate "most wanted" list. A Richmond newspaper denounced the troop as "a bunch of marauding murderers."[3]

The weather, however, had turned brutal. More than a foot of snow lay on Loudoun Heights, and ice had formed along the shores of the river. A covering of sleet tore down limbs, snapped telegraph lines, and left a thick glaze on the roads. The weather discouraged travel, but Mosby considered the capture of Cole important enough to summon his command to meet at Upperville. Men answered the call slowly, cutting paths across frozen fields as they plowed through chest-high drifts. The blizzard had been violent, and some of the older men looked at the leaden gray sky and predicted more snow by morning. They could not go on, they said. It was just too cold.[4]

Early on the morning of January 9, Mosby left Upperville with 106 men, meeting at dark with Stringfellow at Woodgrove, in Loudoun County, some twelve miles from Harpers Ferry. The scout sketched the mountain roads on paper and pointed to a hidden

2. Newcomer, *Cole's Cavalry*, 91; James J. Williamson, *Mosby's Rangers* (New York, 1896), 118; Mosby to McClellan, January 4, 1864, *OR*, XXXIII, 9.

3. R. Shepard Brown, *Stringfellow of the Fourth* (New York, 1960), 238–39.

4. Virgil C. Jones, *Ranger Mosby* (Chapel Hill, N.C., 1944), 164–65; Williamson, *Mosby's Rangers*, 124–25.

path that would take the Rangers between Cole's outposts and the river. A courier from Stringfellow's detachment interrupted the meeting. He had just scouted the camp and reported everyone bedded down but a few lone pickets on the winding road up the snow-covered mountain. He had ten men posted along the path to guide the attack. At 9 P.M. Mosby ordered his command into their saddles, and they jogged into the frigid starlit night. A misty vapor rose from the flanks of the horses. Men thrust their hands into their coats to keep them warm and gripped the reins between their teeth. Frost gathered on the mufflers tied across their faces.

Stringfellow led Mosby around picket posts on the Hillsborough road and up a back trail on Short Hill to Cole's slumbering camp. Two hundred yards from the camp Mosby dismounted in a ravine and waited for his men to come up. Tents loomed like giant igloos, brightened by smoldering fires against the backdrop of an arctic night. Not a soul stirred, as Cole had no sentinels posted on his flank. Stringfellow pointed out Cole's quarters—a tall, framed building with the camp just beyond it—and Mosby told him to take his ten scouts and try for Cole. He then counted off his Rangers, keeping them in squads and cautioning them to wait, to attack in unison, and to not fire into each other.

At 3 A.M. the men remounted, climbed the ravine, and spread out, waiting for Stringfellow to open the attack. Mosby led most of his command up the slope, closed ranks, and waited near the Hillsborough road for Stringfellow to initiate the attack on Cole's headquarters. Stringfellow's men ran into unexpected trouble when they discovered a Marylander astir who refused to surrender. The sentinel dashed behind some picketed horses and fired his carbine. The shot upset Mosby's plans. Stringfellow's scouts stormed prematurely across the hill, shooting wildly into tents. The Rangers mistook the firing to be from Cole and charged Stringfellow's men. In the melee that followed, Cole's Marylanders picked up their carbines and in nightclothes poured out of their tents, dropped to the ground, and delivered a heavy fire at any moving shadow. In the darkness, shots flew indiscriminately through the camp. So confused was the turmoil that one of Mosby's Rangers emptied his revolver at Stringfellow, but missed with all six shots.

When a signal gun boomed from the heights, Mosby knew he had better skedaddle before hundreds of infantry came charging

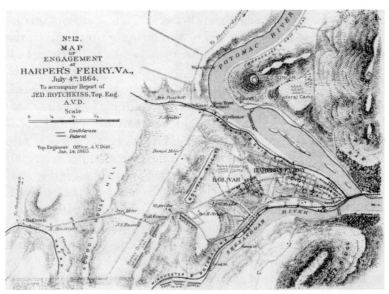

Harpers Ferry dispositions on July 4, 1864, during the invasion of
Maryland by General Jubal A. Early

*From* Atlas to Accompany the Official Records, *courtesy HFA*

up the mountain. He shouted to his men to retreat and sent them
scampering back for their horses. At daylight, both sides counted
their casualties. Mosby lost twelve men but proudly reported capturing six prisoners and "50 to 60 horses." Cole, whose camp consisted of about two hundred men, reported four killed and sixteen
wounded, but Mosby later admitted the attack had been a disaster.[5]

Mosby's raid delivered a wake-up call to Sullivan, who had not
expected to be pestered by raiders during the dark days of winter.
Reports of increased partisan activity at Winchester and Martinsburg convinced him otherwise.[6] Sheaves of misinformation
planted by so-called deserters piled up on Sullivan's desk, and the

5. Mosby's Report, February 1, and Cole's Report, January 10, 1864, *OR*, XXXIII,
15–16, 17. Details of the fight are covered in Jones, *Ranger Mosby*, 162–70; Brown,
*Stringfellow of the Fourth*, 237–44; and Williamson, *Mosby's Rangers*, 124–28,
485. See also Newcomer, *Cole's Cavalry*, 93–96; article in the Washington *Herald*,
June 10, 1914, in Daniel Collection, File HFD-66, HFA.
6. Sullivan to Cullum, January 1, 1864, *OR*, XXXIII, 323, 324, 325.

general wore out his horses by sending them up and down the line chasing rumors.

Kelley, however, was getting as nervous as Sullivan and asked for the 12th West Virginia to be sent to Cumberland. By mid-January he realized there was no serious threat, only scattered companies of partisans, but the scare brought Sullivan mounted reinforcements from Brigadier General William W. Averell's brigade.[7]

Rumors persisted, however, and three days later Kelley informed Sullivan the enemy was marching down the Valley and advancing on Charles Town. Sullivan sent out his cavalry but found Early still in camp and sitting out the winter at Harrisonburg. Squads from Mosby's command caused all the alarm. They made independent raids, helped along by several roving bands of partisans.[8]

Kelley scared easily, but his constant anxiety was instrumental in building his command to 36,274 men. Of those, 13,751 fell under Sullivan's jurisdiction and included 8,379 infantry, 3,796 cavalry, and 72 guns served by 1,576 artillerists. Once again, Harpers Ferry became an armed camp, matching in size the command under Miles in the late summer of 1862.[9]

Captain John Suter of the 54th Pennsylvania sat by a fire in a blockhouse serving as an outpost near Harpers Ferry and on January 13, 1864, wrote his wife: "Averell made a nice raid [but] it lost him considerable horse flesh and prisoners. He came back closely followed by Fitz Hugh Lee who frightened the authorities into an evacuation of nearly the whole country without a fight. Lee took all the conscripts he could find, a train of 300 horses and 75 wagons, a few hundred prisoners . . . and went home drunk and merry."[10]

Suter was more accustomed to the refinements of living and considered the Harpers Ferry area "a sad failure and complete

7. Kelley to Sullivan, January 4, Kelley to Sullivan, January 7, and Kelley to Averell, January 7, 1864, *ibid.*, 341–42, 362.

8. Kelley to Sullivan, January 10, and Sullivan to Kelley, January 18, 1864, *ibid.*, 370, 392.

9. Kelley's Returns, January 31, 1864, *ibid.*, 479.

10. John Suter to his wife, January 13, 1864, Suter Papers, Harrisburg Civil War Round Table Collection, USAMHI. Suter refers to Fitzhugh Lee's raid of December 31. See *OR*, XXXIII, 7–8.

humbug. The principal part of the inhabitants being but little in advance of the aborigines. When we come across an intelligent family the females generally wear black and regard a Yankee as the personification of every thing evil."[11]

Not every soldier shared Suter's dim view of the region. Private Jacob M. Seibert of the 93rd Pennsylvania, who came from a less fashionable family, arrived at the Ferry on January 5, 1864, and expressed a more favorable opinion. "This is a beautiful country," he noted to his parents, "just like Pennsylvania here. Many fine and accomplished ladies reside here. It just seems to me like home."[12]

But cavalry raids continued around Harpers Ferry. On the night of February 11, Major Harry W. Gilmor placed obstructions on the Baltimore and Ohio track at Brown's Shop near Kearneysville. As soon as the Baltimore Express stopped they boarded the train and captured a handful of Union soldiers, but they overlooked a large sum of money in the baggage compartment. The expressman who had the key to the safe jumped before the train came to a stop and hid in the woods. Some of Gilmor's men, however, went from car to car robbing passengers, only to be chased from their looting by the approach of an eastbound troop train. Gilmor's raiders left the scene in great haste, returning to camp with only a few baubles to show for their trouble.[13]

Mosby returned on March 10, this time with a squadron of thirty riders under Lieutenant Adolphus E. "Dolly" Richards. Union pickets near Charles Town mistook the riders for their own men and held their fire. Richards, with about half his men dressed in blue, opened on the pickets at close range. A few fell, but most of them threw down their muskets and surrendered. As Richards rode towards Kabletown with his prisoners, two of the pickets escaped, galloped into Harpers Ferry, and rode straight to headquarters. General Sullivan angrily dispatched a detachment of nine men from the 1st New York Veteran Cavalry under Major

11. John Suter to his wife, January 13, 1864, Suter Papers, Harrisburg Civil War Round Table Collection, USAMHI.

12. Jacob M. Seibert to his parents, January 5, 1864, Seibert Letters, Harrisburg Civil War Round Table Collection, USAMHI.

13. Kelley's Report, February 12, and Stuart to Chilton, February 24, 1864, *OR*, XXXIII, 151; Testimony of Passengers, *ibid.*, 152–54; Harry Gilmor, *Four Years in the Saddle* (New York, 1866), 144–46.

Jerry A. Sullivan. The New Yorkers caught up with Richards outside Kabletown, and in a brisk little fight Sullivan lost his life. The Rangers crossed back into Virginia at Sampson's Ford. The general never explained why he sent only nine men after Richards. In the two skirmishes he lost thirteen men—four killed, five wounded, and four taken prisoner. "I am glad to be able to announce," he added with an inflection of disgust, "that the two officers in charge of the pickets are [now Confederate] prisoners."[14]

But another change was brewing in the Valley. On February 29, 1864, Major General Franz Sigel, a graduate of Germany's Karlsruhe Military Academy, took command of the Department of West Virginia. Soon after emigrating, Sigel had settled in St. Louis. Because of his successful recruiting of the town's large antislavery German population, he was elevated to brigadier general on August 7, 1861. After performing well at Pea Ridge, Sigel received his second star on March 22, 1862, but his subsequent poor performance in the Valley and at Second Manassas raised questions of his competence. Perhaps to protect Sigel from his own ineptitude, the War Department tucked him away in what was becoming peaceful West Virginia.[15]

As Sigel announced his arrival at Cumberland headquarters, more important changes in command were taking place in Washington. At his own request, Halleck stepped aside from his post as general in chief of the Army, and on March 12 Grant took command of the Armies of the United States. Halleck agreed to serve as Grant's chief of staff, prompting considerable speculation over what impact this change would have on the command at Harpers Ferry.[16]

Sigel had a natural preference for Germans, and on April 5 he ordered an old friend, forty-four-year-old Brigadier General Max Weber, to Harpers Ferry. Weber, also a graduate of the German military academy, fought under Sigel in the Hungarian Revolution of 1849. Afterwards, he came to America and spent the next twelve years running a German hotel in New York City. In May, 1861, he raised the 20th New York and became its colonel. Weber

14. Carter's Report, March 7, Sullivan's Report, March 10, Taylor's Report, March 11, and Mosby's Report, September 11, 1864, OR, XXXIII, 234–36, 247, 248, 249; Williamson, Mosby's Rangers, 150–51.

15. General Order No. 80, February 29, 1864, OR, XXXIII, 618; HTI, 688.

16. General Order No. 8, March 10, and No. 98, March 12, 1864, ibid., 664, 669.

238 • *Six Years of Hell*

had led a brigade of the VII Corps at Suffolk and earned recognition as a brigade commander with the II Corps at Antietam. He had been severely wounded, his right arm crippled for life. Harpers Ferrians viewed Weber with amused curiosity. The German kept his gleaming waxed mustache and daggerlike beard as stiff and rigid as his gaudy uniform with its shiny buttons, but Weber, un-like Sigel, had a sense of humor, and the townsfolk liked him.[17]

Sigel moved rapidly to solidify his friend's command by reas-signing Sullivan to a division of infantry being organized under Major General Edward O. C. Ord at Clarksburg. He then consol-idated the cavalry under Averell and buttressed patrols along the Baltimore and Ohio by ordering squads of railroad guards to ride back and forth with the trains in ironclad boxcars equipped with howitzers.[18]

Sigel received orders from Grant to organize a force of 8,000 infantry, three batteries of artillery, and 1,500 picked cavalry for a move against whatever force Lee maintained in the Valley. At the time, Grant was planning his Richmond campaign and wanted Ord to sweep into the Valley and worry Lee's flank while Brigadier General George Crook, with another force of 10,000, struck south and took possession of the Virginia and Tennessee Railroad, one of Lee's lifelines.[19] Grant not only wanted to disrupt the Confed-erate supply line, but he also intended to weaken Lee by forcing him to send reinforcements to the Valley.

To satisfy Grant, Sigel had to dip into Weber's command, but at Harpers Ferry spring floods reached record heights, topping over the Potomac bridge and inundating the lower town. Freshly laid planks ripped loose and floated downriver. Railroad traffic east and west came to a standstill while engineers, for the sixth time in three years, rushed to repair the structure.[20]

At Point of Rocks, Weber ordered three companies of the In-dependent Loudoun Rangers to join Averell's command, but Cap-tain Means refused. He preferred to stay where he was, and said

17. Sigel to Weber, April 5, 1864, *ibid.*, 807; Boatner, *Civil War Dictionary*, 898–99.

18. Special Order No. 68, April 6, and Sigel to Grant, April 2, 1864, *OR*, XXXIII, 813, 791.

19. Grant to Sigel, March 29, 1864, *ibid.*, 765–66; see also Franz Sigel, "Sigel in the Shenandoah Valley in 1864," *B&L*, IV, 487.

20. Hungerford, *Baltimore and Ohio Railroad*, II, 24.

so. Weber advised Averell of the situation and asked what he should do. Averell dismissed Means for insubordination, but War Secretary Stanton sent him on a mission to Waterford. Weber privately celebrated because he needed the Rangers.[21] A year later Means was still at Point of Rocks and still scouting for Stanton. He gave new meaning to military units carrying the name "independent."[22]

Not since Meade's army passed through Harpers Ferry in the summer of 1863 had the town seen so many military supplies and sutlers' wagons roll across the bridge. Equally observant southern sympathizers informed Confederate scouts that mischief was afoot. The spring campaign was about to start, they warned, and Harpers Ferry was once again massing supplies.

Grant asked Sigel to send Ord up the Valley quickly, to take it and hold it. With the enemy driven far from the Potomac, the Baltimore and Ohio would be able to operate unmolested and supply Sigel's force from Harpers Ferry. The German's peppery military style, however, clashed with Ord's preference for thoughtful planning, and the latter asked to be relieved. Ord, a personal friend of Grant's, left the department on April 19, leaving no instructions for his replacement.[23]

On April 22 Sigel marshaled his force at Martinsburg. Because the stores at Harpers Ferry and the roadway of the Baltimore and Ohio required constant protection, he could muster only seven thousand effectives for his invasion of the Valley. Grant thought the number equal to the mission and encouraged Sigel to put the force in motion.[24]

At the last moment, Sigel called Major General Julius Stahel, his chief of cavalry, from Cumberland to take command of the 1st Infantry Division forming at Martinsburg. Thirty-nine-year-old

21. Sigel to Weber, and Weber to Melvin, April 19, 1864, OR, XXXIII, 912; Means to Stanton, August 15, 1864, ibid., XLIII, Pt. 1, p. 799.

22. Stevenson to Chamberlin, March 29, 1864, ibid., XLVI, Pt. 3, p. 279. In Goodhart, Loudoun Virginia Rangers, 123–24, the author states that Means left the service. From OR it appears that Lieutenant Daniel M. Keyes took command of the Loudoun Rangers, but Means continued in the service with a smaller independent unit.

23. Grant to Sigel, April 17, Special Order No. 15, April 19, and Sullivan to Melvin, April 20, 1864, OR, XXXIII, 893, 911, 927–28.

24. Sigel to Grant, April 26, April 18, and Grant to Sigel, April 19, 1864, ibid., 942, 901, 911.

Julius Stahel, one of the German's many cronies, now became an infantry commander. He had served under Sigel early in the war, but his prior military training had been limited to fighting for independence during the Hungarian Revolution.[25] Then, to bolster the force at Martinsburg, Sigel moved Sullivan from Grafton to take command of Stahel's cavalry division, thereby weakening Crook. After a week of reshuffling commands and commanders, Sigel put his force in motion on April 29 and led it slowly up the Valley.[26]

Reaching Winchester at 2 A.M. on May 2, Sigel inexplicably became confused and forgot the purpose of his mission. He wrote Grant, asking, "I would very much like to know what your expectations are." He could locate no enemy in force but decided he needed at least five thousand more infantry to execute an unspecified mission. Sigel's jitters probably kept him awake, because at the same early hour he wired Weber warning that if repulsed, all the troops in the vicinity of Harpers Ferry must retire into the town, and the stores at Martinsburg evacuated to safety. Although Sigel admitted that the force in his front was smaller than his own, his enthusiasm for a fight had noticeably deteriorated. If compelled to retreat, he promised Weber he would "defend Harper's Ferry indirectly because the enemy cannot attack that place when I am on his left flank and rear with my forces."[27] Weber probably wondered why Sigel was so anxious to step aside and give the enemy a straight, uncontested route to Harpers Ferry.

On the heels of Sigel's confusing instructions, Weber received another unsettling message, this one from Kelley, who claimed to be in command of all the troops from Monocacy to Wheeling. Acting on instructions from Stanton, Kelley ordered Weber to report his strength. Distrusting Kelley, Weber refused to comply without Sigel's blessing. Sigel replied from Winchester that since the request came from the secretary of war, "You have to accept it."[28] Weber understood a chain of command, but nobody in the

25. Special Order No. 84, April 26, 1864, *ibid.*, 987, 988; *HTI*, 711.

26. Special Order No. 85, April 27, and Sigel to Grant, April 28, 1864, *OR*, XXXIII, 998, 1006; for Sigel's account of the fight, see his "Sigel in the Shenandoah Valley," *B&L*, IV, 487–91.

27. Sigel to Grant, April 30, and Sigel to Weber, May 2, 1864, *OR*, XXXVII, Pt. 1, pp. 368–69, 369–70.

28. Canby to Kelley, Kelley to Weber, and Weber to Sigel, May 6, and Sigel to Weber, May 7, 1864, *ibid.*, 396, 403.

German military academy had ever explained a matrix organization.

While Sigel loitered at Winchester, Confederate cavalry swarmed around his camp and spread north into Jefferson and Loudoun Counties. Because Weber had been stripped of scouts, he asked Kelley to return Colonel Andrew T. McReynolds' 1st New York Veteran Cavalry, whose riders were familiar with the area. Kelley agreed but sought approval from higher authority.[29] While red tape made its circuit through channels, Grant and Lee fought furiously but indecisively at Spotsylvania, and Major General John C. Breckinridge, scraping together militia and 258 cadets from the Virginia Military Institute, defeated Sigel at New Market.

With more than eight hundred killed, wounded, and missing, and with a loss of five guns, Sigel retreated towards Martinsburg, protecting, as he had promised, Harpers Ferry. When Lincoln learned of the disaster he ordered Sigel relieved and Major General David Hunter placed in command of the Department of West Virginia. Although discredited, Sigel accepted the change with a happy demonstration of relief. Hunter, however, liked the feisty German and on May 22 sent him to Martinsburg to take command of the Reserve Division, consisting of Kelley's force operating out of Cumberland and Weber's garrison at Harpers Ferry.[30] Sigel, although removed from field command, still had twenty thousand effectives and eighty-two guns spread in and between the two towns. Hunter promptly reorganized Sigel's force, stripped away his regiments, and with every intention of succeeding where the German had failed, put the command in motion.

Sixty-three-year-old David Hunter graduated from West Point in 1822 and served at minor stations on the northwest frontier prior to the Civil War. Between May 14 and August 13, 1861, he rose from colonel to major general, his last promotion following a serious wound at First Manassas. In June, 1862, Hunter was suspended from military duty after being badly whipped at Secessionville, South Carolina, following an abortive attempt to capture Charleston. Now back in field command, he developed a thirst for redemption, but whether he was pugnacious enough to battle with the likes of Jubal Early remained to be seen. On

---

29. Weber to Kelley, May 9, and Kelley's Endorsement May 14, 1864, *ibid.*, 416.

30. General Orders Nos. 27 and 28, May 21, and Special Order No. 102, May 23, 1864, *ibid.*, 508, 518–19.

May 22, operating from Cedar Creek, he issued orders for his command to send their tents, personal belongings, and camp equipment back to Martinsburg, as he intended to live off the land.[31]

Stripped of most of his cavalry, Weber passed the month of June harried and harassed by Mosby and Gilmor, but he kept the railroad open and supplies flowing. He took good care of government property and established good relations with the residents of Harpers Ferry by showing concern for their welfare. For a change, local farmers brought their crops to town unmolested, selling wheat and corn to the garrison and seeking permission for licenses to peddle their produce in Baltimore. Weber liked the idea and wrote the War Department for approval.[32]

While he waited for an answer from Washington, rumors circulated down the Valley that Hunter had been defeated at Lynchburg. At Cumberland, Kelley heard the same bad news but refused to believe it. Sigel said nothing of Hunter's defeat but reported him retiring towards Lewisburg.[33] A glance at the map might suggest to any military cadet that if Hunter retreated to Lewisburg he would leave the Valley open to invasion all the way to Harpers Ferry and the Maryland line.

Hunter began his march late in May and made rapid progress up the Valley, arriving at Harrisonburg on June 2, continuing on to Port Republic, and reaching Staunton on June 6. General Crook, after tearing up the track of the Virginia Central, joined Hunter at Staunton, bringing the Union strength to eighteen thousand effectives. Along each leg of the march Hunter stopped to burn buildings and warehouses, and if it suited him, occasionally a private home. Entering Lexington on June 11, he set fire to the Virginia Military Institute and the home of former governor Letcher. Hunter did not get his army back on the road until June 13.

Writing from Lexington, Private Frank Seibert of the 93rd Pennsylvania, who had joined the march from Harpers Ferry, reflected dolefully, "We destroyed . . . the buildings of the Virginia Military

31. *HTI*, 376; General Order No. 29, May 22, 1864, *OR*, XXXVII, Pt. 1, pp. 517–18.

32. Weber to Hardie, June 6, 1864, *OR*, XXXVII, Pt. 1, p. 599.

33. Weber to Meysenburg, and Meysenburg to Weber, June 27, 1864, *ibid.*, 681.

Institute. Very magnificent buildings. Many books were burned. I just wish I had some of them at home."[34]

Because his appetite for destroying property surpassed his enthusiasm for fighting, Hunter did not reach the outskirts of Lynchburg until late on June 16. He dallied moving up his artillery and making dispositions. The delay gave "Old Jube" Early just enough time to bring by forced marches his II Army Corps over from Richmond and check the Union advance. Hunter defeated himself by withdrawing from an inferior force without knowing why. In his haste to reach safety in West Virginia, he never stopped to consider that his line of retreat laid the Valley open to attack. He stopped briefly at Lewisburg to catch his breath before heading deeper into West Virginia and far from the sound of enemy guns. His losses had been moderate, 103 killed and 564 wounded, with some brigades reporting barely a scratch.[35]

Early's corps included the remnants of Jackson's rugged foot cavalry, mostly Valley men themselves. They had slipped away from their Petersburg trenches so quietly that neither Meade nor Grant knew they were gone. Early's road-weary corps arrived at Lynchburg just in time to shock Hunter's advance and send the Federals reeling back in confusion.[36]

Hunter outdistanced his communications to the extent that for several days Sigel lost track of the expedition. On June 27 the German commander became puzzled when he learned Hunter was at Lewisburg, but he became even more bewildered when he learned the army was headed for Charleston, West Virginia. No wonder Hunter's defeat could not be verified. On June 28 the wandering general wrote the War Department, "I have the honor to report that our expedition has been extremely successful, inflicting great injury upon the enemy and victorious in every engagement."[37] Weber, however, was beginning to suspect otherwise.

On June 29 Mosby's Rangers cut the telegraph line at Duffield's

34. Frank Seibert to his parents, June 13, 1864, Seibert Letters, Harrisburg Civil War Round Table Collection, USAMHI.

35. Hunter's Reports, June 8, August 8, and Union Returns, June 10–23, 1864, *OR*, XXXVII, Pt. 1, pp. 94–103, 103–106.

36. For details of the engagement, see Freeman, *Lee's Lieutenants*, III, 542–72.

37. McIlrath to Sigel, June 27, and Hunter to War Department, June 28, 1864, *OR*, XXXVII, Pt. 1, pp. 683, 684.

Station and temporarily disrupted communications between Harpers Ferry and Martinsburg. Weber, fearing the overdue eastbound express had been molested, rushed a small force to the site. The train, two hours late, stopped before reaching Duffield's and backed safely to Martinsburg, but Mosby's men burned the station, plundered storehouses, and captured about fifty men of the 1st Maryland Potomac Home Brigade. Weber sent Garrett, the Baltimore and Ohio's president, an apology for the damage but added that his whole force consisted of only 108 cavalrymen and one effective battery.[38]

With Hunter's force far to the west and no Union cavalry from Sigel's headquarters scouting further than Winchester, Early assimilated the Lynchburg garrison and with 12,000 infantry and 2,000 cavalry marched down the Valley unopposed. Unlike Sigel's railroad guards, Early's men were seasoned veterans who had carried their muskets up and down the Valley through three years of war. As they advanced they heard lurid stories of Hunter's pillaging, and when they reached Lexington they saw the charred remains of the institute where Jackson once taught and where many of them once studied. The soldiers vowed to punish Hunter if they caught him, but Early had other plans and marched swiftly towards the Potomac.[39]

Late on July 2, Sigel's riders clashed with a squadron of Gilmor's horsemen. Prisoners warned that a large force of infantry lay behind the cavalry screen, which was all Sigel needed to hear to accelerate his heart rate.[40]

On July 3 Halleck made several attempts to locate Hunter, but received no reply. Worried that Hunter's army had been crushed, Halleck asked Grant to verify whether Early's force had returned to Lee's army. "The three principal officers on the line of the [Baltimore and Ohio] road," Halleck wrote despondently, "are Sigel, Stahel, and Max Weber. You can therefore judge what probability there is of a good defense if the enemy should attack the line in force." Meade reported he had taken no prisoners from Early's

---

38. Garrett to Stanton, and Weber to Garrett, June 29, 1864, *ibid.*, 694–95; Weber to Meysenburg, July 2, and Mosby's Report, September 11, 1864, *ibid.*, Pt. 2, p. 11, Pt. 1, 3; Williamson, *Mosby's Rangers*, 183n.
   39. Freeman, *Lee's Lieutenants*, III, 558–59.
   40. Sigel to Weber, July 2, 1864, *OR*, XXXVII, Pt. 2, p. 11.

corps, raising concern that trouble was afoot for Sigel's command.[41]

Early morning, July 3, Garrett received an appeal from Sigel for 150 cars to remove all the stores from Martinsburg and ship them to Harpers Ferry. Before Garrett could corral the rolling stock, Mosby's men struck at Point of Rocks, drove off Means's command, plundered the local store, cut the telegraph wires, burned the Federal camp, and ripped up a few tracks.[42]

Garrett wired Stanton that Sigel had abandoned Martinsburg, taking with him six thousand men and leaving half of his supplies behind. Weber, attempting to make a stand on Bolivar Heights, asked for another hundred cars to evacuate the Ferry. Garrett, in a state of distress, wired Halleck, "Cannot General Hunter be ordered from the west to such points east of Cumberland as may be most judicious? Appearances at present indicate a general abandonment of the road."[43]

Weber's weak force, thinned first by Hunter and then by Sigel, lay scattered for miles along the track. He could hear guns booming at Martinsburg, but he could muster only four hundred infantry and three batteries. At 10 P.M. he learned for the first time that Sigel had abandoned Martinsburg and was on his way to the Ferry. Halleck offered to send five companies of artillery, but Weber said they would do no good without horses and equipment to move them. "I need infantry very much," he replied.[44]

Garrett worried about his bridge and cautioned Weber to confer with F. W. Haskett, supervisor of bridges, before doing anything to disable it. "Haskett," Garrett declared, "has been fully advised by our engineer how to accomplish your wishes with the least permanent damage to this costly and difficult structure."[45] Weber promised to leave the trestlework in place unless attacked by a heavy force.[46]

41. Halleck to Grant, Grant to Meade, and Meade to Grant, July 3, 1864, *ibid.*, 15, 16.

42. John Scott, *Partisan Life with Col. John S. Mosby* (Gaithersburg, Md., 1985), 239–44; Williamson, *Mosby's Rangers,* 184–86.

43. Garrett to Stanton, July 3, 1864, *OR,* XXXVII, Pt. 2, pp. 16–17, 18.

44. Sigel to Weber, Halleck to Weber, and Weber to Halleck, July 3, 1864, *ibid.*, 20, 19.

45. Garrett to Weber, July 3, 1864, *ibid.*, 24. Joseph Barry refers to F. W. Haskett as Thomas N. Heskett in *Harper's Ferry,* 138. Either Barry's memory for names is faulty or Garrett forgot the name of his own employee.

46. Burleigh to Garrett, July 3, 1864, *OR,* XXXVII, Pt. 2, p. 22.

With Sigel on the road to Harpers Ferry, Weber prepared his men for a stiff fight and withheld the destruction of military supplies. The panorama of battle unfolded on the summit of Maryland Heights, where signal officer Lieutenant Amos M. Thayer of the 112th New York had a clear view of converging forces. At 4 A.M. on July 4, Thayer observed Sigel's force at Shepherdstown and attempted to establish contact. Sigel declined to set up a signal station. He planned to be at Harpers Ferry shortly and did not want to go to the trouble. Four hours later Thayer observed a large force of Confederate infantry moving down the Charles Town pike towards Halltown. He signaled the information to Weber's headquarters, but the defenders on Bolivar Heights also read the message, abandoned their breastworks, and fled towards town.[47]

All day reinforcements arrived from Washington to shore up Weber, who made every effort to defend the town. "I have been fighting the enemy since morning," he reported on July 4. "They are advancing with cavalry and infantry. I will not evacuate Harper's Ferry until my means are exhausted."[48] While a heavy line of skirmishers exchanged musket fire with the enemy, Weber continued to load supplies on waiting cars.

The German's willingness to fight it out with Early came as a pleasant surprise to Halleck. The outcome now depended upon Sigel reaching Harpers Ferry in time to reinforce Weber, and Halleck remained hopeful. "Everything should be prepared for the defense of your works," he wrote Weber, "and the first man who proposes a surrender or retreats should be hung." But Halleck neglected to send the same message to Sigel, whose arrival at the Ferry was imminently expected. In another telegram to Weber, Halleck offered encouragement: "General Hunter's forces were ordered four days ago to move to [Sigel's] vicinity."[49] Halleck neglected to mention where "vicinity" was located, but the message held enough promise to stiffen Weber's resolve to hold the town.

Late afternoon on July 4, Major Gustavus F. Merriam of the 5th New York Artillery stared down from Maryland Heights and asked permission to fire into Bolivar. "The damned town is full of rebels," he said. He also reported Sigel's army too far up Pleas-

47. Thayer's Report, July [?], 1864, *ibid.*, Pt. 1, pp. 181–82.
48. Weber to Halleck, July 4, 1864, *ibid.*, Pt. 2, p. 38.
49. Halleck to Weber, and Smith to Weber, July 4, 1864, *ibid.*, 38, 39–40.

ant Valley to support Weber.[50] Although Weber's skirmish line was being pressed back upon headquarters, he wanted no shells thrown into Bolivar and tried to check the enemy with a few batteries of light artillery.

Joseph Barry watched the fight from a ringside seat near the 5th New York Artillery. When a shell fired from one of the guns struck Thomas Jenkins' home in Bolivar, Barry walked up to the gunner and asked him to stop firing. The shells, he said, were "doing wanton mischief to inoffensive citizens." The gunners stopped, obviously willing to take orders from anyone who gave them.[51]

Sigel dallied on his march from Shepherdstown, delaying his arrival at Harpers Ferry until 9 P.M. He put his force on Maryland Heights, but part of Stahel's cavalry lost their way in Pleasant Valley. Weber's creditable defense checked the enemy's half-hearted thrust, but Sigel anticipated a strong attack in the morning and ordered an immediate withdrawal and the bridge destroyed. Weber conferred with Haskett and set only two spans on fire. The last men across the pontoon bridge smashed it up and cut it loose.[52] Sigel, flushed out of Harpers Ferry more by threat than by force, succeeded in isolating his command from hundreds of citizens who had chosen to stay in their homes. With total disregard to the safety of the townsfolk, he ordered Weber to shell the town.

Captain James Montgomery of the U.S. Signal Corps watched from the crest of Maryland Heights as Union artillery lobbed shells at enemy positions arrayed around the town. He observed "several fine buildings" in Harpers Ferry and Bolivar break into flames and burn to the ground. After dark the firing continued, and throughout the night guns roared every ten minutes, "shelling out the sharpshooters," Montgomery thought. Joseph Barry examined the damage a few days later and counted civilian casualties. He learned that Thomas Jenkins' stepdaughter had been wounded during the fight, a woman on High Street had been killed, another on Shenandoah Street, and in Bolivar a child had

50. Merriam to Burleigh, July 4, 1864, *ibid.*, 40.

51. Barry, *Harper's Ferry*, 130.

52. Journal of Captain James H. Montgomery, July 4, 1864, Civil War Miscellaneous Collection, USAMHI; Jubal A. Early, "Early's March to Washington in 1864," *B&L*, IV, 495.

died from a wound caused by artillery fire. Barry heard of no Confederate casualties, as the grayclads had skedaddled.[53]

Mary Jane Coates Griffith made an untimely visit to her sister's home in Harpers Ferry a few days before the shelling began. To her sister she wrote, "Linie, you may thank your lucky stars you were not here for you would have died with fright. They shelled this place day and one night [and] threw some of them into several houses. . . . Sis' house, the brick part, is knocked all to pieces. She was obliged to fly to the cellar as that seemed to be the only place of safety. Several balls entered father's house . . . two through the windows, one where I was sleeping and one in the sitting room. Balls fell like hail through the yard, [and] we thought it would kill mother." Mary Jane had nothing good to say about Sigel's order for a hasty retreat. "Every man that could get away went [off] at double quick when they heard the Rebels were coming. I hope I may never witness such a time again. . . . I have seen plenty of cowardice here. The day of the battle it was another Miles affair."[54]

On the morning of July 5 the 43rd North Carolina of Rodes's division sauntered into town to find something to eat. Sutlers had cleaned out their sheds and retreated with the army, but a large cache of wine, whiskey, and beer had been left behind for the Fourth of July celebration. Further grubbing turned up ice cream, cakes, and other sweets. All morning, amid random shots from Maryland Heights, the town's temporary garrison feasted on captured picnic fare. A few townsfolk shared in the meal, washing it down with lemonade, beer, and a variety of intoxicants. By noon the 43rd North Carolina was back on the road, but not before liberating bundles of food from the town's Union sympathizers. Signal Officer Thayer looked down from the summit of Maryland Heights and with guarded disgust reported the enemy leaving.[55]

By sunset on July 5, Sigel must have felt a little foolish. He

53. Journal of Captain James H. Montgomery, July 5, 1864, Civil War Miscellaneous Collection, USAMHI; Mary Jane Coates Griffith to her sister, July 20, 1864, Griffith Letters, File HFD-364, HFA; Barry, *Harper's Ferry*, 130.

54. Mary Jane Coates Griffith to her sister, July 20, 1864, Griffith Letters, File HFD-364, HFA.

55. *Ibid.*; Manly Wade Wellman, *Rebel Boast: First at Bethel, Last at Appomattox* (New York, 1956), 167; Thayer's Report, July [?], 1864, *OR*, XXXVII, Pt. 1, p. 182; for Sigel's Reports, see *ibid.*, 174–81.

could count no more than seventy-five rebels prowling the streets between Harpers Ferry and Bolivar. No record remains of Sigel's reaction when reality penetrated his consciousness—Early's attack on Harpers Ferry had been but a feint.[56]

Equally bizarre was the disappearance of Hunter, whom Stanton finally located on July 5 at Parkersburg. "This Department has for some time been without any information as to where your forces are," the secretary wired irritably, "and how employed. . . . Acknowledge receipt of this telegram." Not knowing Martinsburg had been evacuated, Hunter promised to "push" forty cars of infantry there "as fast as possible." Hunter had been out of touch with his command too long to have any idea of the situation.[57]

Stanton, disgusted with Sigel's blundering, replaced him on July 8 with Brigadier General Albion P. Howe, who gathered up a small force of infantry, filed across the damaged bridge, and reoccupied Harpers Ferry shortly after noon. With the exception of the damage caused by Union artillery, he found the town undisturbed, much like Weber left it.[58]

David Seibert of the U.S. Signal Corps returned to Harpers Ferry a few days later. The temporary fright had passed, and like many Union soldiers, he did not expect to be bothered by rebel soldiers again. Moving to comfortable quarters in town, Seibert sought to socialize, and he wrote home asking for his best black hat, a pair of ribbed velvet pants, and a new pair of boots. He assured his father, "It is now perfectly safe . . . if you desire to come down. How soon the railroad was finished here! The cars now run through again . . . [and] I am hearty."[59]

Joseph Barry had moved back to town in late 1863 and resettled in his old homestead. When Early's skirmishers approached on July 2, Barry joined his neighbors for a hasty departure to Maryland Heights. He maintained a low opinion of the soldiers sent to defend his town, remembering a group of "hundred-day men" from Ohio who arrived at camp with no arms, no military training, and no interest in fighting rebels. To prepare their meal they pulled several large shells from an ammunition wagon, set them

56. Garrett to Stanton, July 6, 1864, OR, XXXVII, Pt. 2, p. 86.
57. Stanton to Hunter, and Hunter to Stanton, July 5, 1864, ibid., 62, 63.
58. Howe to Halleck, July 8, 1864, ibid., 124.
59. David S. Seibert to his father, July 22, 1864, Seibert Papers, Harrisburg Civil War Round Table Collection, USAMHI.

in a circle, and in the center built their cook fire. While they were squatting around the flames with their skillets, "a terrific explosion shook the surrounding hills, sending all the culinary utensils flying over the tree tops and . . . killing or wounding every man in the group." Barry thought the whole episode an unnecessary waste of life. The tragedy served as an example of the caliber of men sent by the War Department to defend Harpers Ferry.[60]

In the morning Barry returned to his home. This time he hoped he could stay.

60. Barry, *Harper's Ferry*, 132–33.

# 16

## The Smoky Days of Autumn

Forty-six-year-old General Howe had been to Harpers Ferry before. He was a captain then, in charge of a battery of the 4th U.S. Artillery, and he had been sent to blow John Brown out of his fort if the old man did not surrender quietly. He and his battery remained until the crisis passed, and Howe, who had taught mathematics at West Point and fought in the Mexican War, returned to Washington to await the coming conflict. Unlike so many of his predecessors at Harpers Ferry, Howe had led brigades in virtually every battle fought by the Army of the Potomac from Yorktown to Mine Run and earned the brevet of major general. Stanton had grown tired of weakhearted generals and detached Howe from his command at Washington. For the first time in the war, the townspeople of the Ferry had a fighting general to look after their safety. But fate played a trick on Stanton. He sent Howe away from the capital at a time when his presence was needed most.[1]

Howe arrived at Maryland Heights on July 8, 1864, and learned for the first time that the Confederate force bypassing the Ferry was indeed Old Jube's veterans. In his flight to safety, Sigel had the foresight to plant infantry down Elk Ridge to cover the Maryland passes, and he sent Stahel's cavalry to harass the enemy's

1. Boatner, *Civil War Dictionary*, 414.

rear. When scouts reported that Early's force consisted of three divisions of infantry and one of cavalry, Sigel stayed at a safe distance, complaining that two-thirds of his command were "100 days' men" and would not fight.[2]

Late on July 7, Early demonstrated against Elk Ridge, and the following morning he pushed through the passes. The grayclads knocked aside a hurriedly gathered force on the banks of the Monocacy and marched down the Potomac. Howe, perhaps anticipating the return of Early, moved most of his infantry to the eastern approaches of Maryland Heights. Thayer set up a signal station on the Catoctin Mountains and on July 10 reported Early in motion. "They are either marching on Washington or Baltimore," Thayer reported, "or are retreating towards Edwards Ferry."[3]

On July 11 Early's exhausted corps lay within artillery range of Washington's outer defenses. He probed the northwest ramparts but found them strongly fortified. A quick count of his footsore effectives convinced him to give it up. The men resisted, complaining they had not come all the way to the Yankee capital just to turn back. Early stayed in front of Washington long enough to see long lines of blue reinforcements file into the earthworks. Had he looked closer, he may have seen a tall, gaunt man in a black chimney-pot hat staring curiously over the bastion. After a brief rest Early put the corps on the road, marched despondently back to the Blue Ridge Mountains, and started looking for trouble. The tall man in the black hat returned to the White House, considerably relieved.[4]

On July 15 Hunter ordered General Crook to relieve Sullivan, form a junction with Major General Horatio Wright, and drive Early out of the Valley.[5] Crook passed through Harpers Ferry on his way to Hillsboro, where he located Sullivan's corps bivouacking peacefully beside a bubbling creek. Sullivan had no scouting parties out and could only speculate on Early's whereabouts. Crook sent Brigadier General Alfred N. Duffié's 1st Cavalry Division with a brigade of infantry towards Snicker's Ferry. On July 17 Duffié struck Early's rear guard on the Snickersville pike, cap-

2. Sigel to War Department, July 7, 1864, *OR*, XXXVII, Pt. 1, p. 179.

3. Thayer's Report, July [?], 1864, *ibid.*, 183.

4. For accounts of Early's raid, see Early, "Early's March to Washington in 1864," *B&L*, IV, 492–99, and Freeman, *Lee's Lieutenants*, III, 562–67.

5. Special Order No. 126, July 15, 1864, *OR*, XXXVII, Pt. 2, p. 342.

turing eighty-two wagons and sixty prisoners. Duffié reported the Confederates "in full retreat for Richmond," but that was only a guess.[6] Early crossed the Shenandoah at Snicker's Ferry and posted a detachment to hold the ford.

Crook sent Duffié to Ashby's Gap to flank Early's wagon train. Three brigades of Colonel Joseph Thoburn's 1st Infantry Division trailed Duffié's riders to a point below Snicker's Ford with orders to cross and strike the enemy from the other flank. In a brisk skirmish, called by locals the Battle of Cool Spring, Thoburn collided with Early's main army and retreated back across the Shenandoah with a loss of 422 men killed, wounded, and missing.[7]

Undaunted by Thoburn's misfortune, Crook seized an opportunity to trap Early at Winchester and asked Hunter to forward the VI and the XIX Army Corps, along with Averell's 2nd Cavalry Division, for a crushing attack. Crook, Hunter, Sigel, and Averell had all clashed with Early before, and at Kernstown on July 24 Old Jube beat them again, driving Crook back to Williamsport and laying Harpers Ferry open to another attack. Nonetheless, Crook reported Early's troops "in no condition to make any hard marches" and predicted they would return to Winchester to collect supplies.[8]

But Crook was wrong. Early stopped at Martinsburg and spent two days tearing up the Baltimore and Ohio, disposing once more of the same trackage he had destroyed a few weeks earlier during his march to Washington.[9] While demolition details twisted rails and blew up roadbeds, Early learned that Hunter had been wreaking vengeance on the homes of citizens in Jefferson and Berkeley Counties. Early, not known for having a good disposition, fumed at the outrage.

Hunter, who consistently fled from Early's shoeless veterans, had expressed his frustration by torching three lovely mansions

---

6. Duffié's Report is in Wright to Halleck, July 17, 1864, *ibid.*, 368–69, and Pt. 1, p. 320.

7. Thoburn's Report, July 29, 1864, *ibid.*, Pt. 1, pp. 290–92; Jubal A. Early, *Lieutenant General Jubal Anderson Early, C.S.A.: Autobiographical Sketch and Narrative of the War Between the States* (Philadelphia, 1912), 396.

8. Averell's Report, July 28, 1864, *OR*, XXXVII, Pt. 1, pp. 326–27; Crook to Hunter, July 20, 1864, *ibid.*, 286; Crook to Hunter, July 27, 1864, *ibid.*, Pt. 2, p. 404.

9. Early, *Autobiographical Sketch*, 401.

not far from Harpers Ferry. The 1st New York (Lincoln) Cavalry, Captain Franklin G. Martindale, drew the assignment and with sixty men rode to the home of Andrew Hunter, David's first cousin. The general instructed Martindale to "burn the dwelling-house and outbuildings . . . not permitting anything to be taken therefrom except the family."[10]

Hunter's determination to burn his namesake's home probably had nothing to do with Cousin Andrew's prosecution of John Brown and his fellow raiders in the autumn of 1859, but the irony prevailed. Hunter meant to pay Early back for a different fire. Old Jube's raiders had burned Falkland, the home of Montgomery Blair, Lincoln's postmaster general, during their demonstration against Washington. Some claimed the fire had been set by accident, but whatever the cause, Hunter felt justified in retaliating upon his cousin. Governor Augustus W. Bradford's home in Maryland had also been burned by Early, but nobody called this one an accident.[11]

Martindale rode to Charles Town on July 17, ordered the women out of the Hunter home, and rebuffed their pleas to save a few clothes and the family portraits. While the house burned, the 1st New York Cavalry made camp on the property and tore up the magnificent grounds surrounding the estate. Andrew Hunter remained a prisoner for a month at Harpers Ferry before being discharged without a trial or an explanation. Throughout his imprisonment he continued to wear a gold ring given to him years before the war "with deep affection" by Cousin David.[12]

Proceeding to the letter of his orders, Martindale gathered up his cavalry and rode to Martinsburg to burn Boydville, the exquisite home of Charles J. Faulkner. Faulkner had been active in Virginia politics, but he had also served briefly as one of the three court-appointed defense attorneys dismissed by John Brown. When Martindale greeted Mrs. Faulkner with fiery tidings, she begged for an hour's delay. Martindale consented and Mrs. Faulkner rode to the telegraph office. She wired General George W. Cullum, Halleck's chief of staff and a friend of the family. Cullum

10. Special Order No. 128, July 17, 1864, *OR*, XXXVII, Pt. 2, p. 367.

11. Dana to Grant, July 11, 1864, *ibid.*, 194.

12. Bier to Averell, July 19, 1864, *ibid.*, 394; Douglas, *I Rode with Stonewall*, 297; Matthew Page Andrews, *The Women of the South in War Times* (Baltimore, 1920), 201–204.

appealed to Lincoln to spare the fine old mansion, and as Martindale was about to strike the first match Mrs. Faulkner rode into the yard waving an order from the president: "The property of Charles J. Faulkner is exempt from the order of General David S. Hunter for the burning of the residences of prominent citizens of the Shenandoah Valley in retaliation for the burning of the governor Bradford's house in Maryland by the Confederate forces."[13]

Martindale blew out his match and on July 19 led his force to Shepherdstown, where he sought to destroy Fountain Rock, the stately mansion of Alexander R. Boteler. In a curious reversal of irony, Boteler had nothing to do with John Brown. He had defeated Faulkner in the 1859 congressional campaign, staunchly supported the Union, and was nominated but defeated as Speaker of the House for the Thirty-Sixth Congress. His transgression occurred when he threw his lot with the South, serving in the Confederate Congress and later as colonel on the staffs of Stonewall Jackson and Jeb Stuart.[14]

When Martindale rode to the door of Fountain Rock he found neither the colonel nor his wife at home. He was met by Boteler's two daughters, one of them a widow with three children, the eldest, five, and the youngest, eighteen months. Martindale showed a little mercy, allowing the occupants to remove a few articles of clothing, but the Federal troopers plundered silver and other valuables before dropping the fatal match on a few bundles of kerosene-saturated straw. At first Helen Boteler refused to leave without her piano, and as the flames gathered about the room she sat at the keyboard and played Charlotte Elliott's hymn "Thy Will Be Done," her voice rising above the crackle of the fire. Choked by the smoke, she calmly rose, locked the piano, and went outside. Martindale destroyed all the outbuildings, leaving only the pigeon house, where Helen Boteler moved her scant belongings, evicted the pigeons, and established a temporary residence.[15]

While embers from the Boteler home still smoldered, Martindale led his firebrands to Bedford, the nearby home of Edmund J. Lee, first cousin of the Confederate chieftain. Edmund was not at home, but his wife, Henrietta, came down from her sickbed with

13. William F. Evans, *History of Berkeley County, West Virginia* (Wheeling, W.Va., 1928), 263–64.

14. Bushong, *Historic Jefferson County*, 407.

15. *Ibid.*, 231.

two small children at her side. She met Martindale at the door and appealed to the captain's sense of history by explaining that the home was hers and not her husband's. She had inherited it directly from her father, a Revolutionary soldier, and the Union army would never sanction waging war on the property of helpless women and innocent children. Unmoved by Mrs. Lee's entreaties, Martindale ordered the house set afire. In less than an hour it lay smoking in ashes.

Mrs. Lee penned a letter of outrage to General Hunter, accusing him of having "the relentless heart of a wild beast, the face of a fiend, and the form of a man. Oh, Earth," she cried, "behold the monster!" Her letter attracted scores of northern sympathizers, one being Baltimore and Ohio's president. Garrett had as much reason as anyone to seek retribution from rebels who relentlessly damaged his railroad, but when he learned that Hunter planned to burn Charles Town and every house in neighboring Clarke County, he wrote Stanton warning that if Hunter carried out his scorched-earth policy, Confederate partisans would retaliate and destroy every engine and mile of track on the railroad.[16]

When word of Hunter's depredations drifted into Early's camp outside Martinsburg, Old Jube decided the time had come "to open the eyes of the people of the North to this enormity, by an example in the way of retaliation." He ordered Brigadier General John McCausland's cavalry to Chambersburg, Pennsylvania, to exact $100,000 in gold or $500,000 in greenbacks. Early intended to turn the proceeds over to the victims of Martindale's arsonists. He told McCausland to proceed to Cumberland after finishing with Chambersburg and demand an equal amount of cash, and after departing from Cumberland to tear up the tracks of the Baltimore and Ohio all the way back to Martinsburg. If either town refused to pay, Early said, "Burn it."[17]

On July 30, 1864, Chambersburg pleaded empty pockets, and McCausland set fire to the buildings in the center of the town. When news of the Early's scorched-earth policy reached Harpers Ferry, the townsfolk cringed and hurriedly organized a fire watch.[18]

16. *Ibid.*, 232–34; Garrett to Stanton, July 18, 1864, *OR*, XXXVII, Pt. 2, pp. 374–75.

17. Early, *Autobiographical Sketch*, 401; Bushong, *Old Jube*, 222–23.

18. Averell to Couch, July 30, 1864, *OR*, XXXVII, Pt. 2, p. 515.

After Early shifted his command to Williamsport, Hunter rolled into Harpers Ferry fully expecting an unwelcome visit from Old Jube's veterans. On July 20 the bridge across the Potomac, rebuilt for the eighth time, had just been reopened to railroad traffic, but Early's presence suspended work on the tracks to the west. Hunter anticipated an attack and halted all westbound rail traffic at Sandy Hook. He massed the entire Harpers Ferry garrison, consisting of four infantry regiments, four cavalry companies, eight companies of the 5th New York Heavy Artillery, eleven batteries of light artillery, and a company of engineers. On July 25 he began making preparations to evacuate the town and ordered all government property loaded on wagons and hauled once again to the Maryland side.[19]

Garrett, fearing his new bridge might be destroyed, wrote Stanton that he did not believe Early would advance on the Ferry and hoped no "unnecessary destruction of property" would be ordered by Hunter. He also suggested that Hunter be reminded of the importance of cavalry reconnaissance, as "some force should be on duty in that territory, or surprise movements may be effected by the enemy." From railroad employees who watched the war from the tracks, Garrett got the impression that Hunter had never learned the value or proper use of cavalry.[20]

Garrett was understandably upset because Hunter's troopers were cavorting about the countryside burning homes, stirring up partisans, and ignoring the importance of the railroad. Averell's force was on the Pennsylvania line chasing McCausland's raiders, and Crook was still near Williamsport watching Early. The only enemy in the vicinity of Harpers Ferry was Mosby's Rangers, who made regular appearances along the Potomac, attacking railroad guards, tearing up track, and keeping Hunter in a state of perpetual nervousness.

Early's Shenandoah campaign had drawn off the VI and XIX Corps from Grant's force at Petersburg, and Old Jube was still in the Valley. Hunter commanded a superior force but lacked the military skills to coordinate the tactics necessary to drive Early back up the Valley. Hunter had no plan, and his sloppy reconnaissance kept him on the defensive and shrinking from shadows. Corporal

19. Garrett to Stanton, July 18, Harpers Ferry Returns, July 31, and Donahoo to Garrett, July 25, 1864, *ibid.*, 375, 548, 438.

20. Garrett to Stanton, July 25, 1864, *ibid.*, 438.

John C. Arnold of the 49th Pennsylvania expressed the frustration of the army when he wrote his wife from Harpers Ferry in early August: "They say the Rebs are at Hagerstown, so I guess [Hunter] will run us up to said place. [By] the time we get up, the Rebs will be some other place, and so they will keep us running around all somer [*sic*]. I wish we could ketch them some place and kill every Son of a Bitch. They are nothing but regular raiders and thiefs."[21]

Grant's patience reached its limit late in July. He had sent trusted generals and veteran soldiers to cleanse West Virginia of Confederate incursions, but Early remained comfortably situated between Martinsburg and Williamsport. On August 1 Grant wrote Washington: "I am sending General [Philip H.] Sheridan for temporary duty whilst the enemy is being expelled from the border. Unless General Hunter is in the field in person, I want Sheridan put in command of all the troops in the field, with instructions to put himself south of the enemy and follow him to the death. Wherever the enemy goes let our troops go also. Once started up the Valley they ought to be followed until we get possession of the Virginia Central Railroad."[22]

David Hunter was not in the field. He was not even at Harpers Ferry. Believing Early intended to attack him, he moved his headquarters east to Monocacy, thereby removing himself even further from the action. After burning the homes of harmless citizens, perhaps the general took comfort in being closer to Washington. He neglected to inform his disjointed command that headquarters had departed downriver, and important intelligence continued to flow into his abandoned headquarters at Harpers Ferry.[23]

On the morning of August 6, Halleck found Sheridan at Willard's Hotel in Washington and directed him, on behalf of Grant, to go to Harpers Ferry and "assume general command of all the troops in the field." Sheridan passed through Monocacy on his way west to inform Hunter of the command change. He arrived at Harpers Ferry at 7:30 P.M. "I find affairs somewhat confused," Sheridan wrote, "but will soon straighten them out."[24]

21. John C. Arnold to his wife, August 7, 1864, Arnold Family Papers, USAMHI. Corporal Arnold was killed on April 6, 1865, at Sailor's Creek.

22. Grant to Halleck, August 1, 1864, *OR*, XXXVII, Pt. 2, p. 558.

23. Wyckoff to Hunter, and Kelley to Hunter, August 3, 1864, *ibid.*, 584, 587.

24. Halleck to Sheridan, and Sheridan to Grant, August 6, 1864, *ibid.*, XLIII, Pt. 1, pp. 709, 710.

Sheridan stepped into an expanded command known as the Middle Military Division, consisting of the Middle Department, Department of Washington, Department of the Susquehanna, and the Department of West Virginia, the latter being Hunter's district. He established temporary headquarters at Harpers Ferry and deployed the cavalry. Under Sheridan, Hunter had little chance of surviving, and on August 30 he was relieved of command and replaced by Crook.[25]

During Hunter's brief stint at Harpers Ferry headquarters, some of Early's cavalry ranged nearby but stopped a short distance from George Hartman's small farm. "Dutch George," as he was known, lived as a bachelor on the outskirts of town, and during the Confederate occupation in the early years of the war he was swept up by conscriptors as a substitute for his employer, a local farmer. Many of his neighbors suffered similarly, but in the spring of 1864 "Dutch George" and his comrades found themselves marching with Early back down the Valley. They took unauthorized leave to visit their homes, and decided, once there, to stay awhile. Whether they ever expected to see Early's corps again is doubtful, but in July Old Jube was back in the Charles Town area with cavalry scouting the approaches to Harpers Ferry.

Fearing capture by either friend or foe, George and his friends hid in an old empty blacksmith shop. Adhering to the finer points of their military training, the group detailed George as picket. Their choice was unfortunate because George leaned against a corner fence post and kept a poor lookout. Surprised by a squad of Yankee cavalry, George told his captors, "By damn, you did dat wery vel, but you ain't schmart enough to find de boys in de blackschmidt shop." According to "Dutch George," the Yankees surrounded the building and made prisoners of the lot. George could never understand how the Yankees found his friends, but some blamed the entire story on a few mischievous youngsters of the neighborhood who enjoyed teasing "the poor fellow." If so, a few lads in Harpers Ferry survived the war without losing their sense of humor.[26]

The incident, however, was indicative of Sheridan's determi-

25. General Order No. 1, August 7, and No. 248, August 30, 1864, *ibid.*, 721, 962.

26. Barry, *Harper's Ferry*, 135–36.

nation to cleanse the neighborhood of partisans and to probe for Early's scattered command. But at Harpers Ferry the townsfolk steeled their nerves for another inept commander. Nobody had ever heard of this man Sheridan, and by the looks of him, nobody was willing to take bets that this feisty little gamecock would last out the summer.

# 17

## Sheridan in the Valley

Major General Philip Henry Sheridan manifested none of the characteristics of his Union predecessors. At thirty-three years old, he was about half the age of Hunter and ten times more energetic. Where Sigel and Weber dressed smartly and enjoyed the pomp and ceremony of European military tradition, Sheridan wore no distinctive uniform and had little use for the officious banter characteristic of headquarters. Whether he came by these traits naturally is difficult to know, but Sheridan had served under Grant long enough to emulate many of the commander in chief's informalities.

None of the townsfolk of Harpers Ferry left an account of their impressions of Sheridan, perhaps because he spent so little time there. Had they done so they might have described him as short, spry, thick through the body, always on the move, and usually on a horse. An observer would notice his rather large head, his dark, penetrating eyes, and a black drooping mustache in need of trimming. Sheridan comported an air of decisiveness and understood his objectives, and Grant probably sent him to the Valley because he knew "Little Phil" was endowed with sufficient ruthlessness to get the job done.

A son of Irish immigrants, Sheridan falsified his birth date by one year and in 1848 gained entrance to West Point. Suspended a year for chasing a fellow cadet with a fixed bayonet, he returned to graduate in 1853, thirty-fourth in a class of forty-nine, and spent the next eight years in the West. In 1861 he was called to duty in Missouri as a captain in the 13th Infantry, where he served under Halleck, distinguished himself as a cavalry commander, and in March, 1863, rose to the grade of major general. As commander of the XX Corps, Army of the Cumberland, Sheridan won praise at the Battle of Chattanooga and at Missionary Ridge, contributing to the defeat of General Braxton Bragg. Grant rewarded him with exclusive command of Army of the Potomac cavalry. Sheridan fought with Grant from the Wilderness to Petersburg, and after arriving at Harpers Ferry he reorganized his force into the Army of the Shenandoah. Grant gave Sheridan specific instructions: to drive Early out of the Valley and to destroy the supplies of the enemy.[1]

Grant dispensed with protocol when he ordered Sheridan to "not hesitate to give commands to officers in whom you repose confidence, without regard to claims of others on account of rank. . . . What we want is prompt and active movements after the enemy in accordance with instructions you already have." Grant's orders gave "Little Phil" virtually unlimited, if not unprecedented, authority to reorganize his force however he wished.[2]

Sheridan established headquarters on Camp Hill on the second floor of "a small and dilapidated hotel" that had served as the armory paymaster's quarters. He disliked the dirty streets and dingy dwellings in the war-scarred town of Harpers Ferry. Preferring to be on the move, he waited anxiously for promised reinforcements to trickle into town. While waiting, he wasted no time and spent hours on end questioning the officers and scouts familiar with the area. Lieutenant Meigs, the capable young engineer who had just rebuilt the Harpers Ferry bridge, laid out the topography of the Valley. Meigs had been all over the lower Shenandoah watershed mapping important roads and streams and noting some of the prominent farmhouses. He had seen the broad, macadamized highway that led south from Williamsport, Maryland, to Lex-

1. *HTI*, 679–80.
2. Grant to Sheridan, August 7, 1864, *OR*, XLIII, Pt. 1, p. 719.

ington, Virginia, along which lay the principal towns through which any mass military movement must pass.[3]

Early had no more than 20,000 men, most of them divided among his five infantry divisions, and Old Jube knew every nook and cranny of the Valley. Union scouts watched him cross the Potomac on August 7 and "take dinner" at Sharpsburg, and then they tracked him back to Martinsburg. Early left a large detail in Maryland to collect the wheat harvest and shuttle it down the pike to the Virginia Central.[4] Sheridan later discovered that some of the scouting reports had been exaggerated, but as long as Early remained in the lower Valley neither the Baltimore and Ohio nor the Winchester and Potomac could safely operate.

Hunter did not wait to be culled out of Sheridan's military organization and on August 7 "humbly beg[ged]" to be relieved. Crook, whose troops were already posted in the Valley, replaced Hunter as commander of the Department of West Virginia. Sheridan sent Howe back to the artillery depot at Washington and on August 8 replaced him with the industrious German, Max Weber, who once again took command of the 4,800 railroad guards in the new Harpers Ferry Military District. Sheridan replaced Averell with Brigadier General Alfred T. A. Torbert, a personal and trusted friend who would eventually find fighting in the Valley as frustrating as his predecessor did. Within a month Sheridan's department counted 45,487 officers and men, composed mainly of three infantry corps: the VI Corps under Wright; the XIX Corps under Brigadier General William H. Emory, brought up from Louisiana; and the Army of West Virginia under Crook.[5]

Among the new arrivals, Captain John William De Forest of the 12th Connecticut entered Harpers Ferry on August 8 and began a search for Company I's lost baggage and camp kettles. He could not believe the size of the army camped between the Ferry and Halltown. The VI Corps was already there, its camp scattered helter-skelter, "all being tumbled together higgledy-piggledy, officers mixed up anyhow with the men, and the brigade commander in the middle. . . . Their guns are dirty," De Forest noted,

3. Philip H. Sheridan, *Personal Memoirs* (2 vols.; New York, 1892), I, 467, 468.
4. Sheridan to Grant, August 7, 1864, *OR*, XLIII, Pt. 1, p. 720.
5. Hunter to Lincoln, August 7, General Order No. 248, August 30, General Order No. 4, August 8, and Organization of the Army of the Shenandoah, September 19, 1864, *ibid.*, 723, 962, 501, 61, 107–12.

"their camps are disorderly clutters of shelter tents; worst of all, the men are disrespectful to their officers. I heard a private say to a lieutenant, 'I'll slap your face if you say that again.' " What the soldiers needed was a victory.[6]

On August 10, four days after Sheridan's arrival at Harpers Ferry, the new department commander left the town in the hands of Weber and with 18,000 infantry and 3,500 cavalry marched south, resting that night with his right wing at Clifton and his left at Berryville. He intended to cut across Early's line of retreat and corral him in the lower Valley.[7]

Sheridan, however, encountered an unexpected problem, especially if Early proved to be a tough customer. High water disabled the Harpers Ferry bridge, and Mosby's Rangers roamed in the rear cutting telegraph lines faster than Weber could repair them. Weber promised to have the bridge restored by August 12, provided the materials he needed arrived on schedule. He asked to have a pontoon bridge on standby, as the trestlework on the flimsy railroad bridge washed out with every flood and could not be repaired until the river fell. "Communication," Weber warned, "may be cut off for six or seven days."[8]

While Sheridan commiserated over delays, an aide handed him a rather nervous message from Weber warning that Longstreet and Hill "are within five days march of Early's present position, moving up the Valley," and that Mosby had captured several wagons and taken prisoners just outside Harpers Ferry. Sheridan wanted to dismiss the notion that Longstreet or Hill was forming a juncture with Early, but the threat served as a reminder that without the bridge in his rear, his own army could be trapped between Early, whose corps was last reported at Martinsburg, and any force Lee chose to send from Petersburg. Weber's warning, however, gathered weight when Grant wired Halleck from City Point, "It is now certain two divisions of infantry have gone to Early, and some cavalry and twenty pieces of artillery. . . . Early's force, with this increase, cannot exceed 40,000 men, but this is too much for Sheridan to attack."[9]

6. DeForest to his family, August 8, 1864, De Forest Papers, YUL.

7. Sheridan's Report, August 11, 1864, and Sheridan to Rawlins, February 3, 1866, *OR*, XLIII, Pt. 1, pp. 17, 42.

8. Weber to Parsons, August 9, 1864, *ibid.*, 747–48.

9. Weber to Sheridan, August 11, and Grant to Halleck, August 12, 1864, *ibid.*, 772, 43.

Mosby's scouts dogged Sheridan's movements from Harpers Ferry, and on the night of August 11 a small party advanced on a house that had been converted into the general's temporary headquarters. Mosby had already captured one slumbering Union general dressed in a nightshirt, but he failed in an attempt for another. Now he wanted Sheridan. John Hearn, wearing a set of Federal blues, advanced on the general's headquarters to reconnoiter but was challenged by a sentinel. In a noisy hand-to-hand scuffle, the Ranger captured the guard's musket but woke six soldiers sleeping nearby. Hearn escaped with the musket and Sheridan slept undisturbed, but the incident demonstrated to the general that Mosby should not be underestimated.[10]

Sheridan had another problem. When he began his march on August 10, all heavy camp equipment and officers' luggage had been left at the Ferry. A thunderstorm threatening from the west served as reminder that everyone from the rank of captain down to private carried nothing but a blanket, three days' rations, and a canteen. He wired Weber, anxiously asking whether the bridge had been repaired, and if not, whether the wagon roadway on the bridge was strong enough to support the movement of troops and supplies. Weber had kept his word. Trains could cross the bridge, and men were already working on the roadbed between Harpers Ferry and Halltown.[11] Mosby, however, continued to pester the workers by sabotaging repairs at night, and Weber could not promise when the Winchester spur would operate.

Early had already slid by Sheridan's trap, withdrawing from Martinsburg on August 10 and retreating towards Strasburg. Cavalry clashed all along the line of the Confederate retreat until Early dug in and took a strong position at Fisher's Hill. On August 13 Grant's warning of advancing enemy reinforcements caught up with Sheridan, who promptly sent a brigade of cavalry east to investigate. Mosby, who remained quite active in Sheridan's rear, gave the impression of being in heavy force. Union cavalry reported the enemy massing at Culpepper, and Early's resistance at Fisher's Hill noticeably stiffened. Sheridan's advance suddenly

10. Jones, *Ranger Mosby*, 192; Scott, *Partisan Life*, 271–72; Williamson, *Mosby's Rangers*, 231. The Union general captured on March 8, 1863, was Brigadier General Edwin H. Stoughton.

11. Forsyth to Weber, August 13, and Weber to Forsyth, August 14, 1864, *OR*, XLIII, Pt. 1, pp. 788, 795.

stopped, and on the afternoon of August 16 he moved headquarters back to Winchester and recalled the infantry.[12]

Sheridan's withdrawal was precipitated by Mosby, whose outposts had been watching the formation of a large supply train at Harpers Ferry. At 10:30 A.M. on August 12, the vanguard of a 525-wagon train rolled out of town with tons of supplies for Sheridan's stalled army. Near the front rode Brigadier General John R. Kenly, whose lengthy orders to the teamsters emphasized, among other things, celerity: "It is of importance that the train should reach Winchester as speedily as possible. Commanding officers will be held responsible that no unnecessary delays occur. Should the train be attacked or any serious obstacle intervene to its march, regimental commanders will transmit the intelligence promptly to the brigadier-general commanding, and give to each other such support and assistance as may be needed."[13]

Kenly's brigade contained three thousand men organized in three regiments, the 3rd Maryland and the 144th and 149th Ohio National Guard. Two companies of Marylanders led the train, followed by another company every twenty wagons. Behind the Marylanders marched the 149th Ohio, a company for every thirty wagons. Next came the 144th Ohio, a company for every twenty wagons, with the last two companies bringing up the rear. The train, divided into five sections, moved out slowly. Each section carried supplies for a specific unit, beginning with the VI Army Corps, followed by wagons for the XIX Army Corps, the Army of West Virginia, the 2nd Brigade of the Cavalry Corps, and the 3rd Brigade Cavalry Reserve. Once on the road the train stretched out for miles, sending dense clouds of dust high into a breezeless sky. Officers rode up and down the line shouting threats and swearing at teamsters, but the train had a mind of its own. Drivers failed to close up, forced back by the reddish-yellow dust that blinded their vision and choked their lungs. A herd of cattle bellowing in the rear stopped to nibble grass, wagons broke down, and one section soon lost contact with another.

Kenly rode ahead and quickly outpaced the rear. Couriers sent to spur along the laggards took longer and longer to return. At sundown guards and teamsters, as fatigued as the animals, won-

12. Sheridan's Report, February 3, 1866, *ibid.*, 43–44.
13. Peabody to Kenly, August 12, 1864, *ibid.*, 628.

dered when the train would stop, but Kenly pressed forward. He wanted to reach Sheridan's camp before dark, but he still had miles to go. By 11 P.M. he could travel no farther and stopped by a small stream running beside the Berryville-Winchester road at Buck Marsh Church to water the animals and give the men time to cook rations and boil coffee. The VI Corps wagons filled one side of the road and the XIX Corps wagons the other. With no space for the other three sections to park, Kenly left orders for where they were to stop and water when they arrived. Two hours later, without waiting for the rest of the train, Kenly put the first two sections back on the road. He left instructions with Captain James C. Mann, quartermaster of the 1st Division, XIX Corps, to wait on the road to guide the others. "I consider this the most dangerous point in the route," Kenly declared. "I desire that you remain here, therefore, until every wagon has passed."[14]

At 2 A.M. on August 13 the VI Corps wagons rattled off in the night, and the teamsters for the XIX Corps train hitched back up and followed. As they moved out, the Army of West Virginia train straggled into the park, followed by the wagons of the 2nd Cavalry Brigade. Teamsters unhitched their animals and led them down to the creek. Guards stretched out on the ground and fell asleep. Mann rode up and down the line hollering for officers, and whenever one replied he encouraged him to hitch up and get back on the road. At 3 A.M. the Army of West Virginia train passed out of sight, and the reserve cavalry's train wearily moved onto the vacated ground.

An hour later Mann felt a premonition of danger. Riding through the cavalry trains he shouted, "Start immediately! We're in danger of attack." But nobody moved. The camp lay asleep. And when dawn streaked the eastern sky, Mann realized a new horror. No pickets had been posted. He rode frantically through the camp and in an hour had the 2nd Cavalry brigade's wagons on the road to Winchester, but the wagons of the reserve cavalry had not moved, nor had the men. One by one Mann jabbed at the teamsters and forced them to their feet. They were still rubbing sleep

14. New York *Times*, August 21, 1864; Investigation of Attack on Union Supply Train, September 8, 1864, *OR*, XLIII, Pt. 1, pp. 619–32; Mann's testimony, *ibid.*, 629.

from their eyes when the first shell from one of Mosby's two howitzers screeched into camp and knocked the head off a mule.[15]

No train this length could pass unnoticed through enemy territory. Confederate scouts had watched from the hills as a thick cloud of orange dust smothered the crawling wagons. From miles away they could hear the constant rumble, much like the sound of an approaching storm or the invasion of a swarm of giant locusts. Confederate scouts watched as the train departed from Harpers Ferry, and they followed it all the way to the creek bottom where Kenly halted for a brief respite.

Mosby collected about 330 men and on the morning of August 13 struck the train as first daylight flooded the sleeping camp. A fog masked the attack, and the Federals scattered in confusion. Mann tried to organize the guards, and as he chased about looking for support he spotted rebel cavalry dressed in blue come charging out of the mist. They wheeled into line and advanced steadily, firing revolvers.[16]

Mosby's artillery encountered unexpected trouble when they set up one of their howitzers on a knoll occupied by a nest of ornery yellow jackets. The bees came buzzing out of their hole and drove off the gunners. Artillery Sergeant A. G. Babcok flailed his hat at the bees, grabbed the chain on the gun, and moved it several yards down the hill. The howitzer belched chaos in the Federal camp until its carriage gave way and rendered the gun useless. By then wagons had been upturned and the enemy scattered in all directions.[17]

For more than two years Mosby's Rangers had disrupted enemy communications and waged a private war in northern Virginia, but never had so few men created more pandemonium than among the supply wagons of Kenly's laggards. The raiders captured 75 wagons, 200 head of cattle, 500 horses and mules, and more than 200 prisoners, leaving Sheridan's reserve cavalry without supplies and in considerable distress. In the confusion, however, Major William E. Beardsley rallied a few guards and rescued $112,000 in payrolls. While the raiders torched the wagons,

15. Mann's testimony, *OR*, XLIII, Pt. 1, p. 629.
16. *Ibid.*; Scott, *Partisan Life*, 239–40; Williamson, *Mosby's Rangers*, 209–210.
17. John S. Mosby, *The Memoirs of Colonel John S. Mosby*, ed. Charles S. Russel (Boston, 1917), 366–67.

Beardsley and his party grabbed loose horses, escaped through the camp, and carried the cash to Winchester.[18]

Sheridan had been warned about Mosby, but this was his first costly brush with the Rangers. Halleck got wind of the attack from one of Grant's scouts and wired Sheridan via Harpers Ferry, asking, "Is this true?" Sheridan, who did not have either Stanton's or Halleck's confidence, replied, "I did not know the extent of the capture until yesterday. It was said everything was recovered except six wagons, but this was not true."[19] On August 15, two days after Mosby's raid, Sheridan brought the Army of the Shenandoah back to Halltown, the base it had left five days before.

Sheridan, irritated and slightly embarrassed, ordered a board of inquiry to meet at Harpers Ferry and investigate the loss of the Cavalry Reserve Brigade's wagon train.[20] The board listened to testimony for nine weeks before deciding no one was to blame, although admitting "there was no sufficient picket established whilst the train halted to prevent surprise or resist sudden attack."[21] The decision made little sense to Sheridan, but by then he had other matters on his mind.

Grant devised a scheme to suppress Mosby and suggested Sheridan send a division of cavalry through counties infested by guerrillas "to destroy and carry off the crops, animals, negroes, and all men under fifty years of age capable of bearing arms." In this way, Grant promised, "you will get many of Mosby's men." Sheridan accepted Grant's advice and sent Major General Wesley Merritt's 1st Cavalry Division storming through the Valley, burning grain and forage and driving off cattle from Cedar Creek to Berryville. "This duty," Merritt reported, "not among the most agreeable assigned to soldiers, was thoroughly and delicately done; no private property, save that mentioned, being injured; nor family molested by any soldier."[22]

---

18. Mosby's Report, September 11, 1864, *OR*, XLIII, Pt. 1, p. 634; Williamson, *Mosby's Rangers*, 208–10; Beardsley's Report, August 14, 1864, *OR*, XLIII, Pt. 1, pp. 484–85; Mosby, *Memoirs*, 292, 367; Scott, *Partisan Life*, 279.

19. Halleck to Sheridan, and Sheridan to Halleck, August 19, 1864, *OR*, XLIII, Pt. 1, pp. 841, 842.

20. Special Order No. 10, August 20, 1864, *ibid.*, 619.

21. *Ibid.*, 632. The investigation is *ibid.*, 619–32.

22. Grant to Sheridan, August 16, Forsyth Circular, August 19, and Merritt's Report, October 5, 1864, *ibid.*, 811, 843, 440.

As Early advanced down the Valley, his rage increased as he passed blackened fields, smoldering haystacks, charred corncribs, and farms barren of livestock. On August 17 he routed Torbert's cavalry at Winchester and pursued Sheridan to Halltown, but he could not penetrate the Federal lines. On the night of August 21 the Confederate army camped about two and a half miles from Charles Town. The sound of artillery once again jarred the nerves of the citizens of Harpers Ferry.[23]

Early probed Sheridan's lines and dispatched Fitzhugh Lee's cavalry to test the Union flanks. For four days Confederate horsemen swarmed through the countryside around Harpers Ferry, taking prisoners and gathering information. Lee attacked Torbert near Kearneysville, driving Brigadier General George A. Custer's brigade back across the Potomac. Torbert withdrew, leaving Custer to feel his way back to Halltown by circling through Maryland, crossing the Potomac bridge, and passing through Harpers Ferry. Early's advance ended with this affair. Convinced Sheridan's lines were impregnable, he reconcentrated his force at Shepherdstown. Finding no advantage there, he withdrew to a more defensible position west of Opequon Creek, near Bunker Hill. For the next two weeks cavalry skirmishes dominated the action, and then Early finally decided to withdraw to Winchester.[24]

Sheridan remained outside Harpers Ferry for several days waiting for supplies. They came by the carload and were piled into the ruins of the old armory buildings. About once a week he loaded up with fresh ammunition, ordered three days' rations, and marched his force to the outskirts of Winchester. After exchanging a few furtive rounds with Early, he withdrew to Halltown. The pattern became so predictable that his men nicknamed him "Harper's Weekly." Early arrived at the same conclusion, surmising that Sheridan was without enterprise and possessed of an excessive caution amounting to timidity. The same feeling pervaded the North among both the uninformed public and a growing number of military critics. Stanton joined the faultfinders, holding to his earlier conviction that the cavalryman was too young and inexperienced for such an important command.[25]

23. Journal of Jedediah Hotchkiss, August 21, 1864, *ibid.*, 570.

24. Torbert's Report, November [?], 1864, *ibid.*, 425; Wesley Merritt, "Sheridan in the Shenandoah Valley," *B&L*, IV, 504–505; Journal of Jedediah Hotchkiss, August 21, 1864, *OR*, XLIII, Pt. 1, pp. 570–71.

25. Joseph Hergesheimer, *Sheridan: A Military Narrative* (Boston, 1931), 193.

Captain De Forest of the 12th Connecticut voiced the travails of his regiment when he wrote, "Here we are, nearly back to Harper's Ferry. . . . Well, we tramped down the Shenandoah Valley, and we tramped back again. If I ever volunteer again I shall remember this vale of sorrows and shall specify that I am not to make war in it. Blazing hot marches, heavy guard duty, a diet of green corn and green apples have made a rough campaign of it."[26]

Criticism had no effect upon Sheridan, who was ready to retire any number of times to Harpers Ferry if he considered his position insecure. On August 28 he advanced the army from Halltown to Charles Town, and six days later the infantry inched into position between Berryville and Clifton. Crook's force returned to Summit Point as a movable column in reserve to protect the right flank and the line to Harpers Ferry. Sheridan's frequent withdrawals convinced Early that he had little to fear from the young Union general, and he returned Kershaw's division and Major Wilfred E. Cutshaw's artillery to Lee. Sheridan observed the movement and made preparations to attack. "Our time had come," he declared, "and I almost made up my mind I would fight at Newton, on the Valley Pike, give up my line to the rear, and take that of the enemy. From my position at Clifton I could throw my force into Newton before Early could get information and move to that point." Sheridan admitted he "was a little timid about this movement until the arrival of General Grant, at Charlestown, who indorsed [sic] it, and the order for the movement was made."[27]

Grant met Sheridan in Charles Town's Rutherford House on Main Street, where they talked for several hours. Neither general was aware of the specter of old John Brown, which hovered nearby in the Jefferson County Courthouse, now perforated by shells and used as a stable to house the horses of war. Brown had died on the gallows just up the street from the Rutherford House. Sheridan and Grant now met to fulfill the martyr's prophecy. They meant to end a war some said the old man started.[28]

On September 17 Sheridan advanced en masse, throwing the VI and XIX Corps, Crook's Army of West Virginia, three brigades of artillery, and 6,400 cavalry against Early's 12,000 defenders. There

26. DeForest to his family, August 21, 24, 1864, De Forest Papers, YUL.
27. Sheridan's Report, February 3, 1866, and Journal of Jedediah Hotchkiss, August 21, 1864, *OR,* XLIII, Pt. 1, pp. 45–46, 573.
28. Bushong, *Historic Jefferson County,* 240.

was never any doubt of the outcome except in the minds of Sheridan and Grant, who both believed Early's army numbered 40,000 men. On September 19 Sheridan routed Early at Winchester, and again, three days later, at Fisher's Hill. In four days the youthful cavalryman destroyed the Confederate hold on the Valley, and Early never recovered from the setback.[29]

Fall settled in the lower Valley, and for the fifth time in more than three years the war seemed to have drifted away. Fewer soldiers drilled on Camp Hill, the Baltimore and Ohio resumed a regular schedule, and less supplies littered the old blackened armory buildings. Martial law still prevailed, but some of the townsfolk busied themselves repairing their homes and preparing for winter. Mosby still ranged around the town, and partisans staged occasional raids, but a war-weariness settled upon the town. The public joined with the army to pray for the end of fighting, and on the eve of winter, hope prevailed.

But with Sheridan gone, guerrilla warfare suddenly erupted in the hills, and the tormented townsfolk wondered if anybody would bother to stop it.

29. Sheridan's Report, February 3, 1866, *OR*, XLIII, Pt. 1, pp. 46–57; Early's Reports are *ibid.*, 554–64; see also Freeman, *Lee's Lieutenants*, III, 577–85.

# 18

## The Last of the Partisans

In characteristic military confusion, General Crook relieved Max Weber of the command of the Harper's Ferry Military District on August 15, 1864, and replaced him with Brigadier General John D. Stevenson, who Crook assumed ranked Weber. Although Weber had become ill, he continued to command from headquarters, and Crook expected him to remain at the Ferry and happily continue with his responsibilities while reporting to Stevenson.[1]

Weber, who had just resumed full command of the Ferry on August 7, was as sensitive to protocol as any officer. Granted a twenty-day sick leave, he departed for New York City and while recuperating complained to Crook that he had "tried in vain to find some cause for the act of the general commanding to relieve me . . . and therefore feel the more hurt and humiliated by it." In the meantime Weber had examined the list of brigadiers and grumbled, "I think the general commanding has not been or is not aware of my seniority over General Stevenson." Crook apologized but blamed the confusion on Sheridan, excusing the oversight by replying, "As you were known to be unwell it was thought in your state of health it would be a relief to you to have the responsibility

1. General Order No. 66, August 15, and Bier to Weber, August 19, 1864, *OR*, XLIII, Pt. 1, pp. 803, 850.

of your important command transferred to someone else for the present at least." Crook also acknowledged that only the president could place a junior officer above a senior. When Weber felt better again, Crook suggested he report to headquarters for reassignment. With Weber out of the picture, at least temporarily, the mission of mopping up the partisans and capturing Mosby's Rangers fell upon Stevenson, whose command of the Harper's Ferry Military District was solidified on September 30 by presidential order.[2]

Forty-three-year-old John Dunlap Stevenson, a lawyer and legislator, originally came from Virginia but cast his lot with the Union. He enjoyed military service and had fought in the Mexican War. He raised the 7th Missouri and in the early years of the war served under Grant in the West. Promoted to brigadier general on November 29, 1862, he fought at Corinth and Vicksburg before resigning his commission on April 22, 1864. He was reappointed brigadier general on August 7, 1864, to date from his original commission. Weber was quite correct in complaining, as his commission dated from April 28, 1862.[3]

Stevenson estimated that a force of "600 to 700 mounted guerrillas" ranged unimpeded through Jefferson and Loudoun Counties and asked Averell to send him a thousand troopers and a section of artillery to clean out the enemy. Torbert refused to release Averell from the vicinity of Martinsburg but agreed to send two hundred horsemen to Brigadier General Alfred N. Duffié, whose 1st Cavalry Division was at Berryville. On August 18 Stevenson planned to send a supply train from Harpers Ferry, and while making final preparations he learned from informants that Mosby intended to attack it. Knowing the wagons would be weakly guarded, he wired Averell asking that the promised cavalry detachment be put on the road early enough to safeguard the passage of the train. Averell promised to provide protection. The train left on schedule, but Averell's squadron arrived late. Mosby captured and burned 50 wagons, running off about 350 mules.[4]

2. Weber to Bier, August 22, 1864, *ibid.*, 886–87; Special Order No. 151, August 19, 1864, *ibid.*, LI, Pt. 1, pp. 1178–79; Bier to Weber, August 30, 1864, *ibid.*, XLIII, Pt. 1, pp. 968–69; Halleck to Stevenson, September 30, 1864, *ibid.*, Pt. 2, p. 221.

3. Weber to Bier, August 22, 1864, *ibid.*, XLIII, Pt. 1, p. 887; Boatner, *Civil War Dictionary*, 798.

4. Stevenson to Averell, August 16, Stevenson to Sheridan, August 17, Rumsey

With Mosby's Rangers cutting telegraph lines, Stevenson resorted to the use of couriers for transmitting his dispatches—only
to have the messages intercepted and the couriers captured. Cole's
Maryland Cavalry scouted Loudoun County, and Duffié's 1st Cavalry ranged through Jefferson County, but neither unit could locate the wily Rangers. Stevenson pleaded for more horses. He had
the 20th Pennsylvania Cavalry in camp at Pleasant Valley, but
they had no mounts. Averell estimated Mosby's force at a thousand, but nobody could find them. An ambulance passing into
Harpers Ferry was captured just outside town by "guerrillas from
Halltown, but nobody knew where they went."[5]

On August 21 a scouting party of Loudoun Rangers under Lieutenant Charles Atwell stumbled upon a small detachment of Mosby's command, chased them into Dry Hollow, and took one prisoner. Finding Mosby with about a hundred men waiting in
ambush, Atwell retreated with his prisoner and returned to Sandy
Hook. Missing his chance to bloody the Loudoun Rangers irritated
Mosby. He considered them traitorous renegades because they
were Virginians fighting for the North, and he vowed to annihilate
them.[6]

Information on the Rangers' whereabouts drifted into Stevenson's headquarters daily, but the best news came on September 15
when a scouting party from the 13th New York Cavalry, Colonel
Henry S. Gansevoort, surprised Mosby and seven riders near Falls
Church. The Confederates retreated in a hurry, but a ball from the
musket of Private Henry Smith struck Mosby's revolver and ricocheted into his groin. Mosby threw one arm in the air, slumped
in the saddle, and rode off. When the Federals learned who Smith
shot, they staged an exhaustive search to locate the wounded partisan.[7] Time passed with Mosby neither found nor seen. Federal
cavalry officers celebrated the partisan chief's death and turned
their attention to locating the rest of the gang. For a few weeks
Stevenson shared their optimism.

Even with Mosby temporarily demobilized, raids on army wag-

to Stevenson, August 17, and Gardner to Meigs, August 18, 1864, *OR*, XLIII, Pt. 1,
pp. 820–21, 826, 828, 836.

5. Averell to Stevenson, and Duffié to Sanford, August 19, 1864, *ibid.*, 850, 851.
6. Burleigh to Cook, August 22, 1864, *ibid.*, 836.
7. Williamson, *Mosby's Rangers*, 233; Lazelle to Taylor, September 15, 22, 1864,
*OR*, XLIII, Pt. 2, pp. 90, 145.

ons and the railroads continued. Stanton lost all patience and ordered retaliatory measures. He told Sheridan that if guerrilla bands continued to molest the railroad he should "destroy every house within five miles of the road" unless the occupants were known friends of the Union. Any male suspected of being a member of a "robber band" was to be arrested and sent to the Old Capital prison in Washington, and all brush within musket range of the railroad was to be cut down and burned. Union soldiers nailed printed notices to trees and public buildings, warning that if hostilities continued a ten-mile strip on each side of the line would be laid waste and the surrounding countryside "entirely depopulated."[8]

The warnings did no good. On October 11 one of Mosby's scouts located a gap in the Union cordon protecting the Baltimore and Ohio tracks between Harpers Ferry and Martinsburg. Mosby, still hobbling from his wound, ordered a rendezvous. Eighty Rangers answered the call, and on the night of October 13 they mounted and rode towards Duffield's Station. Mosby had a copy of the train schedule, and at midnight a squad of fifteen men removed a rail. At 2 A.M. the westbound train veered off the track a few hundred yards from Duffield's Station and careened into the bank. The baggage car slammed into the engine, exploding the boiler and spewing hot coals onto the cars. After relieving $168,000 in greenbacks from two army paymasters, the Rangers set the train on fire and scurried away in the dark, dividing up the money the following day. Mosby took nothing, as was his custom, but the raiders conducted a collection and presented their commander with a fine horse. Lieutenant Charles E. Grogan, a member of the raid, later recalled that the greenbacks circulated so freely in Loudoun County "that never afterwards was there a pie or blooded horse sold in that section for Confederate money."[9]

The war reached a new nadir when the hangings started. On September 23, while Mosby was still recuperating, Captain Sam Chapman, leading Ranger Companies C and E, sighted an ambulance train rolling down the Valley pike that appeared to be lightly defended. Chapman divided his command to strike the train front

8. Halleck to McCallum, October 12, 1864, *OR,* XLIII, Pt. 2, p. 348.

9. Mosby, *Memoirs,* 313–21; Williamson, *Mosby's Rangers,* 260–63; Jones, *Ranger Mosby,* 216, 218–19; Scott, *Partisan Life,* 336–37; New York *Herald,* October 17, 1864.

and rear, jogged down from his lookout above the valley, and charged out of the woods. When he reached the road he spotted Colonel Charles R. Lowell's Reserve Brigade of Merritt's cavalry galloping up from the rear. Lowell was naturally interested in repaying the Rangers for recently destroying his wagons at Berryville.[10]

Trapped, Chapman rode wildly through the train, shouting to his men ahead to fall back, "You are attacking a brigade!" Chapman re-formed his companies and charged through the advancing blue line. When the dust settled Lowell came up and surveyed his casualties. On the ground lay the body of a friend, Lieutenant Charles McMaster, riddled with bullets and broken by the hooves of rampaging horses. When he reported the killing to Torbert, Merritt, and Custer, they flew into a rage. Grant's written words flashed through Custer's consciousness—"Hang them without trial."[11]

With Torbert's consent, men from Custer's Michigan Brigade herded two Rangers, David L. Jones and Lucien Love, into the lot behind the Methodist Church at Front Royal, stood the pair together, and shot them. Another detail took a third prisoner, Thomas E. Anderson, to a nearby farm and killed him under an elm tree. Custer's Michigan Brigade dragged a fourth prisoner, Henry Rhodes, by his mother's home, took him into a pasture, and shot him. In the final act of execution, a squad from the 2nd U.S. Cavalry took William T. Overby and a Ranger named Carter into a empty wagon yard and hung them. Not every trooper witnessing the executions agreed with them.[12]

"The 'dark day' of 1864 is indelibly photographed in my memory," a young girl wrote. "I have often wished I could blot it out, for it clouded my childhood." A seventh prisoner was captured later and executed. Sheridan had his count right but his facts muddled when he wrote Grant, "Mosby has annoyed me and captured a few wagons. We hung one and shot six of his men yesterday."[13]

10. Scott, *Partisan Life,* 318–19; Jones, *Ranger Mosby,* 208–209.

11. Williamson, *Mosby's Rangers,* 240; Jones, *Ranger Mosby,* 208; Scott, *Partisan Life,* 319; Grant to Sheridan, August 16, 1864, *OR,* XLIII, Pt. 1, p. 811.

12. Scott, *Partisan Life,* 320; Williamson, *Mosby's Rangers,* 242n., 454; Jones, *Ranger Mosby,* 210–11, 240; Mosby, *Memoirs,* 301.

13. Williamson, *Mosby's Rangers,* 240–41; Sheridan to Grant, August 17, 1864, *OR,* XLIII, Pt. 1, p. 822.

Retaliation, however, worked both ways. Weeks passed before Mosby recuperated and learned what had happened to his men. On November 6 he lined up twenty-seven prisoners from Custer's cavalry, whom he blamed for the executions, and forced them to draw lots. The numbered pieces meant death by hanging—the blanks prison. Mosby intended to hang the men near Sheridan's camp at Winchester, but two escaped in the dark. The executioners pinned notes written by Mosby on the less fortunate five: "These men have been hung in retaliation for an equal number of Colonel Mosby's men hung by the order of General Custer. . . . Measure for measure."[14]

With Early's corps decimated, Sheridan concentrated on putting Mosby out of business, but the Rangers were not the only so-called guerrilla force operating near Harpers Ferry. While Mosby roamed in Fauquier and Loudoun Counties, a band of partisans led by John Mobley considered the Harpers Ferry area their exclusive domain. Mobley was thought by Stevenson to be a member of Mosby's command, but Mobley operated independently, acting on occasion as scout for Colonel White's 35th Battalion Virginia Cavalry, who also called themselves Loudoun Rangers but were more popularly known as the "Comanches."[15]

Mobley grew up on a small farm outside Harpers Ferry where he lived with his mother, Polly. As a young boy he drove a meat wagon for Joe Hagan, a free black butcher. Mobley was one of the fellows who came to town in October, 1859, to shoot old John Brown and get drunk in the process. Town boys poked fun at the youth, calling him "lubberly" and simple-minded. Mobley enjoyed the attention and manifested none of the hardened criminal spirit that lay latent in his psyche. Mobley had no liking for Abe Lincoln, and when the war started he turned renegade. At the age of seventeen he joined White's "Comanches," and because of his familiarity with the Harpers Ferry area, White detailed him as a scout. With his roving commission Mobley attracted his own gang of thieves and roamed the countryside robbing sutlers and wagonmasters. To the Unionists dwelling in the lower Valley, "lubberly"

---

14. Williamson, *Mosby's Rangers*, 288–93; Edwards to Kingsbury, November 7, 1864, *OR*, XLIII, Pt. 2, p. 566.

15. Jones, *Ranger Mosby*, 204. Atwell's Loudoun Rangers fought for the Union; White's Loudoun Rangers fought for the Confederacy and were attached at this time to Rosser's brigade. In *OR*, Mobley is referred to as Mobberly.

John Mobley earned a reputation as a reckless, cold-blooded murderer, and the town turned against him.

Jefferson County wanted law and order, but a few stalwart secessionists welcomed Mobley into their homes, sheltered him from capture, and acted as informants. In exchange he provided them with clothing and provisions looted from sutlers' wagons and military stores. To starving secessionists he was the Robin Hood of the Valley; to Unionists, the devil himself. Union cavalry hunted him for three years, but Mobley lived as a phantom of many disguises and a man of growing legend.[16]

Brigadier General Erastus B. Tyler intensified the hunt for Mobley in August, 1864, when a patrol scouting the Potomac reported shadowy men "in citizen's clothing" roaming the river and bushwhacking stray Union soldiers. "These men are supposed to belong to a Lieutenant [Mobley's] gang of outlaws," Tyler reported. "I have instructed my command not to bring any of them to my headquarters except for interment."[17]

The net tightened on Mobley's gang, as well as on Mosby's Rangers. In early September Crook's cavalry shot five of Mobley's men, captured an officer, snared four prisoners, and carried off forty horses and a large cache of revolvers. Mosby fared no better, losing twenty-five men. Many of Mobley's dead were recognized as citizens who lived nearby, sold produce to the government, performed odd jobs, and claimed to be loyal. Referring to the growing pile of corpses, Sheridan commented, "They are getting loyalty now," and added, "with a prospect of poverty in the future."[18]

On September 12 Brigadier General George H. Chapman, 2nd Brigade, 3rd Cavalry Division, learned that Mrs. Kline, who lived on the Leesburg road near Snickersville, knew where Mobley could be found. Despite his wily nature, Mobley trusted certain citizens who had no reason to protect him other than to escape his abuse. Chapman picked twenty reliable men and sent them that night to Mrs. Kline's home. She could not attest to Mobley's whereabouts but suggested the squad go to the home of Mr. Carlisle, a trusted Unionist, who was supposed to be arrested after he

16. Barry, *Harper's Ferry*, 127–29.
17. Tyler to Wallace, August 4, 1864, *OR*, XLIII, Pt. 1, p. 693.
18. Sheridan to Augur, September 10, 1864, *ibid.*, Pt. 2, p. 64.

tattled to keep up appearances.[19] Mobley could not be found because he had returned to his usual haunt—Harpers Ferry.

Mobley's men not only dressed in civilian clothes but also owned a remarkably large wardrobe of Federal uniforms. On November 11, dressed in blue, they trotted out of the hills and stopped two wagons of the 2nd U.S. Cavalry, killed the sergeant in charge, captured the teamsters, and disappeared with the loot. The 12th Pennsylvania Cavalry pursued and for their trouble recaptured two recalcitrant mules, but not Mobley or any of his renegades. Mosby added to the confusion a week later by tearing up the Winchester and Potomac tracks outside Charles Town and killing twenty-two pickets of the 12th Pennsylvania Cavalry.[20]

News of the two raids enraged Sheridan, who warned Stevenson, "If the Twelfth Pennsylvania Cavalry cannot keep that country clear of guerrillas I will take the shoulder straps off every officer belonging to the regiment and dismount the regiment in disgrace." A few days later he vented his anger on Halleck, admitting it would take ten men to snare one guerrilla but declaring, "I will soon commence on Loudoun County, and let them know there is a God in Israel. . . . Those people who live in the vicinity of Harpers Ferry are the most villainous in this Valley, and have not yet been hurt much. If the railroad is interfered with I will make some of them poor. Those who live at home, in peace and plenty, want the duello part of this war to go on; but when they have to bear their burden by loss of property and comforts they will cry for peace."[21] The disruptions around the Ferry, however, had less to do with Mosby and more to do with the escapades of Mobley, whose murderous bushwhacking had been consistently blamed upon the Rangers.

On November 27 Sheridan ordered Merritt's 1st Cavalry Division into the lower Valley to round up guerrillas and keep an eye open for Mobley's gang, considered by many locals as the worst criminals in the country. Referring to Loudoun and Jefferson Counties, Sheridan considered them "the hot-bed of lawless bands" and ordered Merritt to scorch the farmland, leaving only

19. Wilson to Chapman, September 12, 1864, *ibid.*, 74.

20. Crowninshield to Dana, November 11, and Stevenson to Forsyth, November 19, 1864, *ibid.*, 604, 648; Williamson, *Mosby's Rangers*, 298–310.

21. Sheridan to Stevenson, November 23, and to Halleck, November 26, 1864, *OR*, XLIII, Pt. 2, pp. 665, 671–72.

the homes of the occupants untouched. Merritt spent five days in Loudoun County carrying off 10,000 head of livestock and more than 500 horses. He torched every farm—some of them Unionist—from the eastern side of the Blue Ridge to the banks of the Shenandoah and Potomac Rivers.[22]

In the cavalry's search for guerrillas, a wandering horseman made a startling discovery outside Harpers Ferry when he crashed through a charred trapdoor of a building burned along the Shenandoah River. A tunnel beneath the door led to a stairway winding downwards and out of sight. With torches to guide them, a scouting party descended into a cavern large enough to hold three hundred horses. Dozens of crude stalls had been built, and a matting of recently stomped straw lay on the floor. At the opposite end was an opening so narrow that only one horse could enter at a time by first wading through three feet of water. The entry was covered with brush and rocks, and above towered a high cliff as if to mark the secret hiding place. There was no question about the identity of the former occupants. It was here that Mosby's band had mysteriously disappeared more times than their pursuers cared to remember.[23]

Merritt's raid netted not one guerrilla, but the Independent Loudoun Rangers, now led by Captain Daniel M. Keyes, captured "French Bill." Most of Mobley's command was made up of old friends who grew up in the Harpers Ferry neighborhood. The exception was Private William "French Bill" Loge of the 61st New York. One day Loge stepped across the Potomac to join Mobley's gang, and he soon earned a reputation as a notorious murderer and bushwhacker. He possessed great physical strength and relished a good fight. On December 1, after several months of successful marauding, he made the mistake of appearing at Johnson's stillhouse to witness a boxing match between Yankee Sullivan and Ben Caunt. French Bill had been involved in the murder of the 6th Pennsylvania Cavalry's surgeon, and Sheridan had standing orders to have him shot. Merritt's raid through Loudoun County had sent Mobley's men into hiding, but a few of the gang resurfaced to see the fight. Corporal Samuel E. Tritapoe of Atwell's company of Independent Loudoun Rangers recognized Loge and hauled him into

22. Forsyth to Merritt, November 27, and Merritt to Forsyth, December 3, 1864, *ibid.*, 679, 730.

23. Jones, *Ranger Mosby,* 240.

Harpers Ferry. Sheridan issued orders for Stevenson to "take him out and hang him."[24]

On December 2, the fifth anniversary of John Brown's execution, French Bill choked to an agonizing death on the gallows. Some said he died game, but Joseph Barry remembered the great brutality displayed by the provost guards as they jostled the prisoner to the scaffold. "On the whole," Barry wrote, "it was the most sickening affair witnessed . . . during the war."[25] Stevenson may have rid the area of French Bill, but Mobley and his gang still roved at large.

With the onset of another miserable winter in the Valley, Captain Suter of the 54th Pennsylvania wrote his wife that he had just moved into a "three cent boarding house" where a rotund landlady "who weighed a ton" spun marvelous yarns about the Harpers Ferry beauties of bygone times. She specialized in a litany on John Brown's raid and blamed the pummeling of her town and the entire war on Brown's mischief.[26]

As the words fell from her lips, more of Merritt's firebrands moved through Jefferson County to continue their destruction of barns and granaries. Smoke billowed skyward to mix with scattered flurries, and at night smoldering fires dotted the landscape. Farmers expressed their outrage. Some blamed Sheridan, others blamed Mobley, and the young renegade's loyal followers began to desert. By midwinter Mobley's force disintegrated to no more than fifteen men, now outlaws turned highwaymen who struck often and drove Stevenson to desperate measures.[27]

On February 3, 1865, Brigadier General Thomas C. Devin sent a squad from the 2nd Brigade, 1st Cavalry Division, after a small body of Mobley's men near the southern base of Loudoun Mountain. Mobley escaped, but another notorious cutthroat, a local boy named Payne, and six others were not so lucky. "What shall I do with them?" Devin asked headquarters, suggesting that "Payne should be tried by a military commission and shot. Since I have

24. Stevenson to Sheridan, December 1, 1864, *OR*, XLIII, Pt. 2, p. 721; Barry, *Harper's Ferry*, 136.

25. Stevenson to Sheridan, December 2, 1864, *OR*, XLIII, Pt. 2, p. 727; Barry, *Harper's Ferry*, 136.

26. John Suter to his wife, December 16, 1864, Suter Papers, Harrisburg Civil War Round Table Collection, USAMHI.

27. Stevenson to Morgan, April 1, 1865, *OR*, XLVI, Pt. 3, pp. 444–45.

been here he has been robbing all around, and shot one man and nearly beat another to death for his money. I ordered that he should not be brought in alive, but he was not recognized in time. If he is tried I will furnish the evidence. I have him tied hand and foot."[28]

Devin kept after Mobley like a hound on a rabbit. Squads of cavalry plowed through hip-deep snow and searched homes from Snicker's Gap to Hillsboro looking for the renegade. Devin captured four men of the 7th Virginia Cavalry and chased a dozen others into the mountains, but he caught neither Mobley nor any of his gang. On St. Valentine's Day he tried again, slogging through fresh snow, searching all houses, "but the alarm had got out," Devin complained, "and the rebs were off. . . . I will get them yet if they don't leave," he promised, adding, "Last night [Mobley] had to cut the horses from his sleigh and leave it in the road."[29]

Early's shattered command had rejoined Lee in the Petersburg entrenchments, and Sheridan departed from the Valley with his force. After cutting the Virginia Central Railroad, he led the cavalry back to the Army of the Potomac. Stevenson, however, remained in the Valley with his railroad guards and a strong cavalry support. People in the vicinity of Harpers Ferry and Charles Town saw the war wearing to an end. Even unreconstructable rebels gave up hope of independence, and a few from Loudoun County agreed to give up Mobley—if there was something in it for them. On March 28, 1865, Stevenson wrote Halleck that "a party of citizens of Loudoun propose to capture [Mobley], if armed by the Government, and ask that they shall have such reward for the service as will enable them temporarily to live elsewhere, which they will be compelled to do if successful."[30]

The gang had dwindled to four—Mobley, Riley, Mocks, and Tribbet. During the preceding months most of the band had been killed, leaving those Stevenson referred to as "the head devils." He thought a reward of $1,000 for Mobley and $500 for each of the others, dead or alive, would clean out the gang. The reward was but a pittance, Stevenson declared. "The Government could readily afford to pay $50,000" to be rid of them. Headquarters

28. Devin to Forsyth, February 3, 1865, *ibid.*, Pt. 2, p. 365.
29. Devin to Russell, February 15, 1865, *ibid.*, 567.
30. Stevenson to Stanton, March 28, 1865, *ibid.*, Pt. 3, pp. 240–41.

agreed but asked Stevenson to keep the whole matter secret and not publicize the reward.[31]

Stevenson quietly offered the reward to the informants, many of them Mobley's old supporters. For men whose small capital had been stripped away by four years of war, $1,000 in greenbacks represented a fortune. A few days later an informant returned and told the commander where Mobley and his trio were hiding. Stevenson sent a small detail armed with repeating rifles to Snicker's Gap, where they lurked in the brush and silently waited. Mobley rode along the path, his three companions trailing behind. A volley blazed from the thicket. Mobley dropped to the ground, three bullets through his head. Riley was hit and slumped over his saddle, but he rode off with the others. The ambushers picked up Mobley's bloody body, dropped it into a sack, draped it over his saddle, and hauled the corpse back to Harpers Ferry. Displayed in front of Stevenson's headquarters, a two-story house at the corner of High and Shenandoah Streets, Mobley's body was propped up for the benefit of the town. A crowd gathered. Some of them may have remembered the gored body of Dangerfield Newby, one of Brown's raiders, which had lain in an alley a few doors away. War had not changed the hardened civilians of Harpers Ferry. Relic hunters drew jackknives and cut off bits of clothing for souvenirs, leaving Mobley's corpse nearly denuded.[32]

There is no record of whether Polly Mobley was allowed to recover the remains of her son, who had not yet seen his twenty-first birthday. Others probably remembered the lad merely as "lubberly" and "simple-looking," but there was nothing simple about John Mobley. He had nearly survived the war and drove a dozen commanders of Harpers Ferry to desperate measures in an effort to capture him.[33]

As onlookers snipped souvenirs from Mobley's bloodied rags, Colonel Mosby gathered together a fresh group of volunteers at North Fork in Loudoun County. Mosby aimed to settle an old score with the Union version of the Loudoun Rangers, and in doing so he performed the final act of aggression in Jefferson County. On April 5 young George Baylor, who had earned distinction in

31. Stevenson to Morgan, and Morgan to Stevenson, April 1, 1865, *ibid.*, 444–45.

32. Stevenson to Stanton, April 5, 1865, *ibid.*, 590; Barry, *Harper's Ferry*, 128.

33. Barry, *Harper's Ferry*, 127.

the Stonewall Brigade and the 12th Virginia Cavalry, became captain of Company H, the last unit organized by Mosby. Learning that the Loudoun Rangers had made a comfortable camp outside Harpers Ferry, Baylor dressed his command in Federal blues and led them towards Halltown. On April 6 the company crossed Keyes Ford and "cleaned them out," capturing forty-five of the Union Rangers, a party of baggage guards from the 5th New York, and about eighty horses. Nearby infantry pursued Baylor, who recrossed at Keyes Ford and disappeared into the hills with his trophies.[34]

Baylor returned to camp, only to find Mosby saddened by the news that on April 9 Robert E. Lee had surrendered to Grant at Appomattox Courthouse. The colonel considered his options. He was cut off from General Johnston's army in North Carolina, and there was a price on his head. For a few days he watched and waited, letting some of his men fade back to civilian life.

On April 9 the few survivors from Harpers Ferry's own Floyd Guards, organized on May 17, 1861, as Company K, 2nd Virginia Regiment, stacked their muskets and signed their paroles. They started home to a town they would barely recognize.

The balance of Mobley's gang fared better than their leader. One surrendered on April 15, the others four days later. Unlike Mobley, they all received paroles, but nobody collected the five-hundred-dollar reward placed on each of their heads.[35]

Major General Winfield S. Hancock, who had replaced Sheridan as commander of the Middle Military District, sent Stevenson his compliments, adding, "Look out for your lines after 12 o'clock [April 20] tomorrow. Mosby will either surrender or the truce with him will end at that hour."[36]

In Washington the jubilation of Lee's surrender ended when John Wilkes Booth shot and mortally wounded Lincoln on the night of April 14. While mourners, both north and south, tried to recover from the shock, rumors filtered out of the Valley that Mosby knew of Booth's plans to kill the president and at the time

34. Williamson, *Mosby's Rangers*, 363–64; Baylor, *Bull Run to Bull Run*, 310–12; Stevenson to Morgan, April 6, 1865, *OR*, XLVI, Pt. 3, p. 617.

35. Stevenson to Morgan, April 15, and to Mitchell, April 19, 1865, *OR*, XLVI, Pt. 3, pp. 774, 840.

36. Hancock to Stevenson, April 19, 1865, *ibid.*, 841.

was with him in Washington.[37] Since the allegation came from General Hancock, Stanton gave the information initial credibility but discarded it later as unlikely.

The majority of Mosby's command, led by Lieutenant Colonel Chapman, surrendered at Winchester on April 21 and received paroles. The remnants of Mosby's band surrendered on May 8, but the wily leader, with a price of five thousand dollars on his head, did not come in until late in June. After stalling for more than two months, Halleck finally granted Mosby the same liberal terms as Lee and Johnston.[38] Attempts to implicate the colonel in Lincoln's assassination may have influenced Mosby's reluctance to give himself up, but he had nothing to do with the tragedy.

The fighting was finally over, but not the misery.

37. Mitchell to Emory, April 19, 1865, *ibid.*, 840.
38. Williamson, *Mosby's Rangers,* 393–99; Baylor, *Bull Run to Bull Run,* 341–42.

# Epilogue

On April 9, ragged veterans from Harpers Ferry and the surrounding countryside collected a few rations from the Union commissary at Appomattox and began the two-hundred-mile trek home. They came in pairs and small groups, mostly shoeless, passing down the Valley by previously well-stocked farms and cultivated fields, many grown over with weeds and grass. Barns once standing in familiar places were gone, as were the fences dividing one lush farm from the next. Towns still stood where the men remembered, but the homes looked as battered and careworn as the people who stared despondently from their porches at the passing rabble. Were it not for the eternal Blue Ridge Mountains, a returning veteran may have thought himself in purgatory.

Floyd Guards passing through Charles Town may have remembered the courthouse where John Brown and his gang received their sentence of death. Only the walls remained. The property had been converted into a fortress, armed with cannon, and used as a stable. Perhaps they recalled the old man's prophecy just before the sheriff carted him through town and led him to the scaffold, but they were probably too tired or depressed to care anymore.

On their way to Harpers Ferry they passed through Bolivar and found a few buildings burned, but most still stood with windows smashed and roofs splintered by artillery. The men looked for their homes, and a few lucky veterans found loved ones waiting to greet them. The remnants of the Guards presented their paroles and entered the military encampment at the Ferry. The armory and arsenal were gone, along with most of the old buildings that once stood near the neck between the two rivers. Federal soldiers occupied the streets, and the only government work being done was the repair of broken guns by a detail under Captain Daniel J. Young. Mills and schoolhouses had disappeared, churches had become stables, and blacks loitered everywhere with nothing to do.[1] For most returning soldiers, Young was easy to recognize. He had been the master machinist at the rifle factory and one of the first men of the Ferry who had remonstrated with Brown on the morning of his raid.

If God had bestowed a single blessing upon Harpers Ferry, it was the preservation of the Catholic church. Father Costello administered the Sacraments throughout the war, and his invocations for protection must have been heard where it counted most. For four long years the priest prayed for peace, and after it came, he died.[2]

Dr. Nicholas Marmion, another of the town's survivors, had lived out the war at Harpers Ferry with his family and eight of his fourteen children. One of his prewar patients was an older man who called himself Isaac Smith—that is, John Brown. The doctor abhorred the war's devastation of his town, but he stayed to cure the sick, the needy, and the young men wearing the blue or the gray. In 1882 he died, leaving among his legacies a good-natured complaint that he had never found "some pious person willing to curse the Yankees for all they had caused him to lose and suffer."[3]

Veterans walking into the lower town observed the Baltimore and Ohio running on its old schedule. They may have sauntered across the new bridge, remembering they had burnt the old, and if they stopped to ask Thomas N. Heskett, the assistant master of the road, how many times the bridge had been rebuilt, he would have told them nine.[4]

In the spring and summer of 1865, families who had fled south during the war returned to the Ferry to restore a forgotten harmony in their lives. They found little to give them hope—only broken windows, shattered walls, leaky roofs, and belligerent occupants. Their homes were in a state of semiconfiscation, having

1. Bushong, *Historic Jefferson County*, 251.
2. Marmion, "Under Fire," 19, HFA.
3. *Ibid.*
4. Barry, *Harper's Ferry*, 138, 140, 144. Garrett refers to Heskett and F. W. Haskett.

been rented out by the Federal government to officers and civilian workers. Other homes were occupied by squatters, who claimed superior ownership by virtue of their loyalty to the Union. Brevet Major General Thomas W. Egan commanded the garrison for a short time during the summer and spent much of his time sorting through claims to establish rightful ownership. He cleared many properties of the riffraff and evicted government tenants. Unfortunately, Egan left for another post before completing his work, leaving the puzzle of restoration to others.[5]

Another visitor during the summer was author John T. Trowbridge, out to collect a series of stories about the South's ruined cities. Trowbridge arrived at Harpers Ferry in a carriage on a dark and stormy night. He checked into the Shenandoah House, the town's brand-new bleak four-story hotel, built on the former site of the Wager House. The floors were bare and the walls unpainted, windows were without blinds or shutters, and the corn-shuck mattresses had been compressed into hard lumps. In the hot, stuffy room overlooking the town's depot, Trowbridge slept little and rose early. Sunlight drenched the valley in perfect "beauty and grandeur," Trowbridge wrote, but his account of the town was far from quaint or picturesque. "War has changed all," he reported. "Freshets tear down the centre of the streets, and dreary hill-sides present only ragged growths of weeds. The town itself lies half in ruins. . . . Of the bridge across the Shenandoah only the ruined piers are left; still less remains of the old bridge across the Potomac. All about the town are rubbish, filth and stench." Trowbridge, wandering through the site of the flame-scorched armory, noted that the only building in good condition was the enginehouse, which stood "like a monument which no Rebel hands were permitted to touch." A man wandered out of a nearby government repair shop and shuffled over to Trowbridge. After chatting a while, he cast a forlorn look at the wrecked buildings and said, "This place will never be anything again unless the government decides to rebuild the armory—and it is doubtful if that is ever done."[6]

But the citizens who returned to live in Harpers Ferry were determined to resurrect the town, with or without help from the

5. *Ibid.*, 140–41.
6. John T. Trowbridge, *The South: A Tour of Its Battle-Fields and Ruined Cities* (Hartford, Conn., 1866), 62–68.

government. Joseph Barry, who had chronicled the war years, now found himself appointed superintendent of Jefferson County's public schools. Buildings were easier to find than teachers. Barry faced a dilemma. He was not permitted to hire a teacher who had "given aid in any way to the late rebels." Since ninety-nine out of every hundred inhabitants of the county had been at one time or another in active sympathy with the rebellion, Barry ignored the law and hired good teachers.[7]

Encouraged by a gradual growth in population, industry and tradesmen returned to town. Abraham Herr rebuilt his mill on Virginius Island, and by the end of the decade most of his twenty-eight buildings on the island were back in the business of manufacturing. Slaters found work patching holes punched through roofs by shot and shell. One workman saved what relics he found in a bucket. When he finished work on the roof, his bucket contained five hundred bullets.[8]

Some believed John Brown had placed a curse upon the South. If so, he must have harbored a special hate for Harpers Ferry. After five years of relentless reconstruction, the great flood in the autumn of 1870 destroyed the homes and factories on Virginius Island and all the new buildings along the Potomac and Shenandoah waterfront. The Winchester and Potomac bridge collapsed where it crossed Virginius Island, but the Baltimore and Ohio bridge, based on sturdy stone piers and framed in heavy iron, survived. When floodwaters began to recede on October 1, Barry's description of the town sounded much like Trowbridge's account five years earlier: "Harper's Ferry was left to present an indescribable appearance of ruin, desolation and filth."[9]

Today, the only buildings standing in the lower town are those preserved by the National Parks Service. What six years of war destroyed and man rebuilt, the flood of 1870 swept away forever.

Beginning with John Brown's raid on October 16, 1859, when he temporarily wrested control of the armory from the government, and continuing through the reoccupation of Harpers Ferry by Union forces on July 8, 1864, the town changed hands fourteen times. There were weeks and months during the war when no force, either military or civil, controlled the town, and the inhab-

7. Barry, *Harper's Ferry*, 141–42.
8. *Ibid.*, 146–47; Marmion, "Under Fire," 19, HFA.
9. Barry, *Harper's Ferry*, 151–58, 164.

itants lived under the rule of bands who wandered through the area on raiding or reconnaissance missions. Aside from Stonewall Jackson's investment of the Ferry on September 14–16, 1862, no major battle was ever fought there, but by the end of the war the town wore the scars of a hotly contested battlefield. By all accounts, the Civil War ended in the spring of 1865, but the Federal garrison at Harpers Ferry remained. A town so hard for the Union to hold in war became in peace a symbol hard to give up. For more than a year after the restoration of the Union, the ear-piercing notes of the fife and the staccato of drums were heard daily on the streets beside the old charred armory buildings. Much of the town is still controlled by the Federal government, but under the peaceful auspices of the National Parks Service.[10]

The scars are there no more, but John Brown lives on in a more commercial way, and some will say in a more reverent way than the old raider deserved. The brick enginehouse, John Brown's fort, still remains as the only vestige of what was once a flourishing national armory. Now standing where the lower town was once located, it is given more financial and public attention than Grant's tomb, which in recent years has been smeared with graffiti and overgrown with weeds—a stomping ground for homeless people and drug dealers. Brown is buried in North Elba, Essex County, New York, but in Harpers Ferry his truth, if not his soul, still marches on.[11]

John Brown failed at Harpers Ferry, but he had a desperate vision of the future. The day he swung from the gallows, poet Henry Wadsworth Longfellow noted in his diary: "This will be a great day in our history; the date of a new revolution,—quite as much needed as the old one. Even now as I write, they are leading old John Brown to execution in Virginia for attempting to rescue slaves! This is sowing the seed to reap the whirlwind—which will soon come."[12]

The purging consumed 623,026 American lives and left the scars of war on 471,427 wounded. Of those who fought, 40 percent shed blood. Nobody tallied the number of displaced civilians who lost their lives because of the war.

Jessie E. Johnson witnessed much of the war from her Harpers

10. *Ibid.*, 140.
11. *Civil War News*, XXI (November, 1995), 25.
12. Longfellow, ed., *Life of Henry W. Longfellow*, II, 347.

Ferry home. In an undated letter, she wrote: "When the [Union] army came they called the citizens Rebels—when the Confederates came they called [them] Yankees. As it was the entire war, most of the male citizens had to leave home . . . some went south and some north to get employment, [leaving] the females almost unprotected . . . and some were old decrefid [*sic*] women."[13]

Harpers Ferry may have passed through the war unnoticed had John Brown not sown the seed to reap a poet's whirlwind on the riverbanks of that pretty little town in the Valley. Some say the war started the day old Brown attacked the Federal armory. Townsfolk like Joseph Barry, Jessie Johnson, eight-year-old Annie Marmion, and Father Costello saw it through, from beginning to end, and from their perspective, no town suffered more than Harpers Ferry.

By all accounts, it had been six years of hell.

13. Johnson (Mrs. Charles Gibbs Johnson) Letters, File HFD-418, HFA.

# Appendix: Chronology of Harpers Ferry

## 1859–1865

| | |
|---|---|
| October 16, 1859 | John Brown's raid. |
| October 18, 1859 | U.S. troops commanded by Bvt. Col. Robert E. Lee are posted in the town. |
| April 18, 1861 | Union troops under Lt. Roger Jones evacuate. |
| April 18, 1861 | Virginia troops under Maj. Gen. Kenton Harper take possession of the town. |
| April 27, 1861 | Col. Thomas J. "Stonewall" Jackson takes command of the Virginia militia. |
| May 24, 1861 | Brig. Gen. Joseph E. Johnston arrives. |
| June 14, 1861 | Johnston begins evacuation of Harpers Ferry. |
| July 15, 1861 | Confederate guard departs from the town. |
| July 19, 1861 | Gen. Winfield Scott appoints Maj. Gen. Nathaniel P. Banks to the command of Harpers Ferry. |
| July 21, 1861 | Union Maj. Gen. Robert Patterson, Department of the Shenandoah, establishes headquarters at Harpers Ferry. |
| July 23, 1861 | Banks replaces Patterson. |
| August 21, 1861 | Banks withdraws Union force from the Ferry and moves headquarters to Sandy Hook. |
| August 22, 1861 | Capt. Turner Ashby's Confederate cavalry reoccupy the town and post pickets. |
| September 17, 1861 | Col. John W. Geary, 28th Pennsylvania Volunteers, retakes Harpers Ferry with a company of the 13th Massachusetts. |
| October 18, 1861 | Geary withdraws from the town after the skirmish at Bolivar Heights. |
| October 22, 1861 | Confederate cavalry occupy the town long enough to destroy Herr's mill and withdraw. |

| | |
|---|---|
| October, 1861, to February, 1862 | Ferry is scouted by both Union and Confederate cavalry. |
| February 24, 1862 | Banks crosses the Potomac and occupies the town with 16,000 troops. |
| March 29, 1862 | Banks moves south and leaves Col. Dixon S. Miles in charge of railroad guards with headquarters at Harpers Ferry. |
| May 24, 1862 | Brig. Gen. Rufus Saxton commands the Ferry. |
| May 30, 1862 | Jackson attacks the Ferry with a small force and withdraws the following morning, being repulsed by Saxton. |
| June 1, 1862 | Maj. Gen. Franz Sigel takes command of the Ferry. |
| June 4, 1862 | Sigel assigns Col. Dixon S. Miles to the command of Harpers Ferry. |
| September 15, 1862 | Jackson captures the Harpers Ferry garrison, and Gen. Ambrose P. Hill paroles the entire force. |
| September 17, 1862 | General Hill evacuates Harpers Ferry, leaving only a small garrison to gather up captured supplies. |
| September 22, 1862 | Gen. Ambrose Burnside reoccupies Harpers Ferry. |
| October 1, 1862 | Lincoln orders McClellan to take possession of Harpers Ferry and make it a permanent base. |
| October 13, 1862 | Maj. Gen. Ambrose Burnside commands the Ferry with the Army of the Potomac II, IX, and XII Corps. |
| October 15, 1862 | Maj. Gen. Henry W. Slocum replaces Burnside. |
| December 11, 1862 | Brig. Gen. John R. Kenly replaces Slocum. |
| December 16, 1862 | Brig. Gen. Benjamin F. Kelley replaces Kenly. |
| June 15, 1863 | Brig. Gen. Daniel Tyler relieves Kelley. |
| June 26, 1863 | Maj. Gen. William H. French takes command of Harpers Ferry. |
| June 28, 1863 | French assigns command to Brig. Gen. Washington Elliott. |
| July 1, 1863 | Elliott evacuates Harpers Ferry after a skirmish with the 12th Virginia Cavalry. |
| July 1, 1863 | Lt. Col. Thomas B. Massie occupies the town with a small force. |
| July 9, 1863 | Brig. Gen. Henry M. Naglee is given command of the Ferry by Maj. Gen. George G. Meade, but the bridge has been destroyed. |
| July 14, 1863 | Naglee sends a regiment to Bolivar Heights and reoccupies the town. |
| July 17, 1863 | Brig. Gen. Henry H. Lockwood replaces Naglee. |
| October 12, 1863 | Brig. Gen. Jeremiah C. Sullivan replaces Lockwood. |

| | |
|---|---|
| April 5, 1864 | Brig. Gen. Max Weber replaces Sullivan. |
| July 4, 1864 | Weber evacuates Harpers Ferry when attacked by Jubal Early's skirmishers. |
| July 5, 1864 | The 43rd North Carolina occupy Harpers Ferry for one day, leaving a small guard behind. |
| July 8, 1864 | Union forces under Brig. Gen. Albion P. Howe reoccupy the town. |
| August 6, 1864 | Maj. Gen. Philip H. Sheridan takes command of the Middle Military District and makes Harpers Ferry his headquarters. |
| August 8, 1864 | Sheridan restores Weber to the command of Harpers Ferry. |
| August 15, 1864 | Brig. Gen. John D. Stevenson replaces Weber as commander of the Harper's Ferry Military District. |
| February 27, 1865 | Maj. Gen. Winfield S. Hancock takes command of Middle Military Division at Harpers Ferry. |
| June 27, 1865 | Maj. Gen. Thomas W. Egan replaces Hancock and begins to return property to its rightful owners. |

# Bibliography

## Primary Sources

LETTERS, DOCUMENTS, AND PUBLIC RECORDS

Alderman Library, University of Virginia, Charlottesville, Va.
    Douglas, Henry K. Letters.
    Imboden, John D. Papers.
    Mosby, John S. Papers.
    Redman, W. H. Letters, 12th Illinois Cavalry.
Chicago Historical Society, Chicago, Ill.
    Brown, John. Papers.
Corry Public Library, Corry, Pa.
Street, John L. Letters, 145th Pennsylvania.
Essex Institute, Salem, Mass.
    Banks, Nathaniel P. Papers.
Harpers Ferry National Park Archives, Harpers Ferry, W.Va.
    1859 Base Map, National Parks Service, Harpers Ferry, W.Va.
    Cook, William. Letters, File HFD-230.
    Daniel Collection, File HFD-66.
    Doubleday, Abner. Journal, File HFB-253.
    Fredrickson, Fred. Letters, File HFD-390.
    Griffith, Mary Jane Coates. Letters, File HFD-364.
    Harper, Kenton. Obituary, from the Staunton *Spectator*, December 31, 1867, File HFD-587.
    Hawthorne, Nathaniel. Article, extracted from "The Conflict of Convictions," 77–85, File HFB-216.
    Hull, Pvt. L. B. Diaries and Letters, Files HFD-277, 278, 279, 503.
    Johnson, Mrs. Charles Gibbs. Letters, File HFD-418.
    Marmion, Annie P. Manuscript, "Under Fire," printed 1959, HFB-206.
    Newcomer, Celeste B. Letters, File HFD-338.

Sheeran, Rev. James B. "Confederate Chaplain," War Journal, 14th Louisiana, File HFB-263.

Shewbridge, James. Letters, File HFD-581.

Smith, Hervey H. Diary, File HFD-70B.

Smith, Horace A. Diary, File HFD-70A.

Wager, Elizabeth. Scrapbook, File HFD-262.

Jefferson County Court Records, Charles Town, W.Va.

Beckham, Mayor Fontaine. Will Book.

Brown, John. Papers.

Library of Congress, Manuscript Division, Washington, D.C.

Carman, Ezra A., "The Maryland Campaign of September, 1862."

Early, Jubal A. Papers, 1829–1911, 15 vols.

Hotchkiss, Jedediah. Papers.

McClellan, George B. Papers.

Mosby, John S. Papers.

Musselman Library, Gettysburg College, Gettysburg, Pa.

"A History of the 145th Pennsylvania Volunteers," in the John H. C. Stuckenberg Collection.

National Archives, Washington, D.C.

Banks, Nathaniel P. Papers, Record Group 98.

Early, Jubal A. Papers, Record Group 109.

Halleck, Henry W. Papers, File 159, Record Group 94.

Harpers Ferry Commission, File KK311, Record Group 79.

Jackson, Thomas J. Papers, Record Group 109.

Mason Committee Inquiry into the Harper's Ferry Invasion, Senate Report 278, 36th Cong., 1st Sess., Ser. 1040, Record Group 36.

Middle Military Department, Telegrams Sent and Received, Record Group 393.

Records of the U.S. Army Commands: Army of the Potomac, 1861–65, Record Group 393.

Sheridan, Philip H. Papers, Record Groups 98 and 128.

Taliaferro, William B. Papers, Record Group 332.

Winchester Commission, File KK311, Record Group 79.

Ontario County Historical Society, Canandaigua, N.Y.

Bassett, Richard. Papers.

Southern Historical Collection, University of North Carolina, Chapel Hill, N.C.

Jackson, Thomas J. Papers.

MacDonald, Edward H. Manuscript.

U.S. Army Military History Research Collection, U.S. Army, Upton Hall, Carlisle, Pa.

Arnold, John C. Letters in Arnold Family Papers, 49th Pennsylvania Infantry.

Curtis, Henry, Jr. Papers, 37th Illinois.

Eanes, Walter A. Letter Book in the Murray Smith Collection, 15th Massachusetts Infantry.

Farr, Charles R. Diary, 1st Vermont Cavalry.

Gaskell, George B. Letters, 1st Rhode Island Light Artillery.

Pardee-Robison Family Collection.

    Pardee, Ario. Papers.

    Pardee, Calvin. Papers.

    Robison, Isaiah. Papers.

Civil War Miscellaneous Collection

    Gasper, James M. Diary, 1st Veteran Maine Infantry.

    Montgomery, James H. Journal, U.S. Signal Corps.

    Moore, Joseph Addison. Papers, 28th Pennsylvania Infantry.

    Von Schlen, John C. H. Papers, 15th Indiana Light Artillery.

Civil War Times Illustrated Collection

    Baker, I. Norval. Memoirs, 18th Virginia Cavalry.

    Bell, Thomas. *At Harper's Ferry, Va., September 14, 1862: How the Cavalry Escaped Out of the Toils.* Brooklyn, 1900.

    DeGraff, Nicholas J. Memoirs, 115th New York Infantry.

    Gardner, Charles E. "Three Years Experience in the First Maine Cavalry Regiment."

    Gillette, James. Letters, 3rd Maryland Infantry.

    Gratton, Charles. "Reminiscences of Camp Life with Stonewall Jackson," 5th Virginia Military District.

    Hodgkins, Thomas. Letters, Battery M, 1st New York Light Artillery.

    Morgan, Hance. Diary, 121st New York Infantry.

    Reser, Jacob. Letters, 34th Ohio Infantry.

    Ross, Orville. Memoir, 133rd Pennsylvania Infantry.

    Thompson, Col. Benjamin W. "Recollections of War Times."

    Tracy, E. D. Letters, 4th Alabama, Lionel Baxter Collection.

Harrisburg Civil War Round Table Collection

    Filbert, Peter A. Diary, 10th Pennsylvania Infantry.

    Hamer, Samuel. Letters, 54th Pennsylvania Infantry.

    Kutz, Bently. Papers, 195th Pennsylvania Infantry.

    Lowery, John E. Memoir, 138th Pennsylvania.

    Mowen, Daniel. "Memoirs of the Civil War," Flegeal Collection.

    Nichol, David. Papers, Knap's Battery, Co. E, Pennsylvania Light Artillery.

    Oestrich, Maurus. Diary, 96th Pennsylvania.

    Seibert, David S. Letters, Co. F, 93rd Pennsylvania.

    Seibert, Frank. Letters, Co. F, 93rd Pennsylvania.

    Suter, John. Papers, 54th Pennsylvania.

Walters, Edgar A. Letters, U.S. Signal Corps.
Virginia Historical Society, Richmond, Va.
Ashby, Turner. Papers.
Early, Jubal A. Papers.
Jackson, Thomas J. Papers.
Langhorne, James. Letters.
Virginia Military Institute Manuscript Collection. Lexington, Va.
Jackson, Thomas J. Papers.
Virginia State Library, Richmond, Va.
Carter, William. Journal, 3rd Virginia Cavalry.
Hill, Daniel H. Papers.
Mosby, John S. Papers.
Virginia Confederate Rosters.
Yale University Library, New Haven, Conn.
De Forest, John William. Papers, 12th Connecticut.


NEWSPAPERS

Auburn (N.Y.) *Daily*
Baltimore *American and Commercial Advertiser*
Baltimore *Weekly American*
Baltimore *Weekly Sun*
Charles Town (W.Va.) *Independent Democrat*
*Civil War News*
*Harper's Weekly*
*National Intelligencer* (Washington, D.C.)
New York *Herald*
New York *Sun*
New York *Times*
New York *Tribune*
Richmond *Enquirer*
Savannah *Daily Morning News*
Shepherdstown (W.Va.) *Register*
Topeka *Tribune*
*Virginia Free Press* (Charles Town, W.Va.)
Washington *Herald*
Wheeling (W.Va.) *Intelligencer*


OTHER PRIMARY SOURCES

Alexander, E. P. *Military Memoirs of a Confederate*. Boston, 1905.
Allan, Elizabeth Preston. *Life and Letters of Margaret Junkin Preston*. Boston, 1903.
Anderson, Osborn P. *A Voice from Harper's Ferry*. Boston, 1861.

Avirett, James B. *The Memoirs of General Ashby Turner and His Compeers*. Baltimore, 1867.

Baltimore and Ohio Railroad Company. *Thirty-Sixth Annual Report*. Baltimore, 1864.

Barry, Joseph. *The Strange Story of Harper's Ferry*. 3rd ed. Shepherdstown, W.Va., 1959.

Baylor, George. *Bull Run to Bull Run; or, Four Years in the Army of Northern Virginia*. Richmond, 1900.

Blackford, W. W. *War Years with Jeb Stuart*. New York, 1946.

Booth, George W. *Personal Reminiscences of a Maryland Soldier in the War Between the States*. Baltimore, 1898.

Boteler, Alexander R. "Recollections of the John Brown Raid." *Century Monthly Magazine*, XXVI (July, 1883), 399–411.

Boyle, John Richards. *Soldiers True: The Story of the 111th Pennsylvania Veteran Volunteer Infantry, 1861–1865*. New York, 1903.

Brown, J. W. *The Signal Corps, U.S.A., in the War of the Rebellion*. 1896; rpr. New York, 1974.

Bryant, Edwin E. *History of the 3rd Regiment of Wisconsin Veteran Volunteer Infantry, 1861–1865*. Madison, 1895.

Caldwell, James FitzJames. *The History of a Brigade of South Carolinians Known First as "Gregg's Brigade" and Subsequently as "McGowan's Brigade."* Philadelphia, 1866.

Casler, John. *Four Years in the Stonewall Brigade*. Marietta, Ga., 1951.

Chamberlayne, John Hampden. *Ham Chamberlayne—Virginian*. Edited by C. G. Chamberlayne. Richmond, 1932.

Clark, James H. *The Iron Hearted Regiment: Being an Account of the Battles, Marches, and Gallant Deeds Performed by the 115th Regiment, N.Y. Volunteers*. Albany, N.Y., 1865.

Cooke, John Esten. *Stonewall Jackson: A Military Biography*. New York, 1876.

Corlis, Augustus W. "History of the Seventh Squadron, Rhode Island Cavalry." In State of Rhode Island, *Adjutant General's Report*. Providence, 1865.

Dabney, R. L. *Life and Campaigns of Lieutenant General Thomas J. Jackson (Stonewall)*. New York, 1865.

Davis, Charles E., Jr. *Three Years in the Army: The Story of the Thirteenth Massachusetts Volunteers*. Boston, 1894.

Davis, Jefferson. *Rise and Fall of the Confederate Government*. 2 vols. New York, 1881.

Dawson, Francis. *Reminiscences of Confederate Service, 1861–1865*. Baton Rouge, 1980.

Dickert, D. Augustus. *History of Kershaw's Brigade*. Newberry, S.C., 1899.

Douglas, Henry Kyd. *I Rode with Stonewall*. Chapel Hill, N.C., 1940.

Dowley, Morris Francis. *History and Honorary Role of the 12th Regiment Infantry, N.G.S.N.Y.* New York, 1869.

Drew, Thomas, comp. *The John Brown Invasion: An Authentic History of the Harper's Ferry Tragedy.* Boston, 1859.

Early, Jubal A. *Lieutenant General Jubal Anderson Early, C.S.A.: Autobiographical Sketch and Narrative of the War Between the States.* Philadelphia, 1912.

Eby, Cecil D., Jr., ed. *A Virginia Yankee in the Civil War: The Diaries of David Hunter Strother.* Chapel Hill, N.C., 1961.

Elwood, John W. *Elwood's Stories of the Old Ringgold Cavalry.* Coal Center, Pa., 1914.

Enderton, Hervert, comp. *The Private Journal of Abraham Joseph Warner.* San Diego, 1973.

Evans, Clement A., ed. *Confederate Military History.* 13 vols. Atlanta, 1899.

Fonerden, C. A. *A Brief History of the Military Career of Carpenter's Battery.* New Market, Va., 1911.

Gilmor, Harry. *Four Years in the Saddle.* New York, 1866.

Goldsborough, W. W. *The Maryland Line in the Confederate Army, 1861–1865.* Baltimore, 1900.

Goodhart, Briscoe. *History of the Independent Loudoun Virginia Rangers, 1862–65.* Washington, D.C., 1896.

Goss, Warren Lee. *Recollections of a Private: A Story of the Army of the Potomac.* New York, 1890.

Greeley, Horace. *The American Conflict.* 2 vols. Hartford, Conn., 1864–66.

Green, Israel. "The Capture of John Brown." *North American Review,* CXLI (December, 1885), 564–69.

Hall, James E. *Diary of a Confederate Soldier.* Edited by Ruth Woods Dayton. Philippi, W.Va., 1961.

Hays, Ebenezer Z. *History of the Thirty-Second Regiment (Ohio Veteran Volunteer Infantry).* Columbus, Ohio, 1896.

Higginson, Thomas Wentworth. *Cheerful Yesterdays.* Boston, 1898.

Hinkley, Julian Wisner. *A Narrative of Service with the Third Wisconsin Infantry.* Madison, 1912.

Hinton, Richard J. *John Brown and His Men.* New York, 1894.

Hitchcock, Frederick L. *War from the Inside: The Story of the 132nd Regiment Pennsylvania Volunteer Infantry.* Philadelphia, 1904.

Howard, McHenry. *Recollections of a Maryland Staff Officer Under Johnston, Jackson, and Lee.* Baltimore, 1914.

Jackson, Mary Anna, ed. *Memoirs of Stonewall Jackson.* Louisville, 1895.

Jefferson, Thomas. *Notes on the State of Virginia.* 2nd American ed. Philadelphia, 1794.

Johnson, Robert U., and Clarence C. Buel, eds., *Battles and Leaders of the Civil War*. 4 vols. New York, 1884–88.

Johnston, Joseph E. *Narrative of Military Operations*. New York, 1874.

Lee, Robert E., Jr. *Recollections and Letters of General Robert E. Lee*. New York, 1909.

Leech, Samuel V. *The Raid of John Brown at Harper's Ferry as I Saw It*. Washington, D.C., 1909.

Longfellow, Samuel, ed. *Life of Henry Wadsworth Longfellow*. 3 vols. Boston, 1891.

Longstreet, James. *From Manassas to Appomattox: Memoirs of the Civil War in America*. Bloomington, Ind., 1960.

Lucas, D. B. *Memoir of John Yates Beall*. Montreal, 1865.

Luff, W. M. "March of the Cavalry from Harper's Ferry, September 14, 1862." *Military Essays and Recollections*. Vol. II. Chicago, 1894.

McClellan, George B. *McClellan's Own Story*. New York, 1886.

———. *Report on the Organization and Campaigns of the Army of the Potomac*. New York, 1864.

McClellan, H. B. *The Life and Campaigns of Major General J. E. B. Stuart*. Boston, 1885.

McDonald, Archie, ed. *Make Me a Map of the Valley: The Civil War Journal of Stonewall Jackson's Topographer*. Dallas, 1973.

McDonald, William. *A History of the Laurel Brigade: Originally the Ashby Cavalry of the Army of Northern Virginia and Chew's Battery*. Baltimore, 1907.

McGuire, Hunter, and George L. Christian. *The Confederate Cause and Conduct in the War Between the States*. Richmond, 1907.

Moore, Edward A. *The Story of a Cannoneer Under Stonewall Jackson*. New York, 1907.

Moore, Frank, ed. *The Rebellion Record: A Diary of American Events*. 12 vols. New York, 1977.

Mosby, John S. *The Memoirs of Colonel John S. Mosby*. Edited by Charles S. Russel. Boston, 1917.

Mulholland, St. Clair A. *The Story of the 116th Regiment Pennsylvania Volunteers*. Philadelphia, 1903.

Myers, Frank. *The Comanches: A Study of White's Battalion, Virginia Cavalry, Laurel Brigade, Hampton's Division, Army of Northern Virginia, C.S.A.* Baltimore, 1895.

Newcomer, Christopher A. *Cole's Cavalry; or, Three Years in the Saddle in the Shenandoah Valley*. Freeport, N.Y., 1970.

Nichols, William H. "The Siege and Capture of Harper's Ferry." *Personal Narratives of Events in the War of the Rebellion*. Ser. 4, No. 2. Providence, R.I., 1889.

Norton, Henry King. *Deeds of Daring; or, History of the 8th New York Volunteer Cavalry.* Norwich, N.Y., 1889.

Opie, John N. *A Rebel Cavalryman with Lee, Stuart, and Jackson.* Chicago, 1899.

Patterson, Robert A. *A Narrative of the Campaign in the Valley of the Shenandoah in 1861.* Philadelphia, 1986.

Peck, R. H. *Reminiscences of a Confederate Soldier.* Fincastle, Va., 1913.

Pettengill, Samuel B. *The College Cavaliers.* Chicago, 1883.

Poague, William T. *Gunner with Stonewall.* Jackson, Tenn., 1957.

Redpath, James. *The Public Life of Capt. John Brown.* Boston, 1860.

Reid, Whitelaw. *Ohio in the War.* 2 vols. Cincinnati, 1868.

Richardson, Albert D. *The Secret Service, the Field, the Dungeon, and the Escape.* Hartford, Conn., 1866.

Ripley, E. H. "Memories of the Ninth Vermont at the Tragedy of Harper's Ferry." *Personal Recollections of the War of the Rebellion.* Vol. IV. New York, 1909.

———. *Vermont General.* Edited by Otto Eisenschmil. New York, 1960.

Sanborn, Franklin B. *The Life and Letters of John Brown.* Boston, 1885.

———. *Recollections of Seventy Years.* 2 vols. Boston, 1909.

Scott, John. *Partisan Life with Col. John S. Mosby.* Gaithersburg, Md., 1985.

Sheridan, Philip Henry. *Personal Memoirs.* 2 vols. New York, 1888.

*Southern Historical Society Papers.* 52 vols. Richmond, 1876–1959.

Stearns, Austin C. *Three Years with Company K, Sergt. Austin C. Stearns, Company K, 13th Massachusetts Infantry.* Edited by Arthur A. Kent. Rutherford, 1976.

Steiner, Bernard Christian. *Life of Reverdy Johnson.* Baltimore, 1914.

Trowbridge, John T. *The South: A Tour of Its Battle-Fields and Ruined Cities.* Hartford, Conn., 1866.

U.S. Congress. 36th Cong., 1st Sess., House of Representatives, Exec. Doc. 2. *Message from the President of the United States* and *Report from the Secretary of War for 1859–1860.* Washington, D.C., 1861.

———. 36th Cong., 1st Sess., Mason Senate Committee. *Report on the Invasion of Harper's Ferry.* Vol. 1, Rpt. 278. Washington, D.C., 1860.

———. 37th Cong., 2nd Sess. Senate Doc. 7, *Message of the President of the United States.* Washington, D.C., 1863.

———. 37th Cong., 3rd Sess. *Report of the Joint Committee on the Conduct of the War.* Vol. 3. Washington, D.C., 1863.

*The War of the Rebellion: A Compilation of the Official Records of the Union and Confederate Armies.* 128 vols. Washington, D.C., 1881–1901.

Waring, G. E. "The Garibaldi Guard." In *The First Book of the Author's Club.* New York, 1893.

Williamson, James J. *Mosby's Rangers.* New York, 1896.

Willson, A. M. *Disaster, Struggle, Triumph; The Adventures of 1,000 "Boys in Blue."* Albany, N.Y., 1870.

Wilmer, L. Allison, J. H. Jarrett, and George W. F. Vernon. *History and Roster of Maryland Volunteers, War of 1861–1865.* 2 vols. Baltimore, 1898.

Wise, Barton H. *The Life of Henry A. Wise of Virginia, 1806–1876.* New York, 1899.

Worsham, John H. *One of Jackson's Foot Cavalry.* New York, 1912.


## Secondary Sources

Abels, Jules. *Man on Fire: John Brown and the Cause of Liberty.* New York, 1971.

Ambler, Charles H. *West Virginia, the Mountain State.* New York, 1940.

Andrews, Matthew Page. *The Women of the South in War Times.* Baltimore, 1920.

Ashby, Thomas A. *Life of Turner Ashby.* New York, 1914.

Bean, William G. *Stonewall's Man: Sandie Pendleton.* Chapel Hill, 1959.

Boatner, Mark M., III. *The Civil War Dictionary.* New York, 1959.

Boney, F. N. *John Letcher of Virginia: The Story of Virginia's War Governor.* University, Ala., 1966.

Boyer, Richard O. *The Legend of John Brown: A Biography and a History.* New York, 1973.

Brown, R. Shepard. *Stringfellow of the Fourth.* New York, 1960.

Bushong, Millard K. *Historic Jefferson County.* Boyce, Va., 1972.

———. *A History of Jefferson County, West Virginia.* Charles Town, W.Va., 1941.

———. *Old Jube: A Biography of General Jubal A. Early.* Shippensburg, Pa., 1985.

Chambers, Lenoir. *Stonewall Jackson.* 2 vols. New York, 1959.

Civil War Centennial Commission, County of Loudoun, Commonwealth of Virginia. *Loudoun County in the Civil War.* By the Commission, 1961.

Clarence, Thomas. *General Turner Ashby.* Winchester, Va., 1907.

Coddington, Edwin. *The Gettysburg Campaign.* New York, 1968.

Conway, Martin. *Harpers Ferry: Time Remembered.* Reston, Va., 1981.

Cullum, George W. *Biographical Register of the Officers and Graduates of the U.S. Military Academy from Its Establishment, in 1802, to 1890.* 2 vols., Boston, 1891.

Evans, William F. *History of Berkeley County, West Virginia.* Wheeling, W.Va., 1928.

Faust, Patricia L., ed. *Historical Times Illustrated Encyclopedia of the Civil War.* New York, 1986.

Freeman, Douglas Southall. *Lee's Lieutenants.* 3 vols. New York, 1942–44.

———. *R. E. Lee: A Biography.* 4 vols. New York, 1947.

Hamlin, Percy G. *Old Bald Head.* Strasburg, Va., 1940.

Hassler, William Woods. *A. P. Hill: Lee's Forgotten General.* Chapel Hill, N.C., 1982.

Hearn, Chester G. "The Great Locomotive March: Jackson's Railroad Campaign." *Civil War Times Illustrated,* XXV (December, 1986), 20–23, 28–31.

Hebert, Walter H. *Fighting Joe Hooker.* Indianapolis, 1944.

Henderson, G. F. R. *Stonewall Jackson and the American Civil War.* New York, 1936.

Hendricks, Sam M. *Military Operations in Jefferson County, Va. (and West Virginia), 1861–1865.* Charles Town, W.Va., 1910.

Hergesheimer, Joseph. *Sheridan: A Military Narrative.* Boston, 1931.

Heysinger, Isaac. *Antietam and the Maryland and Virginia Campaigns of 1862.* New York, 1912.

Hungerford, Edward. *The Story of the Baltimore and Ohio Railroad.* 2 vols. New York, 1928.

Jones, Virgil C. *Gray Ghosts and Rebel Raiders.* New York, 1956.

———. *Ranger Mosby.* Chapel Hill, N.C., 1944.

Keeler, Ralph. "Owen Brown's Escape from Harper's Ferry." *Atlantic Monthly,* XXXIII (March, 1874), 342–65.

Mies, John. "Breakout at Harpers Ferry." *Civil War History,* II (June, 1956), 13–22.

Moore, George E. *A Banner in the Hills.* New York, 1963.

Murfin, James V. *The Gleam of Bayonets: The Battle of Antietam and the Maryland Campaign of 1862.* New York, 1965.

Oates, Stephen B. *To Purge This Land with Blood.* New York, 1970.

Pfanz, Harry W. *Special History Report: Troop Movement Maps, 1862.* Springfield, Va., 1976.

Pond, George E. *The Shenandoah Valley in 1864.* New York, 1884.

Shanks, Henry T. *The Secession Movement in Virginia, 1847–1861.* Richmond, 1934.

Smith, Merritt Roe. *Harpers Ferry Armory and the New Technology.* Ithaca, N.Y., 1977.

Stone, Edward, ed. *Incident at Harper's Ferry.* Englewood Cliffs, N.J., 1956.

Stutler, Boyd B. *Capt. John Brown and Harper's Ferry.* Harpers Ferry, 1926.

———. "The Hanging of John Brown." *American Heritage,* VI (February, 1955), 7–11.

———. *West Virginia in the Civil War.* Charleston, 1966.

Summers, Festus P. *The Baltimore and Ohio in the Civil War.* New York, 1939.

Tanner, Robert G. *Stonewall in the Valley.* Garden City, N.Y., 1976.

Teeter, Paul R. *A Matter of Hours: Treason at Harper's Ferry.* Rutherford, N.J., 1982.

Tischler, Allan L. *The History of the Harpers Ferry Cavalry Expedition, September 14 and 15, 1862.* Winchester, Va., 1993.

Turner, George Edgar. *Victory Rode the Rails.* Indianapolis, 1953.

Villard, Oswald Garrison. *John Brown, 1800–1859: A Biography Fifty Years After.* Boston, 1910.

Webster, Donald B., Jr. "The Last Days of Harpers Ferry Arsenal." *Civil War History,* V (March, 1959), 30–44.

Wellman, Manly Wade. *Harper's Ferry, Prize of War.* Charlotte, N.C., 1960.

———. *Rebel Boast: First at Bethel, Last at Appomattox.* New York, 1956.

Wilson, James Grant. *Biographical Sketches of Illinois Officers Engaged in the War Against the Rebellion of 1861.* Chicago, 1862–63.

Wise, Jennings C. *The Long Arm of Lee.* 2 vols. Lynchburg, Va., 1915.

# Index